THE
MANHUNTER

Also by Cameron Stauth

*The Golden Boys**
The Franchise
The Sweeps
The New Approach to Cancer

*Published by POCKET BOOKS

THE
MANHUNTER

The Astounding True Story of the U.S. Marshal Who Tracked Down the World's Most Evil Criminals

JOHN PASCUCCI
AND
CAMERON STAUTH

POCKET BOOKS
New York   London   Toronto   Sydney   Tokyo   Singapore

POCKET BOOKS, a division of Simon & Schuster Inc.
1230 Avenue of the Americas, New York, NY 10020

Pascucci, John.
    The manhunter : the astounding true story of the U.S. marshal who
tracked down the world's most evil criminals / John Pascucci and
Cameron Stauth.
        p.   cm.
    Includes index.
    ISBN 0-671-88518-9 (hardcover)
    1. Pascucci, John. 2. United States marshals—Biography. 3. Law
enforcement—United States—Case studies. 4. Fugitives from
justice—Case studies. I. Stauth, Cameron. II. Title.
HV8144.M37   1996
363.2'82'092—dc20
[B]   96-3424
                                                                  CIP

First Pocket Books hardcover printing August 1996

10 9 8 7 6 5 4 3 2 1

POCKET and colophon are registered trademarks of
Simon & Schuster Inc.

Printed in the U.S.A.

Author's Note

In some instances, to protect identities and avoid compromising sources and methods, names of people, locations and time frames in this book have been changed.

Thousands of pages of public and private documents, records, and published materials were used as sources for this book, though many of the incidents described as well as virtually all dialogue and direct quotations are based on the author's best recollection. These quotations are intended to convey the spirit and meaning of the conversations, rather than the exact, verbatim words that were used.

Of the reference materials that were used in the preparation of this book, the authors would like to cite the following: *The Flight of the Falcon*, by Robert Lindsey; *The Murderers Among Us*, by Simon Wiesenthal; and *Too Tough to Die*, by Robert Sabbag.

for Betsy
and
for Mike Stauth

Acknowledgments

I would like to thank my editor, Paul McCarthy, and his assistant, Tristram Coburn, for their continued support, respect and faith in this project.

I would also like to thank Detective Lieutenant Paul Bynum, of Hermosa Beach, California, and Inspector Dennis Berry, of San Francisco. I have met few whom I have respected and even fewer whom I have liked. You were both. You let the goddamn job kill you and that's not the way it should be. You will be missed and very hard to replace.

—John Pascucci

Paul McCarthy, our editor, did his usual exceptional job in every phase of this difficult project. Paul is a superb and prominent editor, and we were extremely lucky to have his guidance, advice, editorial ideas, and support. Furthermore, he was a pleasure to work with, and made a difficult job an exciting creative experience. Thanks, too, to his assistant, Tris Coburn.

Richard Pine, my literary agent, represented me with dedication and great energy, as he has for many years. I have also long appreciated the efforts and advice of Arthur Pine, one of the great men in the publishing world.

ACKNOWLEDGMENTS

Jeanne Withrow, who did all the transcribing, organizing, and word processing for this book, contributed her work with great intelligence and efficiency, and I appreciate her efforts very much.

Jim Stiak made important contributions to this book in its earliest stages. His generosity, his good humor, and his kindness will never be forgotten.

This project would never have occurred without the help of Bob Wolfe. The book owes its existence to Bob's special gift: the ability to turn ideas into reality.

Thanks also to Shari, my only constant in a life of change. And thanks to Gabriel, who shared my office during most of the book, and to Miechel Barksdale and Meaghen Porte.

A final word of thanks to Lorraine Stauth, the first person to read this book and to offer editorial advice; the energy and care she put into this project can be found on each of its pages. I'll never be able to replace her help, or her caring.

—Cameron Stauth

Contents

Prologue · **LET ME TELL MY STORY** · 1

One · **THE CHILD KILLER** · 5

Two · **TREASON** · 37

Three · **KILLING PEOPLE** · 62

Four · **MAKING MY BONES** · 84

Five · **TRAITOR** · 119

Six · **THE FACE OF EVIL** · 154

Seven · **POWER** · 193

Eight · **MASS MURDER** · 233

Nine · **THE ANGEL OF DEATH** · 270

Ten · **THE WHORE ON DRUGS** · 315

Eleven · **THE MOST DANGEROUS MAN ON EARTH** · 333

Epilogue · 359

Index · 367

Prologue

Let Me Tell My Story

★

• Heroes and Monsters • The Code of the
West • All the President's Cops •

"The ends justify the means."
—*Hermann Busenbaum*

I know more about the world than most people do. At least, I know more about what's commonly called "the real world." But I'm not bragging. I'm confessing.

Knowledge never comes for free. It always comes at a price, and I paid too much.

Far too often, the price I paid was hurting people, breaking laws, and looking too long at the dark side of life.

But I did what I had to. I was an investigator, and the currency of an investigator's trade is knowledge. Specifically, I was a fugitive investigator, a manhunter. I was chief of International Operations for the United States Marshals Service.

My job was to track down the most evil people on earth: terrorists, killers, spies, Nazis, neo-Nazis, and psychopaths.

I was better at fugitive investigation than anyone else in the federal government—in part because I made myself think like the people I was tracking. That was part of the price I paid.

1

It's true: Knowledge is power. But knowledge is also punishment. It hurts to know the world at its worst. But if you don't, you don't know the real world.

You think I'm cynical? You're right. I am deeply cynical. But I'm also deeply idealistic. I know that sounds contradictory, but if you want a story about a *simple* cop, put down this book and go watch TV.

Please don't misunderstand me, though. I'm not complaining about the life I led. Far from it. I feel nothing but celebration. I had one hell of a ride. I enjoyed the most special privilege life can offer—I got to *do something.* Unlike some "idealists," I didn't just stand by and stay out of trouble. And I wasn't just a cog in a machine. I was *me.* I *lived my passions.* I stomped across the earth like a bull elk. My life was filled with excitement, power, and glamour. It was a privileged existence.

Part of my privilege was being above the law. I took tremendous legal latitude in tracking my targets. I wanted *results*, period.

Some people, of course, think it's wrong to break the law to catch dangerous criminals. I don't. I think that sometimes it's a necessary evil.

In fact, I've always been extremely *proud* of what I did.

My pride was magnified by being part of a glorious history. As a U.S. marshal, I helped uphold a majestic tradition. The Marshals—America's federal police force—were established by George Washington and served bravely throughout the nation's history. After the Civil War, many marshals died fighting the Klan. Shortly after that, marshals like Pat Garrett, Wild Bill Hickock, and Virgil Earp brought law to the West. In the 1930s, marshals went to war against the Mafia. In the 1960s, marshals protected the civil rights workers, and often took dozens of casualties in bloody encounters with racists. Then, in the late seventies, when I joined the Marshals, we began tracking international fugitives.

We tracked them better than any agency ever had. We were extremely aggressive and weren't afraid to twist the law to bring people in. Because we were the "president's police," serving at his pleasure, we adopted the chief executive's style and agenda. Thus, in the 1980s—when I saw

2

most of my action—I became *Ronald Reagan's version of a good cop.*

Under Reagan's kick-ass authority, American law enforcement reached a peak of effectiveness. The national arrest rate for homicides in 1984 was 95 percent—compared to a pathetic 50 percent today. For most serious crimes, national arrest rates were *twice as high* as the current rates.

To be totally honest, though, we could not have achieved this success by following the letter of the law.

But we were not the first marshals ever to bend the law. Throughout the agency's violent history, many marshals—stranded in lonely outposts—routinely broke the law to serve a higher justice. This "cowboy" style of law enforcement was absolutely common in the Old West.

However, marshals have always known that if you live outside America's written code, you'd better follow your own unwritten code. Our unwritten code was: Always put the Service ahead of yourself. If you took care of the Marshals, the Marshals would take care of you.

Because I put the Service ahead of myself, I didn't worry much about the consequences of breaking the law. After all, I represented the president. I was doing *America's work.* And doing it damn well.

Over an eleven-year period, I rocketed to prominence. As chief of International Operations, I held one of the highest positions in the Service. I was one of the most-decorated men in the modern era of the Marshals Service. The future stretched before me like a golden trail.

Then, after a decade of unparalleled success, I violated the unwritten code. And I fell from grace. I lost my position as America's top manhunter.

But through it all, I kept my sense of right and wrong. And I kept my self-esteem. I was able to do more good for this country than most people ever dream of. Many people consider me a modern American hero.

Others, I'm quite sure, think I'm a monster.

I ask only this: Let me tell my story.

It's a story of America in the wild and violent 1980s. It's a story about the twisted and mystifying relationship between good and evil.

It's also the story of a generation of people. I'm part of the American baby boom generation—the one that was going to *save the world*. But we didn't save anything. Instead, we got chewed up by the American system, and by our own unfettered appetites.

But we're still out here, struggling to invent the last half of our lives.

I promise you this: My story will not be a whitewash. I have nothing left to lose. You'll hear everything. You'll see a side of America you've never seen before.

And you'll see me as I really was.

A hero? A monster? Or both? Let me tell my story.

Then you decide.

Chapter One
The Child Killer

★

- First Man Through the Door • Shooting Shitbags Before Breakfast • Hostages and Human Shields • FBI Wienies • Bob Dylan's Blessing • Nazis in Paradise •

"To live outside the law, you must be honest."
—Bob Dylan

I was waiting in a grease pit called The Donut Hole for two cops to show up so we could grab some caffeine and discuss a procedural matter. The question was: Were we going to arrest our fugitive, or just go ahead and kill him?

So of course I grabbed a corner booth, as you always see cops do. It minimizes eavesdropping.

But even if somebody had overheard us, they wouldn't have known what we were talking about. We'd never say, "Let's murder this puke." Instead, we'd say something like, "Let's deprioritize this guy's civil liberties. To a maximum degree."

Any way you cut it, though, it was murder, so that's how I'm describing it. I assume you're sick of the usual line of law enforcement bullshit.

5

Before I could even sink my teeth into a chocolate-frosted doughnut, though, the waitress was in my face. "That your little red car? 'Cause somebody's got into it." She pointed at my fire-apple red '60 Corvette convertible.

I bolted out the door, and sure enough, some little shitbag was trying to rip off my stereo. I jerked my Colt 1911 out of my sport coat and dragged the kid out of the car. I was trying to be as gentle as possible—no excessive force—because I *loved* that car.

I slammed the kid to the ground, but the little skell decided he had to *fight*. He was all over me, even though he was a scrawny bastard—all thin limbs and right angles, like a big praying mantis. I smacked him with the gun, and gave his face a makeover with my free hand, but he just wouldn't go down. Pissed me *off*. Because it was four in the morning, I *still* hadn't gotten my caffeine fix, he was landing some good licks, and we were within *inches* of the car. Heads started popping out of windows, and one old black lady screamed, "*Shoot* the little bastard! *Shoot* him!"

I huffed at the kid, "Stay down, dammit! I'm runnin' outta steam. I'm gonna *have* to shoot ya."

"*Shooooot* him," screamed the lady.

The kid looked up at me and bleated, "Don't listen to *her*! That's my *mama!*"

"I ain't yo mama!" she yelled.

"You got three seconds," I chugged. "Then I'm gonna blast ya."

I pointed the gun at his head. "One!" I pulled back the hammer on my Colt. "Two!"

Then I saw *real* trouble. Two old Philadelphia coppers were waddling straight toward us. I couldn't get to my badge, and I was *sure* they were gonna beat the shit out of me first and do the paperwork later. They *couldn't* be the guys I was waiting for because I was expecting a SWAT team, which invariably meant twenty-five-year-old ex-Marines in spit-shined boots.

I yelled, "John Pascucci, U.S. Marshals!" Next thing I knew, one of them was standing over us—waiting, waiting—*thock!* Kicked the kid right in the balls, and that was the end

6

of him. The other cop called for a backup, and we handed off our mutt.

Turns out, they *were* the SWAT team, which pleased me immensely. Just looking at them—big old guts, veins popped in their noses, arms like ham hocks—you could tell they enhanced my chance of fulfilling the number one rule of law enforcement: At the end of your shift, go home alive. Unlike the ex-Marine SWAT types, these guys weren't burdened with a military "rules of engagement" mentality. Like me, they lived in the real world and knew that there were no rules except the ones we made up.

We went inside, and the waitress was all over us with free coffee and their freshest doughnuts. I had Coke instead of coffee, though; it's my favorite drink. I love the icy, acid way it bites into your belly. "Jesus," I moaned, as the caffeine and sugar kick-started my heart, "I been on the job too long. I was ready to blow that kid away over a fuckin' *stereo.*"

The cops gave each other a look, like, What've we got here, another federal *wienie?* So I let it drop. "Tell me about our fugitive," I said.

"Real piece-a shit," said the shorter of the two cops. "He skipped on a warrant for assault. Poured a can of boiling grease over his own kid's bare ass."

Right away, in my own mind, I knew the germ was dead if he gave us the chance. I can't tolerate abuse of someone who's totally vulnerable, like a child. As far as I'm concerned, that's pure evil. I can't really define evil, because, to me, it's a gut-level, emotional thing. But I know it when I see it.

Therefore, my perp had a *serious* problem. If I got the chance, he'd be meat in the morgue.

I know lawmen aren't supposed to act as judge, jury, and executioner, but if you don't think cops do that all the time, you've watched too much *NYPD Blue.* Besides, this was the *Reagan era of law enforcement,* and it didn't seem like President Rambo was too squeamish about his federal cops making "messy" arrests.

"How *serious* is this guy?" I asked. Meaning: how dangerous?

"He's popped a couple-a caps at police officers," said the

shorter one. "Long rap sheet. Assault. Carrying a concealed weapon. Assault with a deadly weapon. Rape. He's a biker. Sleeps with a sawed-off double-barrel. So this is gonna be a pucker job." He meant we'd all have to pucker our anal sphincters before we hit the door; in moments of extreme stress, the sphincter dilates.

We got all jacked up on caffeine and talked procedure: Do we use any special weapons? Do we cover the back door? Do we evacuate the adjacent apartment? Do we know the floor plan? And most important: Who's going to be the first man through the door? I volunteered for it. Always did. It was just my personality.

Then I eased into a touchy question. "If this guy gets froggy, tries to jump, do we exercise any ... special restraint?"

"No, John," said the less-short one, "he don't merit consideration. Trust me."

"Hey," I said, "if he has to go to heaven, he has to go."

"Can your bosses handle that?" asked the shorter one. He was used to feds being wimps. Because most feds *were* wimps—especially the FBI, which gave us *all* a bad rep.

"I got my bosses housebroken," I said. "Let's roll." I was antsy because this wasn't my only bust of the day. I was in Philadelphia running a Fugitive Investigative Strike Team, and my FIST operations took down about three mutts a day. The first one was usually the easiest because you could nail the puke in bed. After that, they got hairier.

Minutes later, I was standing outside the perp's apartment in Felony Flats with my Colt .45 single-action automatic in one hand and my flashlight in the other. They were my favorite weapons. I loved the Colt because it was a powerful, big-bore gun that needed to be cocked before the first cartridge was fired. In theory, taking time to cock it was a detriment, but in the real world, it gave me a tremendous advantage. When a felon heard the hammer go "click," it sounded like thunder. And once cocked, the trigger needed only three pounds of pressure, compared to fifteen for a double-action gun. You might not know that, but felons do.

Because it was so hair-trigger, the weapon was illegal for law enforcement. But fuck that. It got the job done. Also, it was "square" and didn't look like a cowboy gun. I hate all that cowboy shit. I got sick of people telling me what a cowboy I was.

Even more user-friendly than the Colt was the flashlight. At eighteen inches, with three pounds of batteries, it was meaner than a pit bull. A gun's great, but you're allowed to *hit* a lot more people than you're allowed to shoot, so your flashlight gets a real workout.

We stood outside the door for maybe five seconds. Seemed like forever. As usual, every nerve in my body was screaming: *You do not belong here!*

"Pucker up," the less-short cop whispered. Then: *"Police! Open the fucking door! Now!"* BRAMMM! He slammed his heel into the door and it exploded. We crashed through— screaming, to create confusion and fear. Busted into bedrooms. Kicked over anything in the way. The two fat old cops were a blur.

Suddenly: complete silence. Then the shorter cop backed out of a bedroom. The felon followed—holding a sawed-off shotgun to the head of a little girl. She was maybe ten. She was shaking. Mom was nowhere to be seen. Probably under a bed.

"Get the *fuck* outta here!" the mutt yelled. Half his teeth were black, and even from ten feet away he smelled like rotten meat and whisky. "Get the fuck outta here *now,* or I waste the little bitch!"

We stood staring. Listening to the little girl's shallow breath.

"Think I won't?" he leered.

I smiled at him. Big shit-eating grin. "You fucked *up,*" I said, with a chuckle.

From behind me, I heard the less-short cop snorting, then it snowballed into a laugh. "Inspector Pascucci," he rasped, "maybe you should give Mr. Dumbfuck here the basics on hostage taking."

I put my gun to my side, to show the guy how *badly* he'd fucked up. "When taking hostages," I said, "you must take *at least two.* That way, you can shoot one to make a point, and still have one *left.* But take just *one,* and you have *shit.*"

The mutt looked bewildered, but he wasn't backing down.

I was counting on maternal instinct, though, to break things up. Pretty soon, Mama was going to appear and get his attention. Mama *had* to be here because every instinct in my body said: *This guy does not baby-sit.*

But I wasn't going to wait forever. My motto is: When in doubt, *do something.*

"Furthermore," said the less-short cop.

"Furthermore," I said, still flashing teeth, "when you employ a hostage as a human shield, use one that covers your whole body. At least, all the body parts that you *like.*"

The perp tried to squeeze his crotch behind the little girl, and that gave the less-short cop the giggles again.

"Very soon now," I continued, "I *am* going to kill you, and all that will happen to your 'shield' is that she will get very wet and gooey."

"*Bassss*-turd!" It was Mama. Streaking out of the kitchen with a butcher knife. It was all the distraction I needed. Despite my big talk, there was no way I'd shoot while he was holding the girl. I darted a half-step forward and lashed my flashlight across the bridge of his nose.

The two old cops were glued to him before he hit the floor. They cuffed him, then they each got in a couple of licks. The shorter cop snarled, "You're *lucky,* man." The felon didn't seem to understand. But I did. The bastard would be back on the street in ten months. And that had *not* been the plan. Of course, it's evil to kill people—but sometimes it's a necessary evil.

Before we split, we did a quick sweep of the apartment. The less-short cop opened a closet door and sang out, *"Got* somethin'!" It was a marijuana plant about five feet tall and bushy as a Christmas tree.

"I'll dump the goddamn thing for ya," I offered.

"Thanks." There was no point trying to bust him for it, since we had no search warrant. The beauty of going after fugitives was that you didn't need to worry about having a warrant, or even making a legal arrest. My targets had *already* been arrested, so my job was just to grab their bodies and bring them in.

For me, it was the perfect job: no bullshit, no bureaucracy.

As we headed for the door, the little girl came up to me. "Where you takin' him?"

I gave her a gentle smile. "Where he can't hurt you anymore, honey."

She curled her lip. "You mean *jail,* motherfucker!" She kicked my shin.

I didn't hassle her. What was the point?

Outside, I shook the two old cops' hands.

"You're good coppers," I told them. That was as mushy as I ever got. I'm not good at that male-bonding shit.

I jumped into the 'Vette and streaked onto the freeway. I stuck some old Dylan into the stereo, put down the top, and let the wind and music howl. I punched it, and the acceleration jerked my head back. I'd seized the car from a drug dealer, so it was souped up to outrun cops. The accelerator was as touchy as the trigger on my Colt. *Lovely* car.

Since cops don't get speeding tickets, I revved it up to eighty-five.

I felt totally alive.

"How does it feel? To be all alone?"

I could hardly see over the damn pot plant in the passenger's seat, but I didn't care. I was happy. Tonight, I'd go back to my suite at the Marriott, lay back on my cream-soft leather couch, crank up the MTV on my forty-inch screen, order up a lobster, Caesar salad, and six-pack of Coke, and smoke some of this fine, golden dope.

Presuming, of course, I didn't get killed in the meantime.

The car phone rang.

"Yeah?"

"John, it's Joanne in Mr. Safir's office. Hold, please, for Ron."

The boss's assistant got on the line. "Hey, John, Mr. Safir has a new assignment he wants to task you with. Go straight to the airport. The assistant manager of the Marriott will meet you at gate thirty-one with your suitcase. Your ticket's prepaid. Okay? Hang on for Mr. Safir."

"Hello, John." It was Howard Safir, director of operations of the United States Marshals Service.

"Hi, Boss."

"John, we've got something of extreme importance. It may

be the most critical case we've had since the Marshals took over the apprehension of all federal fugitives."

"Who's the mutt?"

"Nazi war criminal."

"Sounds interesting."

"Oh, it'll be interesting. But, John, before you accept this, I have to tell you that it may be extremely dangerous."

"You always did know how to manipulate me, Boss."

"See you this afternoon."

I trudged through Woolworth's on my way to headquarters. At this time, in 1985, the U.S. Marshals Service was housed in a shopping mall outside Washington, D.C. Despite our two-hundred-year history, we still didn't have our own building. Although we were part of the Justice Department, we were essentially a rogue agency, operating out in deep center field. Which suited me fine.

"Gentlemen," announced Howard Safir as I cruised into his office, "I'd like you to meet John Pascucci, the best tracker in the United States government."

Two baby-faced little guys in matching blue suits stood and shook my hand. Safir introduced us, but their names went in one ear and out the other. To me, they were just Frick and Frack, two more political pimps who'd wormed their way onto the staff of the prestigious Office of Special Investigations. OSI was also part of the Justice Department and was America's official Nazi-hunting agency. It took a lot of political juice to hook up with OSI, so these guys were apparently high-pedigree lawyers. But *Nazi* hunters? They looked more like two little Care Bears.

"I've heard all *about* you," said Frick. "The modern Wild Bill Hickock!" I didn't even try to smile. So what if a bunch of old shitkickers had once been marshals? I worked with computers and international intelligence operations, and I didn't wear *spurs* while I was doing it.

The Boss tried to ease the strain by telling me what hotshot litigators Frick and Frack were. But that didn't defrost me. I had nothing but contempt for OSI. I'd heard that they'd sucked up something like forty million federal dollars and had opened cases on only forty-eight Nazis. That may sound like a lot of Nazis to you, but let me tell you something about the real world that you probably didn't know. At the end of World War II, the Allies identified over *150,000* Nazi war criminals—by name, position, locale, and atrocity. Everyone likes to think that the Nuremberg trials wiped out all the war criminals, but less than 2,000 were convicted there and at the Dachau trials. About 25,000 more were convicted by the Soviet Union, 5,000 were convicted by Poland, 2,000 by France, and 1,000 by England. All together: 35,000. That's about 20 percent.

The other 115,000 slithered off into the sunset. About 10,000 moved to America. Therefore, on average, every American town or neighborhood of 25,000 people became home to one Nazi war criminal. You probably didn't know that because you're not *supposed* to know it. The feds don't like you to think you're surrounded by evil.

The horrifying thing about evil, I think, is not so much its depth in an individual, but its breadth in the everyday world. If you look for it, you find it. If you look hard enough, you even find some in yourself—and that's the most horrifying thing of all.

But I didn't burden Frick and Frack with any of this. I just wanted to get their dossier and get the hell out of Washington.

Frick slid an eight-by-ten photo onto Safir's desk, which was a glossy, polished thing about the size of an aircraft carrier. The picture was a black-and-white head shot of an old man with a cold face and dead eyes. "This is Bohdan Koziy," Frick said.

"Who is Boe-dan Cozy?" I asked.

"His nickname is the Child Killer. He worked in the Ukraine. After the death camps filled up, the Final Solution was decentralized to places like the Ukraine. They murdered over one million people there. But you probably knew that; I understand you've already captured one Nazi for us?"

I wanted to say, Yeah, on a twenty-thousand-dollar budget, after *your* investigation of the guy turned into a million-dollar goatfuck. But the Boss—who *hated* working above a dimestore—wanted me to stop pissing off bureaucrats. So I just nodded.

"Koziy was a Ukrainian policeman," said Frick. "He participated in a local Jewish extermination program that took sixty thousand lives. He earned his nickname by torturing and killing children in front of their parents to extract information."

"OSI already prosecuted him for lying to Immigration," said Safir, "and stripped his citizenship. But nine months ago, he ran. Technically, his only violation is owing $18,500 in court costs. If he's still in the country, you can serve him with papers on the court costs violation. If he doesn't respond, he can be arrested. Then we can deport him to the Soviet Union, where he will be tried for war crimes."

My eyes were glazing over. But Frick and Frack looked very happy. "We think it's a solid, solid strategy," said Frack.

I thought it was solid, solid bullshit. If I served him with papers, he'd just run away. Besides, after nine months in the wind, Koziy's trail would be cold as snow. I thought it was idiotic of OSI to have waited so long to bring in a professional tracker, but that's how government agencies, in general, work; they hog their turf to protect their funding.

If it was up to me, my strategy would be somewhat more streamlined: Track him, whack him, sack him.

In fact, at the end of World War II, Winston Churchill had proposed exactly that. He'd said that when war criminals were found, they should be given six hours to explain themselves, then shot. But he couldn't push it through Parliament.

And now, fifty years later, the politicians were even softer on Nazis. It was the turbulent spring of '85, at the height of the Cold War, and President Reagan was a hell of a lot more concerned about Communists than Nazis. Nor was there much interest in Nazis from *any* of the top men in Reagan's Justice Department—which included the Marshals, the FBI, the DEA, Immigration, and the Bureau of Prisons. As a matter of fact, the FBI was actually considering charges against *me* for some of the things I'd done to bag my last Nazi. They were afraid I'd violated his civil fucking liberties.

"Gentlemen," Safir said to Frick and Frack, "it's obvious you've done excellent work on this case up to now, and Inspector Pascucci will follow through accordingly."

"Well, we deeply appreciate your help," said Frack, "and

you can be assured that the attorney general is very aware of your important role."

I *knew* that was bullshit. The best thing about the A.G., Ed Meese, was that he didn't watch over us too closely. He was an extremely tough law-and-order advocate, and I often got the feeling that he consciously ignored us so that we could crack heads and cut nuts. The Reagan era was an extraordinary time for law enforcement—not equaled before or since. It was a golden oasis of freedom for get-the-job-done cops, like me. We were fast, efficient, and—according to the Justice Department's national arrest and conviction statistics—about twice as effective as cops today.

Safir escorted the little Care Bears back out through his anterooms while I collapsed on a couch and rifled through the file on Bohdan Koziy that they'd left.

Safir came back, alone, and closed the door.

"Jesus, Boss, was that a meeting, or a circle-jerk?"

He ignored me. "Can we nail this guy, John?"

"We can, if we do it like it's *real*." What I meant was, we could if we ignored the fact that it was just a civil case, and not a criminal case.

"It's real to me," said Safir.

I chose to assume that he was giving me the okay to cut loose. But I wasn't sure, and I wasn't about to ask.

I often spoke to Safir in vague terms. I hid the gory details. It made me more valuable. And I was *very* valuable. When Safir *had* to get a job done, he'd turn to me, and it *got* done. No matter what.

I had tremendous respect for Howard Safir. In some ways, he was like me. He was a big, physical guy who'd done plenty of street time. His parents were immigrant Russian Jews, and he was the nephew of the New York City cop who'd busted bank robber Willie Sutton. Safir had worked undercover on dope, had been in several shootouts, and had run the Witness Security Program (which almost everyone refers to, mistakenly, as the Witness Protection Program).

But Safir's crowning achievements had come with the Marshals. Safir, more than anyone else, had quietly dragged the Marshals into power. After its heroic efforts in the 1960s civil rights movement, the Marshals had gradually sunk into

Washington's bureaucratic mush. By the 1970s, the Service had become a club of fat-assed political appointees who "guarded" courthouses and chauffeured federal prisoners. But Safir joined the Service in 1970 and later helped snag the Fugitive Program. That changed everything.

Suddenly, the Marshals "owned" 8,500 of the worst criminals on earth. The fat old boys on the courthouse couches resigned in droves. A new breed of marshals surged forward, willing to risk everything in the Fugitive Program. Safir was a member of that new breed.

So was I. I joined the Marshals in 1979 and flew toward the Fugitive Program like a moth to flame. I'd already been a sheriff's deputy in suburban New York City, and I thought I'd seen serious mutts. At least, they'd been serious enough for me to kill. But in the Fugitive Program, I came into daily contact with absolute evil.

Nothing in my life had prepared me for that experience—even though I'd *hardly* led a sheltered existence. In the early 1960s, when I was fourteen, I dropped out of high school, ran away from home, and moved in with a group of beatniks and drug addicts in the slums of New York's East Village. For a while, I hung around with Bob Dylan's folky crowd, then I joined a gang of leather punks. My buddies were Hell's Angels, killers, and some eventual victims of killers. I got beaten up by cops a number of times. But other cops—good cops—saved my life, literally and figuratively. At sixteen, I was selling furniture on Houston Street for Francis Ford Coppola's uncle, Danny Caputo. Danny taught me how to be a nice Italian boy when I was selling to Italians, and a nice Jewish boy when I was selling to Jews. I found out that I was a pretty good actor. Even learned Yiddish.

When I was seventeen, I joined the army, married my commanding officer's daughter, and was quickly run out of the service by my C.O. End of marriage.

Then I ran through a long string of working-class jobs while I went to college at night. I didn't get a degree, but I studied philosophy and anthropology and discovered I had an IQ of about 150. Shocked the shit out of me. I'd always thought, because I'd skipped high school, that I was kind of stupid. To be honest, I was always pretty insecure about myself, even after I found out I had a high IQ. Maybe it was because of my lack of a college degree, or my working-class upbringing, or just because I didn't get enough approval as a kid. Whatever the reason, I always felt like I had to keep proving myself.

As a young man, I had a wide array of opportunities, but what I really wanted to be was a cop. Like a lot of baby boomers, I was extremely idealistic—in my own cynical way—but I was certain that to do good, you had to have power. And there was no quicker route to power than police work. Even a twenty-one-year-old cop could make life-and-death decisions and go to war against bad guys.

Besides—I'll be honest—it sounded like fun: kickin' ass and drivin' fast.

My Village buddies thought I was crazy—just another acid casualty. Their idea of morality was to recycle their pop cans and grow a tomato on the roof. To me, that was *lame.* I wanted to *do* something. I thought people were *obligated* to do something. I even had a phrase for it: "the moral imperative of action." I tried the phrase out on my buddies, but they just laughed at me—they said I just wanted an excuse to shoot people.

One night, a bunch of us were gathered around Dylan, in our standard sycophants' semicircle, and he said, "What the world needs most is good cops—cops who'll enforce justice, instead of the law."

After that, when my buddies gave me shit, I hit 'em with Dylan's quote. That got them off my ass.

I took the NYC police exam.

Out of 50,000 people taking it, I placed 344th—in the 99th percentile. I was off and running. But, like Safir, I didn't hit my stride until I became a marshal.

It wasn't just coincidence, of course, that Safir and I surged to the top of the Marshals at the same time. We helped each other. I needed him, and he needed me. Now that he was operations director, he needed me more than ever.

"Did OSI miss some leads, John?" Safir asked me. He was looking over my shoulder at the file on Bohdan Koziy.

"Is the pope horny?" I replied. "Hell, yes, they missed

leads. Look at this, they didn't even open his credit card records."

"That's not legal in a civil case," Safir said. I didn't pursue it.

"So I serve him with papers if he's in the United States," I grumbled. "What do I do if he's already split?"

"We'll burn that bridge when we get to it," Safir said. "But I *want* this guy. That's why I tasked *you* with this." Safir gave me a hard, dark look. His rectangular face, topped by a heavy black bar of eyebrows, was rigid with tension.

I thought he was saying that if we found Koziy abroad, I had permission to black-bag him—kidnap him—and bring him back for extradition. But maybe that was just what I *wanted* to think.

Didn't matter. Either way, I was going to get the job done.

I was the Gipper's cop, and the Gip and I didn't worry about details.

I hauled ass out of Safir's office, heading for the Justice Department's historical library, where I'd gather background on Koziy. I felt the thrill of the hunt begin to pulse through me.

I loved my life.

I was a lucky man. Or so I thought.

"Bodhan Koziy," rumbled the tweedy fat man in the Justice Department's library, "or Bogdanus Kosij, as he was known then, was part of the Ukrainian program called 'Judenfrei'—'Free of Jews.' Koziy, who was a policeman, was the son of a wealthy man and the son-in-law of his village's mayor. In other words, he was a man of privilege, who did what he wanted to do."

"Which was *what?*"

"He searched out the Jews in his village, many of whom he'd grown up with, and he shot them.

"He would hunt down hiding families, interrogate them, march them to the cemetery, and shoot them—often repeatedly, if he was using a small-caliber weapon.

"He seemed to be proud of his work. One boy, who was forced to dig a pit to bury bodies, recalls Koziy stacking the bodies before burial, so he could have his photo taken with them.

"Koziy entered the United States in 1948, claiming on immigration forms that the only group he'd ever been a member of was the Boy Scouts. Then he bought a gas station at the New York Thruway exit at Two hundred thirty-third Street."

"I know that station," I said. "Used to buy gas there."

"Small world."

"*Sick* world."

"In recent years, Koziy moved to Florida and bought a motel. It was in Florida, in 1977, that the government first brought charges against him. Of course, that was eight years ago, and not much has happened. He's very anti-Communist, and that's helped him."

As I was getting ready to leave, the researcher gave me a name and address. "It's the niece of one of Koziy's victims," he said. "She lives nearby. She's heard several firsthand accounts about him."

I drove out to see her. It was only about thirty hours since we'd hit the door in Philadelphia, but already that seemed like another lifetime. I was becoming obsessed with Bohdan Koziy. To find him, I had to get inside his head. I had to get a feel for what he liked, feared, trusted, hated: how he thought. That's not how OSI worked. OSI guys had told me, proudly, that they could *never* think like a Nazi.

I guess they didn't have to, as long as they could come to me.

The victim's niece lived in a bad neighborhood, in an apartment with barred windows. She was an old woman who had the kind of plump face that usually looks jolly. But she never smiled, not once, and the effect was creepy.

She told me how Bohdan Koziy used to do *his* investigative work. He'd find a Jewish family—such as the aunt, the uncle, and the two girl cousins of the woman I was interviewing. His goal was to locate everybody in the whole extended family, and all their friends. Then he'd start torturing them, one at a time. Just simple stuff, like burning, or pinching with pliers. But his deal with them was, at any time, they could ask him to stop, and he'd move on to another family member.

"My aunt and uncle, they tried to bear the pain them-selves," said the woman in a monotone. "But who can bear such things?"

Koziy's goal, she said, was to make the family members hate one another—and hate *themselves,* for their weakness. After that, the information came quickly.

"What happened to the family?" I asked.

"When he had his information, he shot my cousins. First the younger one, then the twelve-year-old. He made their parents carry them to the cemetery. Then he shot my uncle. Then he shot my aunt. But she remained alive, and some-how survived."

I sat in silence with her for some time. What the hell do you say? I wanted to tell her how bad I felt. But she didn't need my anguish. She needed my action. So I said to her, "I'm gonna make you a promise. If I find this guy—and I *will* find this guy—he's a dead man." I always got too emotionally involved, and it always got me in trouble.

Then she smiled. But it was the kind of smile I wish I'd never seen.

I bombed into Phillie, grabbed my 'Vette, and screamed down to Ft. Lauderdale, Florida, Koziy's last address. I could've flown, but I loved my car. I had no real home, and I hardly ever got to see my wife. So I'd bonded with the 'Vette.

Besides, the way I drove, I could outrun most airlines.

As I streaked down the highway, I thought about Koziy. What did I know about him? I knew what he looked like. I knew he had money. I knew he had a little knowledge of police work. He had a wife and two grown kids. He was absolutely ruthless. And he was a fugitive.

The fact that he was a fugitive seemed obvious, but OSI, in its half-assed attempt to find him, hadn't addressed that. They'd looked for him as if he were just another citizen and not a runner. But he *was* on the run, and that meant his usual lifestyle patterns would be changed.

I'd look for the patterns of a *fugitive.* I would start with patterns of travel—driving records, travel agencies, airline tickets, etc. I'd look for patterns of money transfer. I'd look for liquidation of assets. I'd look for changing patterns of communication: Was he saying good-bye to people? Was he setting up a mail drop? I'd look for patterns of concealment—because sometimes people reveal things by trying to hide them.

If I couldn't find enough, I'd assume that he was hunkered down somewhere. If that was the case, I'd make him think we were closing in on him, so that he'd run again. You might think it's harder to find somebody if they're moving, but it's not. If you can keep your target running, sooner or later you'll hit him. Because everytime you move, you leave a trail.

In the cowboy days, marshals followed a trail by looking for hoofprints and broken branches, and by smelling the horse shit. These days, people still leave a trail of "broken branches" and "hoofprints," but now it's all electronic information—numerical markers—stored in computers. If you're traveling—especially if I can make you *hurry*—you'll eventually leave a marker on your trail. You'll get a traffic ticket, or use a credit card, or cross an international border. When you do, I may not know where you are, but I'll at least know where you've been.

Tracking somebody is a constant process of cutting down their time line. Koziy, for example, was known to have been in Ft. Lauderdale nine months ago. Therefore, my time line on him was nine months. Let's say that I found out that he'd been in a travel agency in Miami two months ago. If that happened, I would have cut his time line down from nine months to *two* months. I would keep reducing his time line by finding new information, and the trail would get hotter and hotter. Finally, I'd cut it to the point where he and I would be in the same place at the same time.

I flashed down Interstate 95, asking myself, When will Koziy's trail get hottest? One obvious answer was: When I get a hook into his kids. It was very possible that a guilt-ridden puke like him had played Superdad all his life, to convince himself he wasn't such a bad guy. His kids probably adored him and thought he was the victim of a political witch-hunt. They probably knew exactly where he was. And, of critical importance, they'd probably be easier to "play" than Koziy himself. They would be second generation, which would probably mean: softer, more sentimental, less paranoid, less shrewd.

They might even be the kind of dickheads who'd phone the old man's hiding place from their home phones. I'd grab their phone records and find out. Of course, that wasn't legal in a civil case—but fuck that. It was a necessary evil.

As I drove, I activated a worldwide computer search for Koziy with my car phone. I entered Koziy's name into a number of informational systems all over the world, including the Florida Department of Law Enforcement Data Processing System, EPIC (the national computer bank that records people entering America), the Non-Immigrant Immigration System, MIRAC (the international computer network of people applying for citizenship), NADDIS (the Drug Enforcement Agency's secret computer system), the Treasury Enforcement Communications System, several levels of the Florida DMV system, the first level of the entire fifty-state DMV system, and the Interpol system.

By the mid-1980s, these data banks had become the primary resource of all manhunts. With one good modem-equipped computer, and one good gun, I could catch virtually anyone.

Technically, this computer search was illegal, since Koziy wasn't a "criminal." But I was certain it was exactly what Reagan himself would've done.

I also called Simon Wiesenthal's Nazi-hunting group, and they alerted their network. At this point, they were still friendly. Later on, after I proved Josef Mengele was dead and dug up his body, they became pretty cold. Mengele was their "poster boy"—their prime means of fund-raising—and it seemed to me that they resented my closing his case.

When I finished my calls, I leaned back in my baby-soft bucket seat and got down to the ugliest job of the day: getting into Koziy's head. I did it sort of the same way an actor prepares for a role; I pretended I *was* Koziy and tried to *feel* his attitudes, fears, hatreds, and desires. After a while, in a half-trance, I began to think like him. I felt old, tired, and harried. I didn't trust anyone but my immediate family. I didn't want to fight to clear my name; honor meant nothing to me. I just wanted to be left alone. I wanted to escape—from my past, and from America.

As I pulled out of my daydream, I was groggy and sick. My brain felt poisoned.

By the time I hit Lauderdale, information began to trickle in. Best news: We had an address for Koziy's son, out in Albuquerque, New Mexico. I called a marshal out there and told him to make contact. Couldn't locate the daughter, though, because she'd gotten married and changed her name.

Before I settled into a hotel, I set up shop in the Ft. Lauderdale Marshals' office and connected with a couple of great guys, marshal Tony Perez and ex–Miami vice cop Bill Donteri, who was a private investigator. Tony was a legend; he could bite the ass off a bear, and eventually arrested Manuel Noriega. Bill was just as tough but smoother, and would later go to work as an investigator *for* Noriega, after Tony had busted him.

Bill didn't even charge me for his services. He wanted me to owe him one, so that when he needed something illegal done—like looking into a sealed government record—I'd do it for him. His services, though, were invaluable. He was hooked into the southern Florida territory like no one else. He had informants everywhere.

Tony set me up with secretaries, to handle my paperwork, and Bill dug into more difficult matters, like getting a hook into the credit card company that Koziy had used, American Express.

Late in the afternoon, I drove out to Koziy's last address, the Lorelei Apartments, and talked to the manager. Nobody from OSI had ever contacted him. Turns out, Koziy had left there seven months ago, in September of 1984. So already I had cut my time line from nine months to seven months.

"And I know where he *went*," said the manager, a kid who didn't seem too bright. "Albuquerque. Or Toronto. Or Costa Rica."

That really nailed it down.

"Why do you think he went to one of those places?"

"Cuz I heard him and his old lady talking. Couple times."

Of course, Koziy was shrewd enough to plant misinformation, but it was encouraging that one of the possibilities was

Albuquerque, because that's where the son was. Koziy, however, could have included Albuquerque just to give his misinformation veracity.

I started canvassing the neighbors, and picked up another tidbit. Shortly before he'd left, Koziy had sold his refrigerator to one of the neighbors. So he probably wasn't in Florida; if he'd stayed in the area, he would've taken the fridge with him.

I went back to the office and called the local newspaper's classified department. "This is Bohdan Koziy," I said. *"K-o-z-i-y.* I think I was overcharged for an ad I placed." I waited while they punched *Koziy* into the computer.

"Your ad ran September twelfth," said the clerk, "for three days. In the For Sale section. According to our records, the billing was correct."

"Okay, thanks." I didn't have to use subterfuge on something like that, but it was always quicker. More fun, too.

I went to a library, checked the newspaper on microfiche for September 12, and found the ad that corresponded to Koziy's last phone number. He was only selling his big stuff—couch, freezer, dining room table. It wasn't a "yard sale" type of ad.

That meant he was keeping his toaster and lamps and little stuff, which *probably* meant he was staying in the United States.

I started calling every moving van company in the yellow pages, and, sure enough, one of them had moved the Koziys, on September 20, 1984.

It was a good lead, so I drove out to work it up. I wanted to talk to a low-level employee because it's the little guys of this world who'll be straight with you; if you want to know where the bodies are buried, don't ask the owner of the cemetery—ask the gravediggers.

One of the lumpers on the loading dock went into the office for me and got Koziy's bill of lading. An owner probably wouldn't have done that—he would have protected his client's privacy and upheld the *American way of life.*

"Looks like his stuff went to bonded storage out on the docks," the lumper said.

Maybe Koziy *had* split the country. I blasted out to the

docks, thinking I was going to find Koziy's shipping order and get some real heat on the trail.

But Koziy's stuff had only been in storage a couple of days, then had been shipped to Albuquerque. That meant Koziy was either living in Albuquerque, or he'd dumped his stuff with his son before he'd left the country. I was guessing he'd just dumped it. He was too smart to hang around his son.

I drove back to the office. There was a message waiting. Sonny-boy in Albuquerque—Anatoly Koziy—was stonewalling. Totally uncooperative. Yes, he knew where Dad was. No, he wasn't telling. Since this was a civil case, we couldn't compel his cooperation.

It was way past dark, and the office was dead. I hung around, drank Coke, and played with the computers, looking for Koziy-tracks all around the world.

I could never understand it when people left work at five o'clock. But after a few hours, my eyes were burning and my stomach was an acid pit of Coca-Cola. I called it a day. Felt lousy. I was two days into the chase, and I had jack-shit.

So much for the honest approach.

The sun climbed hot and brilliant out of the Atlantic, toasting my body and melting the butter on my croissants as I sat half-naked on the balcony of my suite. I poured down room service Coke and freshly squeezed orange juice and ranted into the phone at my agent in Albuquerque.

For some reason, my agent was annoyed at the time zone difference—it was still night there—and he'd expected me to *share his concern.* But that's not what had set me off. I'd asked him a simple question: Could he develop a contact at the Albuquerque phone company, to get a list of Sonny-boy's calls? And he'd started reciting, like, the Bill of *Rights* or some goddamn thing. He didn't want to invade Anatoly's *space.* This guy did *not* understand the Reagan era of law enforcement.

I reminded him that Safir and I could have him executed. So he said he'd do what he could. But I knew he was just jerking me around.

I told him to go out and interview Anatoly, and left it at that.

I couldn't force him to get aggressive, and I wasn't going to waste my time trying. Knowing what to push is only part of running an investigation; you also have to know what to let slide—because, despite every felon's paranoid fantasies, governmental resources are very finite.

Of course, the most effective procedure would've been to put a trap-and-trace on Anatoly's phone. But even if Anatoly had been the Godfather, it wouldn't have happened. The courts just won't allow it (regardless of what you've seen in the movies).

But then I got Bill Donteri on the phone, and—bingo!—Bill had talked to his confidential informant at American Express and had a list of four guys who could access the files we needed. Bill read me the names. They were like, Mr. Smith, Mr. Jones, Mr. Washington, and Mr. Goldblum.

"I'll go see Mr. Goldblum," I said.

An hour later, I was in Mr. Goldblum's office, watching the poor guy bubble with sweat. As a Jew, he was *dying* to help. I'd told him all about the Child Killer, giving him all the bloody details—and *then* some. I'd guilt-tripped this guy a mile a minute. But he was scared shitless of losing his job.

"If you had *any* kind of subpoena . . ." Mr. Goldblum whined.

"Sit tight. I'll speak to a judge." He was so relieved, you could hear the air hiss out of him.

In the lobby of the building, I pulled a stolen "administrative subpoena" out of my briefcase, filled it out, and signed a judge's name. I'd grabbed a stack of administrative subpoenas (which subpoena evidence, rather than people) from a file cabinet at OSI. I know that sounds dangerous, but I wasn't very worried about getting caught. Ed Meese's Justice Department wasn't very high-minded about punishing mischief. Meese himself had been accused during the 1980 election of acquiring documents stolen from Jimmy Carter. He'd also been accused of financial shenanigans, and of trading jobs for favors. But the Gipper still loved him because Meese always got the job done.

When I gave the subpoena to Mr. Goldblum, he looked relieved—but not *too* relieved. He kept staring at it. He was a smart guy and probably knew my quickie subpoena was the product of a "weasel deal"—a fraud.

He was losing his nerve. "Can you imagine somebody killing *children?*" I asked. He shook his head. But still he hesitated.

"Do *you* have kids?" I asked. He nodded. I just let the question float in the air.

"I'm not sure I can help," he said, finally. "But if I *were* to help, I'd punch in this code." He scribbled some numbers on a scrap of paper. "That would give you what you need. But let me go use the rest room, and I'll think about it. I'll be back in twenty-five minutes."

Then he marched out of the room, with force and conviction, as if he were an Israeli agent sticking a gun in Adolph Eichmann's ribs. Tonight he'd be telling his kids what a hero he was. Fine with me. He *was* a hero. For all I knew, he was blowing his career.

Minutes later, I was back in the sizzling Florida sun with the complete American Express records of Bohdan Koziy.

I scanned the sheet, looking for "triggers." Triggers are pieces of information that lead you to even more pertinent pieces. I found one right away. Koziy had spent money at a travel agency, D'Anne Tours, of Miami. I hit the phones like a bat on speed.

The travel agent at D'Anne Tours told me Koziy had bought tickets for Costa Rica, Albuquerque, and Toronto.

I called the airlines, pretended to be a travel agent, and scammed them into telling me which tickets had actually been used. Two had—the one to Albuquerque, and the one to Costa Rica. But the ticket to Costa Rica had been used by Koziy's wife—*before* Koziy had fled.

That was interesting. It meant she might have been checking out Costa Rica as a possible destination.

Just as interesting, Koziy had traveled extensively just before he'd left Ft. Lauderdale. He'd visited New York, Philadelphia, New Mexico, and Washington, D.C. Then, right after he'd left Ft. Lauderdale, he'd stopped using his credit cards.

To me, it looked like a guy wrapping up all his business and saying good-bye to friends. After his farewell tour, he'd probably left the country—using a ticket purchased with cash so that there wouldn't be a record of it.

As a rule, people who remain in the country—even if they're ducking out of sight—don't exhibit so many patterns of closure. They don't go visit Aunt Minnie in New York if they know she'll still be just a short plane flight away.

Furthermore, his travel records corresponded to key dates in his legal proceedings. Every time the legal noose had tightened, Koziy had made another apparent preparation to flee.

All my instincts told me that Bohdan Koziy was in Costa Rica. But to get the okay to chase him, I had to prove he was there. And I wasn't even close to proving that.

When I got back to the office, I showed the American Express records to a young agent and tasked him with researching some of the purchases.

I hunched over my terminal and worked my way around the world again, looking for tracks. There weren't any. Koziy was a smart bastard.

According to detective novels, I was supposed to be glad that my "worthy adversary" was cunning. What bullshit! The dumber your target is, the happier you are. Problem was, at my level, none of them were ever dumb.

Late that evening, the young agent came back to the office looking happy as a little puppy dog.

He was carrying a Fodor travel guide to Costa Rica. "Know how much this cost?" he asked. "Exactly this much." He pointed to a Waldenbooks charge on Koziy's American Express record.

"Did you computer cross-reference that, to see how many other books in the store cost the same?"

He sagged.

"How late will you be here?" he asked.

"Too late."

He took off again. Three hours later, he was back, with a credit card slip. It was Koziy's original receipt, with the store clerk's annotation: "Fodor/C. Rica." This time he looked like a puppy with a *bone.*

"Well," I said, "I think I've got enough to justify a trip to Costa Rica."

"Cuz of this receipt?" He was *so* happy.

"No. Because when I call Safir tomorrow, I'm gonna lie my ass off."

But it didn't come to that. The next morning I found the trigger that broke the case.

I know that for fictional detectives, *A* leads to *B*, which leads to *C*, and breaks the case. But in real life, *A* leads to *B*, which leads to *dick*, and then the information that breaks the case waltzes in from left field.

But that's not because of luck; it's because you're working in several directions at once.

The minute I walked into the office, a secretary handed me a record I'd been waiting for. It was Koziy's Florida "driver's abstract." The driver's abstract is a semisecret DMV record that goes into much greater detail than the standard driver's profile.

Koziy's driver's abstract contained a fascinating piece of info. He'd been in a minor traffic accident in a car registered to somebody named G. Morelli.

Whoever G. Morelli was, he or she *had* to be close to Koziy. Why else would Koziy have his or her car?

I rushed back to Koziy's old apartment building and started bugging the neighbors: Who's G. Morelli? The third neighbor I talked to knew—G. Morelli was Gina, Koziy's married daughter. She lived in Plantation, a suburb of Ft. Lauderdale.

I thought about going to see her. But I wanted to see what I could scare up before I spooked her. I wanted to grab her phone records before she realized she was under surveillance.

So I swung by my hotel and changed into a dark gray pinstripe suit, white shirt, and solid gold cuff links—a power suit, perfect for corporate manipulation. Then I filled out one of my pocket subpoenas and descended on Southeast Bell like the ACLU's worst nightmare. I had Gina Morelli's phone records in twenty minutes.

And guess what? She'd been making regular calls to Costa Rica. Interestingly, the calls were evenly spaced—every four days—all at 6:00 P.M. The calls tended to be much longer right after key dates in Koziy's ongoing legal skirmishes. I decided to not go see her, in hopes that she'd keep calling Koziy.

I faxed a memo to Safir, telling him what I'd found, and applying for permission to go to Costa Rica.

I sat in the office, waiting, almost sick with nerves. If Safir couldn't sell this to the attorney general, we were finished. Koziy would skate. The thought of that made my stomach hot. At night, I'd been reading the transcript of his trial—particularly survivors' testimony—and it had given me nightmares.

Late in the afternoon, a secretary came to my desk and handed me a fax. From Safir. It said "Go."

My heart burned with joy.

Of course, I knew that the closer you get to your target, the closer you get to danger. But what the hell? Life is short, no matter what you do.

"Inspector Pascucci?" The flight attendant's voice echoed through the empty plane.

I tensed. "What's up?"

"I'm afraid you'll have to deplane for a few minutes."

I stood up, and so did Deputy Marshal Joanne Consuela, who'd been assigned to assist me in Costa Rica. We were the only people on the plane. They'd seated us first, as they always do on-duty officers, even though we weren't carrying guns.

The Marshals, under Safir, had hired a higher percentage of female agents than any other federal law enforcement agency. I liked working with women agents because they often felt they had to keep proving themselves. I could relate to that.

There was a bustle in the cockpit, then two guys in dark suits brushed past us and retrieved something from the back of the plane. I gave the flight attendant a look that said: Spill.

"We found a device," she said quietly. "It looks suspicious, but it's probably nothing."

"And for *this* we've gotta leave the plane?" I said, mostly for the benefit of Joanne. I didn't want her scared, because fear makes people stupid.

The flight attendant looked apologetic. "Rules and regs," she said.

I sighed, like I was just pissed at the inconvenience. But over the last few days I'd gotten a couple of death threats. I'd assumed, though, that they were just *routine* death threats. As a rule, whenever I began to close in on a target, I'd get threats. Didn't bother me. It let me know I was on the right track.

But Nazi threats did concern me somewhat because Nazis were different from regular pukes. They were better organized. While I'd chased my other Nazi, several people had told me that the old Nazi S.S. support group, ODESSA, had been activated, operationally and tactically, as a response to the government's increased activities. In fact, two concentration camp survivors had refused to help me because they'd been threatened by ODESSA.

I was also concerned about a possible alliance between the old Nazis and the neo-Nazis. I'd already tangled with the neo-Nazis, and they knew all about me—where I lived, where my wife was, who my friends were.

It made me wish I had my gun. I loved firearms and was extremely proficient with them. I'd won several national marksman titles. Don't get me wrong, though—I'm not a gun nut. I just like how they blow big holes in bad people.

Joanne and I got Cokes while they secured the plane. "Nice omen," she muttered.

"By tomorrow morning," I promised her, "things won't be so hairy."

I was wrong.

"Good *God,* John!" Joanne wailed as she dug into some weird-looking melon the next morning in San José, Costa Rica. "I got two threats over the phone before I could even take a *shower.* And I think my phone was bugged."

"Why?"

"It sounded funny, so I unscrewed it, and found this." She handed me a little gizmo, and I pocketed it. If it was a bug, I wanted it. The Marshals *never* had any good toys.

"Guess what?" I said. "The bureaucrats didn't get us country clearance. They forgot to tell the ambassador we're coming. So, officially, we're not here. Safir says stay in the hotel and suspend the investigation."

"So what do we do?"

"Nothing."

She eyed me. "That doesn't sound like the John Pascucci everybody talks about. They say you're a *monster.* King of the weasel deal."

"People are kind," I said. "But they exaggerate. Let's be patient."

We finished breakfast. Then I ditched Joanne, snuck out of the hotel through the loading dock, and headed for city hall. I needed to find a "city directory"—it's like a phone book, but the entries are numerical, by phone number, instead of alphabetized by name.

Even with my bad Spanish, I was able to find one. I looked up the numbers that Koziy's daughter had called.

"Shit." The numbers were pay phones in the lobbies of three different San José hotels. That explained why the calls had been at regular times; she'd made them on a prearranged schedule. But why hadn't *he* just called *her?* Didn't make sense.

Still, it was good info. It told me that Koziy had been in the vicinity of San José as recently as five weeks ago. My timeline was shrinking.

I took a cab to one of the hotels the daughter had called, to show Koziy's picture and fish for triggers. In the lobby I spotted a car rental agency.

"Buenos días," I said to the rental guy, "my name's Porgy Tirebiter, and I own D'Anne Tours of Miami. I had a client here who was supposed to pay me commission on his car rental, but I think he, you know, *forgot.* I'd really appreciate it if you could check your records." I wrote down Koziy's name and slid it toward him with a twenty-dollar bill.

Jackpot! He found Koziy's name.

"How far did he drive?" I asked. Most foreign rentals charge by mileage.

"Ninety kilometers."

"When did he return?"

"April sixteenth."

Today was May 15. I'd cut his time line to less than a

month. And I'd cut his probable location to a point somewhere within a radius of forty-five kilometers outside San
José. It was unlikely that wherever he'd settled was beyond
where he'd driven in April.

Good day's work. I went back to the hotel and caught the
last of the equatorial sun out by the pool. Then I went to the
dining room and devoured three shrimp cocktails, four
Cokes, and two platters of onion rings. I can digest and me-
tabolize *anything,* so I prefer food in massive quantities and
bizarre combinations. It's part of my love of extremes. The
shrimp were huge—big as bananas. They were expensive, but
I had a generous expense account. It was my payback for
risking my life about once a week.

Next morning, before I could get my eyes open—bam! bam!
bam!—somebody was at the door. It was a Drug Enforcement
Agency officer. He'd been sent to drive me to the embassy.
Our clearance had come through.

While we drove, he asked, "You people gonna be keepin'
your heads low?"

"Flyin' under the radar," I said. Everybody at a foreign
embassy has the same concern about visiting cops: They
don't want you to screw up the Big Picture. Costa Rica was
an island of democracy in a sea of dictatorships, and
nobody wanted that to change. The Gipper was using Costa
Rica as the CIA base for America's "secret" war against
next-door Nicaragua. Ollie North was shuttling in and out
of San José all the time, and so were dozens of Special
Forces units.

The DEA attaché delivered us to the deputy chief of mission at the American Consulate. DCMs are somewhat lower
in rank than ambassadors, but they're career diplomats, instead of political appointees. Therefore, they often don't have
their heads up their asses.

The DCM, a gruff old bastard in a thousand-dollar suit,
wasn't happy to see us. "We've got a war against the Communists going on about fifty klicks that way," he said, pointing
north, "and we're not crazy about *you* guys fighting World
War Two all over again. So don't get us into any trouble with
the locals, okay? Do what this guy tells you." He nodded at

the consul general, his number two guy, and stood up, as a sign of dismissal.

I considered myself the ultimate realist, but in this guy's book, I was just another starry-eyed do-gooder, trying my best to ignore the real world.

The consul general took my elbow and said, "I've got someone I want you to meet." He steered me to the bottom of a staircase, and down came this very ordinary-looking guy—a gray man in a gray suit—who introduced himself without really telling me who he was.

"Let's go for a ride," the man said. It was clear he meant just me, and not Joanne.

We drove without talking. The countryside was paradisiacal: sugary sand and cobalt sky.

"Mind if I make a stop?" he said as we neared the national airport.

He drove to a back gate, got waved through, and pulled right onto the tarmac, next to a fat C-130 with no markings. There were at least 150 men in green camo fatigues sitting around and under the plane. He hopped out, and talked to a colonel for about ten seconds.

As we drove off, I gave him an inquisitive look; Congress had just cut off *all* of Reagan's aid to the Contras, including CIA support. He gave me a thin, gray smile. "Don't even *think* of askin'," he said.

More silence. Then: "What I wanted to let ya know," he said, "is that our friends are here."

"Friends?"

"Boris." He meant the Soviets—and KGB.

"And they're interested in your work." Silence. "But that may be good."

"Why?"

He shrugged. Silence.

I was pissed. The State Department obviously didn't want me here. The spook who'd driven me to the airport had me paranoid about Soviets. And worst of all, I'd just called home, and my wife, Betsy, had been threatened over the phone by some asshole.

On the other hand: The Kentucky Fried Chicken place

across from my hotel still had *real* Coke—what they now call Coke Classic. Life had its compensations.

After dark, I drifted over to the KFC. I wanted three chicken breasts. *"Tres pollo chi-chis,"* I said to the girl behind the counter.

She stiffened. Turned red. Suddenly every eye in the place was on me. *"Tres chi-chis, por favor?"*

The manager looked apoplectic. A young guy in a Georgetown University sweatshirt leaned over and whispered, "You just asked for three chicken tits."

I backed toward the door, grimacing a smile at the manager. By way of apology, I gave him the "okay" sign, making a circle with my index finger and thumb.

The guy in the sweatshirt jerked his head violently. "That means 'asshole,' " he croaked.

Damn! I'd burned my only source for real Coke. I had to wrap this case up and get home.

I marched down the street, fuming.

I had a tail.

I was being followed by some clean-cut dickhead in a tan suit. Looked like a Century 21 salesman.

Who was it? Boris? Was it the CIA—concerned about my polluting the Big Picture? ODESSA? Neo-Nazis? Private muscle hired by Koziy?

Were they going to *hit* me?

I was tempted to just turn on him and say, Hey, cockbreath, what's the story? Then start punching. But there were too many people around.

I kept going, getting more and more pissed. Big mistake. Other than fear, nothing makes you more stupid than anger. But my feeling was, I'm not just gonna find out who this guy is, I'm gonna *fuck* with him.

I took a corner and ducked into a doorway.

His footsteps quickened. Louder. Louder.

He flashed past. I reached out. Grabbed him. By the scruff of the neck, around the carotid artery, like I always did in a bust.

My alarms went off. Because the guy didn't *have* a neck. He was a sawed-off phone pole—all muscle. A pro.

I could feel his sinews crawling under his skin like a sack full of snakes.

I went to put him against the wall.

And all of a sudden I was looking down the nose of a huge black automatic. Type of gun I'd never seen. That told me one thing: He wasn't American.

My motto in life is, When in doubt, do something.

I did something.

I froze.

Chapter Two

Treason

• Giving Aid and Coke to the Enemy •
Lawyer-Legal and Just Plain Legal •
Sex Appeal • KGB, CIA, and SOB •
A Weasel-Deal • Half-Assed Rambos •

"The only thing necessary for the triumph of evil is for good men to do nothing."

—*Edmund Burke*

Then, in a moment that stopped my heart, I heard him cock the fat, black gun.

I froze very *actively:* an exaggerated pantomime. As if to say: You *got* me—so . . . *don't* . . . shoot.

But I studied his eyes while I did it. Usually, somebody who's just about to pull a trigger will show it in his face— he'll tighten up. If I saw that, I'd have to throw down on him, no matter what.

But he took a step backward, and seemed to relax just a little.

"Calm *down,*" he grunted.

"Put that away, and I *will.*"

"Do *you* have a gun?"

"If I did, you'd be lookin' at it."

He nodded, acknowledging the sense of my statement. He was definitely a pro.

"Then I'll put mine away," he said, "and we can talk." He slipped it into the pocket of his sport coat, but left his hand on it.

"Let's walk while we talk," I said.

"Fine." He nodded for me to lead. As we started to walk, I relaxed my sphincter, and a shudder of relief trembled down my spine. If he was going to whack me, we wouldn't be heading back onto the street.

"I'm John Pascucci, U.S. Marshals Service," I said. Like he didn't know.

"Pleased to meet you." He didn't offer his identity.

"Why were you following me?"

He shrugged. "Just business." He spoke excellent English, with a trace of an Eastern European accent: "Just busy-ness."

He *had* to be KGB. Anybody else, by now, would've identified themselves, or killed me. Of course, maybe the outfit that signed his paychecks was the East German secret police, or Ceausescu's cops in Romania, but it all boiled down to the same thing: KGB.

"Why were you following me?" I repeated.

"Because what you are doing is of interest. My superiors believe that you are here to help the Contras. But I no longer think that is true."

"Why not?"

"Because I do my job." He meant he'd been spying on me and Joanne. "But you *should* be more discreet about whom you drive around with."

I assumed he was talking about my ride to the airport. "I don't always have a choice."

"*Tell* me all about it." He chuckled a little, and I started to enjoy myself. Less than a week ago, I'd been popping shit-bags in Felony Flats, and now I was James Bond. "*I* think what you're doing is a good thing," he said.

"*Do you know where Bohdan Koziy is?*"

"I wish I did. I would tell you."

I believed him. For every American who died in World War II, *forty* Russians died.

We walked some more, and he tried to prompt information out of me. But I was pretty tight-assed. When I needed *him,* that's when he'd get information.

"If you hate Koziy so bad," I said, "why don't you just task somebody with *eliminating* him? I've read all the spy novels—you guys'll whack *anybody."* I was just busting his balls.

He smiled. "How big is your organization?" he asked.

"About twenty-five hundred people."

"We're twenty times bigger than that. Now, you have in your organization a certain number of what you call 'assholes.' Correct?"

"Yeah, sure."

"We have that number, times twenty. *That* is why we cannot just 'whack' someone."

I slapped him on the back. Was this guy my long-lost brother, or what?

Before he split, he scribbled down the number of an answering service, and told me to leave a message if I needed help.

"I'll be seeing you," he said.

"I'll bet you will." I gave him the finger, and he laughed.

When I got back to the hotel, Joanne was on the veranda. Beautiful place—all marble and silk. The stars were lit with fire, and the air was sweet with flowers. Joanne was still in her swimsuit, with some kind of gauzy top over it, and looked great—blond hair and a perfect, sweet face. But I didn't screw around on my wife. Truth be told, the thought of bagging Bohdan Koziy got me hotter than Joanne in her bikini.

"Think we'll get any help from the embassy tomorrow?" she asked.

"I *know* we will."

"Why?"

"Cuz if we don't, I'm gonna threaten to call my buddy at the *New York Times* and tell him what I saw at the airport."

"Watcha see?"

"I don't even *know.* But I bet the boys at the embassy do."

*   *   *

We hit the embassy early, before they could get their full caffeine defense in place, and I started yammering vague threats at the consul general.

Suddenly, he was dying to see me finish my mission—and get the hell out of his country. "I'm going to introduce you to someone who's very well connected," he said. *"Lotsa* juice. He's just a captain in the national police force, but he knows all the right people."

In less than an hour, Joanne and I were in the captain's office.

But the guy was a stiff. Totally square: square face, square shoulders, square attitude. I started down a list of agencies I needed to see: the phone company, the utilities, and the registrar of property. But he had a reason why each was impossible. Too invasive. Not permitted. Sealed records. Yadda, yadda, yadda.

In short, he was a *liberal.* He was Thomas fucking Jefferson of Central America. Ed Meese would've made him dogcatcher.

"Captain Garcia," I said, "I know these things can be very difficult. But perhaps if I could pay you a special administrative fee? Would that expedite the logistics?"

"It would *not.*" He got all huffy. "Do not misunderstand me, please," he said. "I *want* to help. Costa Rica is *very* sensitive about Nazi abuses; the wife of our vice president, in particular, has been extremely active in helping victims of the Nazis. But I cannot solve human rights abuses by engaging in them."

A moral absolutist: my favorite type. "Then take me to somebody who can," I snarled. We traded dagger looks.

"I will take you to someone who should definitely know if Mr. Koziy is in Costa Rica," he said.

We walked to another government building a couple of blocks away, with him marching like he had a corncob up his ass. Joanne tried to thaw him as we walked. Waste of breath. Latin American cops *hate* female cops. They think it's their duty to protect them if things get ugly, so they regard them as a physical danger.

But Joanne did squeeze out one morsel of information. When she asked about the captain's parents, who'd immigrated here after the war, he said they were Swiss. *That* pricked up my ears. As I'd hunted my other Nazi, I'd found that about half the immigrants who'd said they were Swiss were really German, and had been lying to cover a Nazi affiliation. The fact is, after the war, there weren't a hell of a lot of Swiss refugees.

The captain ushered us into a drab tomb of an office—the universal "government" look—and spoke to a secretary in Spanish. Soon a small, dapper man with big jowls came out and was introduced as Señor Carta, an associate director of the government immigration service. Señor Carta listened to my story attentively. Then he said, "If this man is in Costa Rica, I will *find* him."

Señor Carta escorted us to his inner office and started punching codes into his computer. I sipped a Coke—the *real* thing—and tried to hide my nerves.

Finally, Señor Carta, said, "I am sorry. There is no record of entry for a Bohdan Koziy."

"Try Yaraslava Koziy," I said. "That's his wife."

"Not permitted," snapped the captain. "She has committed no crime."

Señor Carta gave me an apologetic look. I made a mental note to come see him later—without El Capitán.

"I don't know what else we can do," said the captain.

"If we've done everything we can," I said, "then I guess we've fulfilled our duty." I gave him my sweetest smile. He seemed to buy it. I'm a good actor. No Ronald Reagan—but still pretty good.

Next morning, while Joanne and I were having breakfast, she said, "Guess who I bumped into last night?"

"Who?"

"A couple of our old buddies." She said she'd seen two prominent drug lawyers who we'd both known when we'd worked Southern California.

"Gee," I said, "I'll bet you my red Corvette I know what *they're* doing here."

Joanne rolled her eyes. We both knew what they were up to.

They were undoubtedly collecting payment from one of

the drug dealers they were defending. It was too risky for them to receive payment in the States, because money paid from illegally gained funds can be seized by the government, even if it's a legitimate payment to attorneys. Because of that, drug defenders often met their clients in the Caribbean, then deposited their fees offshore. That was "lawyer legal," which is often quite different from just plain legal.

Joanne told me the name of the nearby hotel where she'd spotted them, and after my Coke and eggs, I went there. Sure enough, they were registered.

I went up to their room, unannounced. One was gone, but the other was still having breakfast.

The second he saw me, he freaked. He was *sure* I was there to bust him.

I started to play him. "Hey," I hissed, "I *know* you guys are doin' a transfer. And know what? I don't give a shit. *But.* You gotta help me. Cuz I'm on an investigation, and I'm not havin' much luck down here. Now, if I have to go back home with just my dick in my hand, I'll at least look okay if I can go to a judge in the district and say, 'Guess what? I got a *transfer* to talk about.' "

I sat back and waited for his forehead to get shiny. If he was guilty, he'd probably sweat. A lot of people can control their expressions, but not their perspiration. Sure enough, he started brushing his brow.

"If you've got somebody in this country who keeps your presence here a secret—somebody who can quash immigration records—I *gotta* know who it is. Give me a name, and I forget everything. You know my reputation. I won't rat ya out. But *don't* bullshit a bullshitter. You guys walked across the pedestrian border at Tijuana, right? So there's no record of you leavin' the country. Then you flew from T.J. to here, right?"

"There's nothing illegal about that."

"Didn't say there *was.* But don't *bullshit* me. Somebody here is covering your entry."

He took a second to think it over.

"Well," he said, "there's a guy at the airport . . . and sometimes we bring down our girlfriends, you know, quietly."

"Your girlfriends. Fine. Who's the guy?"

He gave me the name. "We got anything to worry about?" he whined.

I shook my head. "You're just another good American, like me."

And *I* was also a *lucky* American. But that was okay. I'd take luck over brains any day.

I dropped off Joanne at the embassy, where she was spending most of her time translating for a local DEA guy. Then I slipped off.

Out at the airport, I stumbled around until I located the immigration official the lawyers were paying. I waited, then approached him when some of his co-workers were around. They weren't close enough to overhear, but were close enough to make him squirrelly. I badged him and put it to him hard and fast: "Look, I know you're letting people into this country, then burying their records. Don't deny it, because I've got two lawyers who've sworn under oath that they paid you. I know how *much* they paid you and I know *why* they paid you. But I don't *care*. All I want you to do is look at this name and picture and tell me if this man slipped into the country. But *don't* bullshit me, or I'll be back here in an hour with Captain Garcia of the federal police force, and you can bullshit *him*."

He got all fucked up and started twisting in his swivel chair.

"Look," I said softly, "just gimme what I need. Captain Garcia's *waiting* on us."

His face turned the color of skim milk. Then he pulled out a notebook, rifled through it, and checked the photo again. He gazed up at me with big glassy eyes and whined, "I swear to you, I swear to you, I *never* have seen him. What did he do, this man?"

"He's an international fugitive. A murderer of children. And anybody who aids him is an accessory after the fact. But I guess you don't have to sweat that, cuz you don't have the *death* penalty in Costa Rica. Or do you?"

He looked like he was going to cry. "Señor, I am going to tell you something. In strict confidence. Up there"—he pointed at a huge mirrored window near the top of the main lobby—"they take photos of all the people who come through the nonresident gate."

"*Who* does?"

He raised the palms of his hands. "Maybe *your* people—the CIA, or U.S. Army. Maybe *our* people. I do not know."

"Can you show me the photos?"

"I am not even supposed to know they exist."

I stopped playing him. When somebody looked as sphincter-dilated as he did, they were usually telling the truth.

I went back to see my bureaucrat, Señor Carta, and he was a much better host without Captain Garcia breathing down his neck. He made a couple of calls for me, to the utility company and the phone company. Unfortunately, he drew a blank.

But then he patched into some Costa Rican computer systems and found a hot lead. It came from a computer network that logged foreign nationals buying property. An elderly woman with American citizenship had just bought a small estate outside San José. It wasn't registered to Yaraslava Koziy, but Koziy's wife could have used an alias.

I grabbed a cab and hit the address. Dead end. Just an old woman trying to stretch her Social Security.

I was tempted to call it a day. Hit the beach. Have a thick steak and a couple of hot fudge sundaes. Watch some CNN.

But fuck that. Every time I felt like punking out, I'd see the heavy joyless face of the old woman whose relatives Koziy had killed, and I'd remember my promise to her.

I went over to Captain Garcia's office. As usual, he looked grim as death—even though he had good news. "The vice president's wife would like to meet you," he said. "She has a great interest in the Holocaust."

"I'll have to run it by my boss." I jotted a memo, and cabled it to Safir.

The captain gave me a lift back to my hotel, and on the way he pointed out his house. *Un*believable. It was like a white marble temple, high on a hill. "It's a replica of the Greek Parthenon," he said casually. His square, inscrutable face was a mask of perpendicular lines.

Maybe he was telling me the price range his bribe would

have to hit. If so, he was pricing himself out of the market. I didn't have the money it would take to flip him.

"I don't mean to pry," I said, "but your house looks very expensive. And you are just a policeman."

"My wife and I did a lot of the work ourselves," he said. Deadpan.

By the middle of the next day, Safir had killed the meeting with the veep's wife. OSI hadn't liked it. State hadn't liked it. The ambassador had *hated* it. But to toss me a bone, the ambassador was giving a state dinner in my honor and allowing me input on the guest list. I invited Garcia and Carta, to stroke them.

So there we stood after dinner, stiff as dead fish, the peons on one side of the ballroom and the heavies on the other. We listened to a grand piano while we made small talk. Not my favorite kind of scene—it brought out my working-class insecurity. I was afraid I'd fart or something.

But it gave me a chance to get all my players together at the same time, which is always a golden opportunity—it makes it much harder for people to bullshit.

I waited until I had Garcia, Carta, the consul general, and the spook who'd driven me to the airport all standing around together. Then I steered the talk to my case, and right away the CIA guy perked up. He probably had to write a report on my mission that night and cable it home.

"It looks bad," I said. "Everybody's telling me there's no way Koziy could be in the country."

"If everyone is saying it," said Garcia, "perhaps it is true."

I made a sour face. It was time to break things loose. Whenever an investigation was gridlocked, I tried to bust things up, even if I couldn't predict the consequences: When in doubt, *do something*.

"I learned something interesting today," I said. "Somebody—either the U.S. or Costa Rica—is taking photos at the airport of all nonresidents as they enter the country."

"That's a new one on me," said the CIA guy. Picture of innocence.

"I have never heard of it, either," said Garcia.

Carta just shrugged, and shook his bulldog jowls.

"Maybe somebody was pullin' your leg, Inspector," said the consul general.

"That may be," I said. "Latin Americans are such a *fun-loving* people." That pissed off everybody, even the Americans. But I didn't care. When you're trying to break things loose, sometimes it helps to make people angry. Anger makes people do dumb things.

I woke just before dawn to a nightmare. This one was about one of Koziy's victims, a four-year-old named Monica Zinger, the daughter of a prominent Jewish doctor in Koziy's village. Witnesses—and this was what I saw in my dream—had seen Koziy dragging Monica by her hair while she screamed, "Mother, he is taking me to kill me! I want to *live!*" Then Koziy had stepped away from her and shot her in the face, twice, while she begged.

When I jolted awake, my pillow was wet with sweat, and the images of my nightmare were still racing through my brain. The thought of someone shooting a little girl made me feel half-crazy.

As I sprawled out in my big king bed, I heard something at the door. I jumped up, stumbled through the suite, and threw open the door. Down the hall, I saw the elevator door close. At my feet was a legal-size envelope.

It held a three-by-five color photo, poorly focused: a surveillance photo. But it was Koziy, sure as hell. Same cold face, beak nose. He was walking through the nonresident gate at the airport.

He was here. This was proof.

I felt good. My little speech at the party had shaken something loose.

But who'd left the photo? My first guess was Señor Carta. He was the only one who'd been helpful so far. And he probably had connections at the airport.

The CIA guy? I doubted it. He was too worried about the Big Picture.

Maybe it had been the captain. If he really did have a friendship with the vice president's wife, she could have swung it.

I chugged two Cokes, hit the street, and was waiting outside the captain's office when he arrived for work.

I stuck the photo under his nose. "Thank you," I said. He
scowled at the picture. "I caught your delivery boy, and he
ratted you out."

"You are making this up," Garcia said.

I didn't push the bluff. "All that matters," I said, "is that
we get some heat on this investigation."

We went into his office, and he collected his overnight
faxes and handed me one. It was from Safir. The Boss said
the bureaucracy was restless. I had forty-eight hours to make
"significant progress." Or come home.

The CIA guy had probably screwed me. He'd probably cabled home that I was running amok. That had probably
freaked out the State Department. Then State had probably
leaned on Justice, which had leaned on OSI, which had
leaned on Safir.

But fuck that. I'd just start hiding from the phone.

"Let's go show this to Señor Carta," I said.

Carta, as usual, was straight out of charm school. He was
all, How is your visit going, Have you been out to the festival,
Have you tried such-and-such restaurant?

"Whoa, whoa, whoa," I said, "don't *start* with me. Look
at this." I held out the picture. "This ain't my uncle. This
ain't my aunt. And this ain't chopped liver. It's my fuckin'
guy, comin' into *your* fuckin' town, and I don't wanna *hear*
no more oh-he-can't-be-here. Okay?" I was half-sick with
nerves. My nightmare was still percolating in the back of
my brain.

Carta started shaking his cheeks and telling me how perfect
his records were, and how hot his computers were, and why
don't we go here and go there—places I'd already been, and
places where Koziy would never have been stupid enough
to hide.

"You're treating me like an *idiot,*" I boomed.

Then Carta got all meek and thoughtful. "I have it!" he
said. "There is a form that is filled out by *all* arriving airline
passengers. Its purpose is to find out if they're bringing in
fruit or plants. I will have the director of that program meet
you at the airport, and find that record for you."

It sounded lame. But it might be enough to stall Safir, or to trigger something else.

So the captain and I drove out to the airport in my four-cylinder, rented shitmobile—a car that made me miss my Corvette terribly. At the airport, everybody was waiting for me and kissing my ass. The director of the fruits-and-flowers program was bursting with pride, telling me how *everybody* who came into the country filled out his form—*without exception.* He led me into this room that was about forty by forty, with one lightbulb hanging from the ceiling. It was wall-to-wall with gray metal file cabinets, and boxes, boxes, boxes.

"These go back . . . *forever,*" the program director beamed.

"What's the system? Alphabetical? By date?"

"No. Just . . . stacked."

I looked at the captain, who was shaking his head. I started spewing curses. The Ugly American.

We double-timed back to Carta's office. Carta was smiling. "I have good news," he said. One of his computer searches had turned up an elderly gringo from Ft. Lauderdale who had just applied, as a resident alien, to rezone a small plantation about fifty kilometers out of San José.

While we drove there, I pumped Garcia about his money. He said his mother had inherited gold. I wanted to say, what kind—gold *fillings?*

We hit the Pacific coast—golden beaches and high white waves—and pulled into a banana plantation. My heart was thumping.

An old man came to the door. Not Koziy. Showed me his ID. Got all pissed off at my attitude.

I didn't talk during the drive back. I drifted into my usual malignant daydream: I'm Koziy—where do I go, what do I do?

When we got inside Carta's cold office, I lost it. "I'm a fuckin' *dick* to swallow this shit!" I yelled. "You guys think you're so goddamn *pure* with your citizens' rights bullshit, but you've got the blood of *children* on your hands."

Garcia looked stunned. He put both his hands on my shoulders and pushed me into a chair. "One moment," he huffed. Then he grabbed Carta by the elbow and marched him stiffly into another office. Their voices started rising. Pretty soon, only Garcia could be heard.

Garcia emerged with his usual dead, boxy face. He growled, "Tomorrow will be a better day." Then stalked off.

Carta didn't reappear. Nobody else was around, so I tried to fool with Carta's computers. But the goddamn things were all in *Spanish,* for some reason.

Garcia called me first thing in the morning. "Let's go to Señor Carta's office," he said.

"No, thanks." I was on my way to meet Boris, my KGB new best friend. I was hoping he had some triggers.

"Please!" said Garcia. His voice was different. I decided to give him one more shot, so I left a message for Boris, canceling.

When we got to Carta's office, there were cartons everywhere and his secretary was smiling. "Señor Carta, he was promoted!" she said. "We are going to work on the *vice president's* staff."

I shot a look at the captain, but couldn't read his face. He disappeared into Carta's office for a few minutes. He emerged looking happy. "The *new* associate director," he said, "is going to look again for information on Mr. Koziy. Perhaps Señor Carta overlooked something. Who can know?"

Five minutes later, a guy in a suit emerged form Carta's office, holding a computer printout. He said something to Garcia in Spanish, and Garcia said, *"Gracias."*

"He located an address for Mr. Koziy," said Garcia. "It is possible that Señor Carta was not . . . dealing in good faith."

"You cops are so *cynical,"* I said. I slapped him on the back. "Let's hit it."

Half an hour later we were watching Koziy's apartment from across the street. We couldn't blow our cover, because we had no paper—no warrant to grab and detain him. If he made us, he'd be on the next plane to Buenos Aires or wherever, and we'd be fucked.

So we sat staring at the apartment, and I got a sick feeling that it was unoccupied. If you know how, you can tell if a place is empty, even with the drapes shut. There'll be all kinds of markers: dust inside the windowsills, no indentations on the doormat, no movement of the curtains from the heater or air-conditioning kicking on, no plants on the porch or balcony.

The mailman was coming. Garcia intercepted him.

"Does not look good," Garcia said. "The postal carrier said Mr. Koziy stopped getting mail here fifteen days ago."

We started knocking on doors, and the neighbors confirmed that Koziy had split about two weeks ago.

I ran back to the car and grabbed the phone records of Koziy's daughter. Her last call to him—at the pay phones in the hotel—had been the day before he'd left this apartment. The call had been two days after we'd interviewed Sonnyboy in Albuquerque.

With hindsight, I could see that we shouldn't have confronted the son because when we had, we'd apparently spooked Koziy. Live and learn.

Now, though, we knew that Koziy had either split the country two weeks ago, or he'd moved somewhere else in Costa Rica.

I tried to think like Koziy. If I were him—old, tired, and arrogant—I'd stay in Costa Rica.

I was bouncing around like a hyperactive kid.

I'd reduced Koziy's time line to fifteen days.

And I had him running.

He was going to leave a track. And I was going to find it.

"What's the population of Costa Rica?" I asked Garcia.

"Two point two million."

"That's not *shit*. Let's go to the phone company." If Koziy had stayed in Costa Rica, he might have ordered a phone.

Garcia gunned it. The cop in him was coming up.

At the phone company, Garcia hooked me up with the head of security. Using Garcia as a translator, I asked if Koziy had taken out a phone in his own name. He hadn't, of course.

Garcia told the security director to review a program that required resident aliens to identify themselves when they ordered phone service.

Again, dead end.

"Ask him how many new phones have been issued in the last two and a half weeks," I said to Garcia.

"He says it is very many," Garcia reported.

"How many?

"He says, a hundred and twenty." Garcia had a glint in his eye. To a cop, that was *not* very many.

I had the security guy take us to the record of new listings. They were in a set of big black books. "Look through here," I told Garcia, "and eliminate the ones that look like businesses."

We ended up with a list of ninety-five residential new phones.

Garcia dropped me at the hotel. I ran up to my room and called for Bill Donteri, my investigator who had a contact at Southeast Bell.

"Bill! Get with your guy at Bell and lay some money on him. I don't give a fuck *how* much he wants. But I gotta get an *hour-by-hour* record of all the phone calls made by Koziy's daughter, starting today."

Then I called a young marshal in Tony Perez's office, a tough, smart kid. "It's weasel-deal time," I told him. "When I give you the word, I want you to go see Koziy's daughter, and toss up a story. Tell her that if it wasn't for that crazy fuckin' John Pascucci, OSI would have signed off on the Koziy case a long time ago. But now word's come down to Pascucci that Justice wants to cut their losses and close Koziy's file. If Koziy—*wherever* he is—will just go to a notary public, and sign a declaration agreeing to not seek residence in America, Justice will drop all proceedings."

Donteri called back. His hook was in place. We could get an hourly report on the phone numbers the daughter called.

I called back the young marshal. "Go throw your story at her," I said. "And *sell* it."

Then I called Garcia, and put him on red alert.

I went out to my balcony, and melted into a soft beach chair. Seagulls were making circles in the sky, and I could hear the laughter of children playing in the pool. I think the best sound in the world is a kid's belly laugh.

How in God's name could anyone shoot a *child?* I couldn't understand it. I can understand craziness—but Koziy wasn't crazy. He was rational. He was able to love his family, and was able to earn their love. He was simply evil. And that's something you never truly understand, no matter how close to it you get.

The phone rang. It was the young marshal. "She bought it." I couldn't sit any longer. I paced, chain-drinking Cokes. Twenty minutes later, Donteri called. "She phoned her brother in Albuquerque, and a law office in Miami. And then she called Costa Rica." He gave me the number.

I ran my finger down the list of new residential phones. *A match.*

I leaped up and called Garcia.

The sun plunged into the ocean as the first sounds of night settled over the countryside.

Joanne and I rode with Garcia and one of his lieutenants—a surveillance expert—to the top of an overlook.

"Down there," Garcia said. "That avocado ranch." He pointed at a manicured estate surrounded by a high barbwire fence. "Koziy."

We had to get close enough to photo Koziy. That would prove he was here—*without* alerting him—and pave the way for his arrest, deportation, or kidnapping. "Maybe we could go through that drainpipe," I said. A long metal culvert tunneled under a marsh and ended just outside Koziy's fence.

We drove as close to the estate as we could, then walked to a rise above the ranch, where the culvert began.

The lieutenant disappeared into the culvert with a camera. He looked worried. We were afraid Koziy might have armed guards. We waited by the car. Forty minutes later he hustled back, with photos, and we hauled ass back to town.

But the photos turned out to be marginal. Koziy's face was blurred. The lieutenant had hurried too much.

The next evening, the lieutenant, Garcia, and I returned, more heavily armed. Garcia and I had rifles, and the lieutenant had a .45 in a shoulder holster.

"Me and the lieutenant will handle the pictures," I said to Garcia. "You stay by the car. And stay ready."

The lieutenant looked froggy, so I grinned at him like, Ain't this fun? "Go through the pipe again," I said, "but this time I'll cover both ends. Take as long as you need—but get a *good* picture."

The lieutenant crawled into the pipe. I hunched down behind the culvert, straining to stay beneath the horizon. The rocks around me were still warm from the sun.

I heard a soft, sibilant sound, like someone drawing a fingertip down a piece of sandpaper.

A snake was gliding straight for me. It was a long, bloated brown thing with a diamond-shaped head. It seemed to see me with its dead brown eyes, and stopped. Its tongue flicked out. It curled onto a rock near my feet.

A few minutes later, another one slithered over. This one wasn't so shy. It parked close enough for me to touch.

For almost an hour, I sat there, breathing deeply, smelling the stink of my own sweat. Trying not to move. Night was coming. I peeked over the culvert, and saw two Indian guards with rifles walking the perimeter of Koziy's ranch.

As it got dark, the snakes blended into the dirt, and I lost sight of them. From time to time, I heard them move.

Finally, the lieutenant's head popped out of the culvert. I put my hand on his shoulder. He stopped. I flicked my lighter.

Now there were half a *dozen* snakes. The lieutenant shuddered.

We tiptoed out, squinting at the ground. As we got farther from the culvert, our pace quickened. When we hit the gravel road, we started running. We didn't stop until we found Garcia's car.

"They're beautiful shots, Boss," I bellowed to Safir over the phone. "One's a classic. It's Bohdan, with that cruel fuckin' face, walking through his garden with his Doberman, stroking a kitten. *Caricature* of a Nazi."

"Sit tight," Safir said, "and I'll see where we go from here." Safir sounded tense. Safir *always* sounded tense.

I strolled out to my balcony, took off my shirt, and let the hot wind and sun soothe the kinks in my shoulders. It felt wonderful. I always loved this stage of an investigation—just before you made the pop. The anticipation made me feel totally alive. But I was *horny* for time to pass. I couldn't wait to see Koziy's face when I ratcheted the cuffs around his wrists.

Our charge against him would be immigration fraud. After that, America would line up extradition to the Soviet Union, then Costa Rica would kick Koziy to the United States, and we'd kick him to Russia, where he'd be tried for war crimes.

If that scenario wasn't feasible, maybe the Costa Ricans would expel him, and we'd board the same plane, then arrest him when we hit international air space. I didn't have a charge to arrest him on yet. But I'd think of one.

It was still possible, though, that we'd have to cut through the formalities and black-bag him. People assume it's illegal to kidnap somebody and bring them back to the States. But it doesn't break any American laws if we kidnap someone on foreign soil.

The courts wouldn't care *how* we'd gotten the body, and I knew Reagan and Ed Meese wouldn't make a peep about it. In my opinion, they'd been indifferent to civil rights for the last twenty years, ever since they'd busted up the Berkeley campus demonstrations in the 1960s, when Reagan had been governor and Meese had been his top-gun lawyer.

Of course, kidnapping Koziy *would* be against Costa Rican law. So after Koziy got finished with being electrocuted in the Soviet Union, he'd have every right to return to Costa Rica and seek justice.

Safir didn't call. The hours began to mount. I started to feel a pit in my stomach. Good news travels fast. Bad news crawls, while people try to change it.

I hoped Safir had just hit a logistical snag—like lining up a military plane for the black-bag job.

Finally, the phone rang. I jumped.

"I'm sorry," said Safir, "but OSI and State think this should be run through the Costa Ricans."

"Run how?"

"Run however they *choose,* John. Civil, criminal—whatever."

"Why?"

"State doesn't want to turn this into an issue down there. Koziy's stridently anti-Communist . . . as you know. . . ."

"But Mr. *Safir,* I *got* this fuckin' guy."

"You did a hell of a job, John. I'm proud of you. In fact, I just nominated you for Federal Investigator of the Year. But it's time to let it go. And come home."

"Wait a minute! I fuckin'—"

"Let it *go,* John."

The Boss was telling me to shut the hell up.

And I always did what the Boss said. No matter how much it hurt.

"Oh, before I forget," said Safir, "the guy you seized your Corvette from was innocent. So remember to turn in the car when you get back."

By dark of the next day, I knew the Costa Ricans weren't going to do shit. The captain had pulled all his strings in the government, but no criminal charges were going to be filed.

Instead, the Costa Rican solicitor general was going to begin civil proceedings—the same slow process Koziy had already run from in America.

I called Boris.

I wasn't ready to "let it go." That just wasn't my style. Besides, I was the *Gipper's cop;* I had to ask myself: What would *Reagan* want?

Reagan might want a more *aggressive* approach. And if America's bureaucracy wouldn't allow that, maybe the Soviet Union's would.

Boris suggested we get together at an expensive restaurant near my hotel. We met on the terrace—no codes, no disguises, no meeting in an alley. Too bad. I loved that 007 shit. But the restaurant was great—best steak I'd had in a year, and we watched the moon get fat and golden as he tossed back frosty glasses of rum and Coke. He loved the Coke as much as the rum. He was my kind of guy.

"I *hate* workin' in someone else's house," I growled. "It's bad enough fightin' the bureaucracy in your own country, but the *second* you go somewhere else, you get *homesick.* Like, if I was in New York, we'd just *destroy* this fuckin' guy. He'd take a fall for heroin, or get hit by a car. Back home, we call it 'necessary evil.'"

Boris nodded knowingly.

"Why don't *you* guys do the right thing?" I said. "Come

in with your helicopters—Bam! Bam! Bam! Koziy goes down, and you zoom back to Nicaragua."

That hit a nerve. *"We* are not *involved* in Central America," he bleated. "The Americans! *They* are involved."

"No shit." That calmed him down.

I dropped the subject of Koziy, and got Boris started on World War II. Turns out, he'd lost about sixteen aunts and uncles in the Nazis' siege of Leningrad. Boris was a mad dog on the subject of Nazis.

I egged him on a little more. "You guys would *never* use helicopters, would you?" I said. "Too crude. You'd take him out with, like, a poisoned BB. Bing! Dead! No wound. No autopsy."

"Our new president, Mr. Gorbachev, he does not approve of such conduct. He is very different from our past leaders."

"Yeah, *right."*

"But you *could* do this for me," said Boris. "You could tell me where Koziy lives."

I could've just given him the address. But I wasn't in the *mood.* I wanted to play him. Play Koziy, too. See if I could shake something loose. When in doubt, do something.

"I'll do better than tell you," I said. "I'll *show* you where he lives. Let's go."

"No. Impossible. We could *never* work operationally to-gether. In my country, that would be treason."

"Not in mine. Reagan *loves* the Evil Empire."

"It is *not done,"* he protested.

"We won't be *workin'* together. I'll just show you where he lives. I'll source you—that's all."

He shook his head, and knocked back two more rum and Cokes.

"You know," I said, "Koziy once heard that this seven-year-old girl had climbed out of a mass grave with bullets in both her arms, and was hiding at a farm way the hell in the boonies. So Bohdan rides his horse out—all the way, on just a *rumor*—and he finds the little girl hiding in the barn. The little girl begs, but he shoots her with his rifle. It takes two shots, but he puts her down. Now, *that's* a bureaucrat!"

"All *right.* You may *show* me where he lives."

Boris seemed to sober up right away. Was *he* scamming *me?* Who knew?

We agreed to meet in an hour.

I went back to the hotel, threw some outdoor gear in a duffel bag, and waited.

Boris pulled up in a customized Land Rover. Sweet vehicle. It had about twenty-thousand bucks in electronics under the dash, eelskin upholstery, a field fax, and a global short-wave. It could jump the Grand Canyon and speak Japanese.

It made me miss my Corvette. My *ex*-Corvette.

He popped the hatchback for my duffel, and I about swallowed my tongue. There was enough ordnance in there to defend Nicaragua. Plus, *superb* toys: night vision goggles, heat sensors, laser sights, and phone tap detectors.

I wasn't sure why he'd let me see the weapons. Probably to make me mind my manners.

One thing particularly caught my eye. He had a Remington model 700 bull-barrel .308 caliber rifle. Got me to thinking: Why an *American* rifle? Who was playing *whom?* Was he going to *hit* Koziy, and let me take the fall? Was I his Lee Patsy Oswald?

As we headed out, I said, "Why an American rifle?"

"Just a souvenir from Vietnam."

About five-thirty, a cold dawn lit the sky behind Koziy's ranch. We drove all the way to the mouth of the culvert. I wasn't concerned anymore about blowing cover. And, to be honest, I was a little snake shy.

Boris opened the hatchback and grabbed a spotting scope and a night vision scope with a daylight filter.

"His guards are armed, you know," I said.

He stood there for a moment, then picked up the Remington. I gave him a look. "Why the old Remington?"

"It's my favorite gun," he said.

That may sound like a line of bullshit to you, but to a gun lover like me, it made sense.

We leaned over the hood of the Land Rover, sighting down on the farm. Boris got annoyed with his night vision scope and started looking through the Remington's scope.

At 6:00 A.M., the front door of the house swung open and somebody in a robe stepped onto the porch. It was Koziy.

He stretched. He looked up at the pink outline of dawn behind the hills.

"Jesus," I said, "I'll bet it would feel *good* to put one right between his *eyes.*" I was just busting his balls. More or *less.*

Boris didn't respond. He seemed transfixed.

Koziy clapped his hands, and his Doberman barked. The dog ran to Koziy, then pranced in a half circle around him, begging. Koziy bent and nuzzled the dog. Then Koziy picked up a sack and poured food into the dog's bowl. He stroked the dog gently while it ate.

"You know," I said, "it's too bad. Here we are, the two most powerful countries in the world, freezin' our nuts, doin' *nuthin,'* while this monster goes free."

No response.

"Squeeze one off," I murmured. "Just to make him piss his pants."

Boris gave me a dirty look.

Koziy ran his hands languidly up and down his sides. He had no fear—and that's what bothered me most. A man like him should dread each day.

"Len-n-ningrad," I whispered. Sometimes when I'm busting balls, I get a little mean.

By way of apology, I said, "Look, you're right, I just—"

KA—BAM!

I jumped three feet. You're *never* ready for the boom of a high-powered rifle.

Koziy was dancing around like a poodle with diarrhea—running two feet one way, three feet the other. He didn't know whether to shit or go blind.

I trained my scope on his face. Then I saw it—the look I wanted: gut-chewing terror.

I heard a muffled *ping.* Then: *Ba-bing!* A fluff of dust kicked up about ten feet away from us. Another.

"The guards! I yelled. "They're shooting!"

We dove into the Land Rover and Boris popped a wheelie as we wailed off.

We'd come in like a couple of half-assed Rambos, but we were leaving like two kids running out of the graveyard on Halloween night.

Didn't matter. The Gipper would've been proud.

I started to laugh hysterically. *"Did you see him dance?"*
Boris smiled. "Leningrad!" he boomed.

When we got back to town, I had Boris drop me at a taxi stand. I didn't want his Land Rover anywhere near my hotel.

Near the taxi stand, I hopped into a bodega and came out with three cases of Coke. "Take this," I said. "They've stopped making *real* Coke in America. Pretty soon they'll run out down here."

"Thank you, my friend."

"We'll meet again," I said.

He shook his head. Smiled. Then he was gone. I never saw him again.

Hours later, Joanne and I were in Captain Garcia's car, headed for the airport. Beautiful car. Used to belong to a Medellín cartel honcho. Garcia had finally leveled with me about his money. He was a DEA "consultant," working "on commission."

My mind was buzzing. Too many loose ends. Who'd threatened me back in the States? Who'd had the picture of Koziy slid under my door—the vice president's wife? Who'd caused the bomb scare on the plane? Had Boris been trying to *kill* Koziy? Or just scare him? Would Boris try to kill Koziy *later?*

I know that movie detectives tie up all the loose ends when the story's over. But I'm telling you about the real world, and that puts me at a hell of a disadvantage. The real world is nothing *but* loose ends.

But guess what? Who gives a fuck?

I was happy. I had seen a look of absolute horror on Bohdan Koziy's face. I knew the rest of his life would be an endless winter of fear. *If* he lived for long.

And I had luxuries ahead. The luxury of seeing my wife. The luxury of being safe. The luxury of returning to Ronald Reagan's America, where a cop could be a cop. The luxury of smoking some pot, cranking up some old Dylan, and *not thinking.* And, best of all, the luxury of casting off the mind-set of Bohdan Koziy.

When we got to the airport, I shook the captain's hand. "I

wanna thank you," I said. "I wasn't sure about you for the longest time, but you did a helluva job." I gave him a little punch on the arm. I felt silly. So did he.

"There is something you deserve to see," he said.

He led me to the room where they kept the "fruits-and-flowers" forms. "Señor Carta's position with the vice president did not work out," Garcia said. He cracked open the door. I peeked in. There was Carta. The little SOB was sorting out the forms. I couldn't help myself. I stuck my head in the door, and said, "Señor Carta! Thank you for your help. Everything worked out *okay!*" I touched my thumb to my forefinger, and gave him the "asshole" sign.

For a second, I was afraid he was going to devour his own jowls.

After two years of legal skirmishes, Costa Rica ordered Bohdan Koziy deported to the Soviet Union. But when the police came for him, he stood at the doorway of his villa with a gun to his head, and said, "I will die here in a free land. I will never go back to communism."

The government reversed its decision. But it ordered Koziy to be locked up in prison.

Sixty days later, he emerged—a free man—to a cheering crowd of anti-Communist supporters.

His legal battles were over. Forever.

Not long after Koziy's release, I got a card from Costa Rica. It said "My condolences." No name. No return address.

I called OSI.

The guy I talked to said he'd heard that Bohdan Koziy had "died suddenly and unexpectedly."

Had Boris finished his job? That's what I like to think.

But then, I'm a sentimental guy.

Let's go back to the beginning of my story. I started in the middle of it on purpose, to grab your attention. As you might have guessed by now, I'm a manipulator.

Besides, I wanted you to see from the get-go that I'm not a monster—that it was my enemies who were the monsters. And who's more monstrous than Bohdan Koziy?

But don't worry. There are more monsters throughout my story. Like the "Falcon and the Snowman" spy, Chris Boyce. And Nazi Konrads Kalejs. And terrorist Frank Terpil—the "most dangerous man on earth." And the "Angel of Death": Dr. Josef Mengele.

There is evil everywhere, if you're willing to look for it.

I paid a price to find that out.

And now I want some payback. Even if that payback is just your attention.

So let me tell my story.

Chapter Three

Killing People

★

• Sharing Girlfriends • The Kill
Zone • Whores for the Stars • Son of
Sam • Bozos with Bayonets •
My Wambaugh Phase •

"If you're not part of the solution, you're part of the problem."
—Eldridge Cleaver

I'm going to tell you how I became a killer.

People have told me I'm a born killer. Not true. I had to learn. It was a necessary evil. But it was the hardest lesson of my life.

Every instinct in your body tells you never to kill. It's almost as strong as the instinct to survive. But you *can* overcome it—if you want to.

When you finally do kill someone, you feel something you never imagined. You feel like you're God.

And, believe me, being God is a shitty job.

You feel a weight of responsibility so heavy you can hardly breathe.

Even if there are no doubts in your mind that you did the

right thing, there are still doubts in your heart. Did this mutt *have* to die? Was there *any* alternative?

But as you satisfy those questions, your doubts diminish and you're left with just a feeling of naked power—and that feeling's almost sexually seductive.

When I was a kid, there was a slaughterhouse near my home. On the killing floor, one man would stun the cows with a prod, then cut their throats. According to the legend of the place, that job was rotated every two weeks. Not because it was horrible. But because the men grew to *like* it.

I could never understand that. Until I killed someone.

When you kill somebody, it does the worst possible thing to you.

It makes you want to do it again.

I remember clearly the first time I ever killed anything. It was 1953, I was five years old, and a daddy-longlegs spider was sitting on one of my toys. I was going, "Shoo! Shoo!" and my dad got pissed off at the commotion. He handed me a rolled-up paper and told me to kill it. I couldn't do it, so dad grabbed the newspaper and swatted my butt. Then I got mad and smacked the spider. Squashed it. When I saw it was dead, I started bawling like a big baby.

Truth be told, I *was* a big baby. I'd been born with a supposedly fatal heart ailment, and my big Italian family had coddled me for years.

But by the time I was ten, I was strong as a little gorilla and was running a one-man Murder Incorporated against the neighborhood bugs. Not all of them, though—just the *mutts.* I spent half my childhood in front of our huge Philco TV, and I learned early on that there are good guys and there are pukes, and that pukes *need* to die.

At the same time, though, my dad was busting ass to keep me away from *real* bad guys, and it wasn't easy. We lived in a tough section of the Bronx, and you didn't have to stay out on the streets for long to see somebody get fucked up by hoods. But I loved the streets, with their gritty, city mystique, and I slipped away whenever I could.

For some reason, even as a little kid, I had a powerful, ingrained sense of good and evil. I don't know where it came from. It didn't come from books or Sunday school. It was just an emotional thing. When I saw some other little kid getting beaten up by bullies, I tried to help him, even if it meant getting my butt kicked. I wasn't trying to be a hero—I just had a gut-level hatred of meanness. The pain of getting thumped by the bullies wasn't as bad as the pain of standing idly by. I guess I watched too much *Lone Ranger*.

To be honest, though, I don't think anybody ever really *learns* morality. It's either in your heart, or it isn't.

When I was in fifth grade, dad got a decent job—house painting—and we moved to Yonkers, the suburb just north of the Bronx. I wasn't thrilled. I wanted to stay around the action.

Dad was a typical working-class Italian guy: tough, loud, and impossible to please. You knew he approved of you when he didn't whip your butt. He was a good guy, but if some touchy-feely types had ever tried to, like, *bond* with Dad, they would've gotten knocked on their asses.

Kids being kids, I still tried to win Dad's approval. When I was eleven, I got a job assembling newspapers and had to be at work at three in the morning. *Earlier* than Dad. Sometimes after work I'd walk four miles to a bakery—all uphill, *both ways*—and help the bread truck drivers make their deliveries in the bad neighborhoods of the city. By the time my mom had breakfast on the table, I'd be home with money in my pocket, war stories to tell, and a box of rolls for our breakfast. Made me feel like I was a tough guy, taking care of the family.

The first time I brought home rolls, my dad didn't even look up from his paper. So the next day I brought home *two* boxes. Then three. *Six* boxes. Never looked up.

Still, I continued to bring home rolls. Even as a kid, I believed that if I tried hard enough, I could make the world around me a better place.

After a while, though, I got tired of trying to defrost Dad. I was restless; I wanted to make my way in the world. I was sick of school. I felt like I was learning more about the real world from the bread truck drivers than school, so in 1963 I talked my mom and dad into signing me out of school. What could they do? When I set my mind on something, I was almost impossible to derail.

I dropped out and left home at fourteen. By then, we had a pretty nice place, because my dad had worked his way up to a supervisory position. He was limited by his education, but he was on fire with the desire to make something of himself. A lot of people in my family were very ambitious; one of my aunts, Flora Fusaro, was among the first five women to graduate from New York University Medical School, and another aunt, Dora Pascucci, was a prominent MCA talent agent who knew all the big movie stars. I think ambition is a genetic trait, and, God knows, I inherited a big dose of it. Too big.

I headed straight for the East Village and moved into a slum apartment filled with beatniks, bikers, nihilists, and heroin addicts. It was a world of extremes—and I love extremes. In that environment, evolution was accelerated, and all the addicts and bikers died in a big hurry, while the beatniks quickly metamorphosed into hippies.

I loved the hippy era. It was like a second chance at childhood. Also, it put us poor kids on an equal footing with the rich ones; even hinting at class status was *totally* uncool.

By 1965, I was in love. It was the real thing. You think I'm being sarcastic, but I'm not. Kids can really *feel* love— better than grown-ups can. In my opinion, it's age and pain that dilute love into the pale, tame affection that adults learn to accept.

Janie was the first girl I ever truly loved, and I loved her so much I didn't care *how* many guys she was fucking. Let's remember, this was the Village in the mid-1960s—Go-Go Gomorrah—and if a girl wasn't sleeping around, she wasn't *trustworthy.*

Janie's other main boyfriend was the most famous hippy in New York. His name was Groovy, he was a master bullshit artist, and he had the New York media wrapped around his finger. By the logic of the era, sharing Janie with Groovy endowed me with *serious* hipness. Not bad for a sixteen-year-old high school dropout.

Janie, the daughter of some rich Connecticut guy, was dark and beautiful, and looked sexy even in granny dresses. And she was the *queen* of innocence—as only a rich kid could be. Even though she, Groovy, me, and several others kids were living together in the most vile ghetto in America, she strolled the streets at night like a debutante at a dance, offering joints to the hippies and wine to the drunks. With *that* kind of karma, I was convinced she could "vibe off" danger.

I remember clearly the last night I spent with her. We ate some amphetamines and stayed up all night watching a cockroach try to crawl out of the bathtub. I told Janie, "That *roach's* struggle is *man's* struggle," and she thought I was *deep.* In a speed frenzy, we figured out the meaning of life, then alphabetized it.

At dawn, we made love by an open window as the city began to burn with orange light. It was like the crescendo of a symphony. I felt totally at peace.

It was the last innocent moment in my life.

Just after sunrise, she left with Groovy to go buy pot from some tough Latino kids. I never saw her again.

She and Groovy were found two days later with their heads smashed apart by bricks. I always blamed the Latinos—but who knew? There were a thousand ways to get killed in the ghetto.

I started walking the streets at night by myself, carrying a blackjack and a bored-out starter's pistol—my idea of serious weaponry. I was trying to attract the Latino assholes. It never occurred to me to go to the police. They were the enemy.

One night, I walked by a tiny neighborhood grocery, and heard a muffled scream. I went through the door, and saw two Latino punks with their hands all over a pretty Spanish girl. To me, she looked like Janie. Another mutt was watching them and laughing. I took a giant step toward Laughing Boy and bashed his head with the blackjack. He folded.

Then I swung the blackjack sidearm as one of the germs leaped toward me. Caught him in the lower jaw. Ugly crunch of bone and gristle.

The third one shoved the girl toward me and went for a gun in his belt. I grabbed for my dinky-ass starter's pistol. But my hands were shaking so hard I couldn't aim it. I thought I was a streetfighter, but I was a fatality waiting to happen.

The kid pointed his gun at my chest and screamed something.

I backpedaled slowly. I'd heard that a gunshot wound burns, so I was waiting for a bang and a burn.

The kid's ugly red eyes bulged out. From behind me: "Police! Drop it!" The girl had punched an alarm. The kid ducked and ran out the back. The cop didn't chase him. He cuffed the punks on the floor and tried to calm the girl.

The cop glared at me. *"You!* I wanchu go over to that coffee shop and wait for me! And *don't* you *leave!"*

I watched from the coffee shop as an ambulance and a couple of police units pulled up. About forty minutes later, the cop came over.

"Are you stuuu-pid?" he said. "Where you from? The *suburbs,* right? Cuz a city kid wouldn't-a fucked with those maggots."

"I'm from Yonkers."

"Yonnn-kers. What-chu doin' *here?"*

"I like the atmosphere."

"You a dope fiend?"

"I smoke a little grass."

"Well, what you did was stupid. I could get you on a bunch-a charges. Assault. Vigilantism. Concealed weapon. You fractured that one guy's skull. Hell, he may *die.* I could maybe get you on murder-two."

He paused, and let it sink in. "But fuck 'em," he said. "Those guys are no goddamn good. You done the right thing."

I smiled a little. "But you're stuuu-pid," he growled. "Whattaya doin', goin' to war with a fucking *starter's* pistol?"

"Well, I didn't want to *kill* anybody, I just wanted to, you know—"

"No, I don't know. Look, if you go against a mutt, you take a *real* gun, and you shoot first, and you keep shooting until his guts are on the floor. That's the *New York way.* Okay?"

All of a sudden, I was struck with admiration for the guy. I'd always thought of cops as robots, enforcing every ignorant law on the books. But this guy was into *justice.* On that street, he was the judge, jury, and executioner—like a sheriff in the Old West.

We talked a little, and to a teenager, his job sounded like heaven: kickin' ass and drivin' fast.

He planted the seed of my dream. A little later, I heard Bob Dylan make that remark about, What the world needs most is cops who'll enforce justice, instead of the law. And I was hooked.

I started to see my Village buddies in a different light. It had never occurred to *them* to track Janie's killers. They'd just sit around and yap, yap, yap about how they were going to *change the world.* But they didn't even change their socks.

In '67, I joined the army. I wanted to be a Vietnam War hero. For about six weeks. Then the army sent me to college classes, where I studied history and politics, and it became obvious the Vietnam War was absurd. The *domino* theory? Please! It taught me a crucial lesson: The American people are sheep, and will let the government get away with *anything.*

Still, I envied the guys who saw combat because it was the ultimate test of courage. I was dying to know if I could look somebody in the eye and blow them away. I was afraid I couldn't. When we had bayonet training and I slid my blade into a dummy's belly, I felt like puking.

Stationed in Virginia Beach, I made metal peace symbols on the base and sold them in Eden's Alley, the local version of Haight-Ashbury. It was there I met Holly, who was seventeen, straight from the Haight, and the daughter of my commanding officer. Two days after we met, we went to North Carolina and got married. It was her fuck-you to her old man. Mine, too.

The C.O. made life miserable for me, and vice versa. Increasingly, I hated the army. Too regimented. No room for creativity.

After nine months, I talked it over with Holly, and cut her dad a deal: We'd get divorced if I could have an early discharge.

He agreed to the weasel-deal, and everybody lived happily ever after.

Back to New York. Back to college. I got hooked into philosophy because I was getting more and more obsessed by the subject of good and evil. If you love extremes, there's nothing more

68

fascinating. Besides, it was '68, and there was evil everywhere you looked: race wars, assassinations, riots, and war crimes. Martin Luther King. Bobby Kennedy. The My Lai massacre. The Chicago Democratic convention. The "new Nixon." Everything in that era felt dark, dirty, and mysterious.

Deep in my gut, I felt that I had an obligation to fight evil. In college, I learned how to articulate my sense of morality, but the truth is, morality was still a gut-level thing with me.

While I went to school, I labored at a long series of working-class jobs: cab driver, steamfitter's helper, truck driver, construction worker—jobs where your raises came a dime at a time. The jobs were tough, but I was always certain that I'd work my way past menial labor. I was extremely grateful for America's wide-open access to success. In most places around the world, I'd have spent my whole life mired in the lower working class.

I know it's not hip to say it, but I really love America. When I think of America, I don't think of corny bullshit like Betsy Ross and Flag Day; I think of loading trucks at night, sweating like a pig—but *knowing it was only temporary.* To me, that's what makes this country a unique place on earth.

I quit school before I got my degree. It wasn't a savvy career move, but I was impatient. School was too much theorizing, and not enough action.

I took the New York City police exam, and did extremely well. Out of about 50,000 applicants, I placed 344th—in the top one-half of one percent.

I was hoping my dad would be impressed, but he shrugged it off. Said there was no money in police work.

I was slated for appointment to the Police Academy, but at the last minute, I got bumped in favor of a councilman's son. I filed for documents on the decision through the Freedom of Information Act. Like a fool.

Meantime, the officer in charge of my appointment kept telling me that he could grease the skids if I'd pay him off. But I was too stuuu-pid to just fork over the tariff and get on with my career.

Instead, I went through an appeals process and finally got my appointment. I was assigned to two seminars: riding with a female partner, and how to apply for vacation.

Then the NYPD got caught in a budget battle and my whole class got laid off.

I resigned.

I was sick of the bureaucratic bullshit.

I joined the Westchester County Sheriff's Department.

Finally! A chance to battle evil! No more corruption!

I went out and bought a gun.

If I'd known what lay just ahead, I'd have probably put the gun to my head.

It was after-hours in the Westchester County divorce court, and the judge and two opposing attorneys were still one member short of a jury.

"It's up to you guys," I chimed in, "but if I had *my* druthers, I'd pick the blond with the big tits."

"Good call," said the judge. The two attorneys nodded distractedly.

And the battle against evil marched on.

I'd been a cop for over a year, and my only accomplishment had been getting tasked with divorce court. All the unmarried deputies competed for divorce court because it was a great place to meet women.

After we finished jury selection, I said good-bye to my courthouse cronies, hopped into my car, and felt my adrenaline start to rise. I was going out to confiscate a pistol from a felon who'd had his gun permit revoked. It was a dangerous job that the other cops hated.

But I liked it. Made me feel like a real cop. Also, it gave me a chance for advancement. I picked up guns every night, on my own time, in my own car.

Also at night, I searched permit records to find the .44-caliber gun used by our famous local killer, Son of Sam. He'd shot about ten people in the area. But there were 50,000 permits. So far, no luck.

When I got to the revocation address, I approached it carefully.

A whisker-stubbled guy with an exploded belly came to the door, and I told him why I needed his gun. He bitched about it. They always did.

He went to get it. He opened the screen door. "Here you go," he said. But all of a sudden, he pointed it at my head.

My body went electric. I grabbed my gun. Hesitated.

I should have pulled the trigger. But I just couldn't.

"Hey-hey-hey!" he blurted. "I'm-kidding-I'm-kidding!"

My stomach felt like I'd swallowed a hot coal. I took a deep breath.

"Look, I know how you feel," I said. "I love guns myself, and if some fuckin' guy came to get mine, I'd do *this*." I swung my fist up under his chin, and his teeth clunked together around his tongue. "But I'd *never* pull a gun on a police officer. Would *you?*"

"Outhss."

"I thought not. We're a lot alike." I left him holding his tongue in his hands.

The next day, I got called in to see the chief of operations. Brutality complaint, I assumed. "John," said the chief, "I want you to go down to the Westchester Premiere Theater and give pistol permits to some part-time security people." He handed me a list of names.

Strange request. The theater was in an incorporated township—the chief of police there should have handled the permits.

"And, John, extend them every courtesy. Do the fingerprints on-site, and take all the forms with you, so they don't have to come in."

"No problem." I was still a rookie, and it wasn't my place to ask questions.

When I got out there, all the guys getting permits listed their occupation as "sanitation worker, City of New York." But they sure didn't *look* like garbage men. They were wearing pinkie rings and leather sport coats.

That night, I went to a steak house near headquarters where all the deputies hung out, and met my buddy Roscoe, a homicide detective. I envied Roscoe. He was a *real* cop.

But his eyes were circled with dark rings. He looked like a sick raccoon. "What's wrong?"

"Nuthin'." He stared at his drink.

I steered him to a booth near the jukebox, where no one

could hear us over the disco boom of Donna Summer. "What's goin' on?"

He threw back his drink and signaled for another. "I been working Son of Sam, right?"

"Right."

"We had *letters* from him, John. We had *fingerprints.*"

"*Hoe*-lee shit! Did you run 'em?"

"Quiet *down!*" He looked around, gulped his drink, and waved for another. Shook his head. "No. And now we can't." He looked stricken. "They were faint, so we tried to bring 'em out. But we fucked 'em up. Our lab just didn't have the expertise."

"*Our* lab? We didn't hand them over to NYPD?"

"No. We had orders to keep it in-house. So Westchester could get the glory."

"Maybe FBI can help."

"They're *gone,* John. After we lost the prints, they made us get rid of the letters."

"Who did?"

He gave me a dirty look. "Who the fuck do you think? The highest level of the department. Okay?"

That was the last I ever heard of it. It never surfaced in the media, or in any of the books about Son of Sam.

I tried to smile. "Don't worry. You'll get him before he hits again."

"Not fuckin' likely. He hit again tonight. John, there are things goin' on in this department that you don't want to *know* about."

He was wrong. I wanted to know everything.

Soon enough, I would.

I got a promotion. The chief liked the way I'd handled the permits at the Westchester Theater, so he stationed me there indefinitely.

My first assignment was to guard Engelbert Humperdinck. More precisely, it was to guard the hooker who the theater's security staff had available for "En-gee," as his retinue called him. She was a wonderful girl, bright and very beautiful. Other than her, though, everybody in En-gee's entourage treated me like I was his fucking valet. We spent many hours at bars and restaurants, and not once did anyone offer me so much as a cup of coffee. It was humiliating.

Then word came down that a female psycho was stalking En-gee. God knows why *anybody* would stalk a flyweight like En-gee, but our intelligence reports said this woman was armed and dangerous. So all day long, I'd scan crowds for her face and stay ready to give up my life for the Hump.

Then my boss gave concealed weapon permits to all of En-gee's half-bright sycophants. Lovely. Now *any* confrontation would go nuclear.

She didn't show during my stint on the Humperdinck deathwatch, but then the theater booked Paul Anka—and Anka heard En-gee's boys had gotten guns, so *he* wanted *his* guys to have them. Then Frank Sinatra came, and Frank wanted an *arsenal* for *his* stooges.

Being in the middle of so many armed idiots was dangerous, but it taught me an important lesson: It's just as easy to die for a punk as it is to die for a noble cause.

Sometimes, after big shows, the security staff would ask me to help them guard box office money as they carried it out to a waiting car. Right off, I was thinking: This is a goddamn *skimming* operation. I ran straight to my boss. No interest. Whenever we did it, the security guys would be jumpy as hell. They were obviously worried that whoever they were stealing from was going to ambush us.

It taught me another lesson: Evil usually doesn't battle good—it battles other evil.

Around this time, I discovered I was a superb marksman—third best in the state, out of about sixty-five thousand officers. For me, the key to shooting was to refrain from staring at the target. I'd put my front sight on it, then forget about it and concentrate on lining up the back sight with the front. But I was haunted by a question: What if the front sight was on a *man?* Could I forget about *him?* Or would I hesitate again—and die?

One afternoon, I ran into a couple of detectives who were leaving for a bust.

"Wanna assist?" one of them offered. "Gambling raid?"

"You bet!"

We drove in a plainclothes car to a barbershop, and they stationed me at a back door while they made their collar.

They came out crowing. They'd nailed a mob bookkeeper with a full set of records. I finally felt like a real cop.

But the next time I saw the guys, they were all fucked up. Their gambling unit had been disbanded, and their cars had been taken away.

I asked them why they were being punished, but neither would talk.

A couple of months later, I came up with something that I thought would get them off the hook. I took one of them aside and told him about it. My buddy Roscoe had pulled a weasel-deal and gotten a trap and trace on the phone of a pool hall, and he'd hit pay dirt. It was a gambling cop.

But the detective wasn't interested. He wouldn't even *talk* about it. "My advice," he said, "my *strong* advice, is run it by senior staff before you take any action."

So Roscoe went to the chief, who told him to stage his raid the following Wednesday afternoon.

That night at the bar, Roscoe was worried. "This ain't *right,* man," he said. "Why's it gotta be at a specific time? It's a tipoff."

"Noooo," I said. I had good reason to trust senior staff: I was stuuu-pid.

On Wednesday we headed for the bust. But on our way there, a call went out for every unit in the vicinity to report to an address in New Rochelle. A neo-Nazi had taken hostages and was killing people.

We could hear shots as we approached, but the second we arrived—taking a shortcut through an alley—the area got deathly quiet. Then, over a megaphone: *"Officers,* you're in the *kill zone!"* They meant us.

Ching! Ching! Just behind us, a stucco wall exploded in puffs of dust.

"Officers! *EVACUATE!"*

Roscoe gunned it. Seconds later, we were at the command center.

The operations commander grabbed my elbow. "Pascucci! Get that cameraman outta there!" He pointed to the other side of an open space, where a TV cameraman was crouched at the corner of a building. I raced toward him, hugging the ground.

A bullet sparked in front of me.

I grabbed the cameraman and shoved him back behind the building.

"You were in the *kill* zone!" I yelled. "You coulda been shot."

I had to run across the same exposed area to get back to the command center.

But as soon as I got there, the commander pointed behind me. The goddamn cameraman was back.

I hauled ass to him. I screamed into his face: "Last warning! Stay back!" He nodded meekly.

From inside the sniper's position, I heard shots and screams. I tore back to the command post and helped a team of sharpshooters load their gear into an armored vehicle. I didn't envy them. How could they kill someone who was so obviously insane?

Ten minutes later: "Pascucci! He's *back!*"

My heart went spastic. After you've done something a couple of times, you *know* how scary it is. But I made myself run back. As I got there, a window above my head shattered and glass hailed onto my hat.

I grabbed the cameraman by the scruff of his neck. "This is *my* fault," I said. "I wasn't specific enough." I balled my hand around my nightstick and punched his face as hard as I could. He started to yell. "Save your comments until I'm finished," I said. I hit him again.

I ran back across the kill zone, and dodged another bullet.

By that time, I was *more* than ready to kill the sniper. Bullets do funny things to your sense of morality.

Then the commander—who knew my rep as a marksman—asked me if I'd take a rifle and go out with the sharpshooters.

"You're goddamn right I will," I said.

The second I picked up the weapon, though, I felt sick.

Minutes later, the shooter killed himself. I was so relieved I shuddered like a wet dog.

Roscoe and I decided to go ahead with our bust. It was way past afternoon, but we were too hyper to go home.

It was a righteous bust. We took down a couple of prominent citizens and confiscated some gaming equipment.

But the next day we got a royal ass-chewing—because we
hadn't made the pop at the appointed time.

That night, I went to the department's hangout ready to *hit*
somebody. I had a few drinks, which is unusual for me—I
hate the loss of control. I started bitching, and the next thing
I knew, I was surrounded by deputies who were as disgrun-
tled as me. Everybody was talking about the same things:
cover-ups, tip-offs, and favors for wise guys and big shots.

The department, in short, was dirty.

Looking back, it's hard for me to believe I hadn't seen it
sooner. But I was young and stuuu-pid.

I had a big mouth, and in the weeks to come, I began
shooting it off on the subject of departmental corruption. Before long, everybody was coming to me with their horror
stories. I got active in union politics, trying to fight within
the system.

But the supervisors started to hate me. I didn't know how
unpopular I was until one night when the sheriff called,
drunk as hell. "Come gimme a ride home," he said. "I banged
up my car again."

"Where are you?"

"Steak 'n Brew. The one near you."

"There's no Steak 'n Brew near me."

"Who is this?"

"Pascucci."

"Oh. Shit. I meant to call a *good* cop." Click!

The next day, as I was driving to work, I got stuck behind
a weaving car. Drunk driver? I pulled him over. All of a
sudden, the driver leaped out of the car—with a *bayonet.*
Huge shiny thing. Razor sharp. He swung it at my belly.
Whoosh! It sliced open my jacket and my shirt, and left a
long red cut from my chest to my stomach. I grabbed my gun
as he hauled back to swing again. I had every legal right to
kill him. And it was the safest course of action. But, Jesus,
he was just a kid. I pointed my weapon toward the sky.
BOOM! He froze.

Then his passenger, an older guy, fell to his knees.
Keeled over.

"Dad!" cried the driver. *"Dad!"*

The older guy was clawing at his heart. I picked him up and put him back in the car.

"There's a hospital just down the street!" I yelled at the guy with the bayonet. "Go!"

They squealed off. I sat down on the curb and started to get deeply depressed. Jimmy Carter had recently been doing a lot of talking about malaise, and I was developing a *bad* case of it. I'd entered law enforcement to fight evil. But I wasn't fighting evil. I was fighting *idiots.* And I was working for crooks. Not only that, I was beginning to wonder if I'd ever have what it takes to kill somebody. I'd heard about other cops who were trigger-shy. They died young.

At that moment, at the ripe old age of twenty-nine, I entered my Wambaugh phase. In Joseph Wambaugh's police novels, the cops are burnouts who release tension with sick pranks. I committed my first one later that afternoon.

We were interrogating a prisoner who'd murdered a cop. We'd all known the cop, and knew his widow and son. So of course we hated this son of a bitch.

About halfway through the questioning, I turned to the other officer. "Okay, I'm satisfied," I said. "You may proceed." My buddy opened the door to an adjoining room— where we'd jerry-rigged an electric chair.

We strapped the mutt in. He tried to laugh. We put a steel bowl over his head with bare wires taped to it. He started wailing. I duct-taped his mouth.

The chair was wired to plug into a 110-volt outlet. It was enough to give him a nice little zap.

I held the plug in front of his bulging eyes. "So long, cop killer."

I plugged it in. *Spraaat!* He let out a huge fart and his crotch went dark with piss.

We howled. But that same day, I started to look for a new job. I was getting jaded.

And there were too many temptations. I was making about $15,000 a year, but deputies who were friendly with the local wise guys were making six figures. Besides, staying straight was dangerous. I was getting notes and phone calls, telling me that if I didn't quit bitching to the union about corruption, I was dead.

It was a bad time, in general, to be in law enforcement. Jimmy Carter seemed to be more concerned about criminals' rights than policemen's rights. Personally, I liked Carter, but he set a tone of national wimpiness that made me want to puke. He seemed paralyzed by his morality, and to me, paralyzed morality is no morality at all.

The only good thing in my life was my deepening relationship with my future wife, Betsy. The minute that I met her, at a restaurant, I was in love. She was pretty and smart, and definitely lived in the real world. She was an operating room nurse, and a frequently published freelance writer. Every day at the hospital she saw at least as much suffering and pain as I did, but she hadn't let it make her cynical. She was still awed by simple things, like seeing a rabbit in the backyard, or growing a pumpkin. She was the perfect balance for me.

In my usual extreme way, I began bombarding her with flowers, gifts, and romantic dinners. She never stood a chance.

Nonetheless, I was starting to get crazy, and it showed in my work. One day, I was assigned to escort a prisoner to Sing Sing, and by the time we got to the prison, I was ready to strangle the guy. He was a real piece of shit—he'd been running nursing homes where the old people were fed dog food, and left unattended while rats and roaches crawled on them. I've got a real soft spot for old people because of their vulnerability, and when I first heard the details of this guy's operation, I got really depressed. But those old people didn't need somebody to sit around and mope for them, they needed somebody to come in, kick some ass, and put this guy away.

On the way up the prison stairs, he started whining about his heart and telling me to carry his suitcase.

"Fuck you. Carry it yourself, or leave it."

He grabbed his chest. "I can't go no farther."

I cuffed him around a little. He kept bitching. Then he swung at me. I slapped his face. He swung again. I popped him good, then popped him again. He fell back onto his ass. He was dead as hell.

I threw him over my shoulder, walked the last flight, and tossed him into a chair in the receiving room. I propped him up, stuck a magazine in his hands, grabbed a receipt for him, and took off.

That night, I kept waiting to feel guilty. But every time I thought of him, sitting there staring at that magazine, I laughed. Something had changed in me. I knew, in my heart, that I was a little more evil than I'd once been. But it seemed like a necessary kind of evil.

At least, I finally had a body count. I was no longer a virgin. I would never again feel quite as unsure of myself. My only regret was that I hadn't lost my virginity in a firefight, like a real cop.

But by this point, I understood an interesting corollary: The less afraid you are to kill, the less afraid you are to die. Proximity to death, for some reason, demystifies it. So I drastically stepped up my fight against the crooks in the department. If they killed me, they killed me.

I started funneling information to a local judge. Without revealing me as the source, he passed it on to the district attorney's office. It was risky. Any good investigator could have nailed me as the source.

After I'd been doing this for about a month, a deputy came to me and told me he'd made a drug bust at a gambling hangout. It was a good clean pop—half a pound of heroin. But his supervisor had called him in and told him to eat the arrest. The deputy had to say he'd failed to Mirandize his perp.

I called the judge to tell him the story. I told him to meet me at a parking garage under the courthouse.

While I was waiting for him, a police car pulled in and cruised past me. Didn't recognize the driver. It slowed down. Stopped. Then it started backing up. Accelerated. Headed straight for me. I jumped behind a pillar. The car banged into a wall. Screeched off.

I never did find out who was in it.

When the judge arrived, I told him about the aborted bust. He was disgusted.

So was I. I wanted out. I applied to the U.S. Marshals Service.

While I was waiting for my application to be processed, I applied for assignment to family court. I thought it would be the safest place to work. I was concerned that if I was involved in street action, I'd catch a "stray" bullet.

But while I was at family court, I heard the worst story yet. One of my colleagues had made a routine traffic bust near the Westchester Theater. But he'd gotten suspicious, had opened the car's trunk, and had found a cardboard box crammed with bundles of cash and packets of white powder.

He'd radioed in his situation, and in a matter of minutes, a department head had arrived on the scene.

The department head had insisted on taking over, and he'd dismissed the officer.

That was the last anybody had heard of it. My buddy had confronted the supervisor but had been told that the cash had been legitimate, and that the powder had just been an industrial product.

I called the judge. We arranged to meet in our usual parking garage.

While I was waiting for him, a call came in on my radio. A punk with a gun had run out of a courtroom upstairs. He was headed for the garage.

I heard a stairwell door open. I ran toward it. Nothing there. I looked under all the nearby cars. Nothing.

A sound. It came from under a van. I looked under it. Nothing.

It was time to bluff. "Okay, motherfucker!" I screamed. "I *see* you."

He dropped from the suspension of the van.

He hurtled toward me. I could see his face. I grabbed my .357 Magnum. Aimed. Then, at the last second, I jerked the gun off-target and fired into the ceiling. BOOM! In the dark of the garage, I was blinded. But I could hear him. He was still coming. Why hadn't I just *killed* him? What was *wrong* with me?

I lashed out in front of me. Caught the side of his head with my gun.

A police car zoomed up. I hit the asshole again. He fell backward, into the waiting arms of the patrolman.

In minutes, the garage was swarming with police. The judge didn't show. I called him later, and he said he'd been there but had been spooked by all the witnesses. We met that night. He said that I'd given him enough to convene a grand jury.

A week later, I was accepted by the U.S. Marshals.

I gave the sheriff's department two week's notice. My goal was to stay alive for fourteen more days. I began a countdown. Fourteen days. Thirteen. Twelve. Ten. Five. Four. Two.

Finally, one more day.

Luckily, I had easy duty: family court.

I thought I had it made.

"John," said Rick, my fellow deputy in family court, "if I tell you somethin', will you forget where you heard it?" His voice was low and his face was cut with lines of worry.

"Sure."

"People in the department are really pissed off at you."

"Tell me somethin' I *don't* know."

"I mean it. *Really* pissed. As in, they're gonna *hurt* you."

"But I'm *leavin'*.*"* It was May 9, 1979, my last day as a deputy sheriff.

"Don't matter—not if you bring charges against guys in the department."

I shot him a scowl. Was he in on it too?

"Look," I said, "if there's an investigation, I'm gonna tell the truth."

Rick looked sad. "Is it worth *dyin'* for?"

"Yeah. Truth *is* worth dying for!" Can you *believe* I said that?

Then I heard a scuffle in the waiting room next door. It was my job to break it up. I headed toward the room.

Brap! Brap!

Gunshots! My body went icy. I lurched toward the door and grabbed my gun.

But the second I got to the door, it banged into my face and a tangle of people poured out. They were congealed into a solid lump, like clay figures wadded together.

"Rick!" But he was frozen. His eyes looked like volleyballs.

I lowered my shoulder and drove into the lump.

I bounced off. Hit it again. A crack opened and I slithered through, keeping my gun at my side so I wouldn't kill someone.

Then I was in the room and seemed suddenly alone. Except for one woman. She was sitting silently on a bench, her eyes locked on the wall. There was a red, round dot on her forehead, as if someone had tapped her with a lipstick.

She began to lean forward. Then tumbled onto her face.

She was mortally wounded.

I scanned wildly. Motion behind me.

I pivoted. I saw the shooter. I ducked and rolled left as his gun began to rise.

I jerked my gun in the direction of his chest.

I didn't hesitate.

I pulled the trigger. He spun sideways and the bullet caught him in the bicep and high chest. He stayed up.

He looked at the hole in his chest.

The gun fell out of his hand.

Behind him, the wall was blotted with a huge red circle. The exit wound in his back was big as a coffee cup, and full of shredded flesh.

He looked at me, and we locked eyes. As I stared into his eyes, I saw the light of life go out of them. It was just like someone turning off the lights in a room.

He toppled forward.

I stepped out of the way, and he crashed onto the floor.

All around me was utter silence.

I felt like God. Or maybe even worse.

About fifteen minutes later, paramedics rushed in. But there were no patients. Just corpses. So they slowed down, and started to clean up the mess. Everywhere you looked, there were strange pieces of anatomy: brains, skull, lung, spine.

It was past my lunch, so I brought in my bag of fast food and started gobbling it, tossing the wrappers into a pile of brain and blood, which needed to be swept up anyway.

One of the paramedics wasn't handling the scene very

well, which surprised me. I thought they saw gore all the time.

Trying to put him at ease, I held out my fries, which were covered with ketchup.

"French fry?" I said.

He stared down at the white fries swimming in ketchup. He started to decline. Then he puked all over my shoes.

I wiped them off with surgical gauze, then went back to my food.

It tasted great.

Shortly after I became a U.S. marshal, the district attorney took all of the information I'd funneled to him through the judge and ripped the department apart. He handed down indictments against thirteen deputies. The sheriff was suspended, and never got his job back.

I returned to Westchester County as the star witness at the trial, and I got my first big write-up in the *New York Times*.

As I finished testifying, a greasy-haired wise guy in a silk suit stood up in the back row and mouthed the words, "You're dead." He sawed his hand across his throat.

I gave him the finger.

I was a changed man. I was no longer innocent. And I was no longer afraid. Almost every day now, as a U.S. marshal, I faced death.

So . . . this punk wanted me dead.

So what?

If he decided to get serious, I'd just have to kill him.

I could do that now.

Chapter Four

Making My Bones

★

• Me versus Richard Nixon • Pimping for
Snitches • Rufus the Mob
Bomber • Watergate Revisited • Tip O'Neill's
Stooge • ATF Dickheads • My First
Manhunt • How the Real World Works •

"Of the two evils, the lesser is always to be chosen."
—*Thomas Kempis*

Hey, Freshmeat!" The boss meant me—the newest deputy
in the San Diego Marshals' office. "Surf's up!"

It was once again time for me to battle the forces of evil:
the surfboarders who'd strayed into the off-limits water in
front of Camp Pendleton.

I tried to smile, but couldn't. "Boss," I said, "can I have a
word with you?"

Bob Dighera, who was in charge of the Warrants Squad,
waved me into his office.

"Bob, I don't wanna be a pain in the ass, okay? But I'm
going *birdshit* on these surfing tickets. What I want, if you
can swing it, is to get onto the Boyce task force."

84

"*Boyce!* You want assigned to *Boyce?*" Dighera's huge, round face began to go orange and purple with anger until it looked like a rotten pumpkin. He was 260 pounds of muscle and bone, and was one of those Italian types that screamed first and asked questions later. "Boyce is the most wanted criminal in the goddamn *country*," boomed Dighera. "Did you hear what *Moynihan* said yesterday?"

"Of course." The whole office was bitching about it. Daniel Patrick Moynihan had stood up in the Senate and said that having the Marshals look for Christopher Boyce—the "Falcon and Snowman" Russian spy—was "just like letting him go free."

At this time—early 1980—the Marshals were the laughing-stock of federal law enforcement. It had been that way for over a decade.

It was currently just five months since the FBI had given the Fugitive Program to the Marshals, and everybody in Washington was waiting for us to screw up the Boyce man-hunt. If we did, the Marshals Service would probably never recover. We were seen as just a rest home for old hacks—*because we were*—and one more major flop would doom us. There was already serious talk of disbanding the entire agency. Carter's attorney general, Benjamin Civiletti, wasn't at all supportive of the Service. I guess he figured we had malaise.

To be honest, if I hadn't been desperate to get out of Westchester, I would *never* have joined the Marshals. But now I had to make the best of my choice.

"Look, Pascucci," said Dighera, "I just don't think you're *ready* for that kind of assignment."

"You're acting like I've never worked a *case,* for Christ's sake."

"I know, I know—you're the Wyatt Earp of Westchester County. But you haven't done anything yet as a *marshal.* The Marshals Service is a federal *bureaucracy,* John, and you've gotta learn how to play it. *Everybody* wants onto the Boyce team, and most of those guys already know how to work the system. What grade are you?"

He meant: What civil service rank was I? "G.S. five," I said.

Dighera shook his head. A "government service grade 5"

was the lowest rank in the federal bureaucracy, paying about $10,000 a year—far less than I'd gotten on the sheriff's department.

"No *five* is gonna make the Boyce team, John."

"When do they name the team?" I asked.

"In a week," said Dighera.

How could I boost my bureaucratic status in one lousy week? "Is there any way I could get on *later*," I asked, "after the team's been formed?"

He gave me a short, hard look. In other words: Forget it.

Just then, the Skeleton stuck his head in the door. The Skeleton, Tommy Whitaker, was a good marshal, and not just another empty suit. But he was *weird*-looking: skinny, bony, white eyebrows, shaved head, beady eyes—a walking X ray. "Ready to roll, Bob," he said to Dighera.

"Meat here wants to track Boyce," Dighera said to the Skeleton, as he slid his gun into his shoulder holster. "I told him that first he's gotta make his bones."

The Skeleton smiled. His teeth got lost in his white face. "If you wanna make your bones," said the Skeleton, "come with *us*. We're gonna hit a house, and bust a real puke."

I looked at Dighera. He shrugged. "Okay," Dighera said, "you can come. But you *owe* me one."

"Thanks," I said.

The Skeleton bleated a squeal. "Don't *thank* him 'til this is over and you're *alive*."

The Skeleton drove me out to the house we were going to hit. While we drove I picked his brain on fugitive hunting. He'd only been doing it for a few months, but he was still way ahead of me. He'd been offered a spot on the Boyce Task Force, but he'd turned it down. He thought Boyce's escape from federal prison had been engineered by the KGB, and that catching him would be impossible.

"When you're lookin' for somebody," he said, "you're always trying to cut down your time line—*where* they last were, and *when*. With a fugitive, that's easier than you'd think, cuz a fugitive usually has to keep committing money crimes to survive. That's why they're so dangerous."

"If they're so dangerous, why'd the FBI give us the Fugitive Program?"

"Well, for one thing, fugitives are fuckin' hard to *catch*. The Feebs *never* had much luck with 'em. *Nobody* has. Also, the Bureau's funding is based on how many *arrests* they make—not how many *re*-arrests. Same goes for local and state cops. Once the initial bust goes down, there's no more money to be made."

"So why'd the Marshals *take* the job?"

"Cuz we're on our ass. If we don't make some waves, we're gone."

"What's the time line on this mutt?"

He grinned. "About fifteen *minutes*. He just stuck up a 7-Eleven. Witnesses traced him to a house a few blocks away."

We pulled up in front of the house. The Skeleton took a deep breath, and got even whiter. "Now, *remember,* John, this guy's a condemned convict. So he *will* kill you, even in a break-even situation."

The Skeleton heaved down another gulp of air, checked his gun, slid out of the car, and scurried around to cover the back of the house. I ran to one side of it, and crawled closer and closer to the front door. When the Skeleton and I were in place, Dighera lunged out of his car and lumbered up the front sidewalk.

He jumped onto the porch, reared back, and crashed the heel of his boot into the door. *BRAM!* The whole house shuddered. The door held. Steel door. He bashed it again. *BRAM!* It held.

I was dying inside. I kept waiting to hear a shotgun blast and see Dighera's guts paint the sidewalk.

But Dighera held his position. He had balls. We were about the same age, but he was sort of a father figure to me.

BRAM! The door ripped completely off its hinges and boomed flat onto the floor.

Dighera leaped into the house and I scrambled after him, puckering my asshole, and trying to keep my hands from shaking.

"Come out! Come out! Come out!" Dighera screamed. We raced from room to room.

But suddenly there was just silence. The house was empty.

"Over here," yelled the Skeleton. He pointed to a broken window. It had been smashed from the inside, and footprints beneath it led to a mesa behind the house. The puke had probably taken off when we'd pulled up.

I headed for the mesa. But the Skeleton grabbed my belt from behind. *"Uh*-uh," he said. "He could be anywhere out there, waiting to pick you off."

I scowled at him.

"Hey," he said, "there's easier ways to make the Boyce team. Believe me."

Dighera seized the telephone and hit 9-1-1. "Code three— we got a ten-thirty-five!" That was the San Diego police code for an emergency situation, with a dangerous-person alert. "Request immediate air surveillance!" He gave them our position, then stayed on the line as we listened to the chopper zero in on us.

"They spotted him!" said Dighera. We jumped back in our cars and raced toward a strip of seedy motels three blocks away. The Skeleton drove like Starsky and Hutch, slaloming pedestrians and jumping curbs. I loved it. While he drove, he yelled, "When we start hitting those motels, *don't* ID yourself to the room clerks! Just act like you got authority. They'll automatically think that you're whatever agency they fear most. Plus, if we fuck up, they won't be able to nail us!"

We screeched to a halt in front of a motel. The Skeleton grabbed a picture of our guy and ran up to a teenage hooker on the sidewalk.

"Seen this guy just now?" he said.

"I think. Maybe."

"Whattaya *want?"*

"Twenty."

"I'll do better than that. After I get my guy, I'll bring you two tricks."

"Like hell you will."

"Or I'll take ya downtown right now—that's your other option."

She looked like a trapped animal. Poor miserable kid. "He went into that one." She pointed at the motel across the street.

Dighera squealed up and set up shop in a phone booth, trying to coordinate some assistance. Most enforcement officers would have stayed in their cars and used their radios, but we were U.S. Marshals. We didn't *have* radios. We didn't have shit.

The Skeleton and I ran over to the motel and rousted the room clerk. But he was a real asshole. Started telling us all about the Bill of Rights. The Skeleton leaned across the desk and grabbed him by the ear, just like the nuns used to grab me in grade school. The Skeleton pulled the clerk out the door, and marched him to the first room.

"Guess what?" said the Skeleton, "I smell *smoke.* Under the authority of the United States government and the hotel safety code of California, I hereby order you to open that fuckin' door or I'll *hit* you." He jerked on the guy's ear. The clerk put a pass key in the door. I cocked my gun. Took a breath. Stood to one side. Bashed open the door. Empty.

We went to the next room. "I smell smoke," I said.

"Okay, okay," whined the clerk. I swung open the door. Nothing.

Next room. "Smoke!" He unlocked it. I stepped away from the door, turned the knob, pushed, then jumped into the jamb.

There he was. Rifle in his hands. He was trying frantically to unstick the bolt, which was bent. I rushed in. Drop-kicked the rifle out of his hands. "Freeze *now!*" I screamed. I shoved my gun barrel against his nose.

His whole body went rigid and he clamped his eyes shut.

The Skeleton grabbed the mutt's arms and cuffed him.

We hauled him outside and threw him in the back of Dighera's car.

"Can you take him in, Bob?" said the Skeleton. "I gotta take care of my snitch." He nodded toward the whore across the street.

"Can't that wait?" said Dighera.

"Come on, Bob—*I owe her one.*"

Dighera shrugged, and split. He knew the importance of paying back favors. Marshals were always talking about "owing one." We had no money or power, so favors were our primary currency. Of course, it was unlikely this hooker would ever again help us with anything, but who knew?

My nerves were still electric with adrenaline. I didn't want to mess around with the whore. "Why don't we just give her the twenty bucks?" I said.

"We're United States *marshals,* John." He scowled at me. "We don't *have* twenty bucks."

We spent the next hour going room to room until we found a couple of customers for the hooker.

It was humiliating.

But I was learning. I was learning how to get the job done. And I was learning more and more about how the real world worked.

As I was going on duty the next day, one of the old, fat-assed marshals started singing "Surfin' Safari." Pissed me off.

So I said, "Hey, be *careful* out there," using the *Hill Street Blues* line. That shut him up, because he was headed for his usual cushy nest—an appeals court where he stood "guard." It was a bullshit job, and he was a bullshit guy, just trying to kill his twenty years and draw a pension. Like a lot of other marshals, he was a retired military man, and was double-dipping—pulling a navy pension and a full marshal's salary. Pretty soon, he'd have two fat pensions, courtesy of the American taxpayer.

Every time you looked at a beer-gutted loser like him, you wondered how he'd made it through the Marshals' Glynco, Georgia, training academy, which had damn near killed *me.* The answer was simple—he hadn't. Until 1973, all U.S. marshals had been political appointees, and they'd been allowed to hire their own deputy marshals. In the early "cowboy" days of the Service, when the marshals had been the only law in the West, the appointees had been tough guys and gunslingers, who'd operated successfully, if not always legally. But as the West had been tamed, and as the mission of the Service had become more bureaucratized, the personnel in the Service had begun to degenerate. By the time the modern era of the Marshals arrived, most of the appointees were political hacks, and their deputies were real Quasimodos. The Service had become a pack of morons. Most of the old Marshals were *happy* with guarding courtrooms and transferring prisoners.

When the Marshals' patronage system had been killed,

though—in '73—new blood had slowly started to flow into the Service. Competent men had begun to rise to the top. Some of these new men had effected the biggest change yet in the Service: They'd snagged the Fugitive Program from the FBI. They'd convinced Jimmy Carter—who was fighting to retain the presidency—that if the FBI gave the Marshals the Fugitive Program, the FBI would have more time to concentrate on headline-making crime, and make Carter look tough.

So in October of 1979, the Marshals had been tasked with finding every bad-ass fugitive in the country. And now, in February of 1980, every young hotshot in the Service wanted to work Fugitives. Including me.

At Glynco, I'd shown an aptitude for criminal investigation, so I'd been assigned to the San Diego office, which had the best fugitive unit in the Service. It had been tough for Betsy to move west, because all her family was on the East Coast. But she made the sacrifice, and it made me love her that much more. I admire strength more than anything else, and, for her, nothing took more strength than leaving her family. But Betsy was extremely supportive of my career and did it without a complaint. She was certain I'd be an overnight success.

But here I was, in hot pursuit of some little dipshit who'd illegally surfed in front of Camp Pendleton. Like a lot of the kids who'd gotten the federal illegal-surfing tickets, he'd apparently considered it too chickenshit to bother with. It was my job to bring him to justice.

I decided, though, to work the case just like I would a *real* beef. That way, I'd learn the techniques.

I got his address and hit it. Found his roommate. But the guy was a real Joe College wise-ass and wouldn't tell me where the surfer was.

I pulled out my cuffs and started ratcheting them in front of the kid. "Pal," I said, "you don't know *dick* about the penalties for harboring a federal fugitive, do you? You probably don't even know what 'accessory after the fact' means, do you?"

"Fuck youuu."

"I think you better call your lawyer." The Skeleton had

told me always to mention somebody's lawyer *before* they did. That established the lawyer as a *defensive* entity, instead of an *offensive* one. It kept you in control.

The kid sneered at me. Utter contempt. So what? I could eat shit longer than he could dish it out. "Call a lawyer, kid," I said softly. "They're not all that expensive."

He caved. Gave me the surfer's workplace.

I found the surfer near Capistrano, where he was the maître d' in an expensive restaurant. He was wearing about fifteen hundred bucks worth of Giorgio Armani and had a perfect tan. His face was immobile, like a porcelain mask.

"I'll call my attorney and have him clear up the oversight by end-of-business Friday," he said. He sniffed the air, as if I smelled bad.

I felt about two inches tall. All my life, I'd had to suck up to upper-class people like him.

But I wasn't just *me* anymore. I was the president's cop.

"Fuck your lawyer," I said. "I'm takin' you in." For just a second, his carefully constructed expression fell to pieces.

I drove him down to see the magistrate because it was too punk of a bust to throw him in jail. But the magistrate was tied up, and told me to hang on for a couple of hours. Instead of tossing the kid in a cell with the other pukes, I took him up to an office, and sat him at a desk. "Look," I said, "if you fuck up, I'm gonna knock you out. But here, if you wanna make some phone calls, go ahead." So he got on the horn while I did some paperwork.

Next thing I knew, the secretary from the magistrate's office was at the door. "The magistrate has canceled his appointments," she said. "He wants to see you two right away." We went down there and, boom, case dismissed—"You're free to go. And Officer Pascucci, do me a favor, please, and drive this man back to his place of business."

The kid left to get his stuff, and I said, "Judge, what's goin' on?"

"You're not going to believe this. I got a call from San Clemente."

"Who's in San Clemente?"

"Who's in San *Clemente?* Don't be stupid." I still didn't know what he meant. So he continued. "This young man is friends with the Nixon family. And they wanted this taken care of."

"Nixon! That asshole doesn't have power anymore."

He looked at me with pity, like, You poor ignorant cop.

"Well, you're the boss," I said. "But . . . does Nixon *owe me one?"*

"Get outta here, officer."

I drove the kid back to his restaurant, and he smirked all the way. Long ride.

When I got back to the office I slumped into my chair and stared at my desk. Piled onto the desk was a stack of Teletypes that nobody else in the office wanted to deal with. They were from Marshal's offices all around the country, alerting us to fugitives from various cities who might be in San Diego. Our deputies hated working the Teletypes because they rarely led to a bust. As a rule, the office sending the Teletype was just covering its ass, foisting off responsibility for someone they'd let slip away.

But one of the Teletypes caught my eye because it was a high-profile case. Rufus Donner, a black guy who was a contract bomber and arsonist for one of the Chicago crime families, had escaped from federal prison. He'd been sentenced to life for killing a bystander in a botched car-bomb hit against another mobster. In the same explosion, a teenage girl had been badly burned. She had barely survived. Before the fire, she'd apparently been very pretty, because she'd been a homecoming queen. But now she was scary-looking. I saw a picture of her, and she didn't have a nose—just a snout, like a pig. The girl had testified at Donner's trial, and his presentence report noted that he'd laughed at her.

How could somebody laugh at a suffering child? It made me want to puke. I knew, theoretically, that hurting a child was no worse than hurting an adult. But I didn't operate on theory—I operated on emotion—and my gut-level sense of morality was just outraged.

I wanted Donner *badly*—and not just because of the girl. I *had* to make a major bust to get on the Boyce team. I believe in utilitarianism: The highest ideal is to do the greatest good for the greatest number—and the ends justify the means. But

I had no hope of doing *anything* for *anybody* unless I elevated my position.

I entered Donner's name into ARJIS, the Automated Regional Justice Information System, but drew a blank. Then I tried some of the other resources that I'd learned about in Westchester. I accessed the California motor vehicle records, did a sweep of local death records, checked with the Social Security Administration, and called the major credit card companies. But I couldn't find any triggers, which was no surprise—this guy was too street-smart to operate under his own name.

It was conceivable his mob contacts had helped him. But not likely. He'd ratted them out in his trial.

It was past quitting time, and all the lard-assed old-timers were long gone. But I drank a couple of Cokes and played with some of the systems that Dighera and the Skeleton had been talking about. I checked computer systems in the Chicago area—Donner's hometown—to see if he'd given power of attorney to anyone. I checked the CompuServe system to locate all the Donners listed in the San Diego area. I plugged into the State Department's computers to see if he'd left the country. He hadn't—at least, not under his own name.

I was getting nowhere. I was working the system—but the system didn't work.

At about 2:00 A.M., I fell asleep on top of my keyboard. When Dighera found me early Friday morning, I pretended that I'd *meant* to stay all night.

But he didn't buy it.

I now had five days left to make the Boyce team.

"I need two bodies!" yelled the Skeleton as he stormed out of the office. "You!" He pointed at me. "And Harvard here." He jerked his thumb at another rookie deputy, a kid from Boston whose patron, everybody said, was Tip O'Neill. I didn't like the kid. He had no experience in law enforcement, and if the Speaker of the House hadn't been a family friend, he would never have gotten into the Service.

I leaped up and double-timed after the Skeleton. It was just eight hours after I'd fallen asleep at my desk, and I was so pumped on Coke that my heart was thrashing around like a fish on the shore.

"What's the drill?" I said.

"I got a snitch who tells me that a bank robber I've been lookin' for is holed up at a sleazebag hotel downtown. I need backup at the door, plus somebody to cover the fire escape."

A few minutes later the Skeleton and I were standing outside a hotel room, guns drawn. The Skeleton whispered, "U.S. Marshals. Open the door."

Then: *BAMMM!* The Skeleton kicked open the old wooden door and jumped into the room with his gun out. "U.S. marshals!" he yelled. About half a dozen bikers were sprawled around. One of them was a woman. They all jerked to attention.

"Any weapons?" shouted the Skeleton.

"A couple," said the fattest biker.

"Let's see 'em," the Skeleton said, "but real slow, and one by one." They began piling weapons on a bed until it sagged.

"Everybody into the bathroom, except you." The Skeleton pointed his gun at a white-trash type with no front teeth. He matched the robber's description.

The Skeleton got the guy's ID and asked him some questions. He wasn't our robber. But we still called the office and ran him through the computers. It turned out that he and his wife—the woman in the bathroom—had an outstanding warrant for a dine-and-dash at a Safeway Deli in San Bernardino.

The Skeleton sat down next to the biker and said, "Looks like you and your old lady are goin' back to Berdoo."

Of course, it was a silly-ass little warrant. San Bernardino wouldn't want to waste jail space on these two. The Skeleton was just squeezing him.

"Come on," said the biker, "let that slide, and I'll *give* ya somethin'."

"This ain't no *swap* meet," said the Skeleton. But it was, and we all knew it.

"I mean somethin' *good,*" said the biker.

"Try me," said The Skeleton.

"There's this rumor—I heard it from two different guys—that there's gonna be an explosion in one of these buildings around the park, or maybe in a car around the park. Next Monday morning at rush hour."

"That's *weak,*" I said. I started ratcheting my cuffs in his face.

"Check this out, though," he said. "There was a burglary out at a conservation station on the Coast Highway. The dude who's gonna do the explosion took seal bombs—those things they use to scare seals off the buoys. He's gonna pack a whole bunch of 'em together, and, you know: boom!"

"For what *reason?*" said the Skeleton.

"Okay, this is what I heard. They're gonna tear down all these old hotels and urban-renew this area, right? But this guy's gonna create, like, chaos around here until the city pays him off."

"He's gonna extort money from the city government?"

"Yeah. It worked in New York. Same damn thing."

"That's the stupidest thing I ever heard of," I said.

"Well," said the biker, "whether it's stupid or not, it's gonna *happen.* I bet-ya."

"Who told you about it?"

"Two different guys in the park. They said, don't be around here Monday morning. Honest, I'd give 'em up if I could—they're not shit to me."

Harvard sauntered in.

"Fire escape get boring?" the Skeleton asked him. Harvard smiled sheepishly, but neither of us returned the smile.

"We're gonna cut you loose now," the Skeleton told the biker. "But I'm assigning this officer to keep in touch with you." He nodded at Harvard.

The biker freaked. "Hey-hey-hey—I'll keep feedin' ya," he whispered feverishly, "but don't call here, okay? My buddies would get hinky."

Harvard nodded vaguely.

When we were back on the street, I asked the Skeleton if he bought the story.

"I think it's . . . not impossible. You're right to think it's stupid. But so are *germs.* They come up with the most stupid goddamn schemes, but they live and breathe 'em."

I told him about my bomber from Chicago, and asked if he

thought there might be a connection. "Stranger things have happened," he said.

We shot back to the office and the Skeleton called in the bomb lead to the local Bureau of Alcohol, Tobacco and Firearms, which was responsible for anything related to bombs.

He got nowhere.

He slammed down the phone. "You know what the dickhead at ATF says? He says he'll take my report later, but that now he's *going fishing*. I told him the fucking thing is set to *blow* Monday morning, but he goes, 'I *always* go fishing Friday afternoon.' He says our lead's too weak to justify 'adjusting his schedule.' That's what he called it: 'adjusting my schedule.' " The Skeleton put his white hands over his white face, and disappeared entirely.

"He's just killin' his twenty," I said.

Then we called the local police. They confirmed the theft of seal bombs at the conservation station. But they just referred us back to ATF.

"Well, fuck all those guys," said the Skeleton. "We'll break this one ourselves. Whattaya got for leads on your Chicago bomber?"

"Not shit."

He looked thoughtful. "You got him tied to any particular car?"

"No. What's the importance of a car?"

"Once you wrap somebody in three thousand pounds of steel, and tag 'em with a license plate, they don't hide so easy."

I called the Chicago Marshals office, which had telexed us the Donner lead. I got the case agent on the phone—an old fart, judging by his voice.

"Two deputies just got back from Donner's parents' house," he said, "but Mom told us to go fuck ourselves. So we don't have much. But we did get something on a car. A neighbor said Donner had a '62 Starfire that's been sitting in the alley behind his mom's house. But last week it disappeared."

"That's when he escaped."

"Well, that's true. What do you think?"

"Well, I think *maybe* Donner took the fuckin' car. Is there anything you can do? Like, check the neighborhood gas station and see if he got a battery charge or tank of gas?"

"Maybe on Monday. But it's Friday here."

"It's Friday *here,* too."

But he wouldn't budge. He gave me the car's license and registration numbers and hung up.

I patched into the California DMV and state police computer systems, but couldn't find any record of the car being in California.

But then I checked into an obscure record the Skeleton had told me about—the "present active vehicles" registry. I hit a lead. A week before, on the Coast Highway, the state police had found a 1962 Oldsmobile Starfire sitting by the side of the road, and had entered it in their "attempt to render assistance" file. The car had been stripped of its plates. Interesting. It had only been there overnight, though. When the patrol had checked the next morning, it was gone.

I hit the phones and started calling every tow truck operator in the vicinity of the abandoned car. I loved the adrenal rush of action. It made me forget all my own doubts and insecurities. After about thirty calls, I found the guy who'd jump-started the Starfire. I told him to stay put, and raced over to show him a picture of my bomber.

He stared at the picture for five minutes. It was a poor picture—a fax of a prison mug shot. "I think that could maybe be him," said the tow truck driver. "Maybe."

"Maybe?"

"Yeah. *Definitely.*"

"Definitely?"

"Well, definitely maybe."

I didn't wait to get back to the office. I went straight to a phone booth and called Chicago. "Look," I said, "I got a possible ID on your bomber. He may be here, and I think he's planning another bombing, on Monday morning. What I need is for somebody outta your office to work leads for me tomorrow."

"How sure are you about this bombing on Monday?"

"I'm not too certain." I felt I had to be honest.

"What did ATF say about it?"

"They go fishin' on Fridays."

"Sounds like ATF. What did the San Diego police say?"

"They said talk to ATF."

There was a long silence. I felt like I should embellish my story, but I didn't want to be a bullshit artist. I was still young and stu-u-u-pid.

"Well, deputy, I appreciate your interest in this, but I think it's too vague to merit weekend overtime. Let's talk Monday."

"Before or after the explosion?"

"Don't bust my balls, son. It's not nice." Click!

I stood there with the phone at my ear, listening to the whine of the empty line. I'd tried everything I could—short of breaking the law, or lying—and nothing had worked. I always say, When in doubt, do something—but according to the rules of the game, there was nothing left to do. I was at a dead end.

My malaise began to flare up.

And the worst part of my day was still ahead.

I had to go to a Friday night dinner with a few other deputies and do some male bonding—which I detested. I'm a loner. I don't trust anyone but myself—and then, only when I'm in a good mood.

I had no idea that the dinner would change my life.

I'd never seen anyone quite like him. He was big—about 250 pounds of fat-stripped meat—and he had a wild animal vitality that was attractive and repellant at the same time. Sharp hawk's eyes. Big piano-key teeth. Booming voice. He was the kind of man you could love and hate at the same time. He sat at the head of the table of deputies like a wolf looking down at a herd of sheep.

His name was Brick. At least, that was his nickname. If I told you his real name, it might destroy his current career with the CIA. You'll see why later.

There were fewer deputies at the dinner than I'd imagined. Just the young guys. The only two I knew were the Skeleton and Harvard.

Brick stood up, and towered over us. Looking at him was like gazing up the trunk of a tree.

"Gentlemen," he said, "let's slice through the bullshit, and get down to our *serious* business. Which is . . ."—he clapped his hands, and two waiters appeared with frosted half-gallons of tequila—". . .tuh-*kee*-lah!" Brick grabbed one of the jugs and started pouring liquor into our glasses. Then he dumped about four inches into his own and said, "To the Service!" He threw down his drink, and pounded both fists on the table.

We all followed.

Then we did another round. And another. My eyes felt disconnected, as if they could look two places at once.

"Okay, guys," Brick boomed, "let's talk turkey. You know what Hemingway said? He said that once a hunter stalks a man, he's never again content with any other kind of prey. He's a *manhunter,* and that's *all* he is. And that, gentlemen, is what *you* are going to become."

He let that sink in, as alcohol shot from our bellies to our brains.

"As you know, we just grabbed the Fugitive Program from the College Boys"—he meant the FBI. "And with it, we took a *hell* of a gamble. In the next year, you men will either become the greatest manhunters in world history, or you'll become . . . unemployed. You'll be night watchmen at Kmart.

"The College Boys gave us the Fugitive Program because they couldn't *hack* it. And they don't think *you'll* be able to, either."

He slammed his fist onto the table. "But I say *you will!* And I'll tell you *how* you will, in two words. *Aggressiveness.* And *imagination.*"

Through the booze-fog, I felt a jolt. *Aggressive* and *imaginative* were two of the oldest cop code words. They meant: *breaking the law.*

Around the table, I could see deputies—suddenly sober—stealing glances at one another. If this guy was serious, it could change everything. Brick was not just another old-timer killing his twenty. He was a deputy director of the Enforcement Division, and he had serious clout.

"Tell you what, men," Brick said, "you tell me your problems, and I'll try to throw out some imaginative and aggressive solutions, okay? But hear me out: I'm speaking *theoretically,* and I'm not advising or condoning any of these *theoretical* solutions. Okay?"

I stuck my hand into the air. I wanted to be first. I *always* wanted to be first. He pointed at me. "We've got no money for snitches," I said.

"But you *do* get money for out-of-pocket stuff like gasoline, right?" Brick said. "Well, once me and my partner were working a case in Miami where we used a whole *bunch* of snitches. And wouldn't you know it—that week we spent over five hundred dollars in gasoline. For his *Pinto.* Little sucker just *gobbled* gas. Bottom line: You *get the job done,* and I'll sail your expense vouchers through."

Another deputy raised his hand. "Every time I try to get information by offering a snitch immunity, the Justice Department breaks my balls with red tape."

"You ever hear of a thing called 'do-it-yourself immunity?' " Brick said. "It's simple. You tape-record your first interview with a perp, and you 'forget' to read him his rights. Then, if you want to cut him a deal and let him walk, you produce the tape and go, 'Oh, gee, I forgot to Mirandize my perp.' " Around the table, eyes went wide.

Another guy raised his hand. "It seems like whenever we hit a house, the guy we're lookin' for is hidin' in a back room. So we cover all the other occupants, and by the time we get to the bad guy, we're short-handed. How can we get more people?"

"I *can't* get you more people. You know how many FBI there are? About twenty-four thousand. There are less than a hundred U.S. marshals, and about fourteen hundred deputies—and there's a tight lid on more hiring. The USMS is *one-tenth* the size of the New York City Police Department. So more manpower is not an option. But here's what *some* people do when they hit a house. Not that it's legal, of course. They use human shields. You grab one of the mutts in the living room and you let *him* give you the guided tour. But remember—use the *biggest* guy available. You can't hide behind a midget."

"With all these new phone companies, how do we get hooks at each company?"

"You *don't.* Here—write this down." He dictated a phone

number. "I call that number 'Ma.' It's Ma Bell's in-house ID service. Only top phone company executives are supposed to have it. You call that number, and ask them the phone number of anybody in America—listed or unlisted—and they'll give it to you. You don't even have to know what state they're in. Or you give them a phone number, and they'll tell you who it's assigned to.

"Also, there's another way to get a whole bunch of unlisted numbers at once. Wait until you've got a legitimate subpoena for one unlisted number—then add the others you want. It's unlikely that anybody will check up on your subpoena. Of course, if they do, you're fucked. The same goes for *most* of what I'm telling you. Being aggressive and imaginative is *dangerous.* It's a good way to lose your job. Or worse."

Some of the guys got weird when he said that. Not me. I was soaking this stuff up. I didn't fear failure or danger. What I feared was not being able to *do something* with my life.

"How do we get banks to give out information?" I asked.

"Find a bank where your mutt has a loan, or mortgage. They'll be happy to bend the rules. All they want is their money back."

"What about credit card companies?"

"They're harder. But remember. Big companies are just groups of little guys, and lots of times secretaries or assistants have access to what you need. So develop contacts at all the major banking and communication companies, and take *care* of them. Tell 'em war stories. Listen to their theories. Make 'em feel like Junior G-men."

"How do you tap the records of a perp's family?"

"By law, you can only go after records of lawbreakers, or suspects. So be *suspicious.* If some perp's dad *might* be helping him, then he's a *suspect,* as an accessory."

"Can we lie during an investigation?" I asked.

"Yes. You can lie your ass off. Now, juries *hate* that. But, remember, most of the time there won't be any jury involved, cuz you're workin' fugitives. You grab a guy, and—bang!— he's back in the joint. End of story.

"The same general principle applies to search and seizure laws: Don't *worry* about 'em. You're out to grab a *body,* not evidence. So *what* if you violate search and seizure laws, and blow an arrest? It doesn't matter. You've still got your puke on his original warrant.

"You've also got the same latitude on breaking into your fugitive's house while he's gone. Go ahead, break in, disarm his weapons, and *then* bust him. Normally, that would put your arrest at risk. But with fugitives, it's different, because they've *already* been busted."

"What about violence against prisoners?"

Brick paused for a while. "Let's be realistic, men. There may be times when hurting a bad person will stop *them* from hurting a good person. In that situation, it's a necessary evil."

Even I was shocked. This was a highly placed representative of the U.S. government, advocating torture. I believed that ends justified means. But . . . *torture?*

"Can you squeeze a snitch if he's holding out on you?" blurted Harvard, who looked drunk and tousled. "I've got this biker snitch that probably knows more than he's telling me, but now he won't even take my calls—"

The Skeleton jerked to attention. "You been *calling* that biker on the *phone?*" he snapped. "He told you *not* to, that his buddies would put his nuts in a vise!"

"I don't *work* for that punk," said Harvard.

"The senior deputy is right," Brick said to Harvard. "You gotta treat your snitches with TLC."

For a few moments, there was an uneasy silence. The Skeleton glared at Harvard. They were *not* bonding.

"Is there anything we *can't* do?" I asked. That broke the tension.

"Yeah, deputy, there is," he said. "Don't break rule number one."

"What's rule number one?"

"Don't get caught."

"Well, let's say we *do* get caught," I persisted. "What's Jimmy Carter and his weak-ass A.G. likely to do? Let it slide?"

"They'd can your ass," said Brick. "But if Reagan gets in, things are gonna change. *Believe* me. For now, though, we serve the boss we've got.

"And lemme tell ya another rule," Brick said. Suddenly he was solemn. "This is a rule you've *got* to follow. Every minute of every day. You won't find it in your training manual. But, so help me God, you'd better honor it.

"It's this: Always put the Service ahead of yourself."

His words drilled right into my chest. I felt like he was speaking directly to me. He was talking about *family:* You take care of your family, and your family will take care of you, no matter what. It got to me, because a few months earlier, my dad had died, and I'd felt like a kid again, stripped of protection.

Suddenly, I had a new family.

Then Brick started talking about the history of the Service. He told about the civil rights wars of the 1960s, when being a marshal meant something. He spoke of the Indian Wars, and Pat Garrett, Virgil Earp, and Wild Bill Hickock.

I had a family with a proud past. I had a true American heritage.

I could barely sit still. I had to get back to the office. I had a bomber to catch.

I drove back to work alone. I thought about inviting the Skeleton, but he was drunk. Besides, I didn't want any witnesses.

I dropped into my swivel chair and punched in my new "Ma" number. I asked for the unlisted home phone number of the old marshal in Chicago who was busting my balls. I got it.

I called him immediately—at 4:00 A.M. Chicago time. I needed the element of surprise.

"Deputy!" I barked at him. "This is Howard Safir. It's come to my attention that you're hindering a vital investigation in San Diego by refusing to authorize overtime. Can that possibly be correct?"

"Well, I guess," he croaked.

"You *guess?* Deputy, you call your best investigator *now,* and have him in the office at six A.M." I slammed down the phone.

When I called the Chicago office a couple of hours later, I got a whole different reception. A young deputy kissed my ass so hard it left marks. He was almost *too* gung-ho for 6:00 A.M. Later, I'd find out that he was dipping deeply into his office's cache of seized cocaine.

"Go out to Rufus Donner's old high school," I told him, "and get hold of the school annuals for the years he attended. Check his presentencing report to make sure of the dates. There should be custodial staff at the school by now, but if there's not, get the principal outta bed. When you get the yearbooks, fax me every possible reference, and picture, of my perp. I want every trigger I can get my hands on. Got it?"

"Got it."

I acted like I'd done this a hundred times.

Ninety minutes later, the faxes came through. They didn't offer much—no associations with other people. But we found out some of the classes he'd been in, and I started calling his teachers.

It took me less than an hour to get a decent lead. His shop teacher had remembered that he'd had a girlfriend. He couldn't remember her last name, but he remembered her best friend.

I called the friend. "Carmelle Rollins?" I said, "this is Woodrow Guthrie of the Publishers Clearinghouse Sweepstakes. I've got some *very* good news for your friend LaDonna, but I need your help to contact her."

"LaDonna Edwards?"

"Yes, LaDonna Edwards. The phone number she listed on her entry form doesn't seem to be in working order."

"How'd you get *my* number?"

"She listed you as someone our telephone sales people should contact. But here's the good news. LaDonna has been chosen from our general pool as a grand finalist. That means she now has exactly *one chance in twenty* of winning over two *million* dollars."

"Well, LaDonna moved. That's why you can't find her. Out to San Diego."

I bolted upright in my chair. "Yes," I said calmly, "that's what our records indicate. But we must have the wrong phone number for her out there."

"Well, I guess I can give you her number. But not the address, okay? She wants where she's livin' kept private."

"That's fine."

She gave me the phone number. I called "Ma" and got the address.

I was literally bouncing up and down in my chair when Brick came through the door.

"Hey, it's good to see somebody *else* workin' Saturday," he boomed. He didn't look as if he'd spent all night drinking. He looked as if he'd just spent a month at a health spa.

"I'm makin' a major collar," I said. "And when I do, I'm gonna apply to be on the Boyce team."

"You don't *apply* for Boyce, deputy. You're chosen. And, hell, I'll be honest. One good collar's not gonna make the nut."

My face fell.

"But you know who could *help* you back at Tysons?" He meant Tysons Corner, the national headquarters. "This guy." He pointed his huge thumb at his chest.

"Well," I said, *"will* you?"

"I will. If you help me. I've got a delicate problem, and I'll bet you're just the man to task with it. As you know, it's an election year, and things don't look so hot for Carter. He's up to his ass in this hostage crisis, and he's goin' crazy fightin' off these ultraliberals, like Teddy Kennedy and Jerry Brown. Now, I've got an associate in the White House who thinks Brown's getting all his money from the Japanese. So I need to have somebody out here in California check that out."

"Check it out, how?"

"First thing would just be to see if he's got a lot of calls going out to Japan. If he doesn't, there's probably nothing to the rumor."

"I can do that."

"Good man! You do that, and I'll give you a hand. But you gotta make your collar, too, because I can't be mentioning this Brown thing to anybody. You understand?"

"Of course."

He beamed at me, and I felt queasy. I had absolutely no *idea* how to get Jerry Brown's phone records. I didn't have a hook into the phone company, or anyplace else.

Besides, it seemed surreal. Jimmy *Carter?* Mr. Clean? Up to the same kind of bullshit that had brought down Nixon? I didn't want to believe it. But I made myself accept it— true or not—and when I did, I took a giant step closer to understanding the real world. In the real world, you trust people to do just one thing: whatever's in their own best interests.

But I couldn't worry about Jimmy Carter's guilt or innocence. I had a bomber to pop.

I jumped in my car and ripped out to the address of Donner's girlfriend.

But the second I set foot on the place—a little bungalow out in the eastern suburbs—it didn't feel right. It felt like they were gone. I looked in the windows. The place was bare.

I hit the closest post office and badged my way into the postmaster's office. "I need the change of address card for somebody on your route," I told him.

"I'm sorry, those are confidential."

"She's a suspect in a crime. So your confidentiality obligations are waived."

"What crime?"

"Harboring a fugitive."

"Have you arrested the fugitive and taken his statement?"

"No."

He looked dubious.

"But that's not all," I said. "She also robbed a rural postal carrier in Illinois—a *female* carrier. She beat the carrier half to death."

"Oh, my." He started searching for the change of address card. But Donner's girlfriend hadn't left one.

I went back to her abandoned house and started interviewing neighbors. Nobody had much, but I got a better feel for the girl. Supposedly, she hated her landlord because she thought he was "snoopy." None of the neighbors had seen Donner, though, or his Starfire.

By the time I got back to the office, it was dusk. The days were beginning to melt together. But I didn't feel tired. I was exhilarated. I was going to *catch* this son of a bitch, and I was going to do it before he blew anything up. I still had about thirty hours before Monday morning.

I grabbed the phone and called the telephone company's local business office. I had a hard time finding anyone on duty, because it was Saturday night. "Hello," I said, "this is

Edmund G. Brown." I was hoping Jerry Brown's real name wouldn't ring any bells. But it did.

"*Governor* Brown?" said the phone company executive.

I hung up. Tried another office. "Hello, this is Ed Brown."

"Yes?"

"I'm hoping you can help me resolve a personal problem. I was recently divorced, and I'm obligated to pay for phone calls made before the separation. But I'm not supposed to pay for any *international* calls. My wife's lawyer sent me a bill for what he says I owe, but I don't see how it can be as high as it is without any international calls."

"I'll check." Divorce was always a great scam. It triggered pity like nothing else.

"Spell your name, please."

"*E-d-m-u-n-d*. Middle initial *G. B-r-o-w-n*."

"Employer?"

"State job. State of California."

"Looking six months back at your bill, Mr. Brown, I see only six international calls. Four to England, one to France, and one to Germany. They total less than fifty dollars."

"Anything international on her *other* line?" I gave her Jerry Brown's office number, which I'd gotten from a state pamphlet.

"Nothing there, either," she said.

"Thanks." My pulse galloped. I could do *anything*. I could *destroy* Donner. I had a mental flash of Donner laughing at the girl with the snout. By Monday morning, I'd be laughing at *him*.

Donner's girlfriend was paranoid about snoopy landlords? What was her best remedy for that? I tried to think like her. If I was her, I'd *buy* a place. No more landlord.

I started patching into municipal property tax rolls, city by city, all around the San Diego area. It was slow and tedious. Around midnight, I dozed off. I woke up a couple of hours later, and chugged four sixteen-ounce Cokes.

Just before dawn, I found her. In a cheap little house in Chula Vista.

I was headed out the door for Chula Vista when I ran into Brick. "Hell, man," he boomed, "you really *are* a go-getter, aren't you? I just called your home, and your wife said you'd be here."

Trailing in Brick's wake, and barely visible behind him, was a rumpled little man who looked nervous. Brick encircled my shoulders with one of his huge arms—which wasn't easy, since I'm a big guy myself—and pulled me back into the office.

"Your target on that phone thing is clean," I murmured to him.

He studied my face. "You wouldn't shit me, would you?"

"No, Brick. You're my favorite turd."

He clapped me on the back. "Good enough," he said. "I'll tell my associate at the W.H." I assumed he meant the White House. "He'll owe us one. And I owe you one."

"Are you gonna take care of me on Boyce now?" I looked him hard in the eye.

"I am," he said. "But I was hoping that first you'd do a couple *tiny* little things for me."

"How many times you gonna up the ante?" I snarled.

"These things are *nuthin.* Both of 'em together won't take two hours."

What the hell could I do? I had no power. I didn't have Tip O'Neill behind me, or anyone else.

He introduced me to the weasly little guy, a private investigator from Arlington, Virginia, who pulled a list of names and addresses out of his briefcase. He held the list with two fingers, like it was covered with shit.

I recognized a few of the names as political associates of Jerry Brown. Some of them were prominent people. The addresses were where they lived, or where they'd gotten parking tickets or traffic citations, or, in a few cases, where they'd used credit cards. The neighborhoods were mostly in Sacramento, Los Angeles, and San Diego.

"What we're looking for," wheezed the rumpled guy, "is a correlation between these areas, and areas of a particular nature. Specifically, I mean areas with adult bookstores and theaters, gay neighborhoods, red light districts, and streets frequented by male prostitutes. That kind of thing. Hmmm?"

We had a computer program that targeted vice-related areas

throughout California. Interfacing his list with that program would have been easy.

But would it be *right?* Obviously, they were trying to cash in on the old rumor that the unmarried ex-governor was gay—a rumor Brown had just tackled head-on by taking Linda Ronstadt on an African safari. I handed back the list. "I think a city vice cop would know more about this than me," I said.

"Perhaps so," wheezed the weasel, "but we feel you're someone who can be . . . reliable . . . in a sensitive matter." He handed me the list again.

"Come on, guys," I said, "this is the kind of shit that brought Nixon down." I handed it back.

"Let's talk turkey," said Brick, his voice oozing charm. "I know about the bomber case you're working, deputy, and it really *should* be handled by somebody with more seniority. Now, I'm perfectly willing to let *you* handle it. But you gotta give *me* some consideration."

Brick made his threats very diplomatically. I made a mental note to learn that skill. It wasn't a classic working-class trait. I always thought you were supposed to smack people around when you threatened them.

I took the list and sat down at my computer. I fed it into my vice program, looking for "hits"—links between the two sets of information.

None came up. Jerry Brown's people were clean. Or careful.

When I finished, Brick was beaming. Even though I hadn't found dirt, Carter's people would be in his debt.

"Okay," I said, "what's the other thing you want? And it better not *take* long."

"Just need you to move a prisoner. He's down in the San Ysidro city jail."

"Where do you want him moved?"

"I want him moved to *me.*" Brick put his arm around my shoulder. "Deal is," he said softly, "this prisoner works for Mexican Army Intelligence. And he also works for *us.*" Brick gave me a long look. "We've got about a dozen men like him working south of the border, and they're extremely valuable. 'Course, we're not *supposed* to have 'em down there. It's illegal as hell. But they're there. This guy got in a beef with a cab driver this afternoon, and some Barney Fife in San Ysidro popped him. I want him *outta* there, fast, before the shit hits the fan. Make sense?"

I drove down to San Ysidro and took custody of the prisoner, whose name was Manuel Fuerte. He looked scared to death—probably because he was accustomed to torturing *his* prisoners before he charged them. When I got him in my car, and explained that he was being weasel-dealed out of jail, he was overjoyed. He said he would never forget me, and that any time I needed a favor, all I had to do was call.

Back at the office, I handed him over to Brick.

"I'm gonna go grab my perp now," I said. "If that's okay." I eased toward the door.

"Do you want backup?" Brick asked. "Cuz I got the rest of the day off."

"It could be pretty dangerous."

"Not a problem."

My anger at him evaporated. He expected a lot—but he offered the same.

"Thanks anyway. But I'll be totally honest. I don't want backup. The less glory I have to share, the easier it'll be for me to make the Boyce team."

"You are flat-ass wrong, deputy," Brick snapped. "The last thing Safir wants is a Service full of hotdogs. Weren't you *listening* the other night? Put the Service *ahead* of yourself."

He calmed down. "Tell me who you trust most in this office."

"Tommy," I said. "The Skeleton."

He pushed the phone toward me. "Call him."

In less than an hour, the Skeleton and I were parked near the little house owned by Donner's girlfriend. It looked occupied—there were a couple of cactus plants on the porch. There was a separate garage; maybe the Starfire was in it.

We started our stakeout. The Skeleton got in his own car and covered the alley behind the house. We communicated with crappy, plastic walkie-talkies. On the way over, we'd bought them at a Toys "Я" Us. $19.95.

The plan was to take Donner as he was leaving the house. He'd have less cover that way, and we'd have a greater element of surprise.

I sat there, exhausted and elated, and daydreamed about making the bust. As the Sunday morning sun began to bake my car, my daydreams got more and more vivid, and I found myself drifting in and out of a half-sleep.

I slapped my face as hard as I could. It shocked me out of drowsiness. But within minutes, the fatigue creeped back in.

The next thing I knew, a car with a bad muffler bombed past me. Before I could focus my eyes, the car was gone. But I thought it was the Starfire.

I grabbed my walkie-talkie. "I fucked up," I said. "I think he just drove past me."

"He'll be back," said the Skeleton.

I cursed at myself, got out of the car, and slammed the door. I hated weakness in myself. Whatever else my dad had been, he'd been tough. Right now, he'd have been ashamed of me.

I marched onto the girlfriend's front porch and knocked on the door. If they were there, I was going to pretend to be a salesman. But no one answered. I kept knocking. No answer.

I went around to the back door. It was locked. I banged on it. I yelled, "Meter reader!" No response. I jimmied the lock with my pocket knife. It sprang open. I stuck my head in the door. "Utility company! Anybody home? . . . Anybody home?"

I walked through the house. The silence made my spine cold. I felt naked.

I wanted to find proof that Donner was here, and get the hell out. But I felt like I was moving in slow motion.

In the back bedroom I found men's clothes. And a shoebox of letters addressed to Rufus Donner.

My mind raced. *I'm Donner—where's my gun?* In the closet? I checked; it wasn't there. Under the dirty clothes? No. Under the mattress? Not there. *I'm Donner—I want my gun as close as possible.* Under the pillow! There it was—a stainless steel Coonan Arms .357 Magnum automatic. I broke off the firing pin, slipped the gun back under the pillow, and streaked out of the house.

I walked as casually as possible to my car, then drove around the block and parked on the other side of the street.

Smart cons always checked for stakeout cars, so you had to keep moving them.

The morning crawled past. Then the afternoon. My nerves were jumpy and hot-wired. What if he didn't come back?

Just after sunset, the Starfire cruised home, and parked in front of the house. I picked up my gun. "He's back," I muttered into the walkie-talkie. "Get ready to rock 'n' roll." My heart was pounding. Donner got out of the car. He was big and very black, with strange, twisted features. A homely, honey-colored girl was hanging all over him.

I put my fingers on the handle of my door. But at that same moment an old Caddie pulled up behind the Starfire, and a couple of loud Mexican kids carrying six-packs jumped out. I froze. They might have weapons. "Hang on!" I said to the Skeleton. "Stay put!"

As soon as their six-packs were empty, I thought, the two kids would take off.

I waited.

All night.

Throughout the night, every light in the house stayed on, and music blared. From time to time, the girl would leave, then return with a couple more six-packs.

Time was running out. It was getting closer and closer to Monday morning rush hour.

Of course, we still had absolutely no proof that Donner was going to do *anything* at rush hour. The bomb rumor might be pure bullshit.

But that's not what my instincts said.

If Donner didn't make his move soon, we'd have to hit the house, no matter how many men were in it.

At five in the morning the music stopped. A few minutes later, the two Mexicans dragged out of the house and piled into their old Caddie.

To the east, the sky was growing opaque. On the street, blackness was turning to shadow.

I punched the "transmit" button on my walkie-talkie. "Let's give him fifteen minutes," I said. "If he doesn't come out, we better hit the house."

"Check," said the Skeleton.

Three minutes later, the door to Donner's garage opened.

"He's out!" I whispered hoarsely to the Skeleton. I could hear the Skeleton's car start. Donner backed out of the driveway.

"Gimme a direction!" yelled the Skeleton.

Donner curled his car north, heading away from me.

"North!"

"In pursuit," said the Skeleton. "Let's do it *fast*," he barked. "At the next corner, if we can."

I turned my key, hit the gas and swooped up behind Donner. I could see his head swivel to his rearview mirror.

The Skeleton's car shrieked around the corner and screeched to a stop in the intersection. Donner swerved, but I punched it and cut him off.

I jumped out. Donner's door flew open. His gun came up toward my chest. It was the Coonan Arms. It went "click."

I smashed my revolver into his throat. He made an ugly gurgling noise and doubled over. The Skeleton ran up behind him and kicked him in the ass, banging Donner's head into the Starfire.

I grabbed Donner and cuffed him before he could straighten up.

I got in Donner's face and screamed, "Where's the explosives, motherfucker?"

Drops of my spit landed on his mouth and cheeks.

"I-wan-ma-lawyer," he garbled.

"Where's the *bomb*, goddamnit?"

"I got nuthin' to say to you." The Skeleton kicked him in the ass again but Donner ignored it. Didn't even glance around. He was a tough con.

I shook him down and found a hotel key. The room number and name of the hotel had been filed off. "Is this where the bomb is?" He looked away.

"Look," I said, trying to sound gentle, "if anybody gets killed this morning, you *fry*. Right now, we got you on just a bullshit escape warrant. You'll be back on the bricks in seven or eight years. Then *you* can come fuck *us* up." I tried to smile.

"Fuck you, cop," he said. "I *know* I get a lawyer."

I felt helpless. By the rules of the game, we could do nothing more.

We were in the gutter off to the side of the street. Donner was standing in front of a board with a nail sticking through it. I grabbed him by his cuffs and pulled him back, until his foot was over the nail.

Then I stomped on his foot.

He screamed and hopped. As he jumped, the board stayed with him.

I grabbed the board and pried the nail out of his foot. It made a hard, grating noise; it was lodged in bone. It was bright with blood.

Donner collapsed in a heap. I knelt beside him. "See this nail?" I said softly. "If you don't tell me where your bomb is, I'm gonna put this in your fuckin' eye."

"*You* can't do that," Donner hissed.

"Sure I can." My voice was flat and cold. "It's a necessary evil."

Donner stared at me, then at the Skeleton. The Skeleton made a point of walking away.

Donner started to tremble, and a fat tear rolled onto his cheek.

"I wouldn't expect you to *believe* me," I growled, "except for one thing. I'm the fuckin' guy who just *crucified* you."

I put the board by his eye, and gently popped the tear on his cheek. The tear mingled with his blood and trickled pink down his face.

He looked so fucked up that I couldn't help but laugh.

It was a sick, dirty laugh. It seemed to scare the shit out of him. To be honest, it scared the shit out of me, too. Was I losing my soul?

"*I'll tell ya where it is,*" he bleated. "Just get that fuckin' thing outta my face."

"Let's go."

By five-thirty we were standing outside a first-floor room in the same hotel where we'd found the bikers.

The Skeleton put Donner's key in the lock. I shoved Donner toward the door. "Ladies first," I said.

"It ain't booby trapped," he protested.

"Then go right ahead."

He limped into the room, and showed us the explosives. There was a hell of a pile of them. Some were seal bombs, and some were sticks of dynamite that had been stolen from

115

a construction site. Sitting on top of the pile was an old mechanical alarm clock. Two wires ran out of the clock and into a blasting cap. It was set to blow at 8:00 A.M.

When we'd caught Donner, he'd been on his way to watch the explosion. Donner liked fire.

I pulled the wires out of the clock and called the city police bomb squad. I could have called ATF. But fuck 'em.

The police arrived within minutes, and there was a big commotion. In the hallway, people from the adjacent rooms peered through the doorway. Seeing their faces gave me an eerie buzz. If it hadn't been for me, some of them would have died. Others might have ended up like the girl with the snout.

I can't describe the feeling that I got looking into their faces. It was the best feeling I'd ever had.

For the first time in my life, I'd done something important. I'd given the ultimate treasure—life itself—to a number of people.

God knows, they owed me one.

But it was funny. Standing there, I felt like I owed *them* one.

We handed off Donner to the San Diego police.

I felt high.

Just for the hell of it, the Skeleton and I walked back upstairs to see the biker we'd rousted. He'd been instrumental in this, and I wanted him to know it. If some of what I was feeling rubbed off on him, it might help him redeem his shitty little life.

We knocked on the door. There was no answer. There was a smell coming from the room. We got the room clerk to unlock the door. As it swung open, the stench rushed out.

The biker and his wife were sprawled on the bed, dead, with syringes still near their hands. They had no apparent wounds.

"Oh, Jesus," said the Skeleton. "This is what happens."

"What do you mean?" I said.

"This is what happens when you work your snitch in front of his buddies. I *told* Harvard not to call this guy. His buddies got hinky. They loaded his syringe with an overdose. His old lady's, too."

The crime would never be prosecuted. We had no proof—just instinct.

I picked up the phone and called the local police again. But before we left, we found out the names of the biker's buddies.

If I could, I was going to fuck with them. It wouldn't help the biker now. But I owed him one.

I called the office, to see if there was anything I could do to fill the rest of the day. I volunteered for surfer warrants. Suddenly, that seemed like good duty.

"No more surfer warrants," said the duty officer. "The feds just made the Camp Pendleton beach a national park."

Nixon, I suspected, had pulled strings in the federal bureaucracy to make that happen.

I flashed on an ugly image: Dick Nixon sitting in a dark office, still making deals, while punks like me did the dirty work.

Maybe dirty work was all I would ever do. Sometimes it seemed like dirty work was the only kind of work there was.

When I got to the office the next morning, Harvard was cleaning out his desk. The Skeleton had chewed him out with words Harvard didn't know existed. So he'd quit. Before Harvard could get out the door, I took a bite out of his ass myself. It tasted good.

Maybe Tip O'Neill had something else lined up for Harvard. Rich bastards always landed on their feet.

Bob Dighera called me into his office. Dighera shook my hand warmly and squeezed my shoulder.

"I'm proud of you, John," he said. He seemed to be moved, and I was, too.

His praise put a glow into me, because I had great respect for him. He was very brave—a true warrior. Being in a brotherhood with men like him made me feel like I'd found a true family. We were going to *change the world*. Maybe we weren't Virgil Earp and Wild Bill Hickock, but, by God, we were trying to *do* something.

Dighera said that everybody at headquarters was talking about me—including the Big Boss, Howard Safir—and that Brick was my biggest promoter. He said that Brick had told him I was officially on the short list for the Boyce team.

In other words, the fix was in.

In the past, I might still have felt uncertain about making the team. Not anymore. I had a better idea about how the real world worked.

It worked in strange and twisted ways.

Over the past few days, I'd committed the most brutal act of my life, against Donner. But it had broken a major case. I'd also committed the most corrupt act of my life, against Jerry Brown. But it had won me Brick's permission to pursue Donner.

And when I'd found that bomb, I'd done the best thing in my life.

It was funny. A brutal act and a corrupt act had made a good act possible.

Somehow, all of that made sense. It fit perfectly with my philosophy of utilitarianism: When you're trying to do the greatest good for the greatest number, the ends justify the means.

I was finally getting to know who I really was. Supposedly, my job now was to find other people. But I was finding myself.

I could, of course, have thought: Yeah, you've found yourself—and you're Dick Nixon, pulling weasel-deals in dark rooms.

But fuck that. I didn't have *time* for guilt.

I had things to do.

I was going after Christopher Boyce, the worst traitor in modern American history.

"It's a great time to come on board," said Dighera, who'd been working on Boyce for months.

"How come?"

"Because," said Dighera, "I think we've found him. And you're gonna go out and make the pop."

"Why me?"

"We need a marksman. This is gonna be ugly."

"When do I go?"

"Now."

Chapter Five

Traitor

★

• The Falcon and the Snowman • The Criminal
Mentality • My Bullshit Detector • How to
Squeeze a Snitch • How to Squeeze a Judge •

*"The good life is not a passive existence where you live and
let live. It is one of involvement where you live and help live."*
—*Isaac Bashevis Singer*

Where *is* Boyce?" I asked Dighera.

"On a Greyhound bus, headed here from Santa Barbara.
The driver called from his last stop and said he's got a guy
on board that's the spittin' image of Boyce." Boyce's picture
had been in the papers many times since his escape from
prison a few weeks earlier.

"You figure he's headed for the border?" I asked.

"Most likely."

"What's the takedown plan?"

"At the Oceanside stop, you and three other deputies board
the bus. You ID Boyce. Then you overwhelm him."

"Is he armed?"

"My guess? Yeah, probably."

I felt my testicles shrivel. I pulled a bulletproof vest against

119

my chest, and I could feel my heart kick against it. The hard pulse put a roar in my ears, like you get when you listen to a seashell.

I cinched the vest tight.

"Let's do it."

But it wasn't Boyce.

The suspect didn't even *look* like Boyce.

I was almost sick with disappointment. But I made myself get over it. My reaction was stupid. Grabbing Boyce before I was even on the Boyce Team would've been too good to be true.

And too-good-to-be-true was *never* how the real world worked.

I spent the next two months locked in a refrigerated mainframe computer room, organizing a program that analyzed all the phone calls made by Boyce's family and friends. After all that work, I found almost no "hits"—connections among the various callers.

Apparently, that indicated that Boyce had no network of conspirators. But I didn't buy that. It didn't fit my concept of Boyce's mentality.

Every day, I was learning more about the criminal mentality, and I'd come to believe that a cornerstone of the criminal mind is vanity: Criminals group into gangs not just for practical reasons, but because they *need an audience.* They *demand* attention. Virtually all criminals are steeped in self-hate, and are desperate for approval. By their perverse logic, their criminal acts are their greatest achievements. Boyce, in particular, was a criminal exhibitionist; he had an extreme need for people to brag to. So I was certain that he had a retinue of cronies who were helping him stay on the run.

I was just as certain that one of Boyce's cohorts would eventually betray him and break the case. People drawn together for criminal activity usually don't stay friends for long. The same self-involved traits that bring them together tear them apart. They all want to be the center of attention, and none of them really care about the needs of their "friends." So they inevitably turn against one another.

But my FBI contacts were telling me that Boyce did *not* fit the standard criminal profile, and that I'd never catch him with conventional investigative methods, like locating one of his cohorts and getting him to rat Boyce out. But I thought the Feebs were full of shit.

The FBI thought Boyce's crime—stealing secrets from a government contractor and selling them to the Soviets—had been triggered by his political beliefs. They saw Boyce as basically a "prisoner of conscience," and not a common criminal. The secrets he'd stolen were about CIA spy satellites, and Boyce claimed he'd stolen them because he hated the CIA.

I didn't buy that. The more I learned about Boyce, the more I believed he had a standard criminal mind-set. His philosophical argument was just a rationalization.

Criminals almost never break laws because of their philosophical beliefs. They're not driven by ideas, but by feelings—primarily anger, greed, adventurism, and self-loathing. I saw all of those traits in Boyce. Particularly adventurism. He was a born risk taker—an adrenaline junkie.

I knew all about adrenaline junkies, because I was one myself. But I tried to use the trait to further my philosophy of utilitarianism. Boyce, despite his IQ of 142 and his upper middle-class privileges, had never *bothered* to develop a philosophy. He just hopped from one thrill to the next.

By doing that, he'd become the most damaging American spy in modern history. The satellite program he'd derailed was extremely important to maintaining world peace. The satellites had told the United States when the Soviets were cheating on their missile building. Because of Boyce, the SALT missile treaty was scrapped; we could no longer verify if the Soviets were honoring it. After Boyce's thefts, the Cold War intensified, the arms race accelerated, and every person on earth was put in greater peril.

But Boyce didn't give a shit about any of that. Like all sociopaths, he was blind to the pain of other people. Personally, I can't stand it when somebody hurts people and isn't even aware of it. To me, that's the worst kind of indifference to the real world.

Because I considered Boyce a garden-variety criminal, the first person I hit after I joined the Boyce Task Force was his ex-girlfriend. There was a saying in the Marshals: "Behind every fugitive is a woman." I thought Boyce, a weak little worm, would come running to his girlfriend. After all, she'd become a primary character in the book and movie about Boyce's crime, *The Falcon and the Snowman.* In the criminal mind, that meant she *owed him one.*

I drove out to see her and developed some tantalizing information. For weeks after Boyce's escape, she hadn't been "in-pocket" (in her normal routine). Instead, she'd gone out of pocket on a long van trip through western America.

But her stories all held together. The van trip had been a honeymoon with her new husband, and there was no evidence that her marriage was a scam. She offered details freely, and all of them were corroborated by hard evidence, like phone records and receipts.

Also, I got a gut-level feeling that she was telling the truth. Already, I was known for having an excellent "bullshit detector." I could tell when people were lying. Part of it was intuition, but mostly it was just being able to notice and correlate subtleties, like body language, discrepancies, evasiveness, eye contact, tone of voice, and attempts to manipulate me.

I cut Boyce's ex-girlfriend loose and went after other people who knew him. But no one had much to offer.

The heat hissed out of the investigation. We had no leads, and no plan. The task force had only a $10,000 budget, and once that was gone, the task force would be disbanded. The piddly budget was a painful reminder of the Marshals' lack of congressional and presidential support. It also seemed to indicate how little faith the USMS hierarchy had in its own investigators; it looked as if they fully *expected* us to fail, and were already cutting their losses.

Unfortunately, we were getting no help at all from the Federal Bureaucracy of Investigation. The College Boys obviously wanted us to fall on our butts. The Marshals and the Bureau hated each other—standard bureaucratic rivalry.

Occasionally, Brick would call and fill me in on the atmosphere at headquarters. It was grim. If we fucked up on Boyce, he said, the entire agency would probably be shitcanned.

But then, one night in October of 1980, an anonymous

caller telephoned the Lompoc, California, prison that Boyce had escaped from. The caller said that Boyce was making a move to Mexico the following day, but that Boyce could be captured that night.

The caller gave us Boyce's address. And also a warning: Boyce was with two buddies, and he had an M-16 assault rifle.

We even got the names of the buddies. We ran them through the ARJIS computer. One had served time with Boyce.

I volunteered to storm the house.

Dighera found me a bulletproof vest.

After nightfall, we hit a glitch. The judge Dighera needed for a search warrant pussied out. He was at a party and re-fused to go back to his office.

"I got a judge who owes me one," I told Dighera.

"Go for it," he said.

I called up the judge who'd helped Dick Nixon's surfing buddy. I'd never made a stink over that weasel-deal, and I was hoping the judge would be appreciative.

But he told me to fuck off. "Please, judge," I said, "this is important. Besides, you kinda owe me one. Remember that call you got from San Clemente?"

Long silence. "What call?" The bastard was stonewalling. Taught me a lesson. If you're squeezing somebody, have hard evidence. Otherwise, it's just a pissing match.

I tried another judge who owed me one—U.S. Magistrate Harry McCue. For years, Judge McCue's court had been cha-otic with illegal aliens—until I'd been assigned to guard it. Being a control freak, I'd devised a numerical system and had written a number on each illegal alien's wrist. The defense attorneys had screamed that it was dehumanizing—"like Auschwitz." But pretty soon, everybody had started going home two hours earlier. Then they *loved* me, especially the judge.

When I called him, Judge McCue was a real gentleman. He got out of bed and drove to the courthouse.

By 3:00 A.M., we were in the San Diego suburb of Santee, gazing up at an apartment building. For all we knew, Boyce was staring back at us through the scope of his M-16. Between us and the apartment was a large, deserted parking lot—a vast kill zone that was our only approach.

Dighera and I were going to hit the door. We were flanked by a tough, smart kid named Jerry Smith, and by Tony Perez, the war hero who later busted Manuel Noriega. A dozen guys from the San Diego SWAT team were providing backup. If we drew fire crossing the kill zone, they'd suppress it. That way, not *all* of us would die.

"I think we oughta smoke him outta there with gas," said one of the SWAT guys. He looked white and trembly.

I gave him a cold look. "What are *you* worried about?" I said.

"We *can't* use gas," Dighera said, "because there may be an elderly couple in the apartment, and old people can go into cardiac arrest from gas. The apartment's being rented by the parents of one of the pukes who's up there with Boyce. The germs are named Thomas and Black, and we have to consider them armed and dangerous. We've got the adjacent apartments evacuated, but let's still be careful about through-wall fire, okay? Questions!"

Nobody said anything. I gaped at the parking lot; it looked a mile wide. I clenched my jaw to keep my teeth from chattering.

Dighera clapped me on the back and took the lead across the parking lot. He could have tasked one of the lower ranks with taking the point, but he wasn't that kind of man. I ran up in front of him. I wasn't trying to be a hero. It was just instinct. I wanted to go home alive, and I didn't trust anybody more than I trusted myself.

We ran like hell, but stayed silent. My breath came in short, mechanical stabs. My lungs felt like they could only hold a cup of air. The doorway to the building got closer. Closer. Made it.

We tiptoed up to the landing outside the apartment and stationed two men on each side, guns drawn. I looked into Dighera's eyes. He nodded.

I jumped in front of the door and crashed my boot heel into it. It exploded open. We ran in screaming.

My body was electric with perception. I could hear, see,

and feel *everything*. And my first sense was: This doesn't *smell* right.

It smelled like old people. Not young punks.

I busted into a bedroom and found Thomas and Black. They looked totally awake, and not very surprised. Something was *wrong*.

"Get on the floor, fuckmeat!" They obeyed meekly. They were totally jailhouse: tattoos, pale greasy skin, and jagged teeth.

I cuffed them. "Where's Boyce!"

"I'll tell you," said Thomas. He lifted up, and I bent down. "Boyce is out fuckin' your mom," he said.

I kicked him hard in the ribs. He grunted but then looked at Black and smirked. What did the smirk mean? Something was *wrong*. I didn't think we were going to find Boyce.

I hauled them out to the living room, where an elderly man and woman sat, frightened and befuddled. I felt sorry for them.

"No Boyce?" asked Dighera.

"No Boyce."

Dighera, suddenly spent from tension, dropped his huge bulk into a chair and gulped air.

We drove Thomas and Black downtown, separated them, and started the questioning.

They both denied knowing anything about Boyce. Neither of them seemed very worried, and they kept goading us— like they *wanted* to get smacked.

While Black sucked down a cigarette, I studied his rap sheet. Both he and Thomas had been busted for airline fraud. Interesting. If they knew how to manipulate the airlines, maybe they'd already gotten Boyce out of the country without triggering the State Department's computers.

"You put Boyce on an airplane, didn't you?" I said to Black.

"You've got *nuthin'* linking me to Boyce," Black sneered. "You made a false arrest. You fucked up."

"No," I said, "*you* fucked up." I picked up my briefcase. "See this? It's got Boyce's fingerprints all over it. We found it in your old man's apartment. So you *are* goin' down for harboring. Your parents, too. But we don't give a shit about you—we want Boyce. Tell me where he is, and I'll lose the briefcase."

"You lying fuck," said Black. "You planted that."

"All's fair, asshole. Think about it." I left the room.

I found the communications room and started playing with the computers, to enlarge my profiles of Thomas and Black. We hadn't had time to get details on them, and I wanted all the triggers I could get. If we were going to squeeze them, I wanted hard evidence.

First, I researched the airline charge. Working as a team, Thomas and Black had been convicted of filing false claims on lost luggage. Their MO was to check in several bags—one much larger than the other, and all of them empty. Then, after the flight, they would stuff the smaller suitcases into the large one, and make a claim for lost luggage. They'd collected over ten grand before they'd gotten popped.

Another conviction was for defrauding a bank. They'd opened a checking account, then had reported their checks stolen. The bank had put a hold on the checks. A couple of days later, they'd tried to cash one of the "stolen" checks and had been arrested. They had protested that they'd just found the checks, and had already notified the bank. They'd sued for false arrest. They'd succeeded with this scam several times before somebody had figured it out.

During one of these scams, they'd also sued the arresting officer for police brutality and had settled that claim for $5,000.

My heart sank as I read this stuff. These guys were just gyp artists. They'd probably called in the anonymous Boyce tip themselves, so they could file a false arrest suit. Thomas would probably also file a brutality suit against me for kicking him in the ribs.

I went into the other interrogation room, where Dighera was grilling Thomas. Dighera was so pissed that it looked like his eyes were about to explode.

I pulled Dighera aside, explained what I'd learned, then got in Thomas's face. "You guys fucked up *righteously*," I barked. "When you phoned in the tip yourselves, you were furnishing false information to a law enforcement officer.

That's a violation of federal statute 1001, and you're goin' away on it."

Thomas showed no expression. "Don't look so happy," I said. "Lompoc's got your call on audiotape, and we're waiting for a judge to let us take a sample of both your voices, for a voiceprint."

Thomas tried to play cool, but I could see the lines around his eyes start to crawl. I made a point of smiling.

"Your partner's already started whining about a false arrest suit," I said, "and I read both your jackets. So I *know* your motive.

"And, lemme tell ya, it gets worse. When we were evacuating the apartments, an old lady fell down and broke her hip. Technically, you're responsible for that injury, so we could file an assault charge. So you're gonna go on 1001, plus an assault, *plus* endangering."

His forehead got slick, and a hot, stale smell started to rise off him. I had him by the balls. Time to twist.

"We can forget all that, though," I said, "if you'll help us solve our real problem: *Boyce.* Have you had *any* contact with him?"

I could see the wheels in his mind spin: What could he tell us that would get him off?

"Hey!" Dighera yelled. "Answer!" Dighera didn't want him to think—he wanted him to *talk.*

"Yeah," Thomas said, "Boyce showed up one day, but he took off before I could, you know, turn him in."

I laughed spontaneously. Turn him in, my ass!

"What did Boyce say when you saw him?" asked Dighera.

"He said he was going up to Canada. Said he was gonna walk across the border in Washington, and go live in Vancouver."

My eyes met Dighera's. This was tremendous information. Or pure bullshit.

"Did he tell you how he escaped?" I asked.

"He told me all about it. He said he left a dummy in his bed, and went over the wall. He got the idea from *Escape from Alcatraz.*"

Everybody knew about the dummy. It had been in the newspapers. But Dighera and I acted impressed.

"Was he embarrassed about his hair?" Dighera asked. "About having to shave it off to glue to the dummy?"

"Oh, he felt funny," said Thomas. "But he knows it'll grow back."

"What about his hand?" I said. "We know he cut it on Lompoc's razor-wire. What we need to know is, can he hold a gun yet?"

"It's mostly healed, except for the thumb. But he can probably use a gun, cuz he asked me to get him one. I told him no way—to just get the hell outta my life."

Dighera and I let Thomas sit while we got Cokes. We'd lost all interest in him. Boyce had not cut his hand. And Boyce had cut off only a couple of locks of hair to glue to the dummy.

Thomas was a lying sack of shit.

But I was still high from adrenaline, and it felt incredibly peaceful just to sit there, sipping Cokes, feeling safe. I felt a real sense of brotherhood with Dighera. Tonight we'd faced death together. We'd trusted each other with our lives. Nothing draws people closer than that.

"Is that the last we'll see of Thomas?" I asked Dighera.

"Oh, yeah."

But Dighera was wrong. Even though we soon released Thomas and Black, Thomas surfaced again.

The plot sickened.

"Here he comes!"

Everybody jumped up, as if the president were approaching.

For us, the big, box-faced guy lumbering up the walk was *more* important than the president. His name was Tommy Lynch, and he had a secret meeting scheduled with Christopher Boyce.

Unbeknownst to Boyce, though, we'd collared Tommy Lynch a week ago. We'd squeezed him, and flipped him. He'd rolled over on Boyce, and now he was working for us.

The first man at the door to greet Lynch was Howard Safir's right-hand man, Chuck Kupferer.

I'd never seen Chuck Kupferer look so happy. In fact, I'd never seen Kupferer look happy at all. Several months earlier, Howard Safir had put Kupferer in charge of the Fugitive Program. So now—in February of 1981, about four months after the Black-Thomas raid—Kupferer had his nuts in a vise. Ronald Reagan had just been inaugurated—as President Rambo—and the pressure on us was greater than ever. Reagan, Congress, the Bureau, and the press were all screaming for Boyce's head, and Kupferer was the official whipping boy. Kupferer—who pronounced his name "Cup-fur"—was desperate for a good lead.

Prior to Tommy Lynch, we hadn't had any. What we'd had, instead, had been bizarre: After his release, Thomas— the scam artist we'd busted in Santee—had gone psycho and decided that he was Chris Boyce's "alter ego." He believed that he *had* to help Boyce stay free. So Thomas had started anonymously calling the media with fake leads on Boyce. It was a terrible distraction, and pumped up the pressure to find Boyce.

Kupferer, with a big smile on his face, introduced Tommy Lynch to the men on the task force, and we all adjourned to the living room to drink and talk. For the past several weeks, the whole task force had been living together in a condominium in Palos Verdes, the classy LA suburb that was Boyce's hometown. The investigation had been centered on Palos Verdes lately, and it was cheaper for Kupferer to rent one $2,000-per-month condo than ten motel rooms. The task force's $10,000 budget was almost gone, so we were stretching it every way possible—making our own meals, doing our own housework, not taking overtime, and not using any "flash money"—money to buy information, and to flash around in bars, so that we'd look like players, instead of cops. We weren't even inflating our expense accounts, which was a remarkable sacrifice for government employees.

Having no money was a bitch. The condo smelled sweaty from unwashed laundry, and there weren't enough beds. For weeks, I'd been sleeping on the floor because I was the lowest rank of anybody on the task force. The night Lynch came, I was excited because one of the marshals had gone on leave and had opened up a bed.

"Whattaya drink, Tommy?" asked Kupferer, as Lynch settled into the room's only easy chair. Lynch pointed at somebody's glass of red wine, and Kupferer went to get it himself. Kupferer was a naturally friendly, good-hearted guy. He was informal, earthy, and fun-loving. He insisted that everybody call him Chuck. Kupferer was a perfect next-in-command to Safir, because he was as warm as Safir was analytical. They did a terrific job of good cop/bad cop.

"Tommy," said Kupferer, handing him the wine, "you *gotta* show us the telegram."

"No problemo, Chuck," Lynch said with a shit-eating grin. With a flourish, he popped the snaps on a briefcase and produced a slightly tattered telegram. Everybody huddled around it, but Lynch handed it to Kupferer.

The telegram was dated January 7, 1981, and had been sent from San José, Costa Rica. It said: CANCEL MEETING IN MEXICO CITY. CHANGE TO SAN JOSE, COSTA RICA. MUST SEE YOU. It was signed "C.B."

"Oh, that's beautiful," said Kupferer. From beneath Kupferer's big cowboy mustache a gleam of white teeth erupted. "It's just bee-*you*-tiful."

All the marshals were straining to see it, and were slapping Lynch on the back. Lynch was devouring the attention like a starving dog. I'd never seen a happier man.

Among the Boyce-investigation insiders, Lynch's telegram was famous. A month earlier, Lynch had approached prominent television journalist Don North—who'd once tracked down the famous assassin and terrorist Carlos "The Jackal" Ramirez—and had told North that he'd been in contact with Boyce. Lynch, a mercenary soldier who'd done freelance work for the CIA, told North that he'd visited Boyce in Mexico City, where Boyce was smuggling guns for Cuba.

North had done a TV piece about Lynch's claim without revealing Lynch's name, and the story had died down. But then Lynch had gotten his telegram, and had shown it to North. The telegram had fired North up again. North had called NBC, and had talked them into paying for him and Lynch to go to Costa Rica, where they would secretly interview Boyce.

But North had made one mistake. He'd offered the Costa Rican job to one cameraman, and then given it to another.

The spurned cameraman had gotten pissed off, called Dighera, and blabbed the whole story.

Dighera had hunted down Tommy Lynch, squeezed him, and had then offered him a reward to roll over on Boyce. Lynch had taken the deal.

So now the plan was to debrief Lynch here in Palos Verdes, then follow him to Costa Rica, and take down Boyce.

Everybody was giddy with anticipation. The wine was flowing and the aroma of baking pizzas flooded in from the kitchen.

All the guys on the task force settled into a semicircle around Lynch. They wanted to hear his CIA war stories.

"Hey, Tommy," said Tony Perez, "tell us about the Allende coup in Chile. Pretty hairy?"

Supposedly, Lynch had done something for the Agency in that ugly coup, but it looked to me like Tony was just stroking him. To Tony, *nothing* was hairy—as a teenager, he'd rowed from Cuba to America, and he'd won combat medals in Vietnam.

Lynch leaned back and got a faraway look in his eyes. "Oh, Chile was *interesting,* I'll say that," he said. "I was there around September, and it was hot as hell, and—"

"In *September?*" Tony interrupted. "It's springtime there in September."

"You're right—I get mixed up," said Lynch. "Anyhow, it was just after the coup, and the Agency was wondering, How do we sell the story that Allende committed *suicide,* when the fatal wounds were from a *machine* gun—*in the back?* They were worried about the blowback—you know, the bad PR. So I go, Here's how to sell that. You just say, He's a *Commie,* he's a *Commie,* he's a *Commie*—and the story'll sell *itself.* And, by God, that's exactly what they did. P.S. It *worked.* Like a charm." Lynch belly laughed. So did some of the guys. Not me. Nixon's shitty little adventure in Chile had caused a decade of torture and murder.

Somebody asked Lynch what Boyce was doing in Mexico. "Mexico is just a staging area for him," Lynch said. "His primary plan is to smuggle ten thousand pounds of rifles from Cuba to El Salvador. Of course"—Lynch squeezed out a tight smile and winked—"we've got our *own* plans in El Salvador. But I can't say anything about that."

He took a long pull on his wine. "Tell you what I *can* talk about," he said. "But this is just between us girls. I know what the Agency's got cooked up for the Beard." I assumed he meant Castro. "They wanna explode fireworks all over Cuba, outlining the face of Jesus. It'll show the peasants that God's pissed at Fidel." He smiled and shook his head.

"Where in Mexico did you see Boyce?" Dighera asked.

"I shouldn't say. But what the hell. I know it won't leave this room. Mexico City."

"Wasn't that where Boyce met his KGB contact?"

"Exactamento, my friend. His old stomping grounds. It's a perfect place to meet. His pals are there, and it's a nice town. No offense to you LA guys, but you can actually *breathe* down there."

Lynch held court until well after midnight, shoveling down pizza and slurping wine. He trotted out all his stories, and kept everybody entertained. I could see, by the way they looked at him, that their confidence in him was growing. To be honest, it made me jealous. I'd have given anything to have the men in that room look at me with that kind of respect. But I was starting to feel more than just jealousy. I didn't trust Lynch. To me, he sounded like a consummate bullshit artist.

At one point, when he was reaching for his wine, his sport coat fell open and I saw that he was carrying a gun.

"Where'd you get the piece?" I asked. I knew he'd flown here with a marshal, with only carry-on luggage. I couldn't see how he'd gotten the gun onto the plane.

"You know the drill," Lynch said, with a little closed-lip smile. "When two 'marshals' go through security, they're allowed to board with their weapons."

The marshal he'd flown in with looked at the floor—but Kupferer didn't jump on him for cooperating with such a stupid stunt. Kupferer was just glad Lynch was with *us,* and not Boyce.

"I'd never go *anywhere* without my friend," Lynch said, patting his shoulder holster. "I got *one* little problem, though; I'm outta ammo."

"That's not a problem," said Kupferer. "John will score you some in the morning."

As low man in rank, I was the task force's gofer. "I'll be happy to," I told Lynch. "Whattaya need?" He had a Colt .38 Super.

"Forty-fives," he said. "I need some man-stoppers."

"I'll get 'em first thing in the morning."

Lynch went back on his tongue cruise, but the guys were starting to nod off. We were all working eighty-hour weeks.

"Tommy," said Kupferer, "I gotta get my men some rack time. So come with me, and I'll show ya where to bunk." He led Lynch toward the vacant bedroom. As Kupferer walked by me, he smiled apologetically. "You *almost* got a bed," he said.

"Don't matter, Chuck." But it did. I hated being low man. It brought out all my insecurity. I also hated living away from home. It wasn't fair to Betsy. But she never complained, not once. In her own way, she was as strong as any of the men in this house.

After Kupferer tucked Lynch in, I pulled Kupferer into the kitchen, where a few guys were nibbling cold pizza. "I'd be happy to run down backup info on Lynch's telegram," I told Kupferer.

"Think we need to?"

"Well, he's given us some paperwork here, some hard evidence. Might as *well* check it out."

"Sure, why not." Kupferer studied my face. "You don't buy off on it?"

"I'm not saying that. But—you want us all to be out front with you, right?"

"Absolutely."

"To be totally honest, my bullshit detector is goin' ape on this guy," I said.

A couple of marshals groaned.

"Come on," I protested, "think about it. He doesn't know tradecraft from his ass."

"Why do you say that?" Kupferer challenged.

"Lotta *little* things. Like not knowing the seasons reverse when you get below the equator. Or saying that the air is better in Mexico City."

"John Pascucci, junior weatherman," sneered a senior marshal.

"Okay," I said, "here's another one. That gun of his. At first, I was thinking it's a point of credibility, because the thirty-eight Super is popular as hell down in Mexico. But he wanted *forty-fives* for it. He didn't even know what the hell kinda *bullets* it takes.

"And think about this. I'm Chris Boyce, and I'm trying to stay hidden, and I send a telegram to somebody who already *knows* it's from me. Do I put my *own initials* on it? Hell no, I don't. Maybe Lynch sent that telegram to himself, just to sell his story.

"And that thing about Cuba. The fireworks shaped like Jesus? I heard that story ten *years* ago."

"I know," said Kupferer, "so did I. But cut him a *little* slack."

Kupferer put his arm on my shoulder. "Those are reasonable points, John. So go ahead. Run down the telegram.

"But put yourself in my place. What else have I *got?* Lynch is goin' to Costa Rica tomorrow. And we're goin' with him."

"RCA, security division, how may I help?"

"Hello," I said, "my name is John Pascucci; I'm a U.S. marshal. I'm in the office of the U.S. attorney general, working with him on the American government's most important spy case. The A.G. and I—and President Reagan—*need your help.*" I was on the kitchen phone, keeping my voice low so Lynch wouldn't hear me. For five minutes, I schmoozed with the RCA security guy until I had him feeling like 007. I didn't give him my badge number, or a call-back number, so that he could verify that I really was a marshal. I never did that. I just acted like I was for real, and no one ever seemed to doubt me.

"What I need," I said, "is the point of origin for a telegram that was sent through your system. I suspect—and this is top secret—that our target somehow sent this telegram to himself."

"Give me the number on it."

I gave him the number, and he said he'd have an answer in ten working days. "Hang on," I said. I put my hand over the receiver, and waited for a few seconds. "The attorney general asked me to tell you that anything you could do to expedite the process would be *greatly* appreciated by your government." I lowered my voice to a conspiratorial whisper. "Frankly," I said, "he's under a great deal of pressure from the president."

I got off the phone and ran out to get Lynch's bullets. When I gave them to him, I said, "Give them a try, to make sure I got the right ones."

When he pulled his gun out, I memorized the serial number. The bullets, of course, didn't fit. "I'm sorry," I said, "I screwed up. I'll go back and get the right ones."

I hopped in my car and drove to the Marshals' LA office. I entered the serial number of Lynch's gun into the National Crime Information Center computer, an FBI system that holds data on all fugitives, missing persons, and stolen property. Lynch's gun came up as stolen.

What did that mean? It could mean Lynch was a common criminal. At the very least, it meant he was too flaky to buy his firearms from a reputable dealer.

When I got back to the condo, I told Kupferer about the gun. Kupferer grimaced, and got on the phone with Safir.

New plan. Before Lynch went to Costa Rica, he would go to Washington—for a lie detector test.

The next day, I got a call from Kupferer, who'd gone to D.C. with Lynch.

Lynch had taken three lie detector tests from the DEA's best polygraph analyst. He'd passed all three.

"The examiner said Lynch is good as gold," Kupferer told me. He sounded vastly relived.

I didn't trust polygraphs. But this was no time to argue about it. "So you're sending him on down to Costa Rica?"

"He's already on a plane."

Tommy Lynch flew south with Dighera. They were accompanied by Larry Homenick, an excellent agent who was absolutely vital to the Boyce investigation. Also in Costa Rica were war hero Tony Perez and my gutsy buddy from the Thomas-Black raid, Jerry Smith.

As soon as Lynch got off the plane, he began organizing a raid into the jungle. He said he knew where Boyce had set up a "hootch." The first raid, though, was a flop. So were the second and third.

But at headquarters, everybody was getting more and more excited. They felt we were closing in on Boyce. Our budget was reapproved and substantially increased.

Kupferer called. "We've decided that when we get Boyce, we're going to do a black-bag job. We've gotta get him back into the States, with no interference from Costa Rica. We need to task you with a couple of crucial things. And we're gonna give you big money to work with, so for Christ's sake, don't blow it."

My job was to get a straitjacket, so that if authorities confronted our team after Boyce was in custody, they could try to sell the story that he was a mental patient, whose claim of being "a kidnapped Russian spy" was just lunacy. I also had to get a kit for dressing gunshot wounds in the field. If there was a firefight, we couldn't risk going to a Costa Rican hospital.

"The other thing you gotta do," said Kupferer, "the *expensive* thing, is to rent a Lear jet that can go two thousand miles without refueling. We don't want to stop in another country and explain why we have a kidnapped man on board. And get one that can land in Costa Rica on the Pan American Highway. We can't use a regular airport. Of course, you'll have to pay cash, because you can't reveal the nature of this job. I've authorized headquarters to wire the money."

"Jesus, Chuck, the airplane people are gonna think I'm a drug smuggler."

"I know," he said. "So act like it."

Straitjackets, I discovered, were illegal in California. So I had to get one under the table from a local sheriff. Then I special-ordered the gunshot kit from a hospital supply house.

Next, I drove down to a private airport in Huntington Beach, the rich LA suburb, and bopped into a charter rental company in jeans and a T-shirt.

"Wha's happenin'?" I said. "I hope you can help me. I gotta have a plane that can go two thousand miles without refueling, and my employer insists that it be able to land on the highway outside his villa." The guy gave me a long, cold look. He was accustomed to dealing with wealthy business-men and movie people, and turning away customers like me.

"First off," he said, "we can't let you land on a highway unless you can assure us no rocks will be sucked into the engines. And second, we can't go that far without refueling."

"Well," I said, "I've heard it's possible to take up a bladder tank to get more distance." That was an old dope-runner's trick—filling a waterbed mattress with fuel, then throwing it out after it had been emptied.

He scowled and clenched his teeth. "No offense," he said, "but I just don't *do* this kind of business." He started to duck into his office.

"Wait a sec," I said. "What would you normally charge for this?"

"About seventy-five hundred." I could tell he was exag-gerating.

I opened a satchel full of hundred-dollar bills. "Then how would fifteen thousand be?" Kupferer had wired me a small fortune. The bosses were going all-out on this gamble. They smelled success.

He smiled sweetly. "It would be *fine.*" He got me a Coke, found some ice for it, and started the paperwork.

I paced while I waited. I was sweaty and jumpy, and my nerves were frayed. Not just because this guy thought I was trying to smuggle drugs, but because *I knew* I was trying to arrange a kidnapping.

The fact that the operation had been approved by the White House didn't make me feel more comfortable. It made me feel worse.

When the U.S. government started kidnapping people—as official policy—what would be next?

Of course, I could see Reagan's point of view. The pukes on the street didn't play fair. Why should *he?* Reagan pro-jected kindness to the public, but within the Justice Depart-ment, people considered him the toughest son of a bitch ever to occupy the Oval Office. He loved to kick ass. Overall, I was never the world's biggest fan of Ronald Reagan. From the get-go, it was obvious he was spending the country into permanent debt with his military buildup. And he screwed the working class horrendously. He obviously felt the rich should get richer and the poor should get what they deserved. But in terms of law enforcement, he was the champ. America may never again see enforcement stats like the ones we racked up under the Gip.

Still ... somebody had to do the messy work. And that somebody, as usual, was me. But at least I wasn't walking the low road alone. Throughout the Service, marshals were becoming more "imaginative" and "aggressive."

The Reagan era of law enforcement was swinging into high gear.

We were becoming *Rambo's cops.*

In Costa Rica, things were getting weirder by the hour. Lynch had much more interest in Latino whores than he did in Chris Boyce, and he was demanding we use our meager flash money to buy him prostitutes. Our deputies thought they were being followed by the KGB *and* the CIA, and Lynch was starting to claim that the best way to find Boyce would be to wait in Boyce's favorite hooker bar—pounding down booze and screwing whores to "keep our cover."

But Kupferer wanted to stick with Lynch.

I called back my hook at RCA and begged him to speed up his search on the telegram. I told him two CIA operatives would die tomorrow if he couldn't nail down my info right away.

Two hours later, he called back.

"The telegram actually *did* originate in Costa Rica," he said. "There's no evidence that it originated in America."

I was crestfallen. "Thanks for the help," I said. He started to hang up. "One other thing," I blurted. "I wonder about the billing of the telegram. How hard would it be to find out if it was actually *paid for* in Costa Rica?"

"Not hard at all. Gimme an hour."

Forty minutes later, he phoned. "It was *not* paid for in Costa Rica," he said. "It was prepaid in California. It was paid for two days before it was sent, by a Mr. Thomas Lynch."

I called headquarters immediately. The news had a devastating impact.

Within a couple of days, the man who had sent the telegram from Costa Rica was located. His name was Carlos; he was an old friend of Lynch, and he'd written the telegram just as Lynch had asked him to over the telephone, signing it "C.B."

The Lynch investigation collapsed. The marshals in Costa Rica straggled home.

Why had Lynch led us on a wild goose chase? Because he wanted to feel important. I know that sounds absurd—but people like Lynch *are* absurd. Lynch's scheme was even more ridiculous than Rufus Donner's goofy extortion plot, because there was no payoff to it, except for momentary attention. To me, that was totally illogical. But the real world is rarely logical. That's why logical people don't really understand it.

I probably should have felt like a hero for breaking Lynch's story. But I didn't. And nobody treated me like one. In fact, some of the deputies were pissed off at me. They *still* bought off on Lynch.

Boyce had been on the streets for thirteen months. His time line was cold as snow. I had no solid leads and virtually no triggers.

And then came the news of Frank Burton Riley.

"Have you heard of Frank Riley?" Kupferer asked me as he tweaked one end of his Wild West mustache.

"I've heard the name," I said.

"Right now," said Kupferer, "we've got him linked *this close* to Boyce." He held up his thumb and forefinger, and squeezed them together.

Riley, Kupferer told me, was a career mutt with a three-page rap sheet. He was a bank robber, gun nut, and mail fraud operator. He'd once held off the New Jersey state police from his house with a Thompson submachine gun. In that standoff, his parents had begged the police to hold their fire, had run into the house, grabbed the family dog, and had then told the police to resume firing. Close family.

After his capture, the ultraracist Riley had been moved

from the New Jersey penal system, because New Jersey authorities were afraid he'd slaughter some of their large population of black inmates. Even more ominous, as a mercenary soldier, Riley had been kicked out of the bloodthirsty Rhodesian Army for being "too brutal."

Over a year ago, even before the Thomas-Black raid, Riley had come to our attention. At that time, an anonymous tipster had told us Boyce was in South Africa. We'd run all the data we had relating to South Africa, and had made a "hit" between Riley and South Africa, and a hit between Riley and Boyce. Riley had once traveled to South Africa. And Riley and Boyce had done time together at Terminal Island prison. But nothing had developed from the lead.

During the Costa Rican episode, however, Dighera had gotten another tip—an anonymous letter—saying that Boyce was in South Africa. Boyce was supposedly using the alias "Hollenbeck," and he was being helped by someone named "Schmeiser."

Both names raised red flags in our computers. "Hollenbeck" was the maiden name of Boyce's mother. And "Schmeiser" was an alias that Riley sometimes used.

Kupferer had immediately ordered marshals to sit on Riley's house in New Jersey. During that surveillance, Riley had flown to San Francisco, accompanied by an old ex-con named Henry Rabinowitz. After Riley had left New Jersey, marshals had searched his house, and had found documents indicating he was headed for Australia—another one of the places where we thought Boyce might be hiding.

"I need you to help sit on Riley in San Francisco," Kupferer said. "I need somebody there I can trust." The SF office, he said, was still full of old farts and fools. Kupferer looked exhausted; his face was so pale that his black mustache looked painted on. Some of the guys had started calling him the Undertaker.

The last few months had been pretty hellish. It seemed as if Ronald Reagan's worst fears about criminal chaos were all coming true. In December, John Lennon had been murdered. Then, in April, Reagan himself had been shot. When Reagan had gotten hit, virtually everybody in the Service—regardless of their politics—had felt like shit. He wasn't just the Boss—he was the ultimate father figure.

Then, a month later, the pope had taken a bullet. Another "father" had gone down.

What was going *on?* And what would it take to end it?

I took the next flight to San Francisco and hustled out to the hotel room that was serving as stakeout headquarters. But as I knocked on the door, I could hear the theme song from the TV show *Dallas.*

The door opened, and sure as hell, there was the entire six-man stakeout squad glued to the tube, arguing about who'd shot J.R. I walked straight to the TV and switched it off. "You! Stupid! Motherfuckers!" I screamed. "What's goin' *on?*"

"Riley gave us the slip," one of them muttered.

I marched to the phone, called Kupferer, and in front of everybody I said, "It's worse than you thought. They're not even *trying.*" I got some vicious looks. At that moment, my reputation as the Marshals' "headquarters' man" began. From then on, when a local office fucked up, I'd get sent in. Nobody ever liked to see me arrive.

I asked Kupferer to send me some men from the task force, and I sent the San Francisco deputies home. They hated me for that, because they'd been drawing stakeout pay overtime.

The next day, I started the Riley surveillance with fresh troops. I had to admit, Riley was a pro. His countersurveillance tradecraft was excellent. First thing that morning, he left his hotel in a jogging suit. Walked twenty steps. Pivoted and went the other way. At the corner, he waited for the light to turn red, then jumped out at the last second and ran across the street just ahead of the traffic. We couldn't follow, or he'd spot us. My men were going crazy. We had no decent communications equipment, just cheap radios with detached microphones that we ran up our sleeves. At the next intersection, Riley went out with the last group of pedestrians, and the only marshal who was still with him lurched along in his wake. Halfway across, Riley turned and came back. The marshal had to keep going. Riley disappeared into the crowd and was gone. We didn't find him until several hours later, when he returned to the hotel.

I went up to my room and devised a new surveillance system. I called it the "box system," and it's still being taught at the Marshals' training academy. The key to it was not following the target, but waiting for him. If I knew the target would be coming out a door, I would station one man at each street corner, and another across the street, spotting. If the target went right, the spotter would radio that message, and the guy on the left corner would leave his position, cross the street, and go right. The guy who was already on the right corner would wait for the target, then radio the target's new direction. If the target went right, another officer would be waiting for him at the next corner. If the target went left, the officer who'd just left his position would be waiting for him. If the target went straight, the officer on the corner would follow him. If the target ducked into a building between corners, we'd watch the front and back and wait him out. Using this system, four men could cover almost any target.

Next morning, we tried it out. It worked perfectly. I tracked Riley to the Tenderloin District, where he picked up a whore. When he left, I moved in on her. I thought she'd be easy to flip. But I was wrong. Riley had *proposed* to her, and she was going to take him up on it. Riley had inherited about $300,000, and to Vicki—the prostitute—that made him Mr. Right. But I talked a blue streak, and by the end of it she was convinced that the only way for her to help Riley stay out of trouble—and for her to get her hands on his inheritance—was to help me.

"Do you know why Riley brought Rabinowitz with him from Jersey?" I asked her.

"He's Frank's muscle," she said.

"Muscle for what?"

"He won't say. He just says he's working on something big, and needs protection."

"Has he been talking to anybody regularly?"

"He's been phoning somebody he calls 'the Colonel.' "

"Who's that?"

She didn't know. But she did promise to tip me off on Riley's movements.

I didn't hear from her for several days. They were rotten,

exhausting days. We were understaffed and underfunded, and Riley was running us into the ground. We booked the hotel room across the hall from him, and I spent half of every night lying on my stomach, looking through the crack under the door, waiting for Riley to make a move.

Then one morning the phone rang. It was Vicki. "He's going to Australia," she said.

We ran to our van in front of the hotel and waited. After three hours, my partner left to go to the bathroom. Riley appeared. Hailed a cab. I jumped into the van's driver's seat and groped for the keys. Gone. My partner had them.

I bolted out of the car and badged the first cab I saw. "U.S. Marshals!" I yelled. "Follow that car!"

The driver, an old Chinese guy, looked ecstatic. "For twenty-two *years* I've been waiting for somebody to say that!" he said. "Let's go!" He peeled off.

I followed Riley to the Union Square office of Australia's Qantas Airlines. After Riley left, I talked to the agent who'd served him. Riley had booked a flight to Sydney, Australia, on July 10, which was about a month away.

I called Kupferer, and he was thrilled. For some time, we'd suspected Boyce might be in Australia. Several months earlier, we'd turned up a magazine subscription for Christopher J. Boyce in Alice Springs, Australia. The lead had been tantalizing because, before his arrest, Boyce had been in almost daily contact with a U.S. intelligence base in Alice Springs. We were certain he had friends there.

"Get a ticket on the same flight," Kupferer told me.

That night, while Riley was out with Vicki, we searched his room and came up with a scrap of paper that had a couple of phone numbers on it. One of them was labeled "the Colonel."

Deputy Marshal Larry Homenick ran the phone number through the General Telephone records and found that it had been issued to Colonel Raymond Lincoln. Then Homenick ran Lincoln's name through the California DMV computer. "Colonel Lincoln" did not exist. Homenick went to the apartment serviced by the phone number and found that "Colonel Raymond Lincoln" was actually "Colonel Paul Hudson." Homenick was shocked: He *knew* Colonel Hudson.

The Colonel was an old-time con and wild-ass politico—just the type to be impressed by "activists" like Riley and Boyce.

Homenick got a warrant and hit the Colonel's apartment. The Colonel was gone, so Homenick started searching the place. It was absolutely filthy, full of garbage, maggots, and shit. Homenick put on a pair of gloves and started digging through the trash. That's when he found it. The "smoking gun."

The smoking gun was an eight-month-old letter about Boyce that Riley had sent the Colonel.

It read, "Dear Colonel, Two marshals interviewed me yesterday about our escaped friend. Somehow they've discovered that I helped him get into South Africa. If the feds contact you, say nothing. Don't mention that I contacted you."

Then he found *another* letter, mailed shortly after the first. It said, "There's a big push on for Boyce. I told the bums nothing. However, they seemed very suspicious, asking about my recent trip to South Africa. If the feds question you about Chris, please don't mention me."

Homenick called Kupferer at home. "You're not going to believe this, Chuck," he said. "I've got two letters signed by Frank Riley, to Colonel Hudson, in which he *admits* everything we think he's done."

Kupferer shouted with joy.

We were closing in.

Riley caught a plane back to New Jersey, where the local marshals picked up surveillance and waited for Riley to contact Boyce.

Riley's "muscle," Henry Rabinowitz, flew to Reno. The Reno office was supposed to tail him, but Rabinowitz slipped them. Kupferer was infuriated and ordered me and deputy Joe Cludy to go to Reno and track down Rabinowitz.

I was dying to match wits with Riley or Rabinowitz. I thought I could squeeze Boyce's location out of them, no matter how hard they tried to conceal it.

I also thought I could break their story, if this was just another wild goose chase.

Kupferer believed that Riley was "gold." But I was beginning to wonder. So far, Riley had *not* done what he'd indicated he would: Hook up with Boyce. In my eyes, that made him suspect. Maybe he was just another fraud.

But Kupferer was fixated on the letters Riley had sent the Colonel. His reasoning was: *Nobody* would admit guilt in writing if he wasn't really guilty.

But I thought that ignored a key aspect of the criminal mentality. The criminal mind is diametrically different from yours and mine; the same things that would shame us make the criminal proud. For example, both John Lennon and President Reagan had been shot by guys who were trying to show how *cool* they were. By the same token, Riley could have been linking himself to Boyce just for the *honor* of it. I know that's stupid, but that's how pukes think.

When we touched down in Reno, we were almost killed. It was the first day of the 1981 air traffic controllers' strike, and our plane just missed crashing into another one.

We headed into town. As we cruised, I tried to get into my "Rabinowitz mind-set." If I was an aging skell with no money, where would I go? I drifted into a whole different attitude; sleazy places started to look attractive, and nice hotels and restaurants made me uncomfortable. We meandered around the industrial outskirts, getting a feel for Reno's low-rent district.

Before long, we found ourselves on a street with a Salvation Army post and a strip of seedy motels and porn joints. I could practically smell Rabinowitz. My instincts were buzzing.

We took a stack of his mug shots and started canvassing the area. In less than an hour, we got a hit. The clerk at roach-infested motel said Rabinowitz came in almost every evening to pick up discount coupons for a casino buffet.

At eight-thirty that night, we collared Rabinowitz. I called Kupferer. He was ecstatic. In my mind, I could see Kupferer's teeth flashing white against his black mustache. I was becoming one of Kupferer's favorite agents, and it was a godsend to my career, since Kupferer ran the Fugitive Program.

After I told him about catching Rabinowitz, Kupferer said

he'd sent men to South Africa, to research Riley's activities there. They'd connected Riley to a young woman, and were closing in on her.

We hauled Rabinowitz to the Reno police station on a parole violation charge and started interrogating him. I thought about starting the interview by punching Rabinowitz around, but decided not to. You couldn't scare a tough old con like him with rough stuff. So I tried the friendly approach, and he seemed cooperative. He was a career perp—a forger, robber, and thief—so he wouldn't just tell us to go fuck ourselves. He'd wait to see what we wanted, and play the game out.

I didn't mention Boyce but started asking Rabinowitz about things Vicki had told us, to test his level of honesty. He told the truth.

Then I began wandering around the subject of Colonel Hudson—but not mentioning him by name—to see how Rabinowitz would react. If he stonewalled, I'd be suspicious that Rabinowitz was part of a Boyce conspiracy. But if he voluntarily brought up Hudson himself, I'd be more prone to think Rabinowitz was innocent.

He brought up Hudson himself. He called him a "crazy old fuck."

I edged toward the subject of Riley's contacts in South Africa. Rabinowitz freely offered the name of the young woman the marshals were hunting—Simone Godchaux.

Why would he be volunteering this stuff if he had anything to hide?

I kept probing him, and didn't get a single blip on my bullshit detector. Either he was in the clear, or he was one of the best liars I'd ever met.

For nine hours, we went over and over the same material, approaching it from different directions to find inconsistencies. But there weren't any.

We started asking pointed questions about Boyce. But Rabinowitz thought Riley had no connection to Boyce. "Riley's just a fuckin' mope," he said. "He just sits around and runs his mouth. He never *does* nuthin.' "

"Then why would he want to make people think he's hooked up with Boyce?"

Rabinowitz grinned and gave me a good look at his shitty prison dental work. "For the fuckin' *glory*, man. Boyce is *big*."

When dawn hit, I called Kupferer. I told him I thought Riley was just another bullshit artist, like Tommy Lynch, and like Thomas and Black.

I could almost hear Kupferer deflate.

"If it was up to me," I said, "I'd stop waiting for Riley to contact Boyce. I'd pick up Riley and try to break his story."

"Well, we found Simone Godchaux," Kupferer said. "I'll tell the guys to try to flip her, and get her to trick Riley."

"Sounds good."

"In the meantime, give your guy a poly."

"Sure." As I mentioned, I don't trust polygraphs, but an order was an order.

My problem with lie detectors is that they're too easy to manipulate. First of all, they don't detect lies; they detect stress, through pulse, blood pressure, and perspiration. But if the subject isn't particularly stressed out by fear of punishment, he can beat the machine. Even if he is stressed, there are ways to disguise stress. One is to coat the fingers with clear nail polish, to stop perspiration. Another is to take a relatively strong tranquilizer; Valium won't work, but Miltown will, and so will beta-blockers, because they inhibit adrenaline. Another way to beat the box is to think of something scary when you're telling the truth—or even press your toe against a tack in your shoe—so that your true responses and your lies will look similar on the graph.

Before I made Rabinowitz take the polygraph, I grilled him five more hours. By the end of it, I was certain he was straight. There was no one big answer that convinced me, although that's always what you're looking for. Instead, there was an endless series of small truthful answers, which combined to create credibility.

Besides, there was one undeniable fact: Rabinowitz could have rolled over on Riley and Boyce at any time, and walked. But he never did.

We took him down for the polygraph, and he passed it unequivocally.

I called Kupferer. Gave him the bad news. His voice got hollow and despairing. "Shit," he said, "we *gotta* confront Riley."

Kupferer arranged for Simone Godchaux to phone Riley. When she did, Riley incriminated himself again. He told her he'd seen Boyce. He was busted immediately in his New Jersey home.

For several days, Riley was questioned. Slowly, his story crumbled to pieces. He had no current link whatsoever to Boyce. He was just another sick mutt, desperate for negative attention.

The Boyce investigation was now twenty months old. And we had nothing. Absolutely nothing.

But in two weeks, we would have Christopher Boyce.

"You know what the real bitch of this whole thing is?" Bob Dighera asked, as he shifted his 260 pounds in his sagging office chair. "The *real* bitch is that even after we catch Boyce, he's probably gonna be out on parole in about eight years."

"Eight?"

"Yep. His escape beef will only add about two years."

"Jesus!" I slumped. I was half-crazy with exhaustion, and the idea of a traitor like Boyce weaseling free made me want to vomit. Boyce had destroyed America's best shot at detente and had guaranteed continued Cold War murder and torture in places like Afghanistan and Nicaragua. Still, the egotistical little bastard thought he was a *peacenik.*

Besides, I had a gut-level hatred for somebody who'd betray America. People like me, who've climbed America's ladder from the bottom, appreciate this country in a way others can't quite understand.

Dighera's phone rang. It was Deputy Marshal Dave Neff. A new informant had just approached Neff, promising to take us to Boyce. But Dighera and Kupferer were sick of being burned by phonies, and they weren't giving Neff much support.

After he got off the phone, Dighera said, "Neff's informant sounds like another flake. He says Boyce got steered to a fugitive hangout up in the Northwest, and robbed some banks up there. So Neff asked his informant, 'Who steered him?' And the snitch goes, 'Well, Chris says it was a big, strong guy.' "

"That narrows it down," I said.

"You want to work up that lead? Go find a big, strong guy?"

"I can find him," I said. I smiled. But I had an idea.

Christopher Boyce was a wimpy-ass, scrawny punk who considered himself an intellectual. His friends were all effete little brainiacs. Only one thing would attract Boyce to a "big, strong guy": the need for protection. And there was only one place he'd need physical protection—in prison.

In prison, a celebrity skell like Boyce would be a prize "bitch"—a status symbol for any homosexual who could overpower him.

I drove up to Lompoc prison and started interviewing guards, to find out who the top-dog homosexuals were. The guards all pointed me to a psychopathic jocker named LeRon.

LeRon, a black guy with red tattoos down both arms, gave me exactly what I needed, and he seemed to enjoy doing it. LeRon had badly wanted to turn out "Sweetmeat Chris." But he'd been thwarted by a huge con named Cameron Johnson. Johnson was Boyce's prison muscle. And he'd gotten out shortly *before* Boyce had escaped. He was my top candidate for the "big, strong guy."

Johnson was on parole in Santa Cruz. I jumped a commuter flight and started screaming threats at Johnson before he even knew why I was there. As soon as I mentioned Boyce, Johnson ratted him out. Johnson told me about the same fugitive hangout, in the Northwest, that Neff's snitch had described. Johnson was street-smart. He knew the only way to get rid of me was to roll over on Boyce.

By the end of the day, I was back in Dighera's office, pacing up and down while fatigue sweat ran in rivulets down my back. "I think it's solid, solid, *solid*," I ranted. "My bullshit detector did *not* go off on this guy Johnson. He's gold. He's *platinum*. I think we got a real *lead* here, Bob."

"You got a gun?" asked Dighera.

"Yeah, sure."

"Loan it to me," he said. "I don't have one on me, and I'm headin' out the door."

"Where you goin'?"

"Up north. After Boyce."

"What about me?"

"I need you here, in charge of communications for the entire operation."

"I'd rather be in the field, Bob."

"I know. But I need somebody in the middle of this who's not afraid to call bullshit on the bosses if things go sour."

"Anybody can do that."

He shook his head. "Most guys are scared to do that." He stood up, and put one of his big, ball glove–size hands on my back. "But I'll tell you one thing," he said. "You better not be *wrong* on this."

I tried to smile.

Dighera took a huge force up to the Northwest—about twenty-five men. It was the most expensive operation the USMS had fielded in years. Obviously, the bosses thought it was time to do or die.

Kupferer went along to supervise. The investigation centered on Port Angeles, a little town near Seattle where Neff's snitch claimed Boyce was now hiding. Boyce, according to the snitch, had first hidden out at the fugitive hangout in northern Idaho, then had migrated to Port Angeles.

Our Port Angeles operation was simple—just a massive stakeout. We divided the town into quadrants, and stationed forces in each section. From the communications center in California, I began strategically moving the various teams, trying to cover the most promising locations, like motels, bars, and restaurants. We organized the teams into a circle and began tightening it toward the center of town.

Our snitch provided us with lifestyle characteristics that might help us locate Boyce. He said Boyce had grown fond of bars and beer joints, where he could find the type of low-lifes whom he felt safe bragging to. Boyce couldn't keep his mouth shut about his exploits, or even his identity.

Meanwhile, I quizzed Neff's snitch, trying to break his

story. First, I wanted to know his motive for flipping on Boyce. He said he was pissed at Boyce for stiffing him on a hundred-dollar loan, and for involving him and his brother in the bank robberies.

To me, the whole scenario had the ring of truth. It didn't involve any grand schemes of running guns for the Cubans or escaping to the Australian Outback. It was a simple story of an escaped criminal hiding out among other criminals, and then blowing his own cover through greed and exhibitionism.

When I'd investigated Thomas, Black, Lynch, and Riley, I'd learned another important lesson. When you're trying to understand the real world, look for the most commonplace, prosaic scenarios. The complicated ones never seemed to pan out. My new motto was: In the real world, expect the ordinary.

But the Marshals' staff psychiatrist got involved, and he didn't buy my scenario. The psychiatrist said Boyce was too nonviolent to rob banks, and too smart to reveal his identity.

I thought the shrink was full of shit. Sure, what he said was logical. But what did logic have to do with the real world?

For seven days, the ring around Boyce got tighter and tighter.

Dighera and Kupferer called several times a day. They were both on the edge of hysteria, laughing and cursing for no particular reason. We all thought this was our last chance. Either we made this operation work, or we presided over the death of the two-hundred-year-old United States Marshals Service.

Early in the morning of August 20, Kupferer called. His mood was black. The circle had cinched to the center of town, with no sighting of Boyce.

So far, we'd kept a zero profile, not questioning anybody, for fear of spooking Boyce.

"Chuck, it's your call," I said, "but maybe we should start running this like a *regular* fugitive investigation. Ask around. Talk to people. Break somethin' loose. I always say, when in doubt, do something."

Kupferer sighed. "Maybe you're right."

*   *   *

August 21. Late night. The office was still as death. The phone rang and I jumped.

"John! John!" It was Dighera. In the background, I could hear loud voices and laughter. "Guess who I've got sitting across from me?"

I didn't want to jinx it, so I just said, "Who?"

"Boyce." I didn't say anything. I felt like I had something stuck in my throat. "It's *Boyce!*" Dighera yelled.

"Where'd you take him down?" My voice was tight and croaky.

"We took him at a hamburger stand. We started running this like a routine investigation yesterday, and we closed in on him fast. I got the collar myself.

"And, John—the gun I put in his ear? It was your gun, John."

"Thank you." I suppose that was a stupid thing to say— but it came from my heart.

The next morning, Kupferer again called. For the first time since I'd met him, he sounded relaxed and happy. "I'm in Howard Safir's office, John," he said. "And we both want to thank you for an outstanding job. You kept us on track. If it wasn't for you, we might still be in Costa Rica, or South Africa, or God knows where. So we're puttin' you in for a GS seven. I know it's gonna be the first promotion of many."

"Thanks, Chuck."

"Here's why I called. Howard and I do not—we do *not*— wanna see Boyce out of prison in seven or eight years. We think he was involved in the bank robberies you've heard about, and we think that's our hook to keep him down.

"So we want you to move up to northern Idaho, and prove Boyce hit those banks."

"Who's the lead agent on the case, Chuck?"

"You are."

"Me?"

"Yeah, it's *your* show this time. So take that bullshit detector of yours, okay? But, listen, John—you ever been to northern Idaho?"

"Nope."

"Well, it's beautiful. But it's crawling with neo-Nazis, fugitives, drug runners, gun nuts, and every kind of sicko you can imagine. Right now, it's the most dangerous place in America."

"How bad can it be?"

"Well, the guy you need to work with up there—John Durant, the prosecuting attorney—last week they tried to kill him. Bombed his car. Blew it to pieces."

"*Who* did?"

"Apparently, Boyce's people. So, John, you can turn this down if you want."

"I'm not going to turn it down." Was he *kidding?* I was President Rambo's cop.

"Good man."

"Lemme call my wife."

"Howard's secretary called her. She's already at the airport."

Chapter Six

The Face of Evil

★

• Neo-Nazis in White Trash Heaven • Car
Bombs • Meth Monsters • The Reagan Era
of Weasel-Deals • *My* Sons of Bitches •
Sex, Drugs, and Rock 'n' Roll • The Spy
Goes Down •

*"The hottest places in Hell are reserved for those who, in a
period of moral crisis, maintain their neutrality."*
—Dante

Gunshots popped in the distance but I paid them no mind.
I was hypnotized by the heavenly water.

It fell in a glassy sheet from a ledge overhead, and
splattered into an icy clear pool that shivered with sun-
light. I'd never seen such water. It sparkled like a
melted diamond.

I bent over, cupped my hands, and drank from the pool.
It was sweet and freezing. I scooped up more.

"Hold it!" The shout came from behind me. I spun around.
Grabbed for my shoulder holster. But I wasn't wearing it. I
thought I'd be safe here.

A kid emerged from behind a green curtain of forest. "Drop that water," he said.

"What! Why?"

"Moose shit in it."

I gagged and spit.

"Caribou, too. This is a watering hole." He eased down to the pool, kicked off his moccasins, and pulled his buckskin shirt over his glossy flowing hair and headband. "It's really more *their* place than ours," he admonished.

Just what I needed. A mouthful of moose shit and an ecology lecture from Tonto the Indian boy.

The kid dangled his feet in the water, and minnows darted over to nip at his toes. He pulled a joint from behind his ear and fired it up—*very* casually, to show me what a *free dude* he was. "The herb superb," he grunted, holding his breath. He took another hit, then held it out to me.

I took it. What the hell? I was a *free dude,* too—when nobody was watching. Besides, I had two hours before my meeting with Idaho prosecutor John Durant, and I needed a break. Boyce had been in custody for only a day, and it was obvious that I wasn't going to get any time off before I started investigating his bank robberies. I was replying on pot more and more as my only real escape from work. I called it my sixty-minute vacation.

I took a toke and handed it back. The kid's arm was brown and weathered. He had big blank eyes, like a dead deer. From the looks of him, he was on a sixty-*year* vacation.

"Are you Indian?" I asked.

"Not yet."

"Not *yet?*"

But he was lost in the ozone.

The pot flooded through my system and began to pull the tightness out of my nerves. The green moss by the blue pool began to glow.

"Lived here long?" I asked.

"Oh ... *yeah,*" he said, after half a minute. "I been here for *weeks.* I got myself a tepee just upstream. I'm an old-timer. Lotta people just *sail* through here. You kinda hear 'em, but don't *see* 'em."

"Why-zat? This is good dope."

"Thanks. Grew it myself. It's cuz a lotta people don't *wanna* be seen. This is *outlaw* country."

"That's what I hear."

"*Always* been that way. During the Gold Rush, train robbers lived up here and ripped off the Great Northern when it ran to the silver mines. Can you *relate?*"

"What's goin' on these days?"

"Oh, people poach deer, grow pot, make whiskey. This is the *future of America,* man! The poor are gettin' poorer. Dig it!" He grinned and blew a smoke ring.

"Whatta you do?"

"I live off the land."

"Oh, yeah? You hunt and fish?"

"No, man, I collect." I gave him a blank look. "I collect *welfare,* man—I live off the fuckin' *land.*"

Again, the muffled pop of gunfire filtered through the pines.

"Is that a poacher?" I asked.

"Ummm, I doubt it. Probably Nazis. They have a target range downstream."

"They a problem? The Nazis?"

"Not if you don't invade their space."

My nerves started to tighten again. My job was to invade *everybody's* space.

Even in the peace of the forest, I began to get the same feeling I got whenever I hit a house: *You do not belong here.*

I said good-bye to Tonto, ambled back to my car, and headed up Highway 95 toward Bonners Ferry, where Boyce had lived, and where John Durant was headquartered.

After five miles, I hit the county line. By the side of the road was a makeshift sign, a caricature of a black man sprinting and sweating. It said RUNNING NIGGER TARGET. It was full of bullet holes. Just behind it was another sign: WELCOME TO BOUNDARY COUNTY. YOU HAVE JUST GONE BACK 100 YEARS IN TIME.

"Welcome to Boundary County," boomed John Durant. "It's *God's* country. Unless you're afraid of, you know, *death,* or something." He laughed without smiling. It was unnerving.

"My boss doesn't *allow* me to fear death," I said.

"Good for him. Tell me what I can do to help." Durant was thin, well-barbered, and carefully dressed—a Brooks Brothers guy in a Wild West town.

"First of all," I said, easing into the only other chair in his Spartan office, "tell me who tried to kill you."

He shrugged. "Maybe Boyce. Maybe Celia James—the woman who was hiding him. Maybe the neo-Nazis. Maybe the dopers. The hell of it is, all these people seem to be *intertwined*—so it could have been the whole bunch of 'em, working together."

"How'd it happen?"

"Car bomb. Just outside my house. It blew twenty feet from me, my mom, and sister. Totaled the car, but we were okay."

"Anybody claim responsibility?"

Durant shook his head, and his close-cropped blond hair trembled.

"Tell me about Celia James."

"Celia's one of our favorite types: white trash trying to look like a hippy. Earth mama: long, straight hair, granny dresses, and a diamond set into one of her teeth. She lives in a big log cabin she built herself, and uses it as a crash pad for hippies, fugitives, and ex-cons. Always bitching about 'the Establishment.' Six kids and three husbands. Sleeps around. She's been busted for bad checks, importing marijuana, and aiding and abetting a bank robbery. So far, she's beat all her charges. For a long time, we've thought she's been smuggling drugs and guns, and using her place in the woods as a safehouse."

"You get a lot of fugitives through here?"

"They *love* it here. We're thirty miles from the Canadian border, and it's an easy border to sneak across. There's plenty of wilderness to hide in, and not much local law enforcement. We've got more outlaws now than we did a hundred years ago."

"Talk to me about the Nazis."

"*Those* assholes? They started coming here about ten years ago, after police down in California busted them with somethin' like five tons of munitions. Mortar. Machine guns. Land mines. Napalm. All kindsa stuff. Their guru's a correspondence-course preacher named Richard Butler. He's into all kinds of apocalyptic bullshit and half-ass theories about race and religion."

"Such as?"

"Such as the Christian Identity movement. It's been around for over a hundred years, and the whole point of it is that Jews aren't the Chosen People. Anglo-Saxons are. No way was *Jesus* a Jew. He was like, Swedish, or something—maybe *Australian.* Jews are 'mud people'—like blacks—and they're gonna annihilate the white race with stuff like birth control and water fluoridation."

"Do these guys do anything other than talk?"

"Oh, *yeah.* Butler *loves* Hitler, and he's set up a thing called the Aryan Nations, which is the political arm of the movement. They harass nonwhites around here, and they're real active in prisons all over the country. Butler's got a mailing list of fifty thousand people. About five hundred of 'em live up here now—and Bonners Ferry's population is less than two thousand. They like it here for the same reasons the fugitives do—it's remote, it's close to Canada, and people here mind their own business. Plus, there's hardly any blacks or Jews up here—twenty or thirty, all told.

"Butler's got a twenty-acre compound, and every year he hosts the world's largest convention of racists.

"He's a scary son of a bitch, no doubt about it. But I'll tell you, some of the mutants he's bringing up here are *worse.* They just wanna kill somebody, and don't care who. Some of 'em probably do business at Celia's—drugs or guns."

"What have you got tying Celia to Boyce's bank robberies?"

"Right now, not much. As I understand it, your snitch on Boyce can tie her to the robberies, but your snitch was apparently involved himself. So I assume he'll be prosecuted, and his testimony won't be worth anything."

Durant's secretary buzzed him on the intercom. "Mr. Durant? Mr. Pascucci's supervisor is on line one, and says it's urgent."

"Take it in there," said Durant, pointing to an adjacent room.

I closed the door and picked up the receiver. A deep voice boomed, "Hey, Go-getter! Let's talk turkey!"

"Brick! What's up?"

"So! You got another promotion! You're a *force of nature,* Deputy! Now, here's the deal. Safir says it's *imperative* that we nail Boyce on those bank jobs. He thinks the best way to get a conviction is for you to figure out what Boyce was doing *every damn day* he was on the loose."

"Jesus, Brick, how am I gonna do that?"

"Hell if I know. The FBI's *already* declined to prosecute him on the banks. They say there's not enough hard evidence. None of the bank photos show anything but fake beards and big hats, and none of the tellers can ID him."

"So how do we make the case?"

"I don't *know,* and I don't *give* a rat's ass. Just get the job *done*—and spare me the gory details."

"Okay—then let's start right off with a weasel-deal. How about givin' me the snitch who turned Boyce in? I know he was in on the robberies, and we don't make deals with bank robbers. But in *this* case—"

"That's not a problem."

"Not a problem?"

"No. My guys in the field, uh ... forgot ... to read the snitch his Miranda rights. So we got no beef against him. Actually, we're giving him reward money. So the little bastard *definitely* owes us one."

"You're very efficient, Brick."

"You're too kind. Actually, things are lookin' up back here. The new Reagan guys at Justice aren't so goddamn *picky* about criminals' rights. I *love* this new A.G., William French Smith. He's a *mean* bastard. And he's actually givin' us a little *money* for a change. Hey, one more thing, make sure you take down that bitch who was hiding Boyce. It'll strengthen your case against Boyce, and a high-profile harboring bust will teach people not to hide our mutts."

I got off the line and sat back down with Durant.

"Got myself a witness," I said.

"Who?"

"The snitch. We didn't Miranda him. So he's a citizen again."

Durant's eyes got big. He wasn't used to weasel-dealing. He didn't work for the Gipper.

"I think I'll go take a ride with my snitch," I said. "Go visit every bank they hit."

"That'll be a lon-n-ng ride."

"First, though, I'm gonna go back to my motel and get my wife. No offense to your town, but I'm getting her the hell outta here."

Durant looked sad. "That's a good idea," he said.

Betsy got pissed when I told her she should go back to San Diego.

"I'm staying," she hissed. "If it's not too dangerous for you, it's not too dangerous for me."

"C'mon, Bets, you're a woman—you're more vulnerable."

"That's sexist." Her nose jutted into the air.

"Betsy, these people are scum. They'll do anything."

"What? Like you're usually out after *nice* people?"

"Don't try to be a hero."

"Don't *you* try."

"It's my job, and you know it."

"It's my job to back you up. You *need* it. You know *that.*"

Finally, I did what any head of the household does in a crisis. I begged.

She relented.

But when she left, I felt empty. The truth is, I did need her backup.

When the speedometer hit ninety, the falling snow settled over the windshield like a bedsheet. *"Don't back off!"* wailed Mike Perry, the snitch who'd turned in Boyce. "They'll think we're *pussy.*"

Just ahead of us, setting the pace, was an FBI car. After the Feebs had found out we were going to prosecute Boyce for the banks—a job they declined—they'd decided to tag along while me and the snitch retraced the robbery routes, interviewing witnesses and building the case.

To prove they weren't *total* wienies, the FBI guys insisted on driving like hell through the backroads of Idaho and Montana.

When we hit ninety-five, and started sidewinding down the road like a big snake, Mike Perry croaked, "I need a *drink. Bad.*"

From the backseat, Perry's brother, John, moaned, "Me, too."

Turns out, *both* of the Perry boys had helped Boyce rob banks. And now they were both helping me put him away.

I heard the pop of a can and felt a mist on the side of my neck. Mike Perry handed back a beer to his brother John, then cracked one for himself.

"You better have one, Pascucci," Mike said, "or you'll be too *nervous* to drive this fast."

"No, thanks." The FBI car began to pull away from us, so I nudged the throttle up to ninety-seven.

"*I* know how to slow 'em down," Mike said. "Pull up alongside 'em."

"You're crazy," I yelled.

"Please!" shrieked Mike. "I *hate* danger."

That made all of us laugh. Mike and his brother *loved* danger. The Perrys were, in fact, a liberal sociologist's dream case study: decent kids ruined by their environments. They'd come from a malignant home, and just wanted to live fast and die young. Boyce had seduced them with danger, not money.

In my heart of hearts, I knew they were sons of bitches like Boyce, just self-centered thrill seekers.

But they were *my* sons of bitches.

I floored it and moved up on the FBI car. The car was every cop's fantasy: a "police package" with a jacked-up suspension, a four-barrel carburetor, a monster V-8, and mile-wide radials. It held the road like a prehistoric bird.

Our car, on the other hand, was pure U.S. marshal: a rented Ford Fairmont with blackwall retreads.

Mike rolled down his window and stuck out a beer. The FBI agents—two local Mormons with bugs up their asses—looked shocked and disgusted.

Mike shook the beer, popped the tab, and sprayed the Mormons' windshield. It frosted on impact. The Feeb car braked, fishtailed, and ground to a halt.

As I slowed, Mike screamed back at the Mormons, "That'll teach you to fuck with us *U.S. marshals.*"

I turned on the radio, just in time to catch a news bulletin saying Anwar Sadat had been assassinated. The Mideast was in chaos, and it felt like the world was again at war's doorstep.

Who'd hit Sadat? The Jews? The PLO? Had Reagan done it, to impress Jodie Foster?

The early 1980s was a strange, violent time. It was an era of extremes. Nothing seemed impossible, and paranoia felt like common sense.

Mike grabbed the dial and twisted it to a rock station.

"Can we get some work done now?" I said, easing back down to eighty. "Tell me again what Boyce did immediately after he showed up at Celia's."

I flipped on my tape recorder and Mike started filling me in with the details that would sell our case to the jury. For the past four weeks, as autumn had waned, I'd put together a picture of Boyce's nineteen months of freedom. Boyce had bragged incessantly to the Perrys about his life on the run, and now I was using Boyce's braggadocio to ruin the rest of his life.

In the rearview mirror, I saw the FBI car head back onto the road. "Let's talk about the time the bank teller put the dye bomb into Boyce's bag," I said. "Where did he try to wash off the stained money?"

"At the Bonners Ferry laundromat. Him and Celia."

"Anybody else help?"

"Yeah," said Mike, "Rick the Spic. This little kid that used to hang at Celia's."

"What's his last name?"

"I dunno," Mike said. "But he saw a lotta shit, for a little kid."

The FBI car pulled up next to us and the driver motioned us over.

When we stopped—out in the middle of some windy, god-forsaken plain—the driver called Mike over to his car.

"What the *heck* kinda stunt was *that,* young man? Are you buckin' for a *citation?*" The Mormon's fat neck, which flopped out over his string tie, was red as a buzzard's. He was an R.A.—a resident agent—and he was accustomed to all the locals treating him like J. Edgar Hoover.

Mike wouldn't respond. He just smiled.

"You're cruisin' for a bruisin', mister," said the R.A.

"Look," said Mike, "lemme *give* ya somethin', to show ya I'm sorry." He fished a joint out of his windbreaker, lit it, and offered it to the agent. "This'll help ya see the *lighter* side of violent crime," he said.

"You're *busted, son.*"

"I doubt it. My country *needs* me."

I walked over. "Please, guys," I said to the agents, "the bosses will *kill* us if we start any paperwork on this guy. He's a major witness."

Mike blew a cloud of smoke into the FBI car. The agents waved their arms wildly, and peeled off.

"Get in the car!" I yelled.

As we took off, I barked, "*Gimme* that joint."

Mike handed it over.

"Now gimme a *light!*"

From the backseat, John handed up an open bottle of Kahlua. He'd packed a bootleg Quaalude in snow, then stuffed the little snowball into the neck of the bottle. "Suck the booze through the 'lude 'n' snow," he said. "I call it a White Russian Baby Bottle. I *invented* it. I'm gonna *patent* it. Make us *all* rich."

Mike took a long draw on the bottle. "Where we goin' tomorrow?" he asked.

"Back to Bonners Ferry," I said. "I got a *date.* And I'm *horny* for it."

"Who with?" said Mike. "Your wife?"

"No. *Better.*"

"*Who?*"

"Boyce."

Christopher Boyce had a smirk on his face when they led him in. He was jailhouse pale, and he looked thin and shriveled, like a wilted daisy. But he still managed the smirk.

"So," he said, "you're the guy who knows all-l-l about me."

I nodded.

"I assume, then, that you've read the book." He meant *The Falcon and the Snowman.*

"Nah. I don't care about how you did your crime."

That wiped the smirk off his face. "But you can't know the *real me* without reading the book," he protested.

"There *is* no 'real' you, Boyce. You're not a *real* person. You're just a *type.* You're a narcissistic sociopath. End of story."

He forced out a smile that was thin as string. "We'll find out who's real, before this is *over,"* he said. "Go ahead. Tell me what you've got."

I returned his smile, just to piss him off. I opened my briefcase, took out a stack of papers labeled BOYCE TIME LINE and started telling Christopher Boyce where he'd been every day of the last nineteen months.

January 21, 1980

Christopher Boyce stood over a cliff and peered down at the river below. He'd been jogging for about ten hours—ever since he'd gone over the wire at Lompoc prison on a make-shift ladder. Behind him, tracking dogs brayed. Several times, he'd narrowly escaped his pursuers. Helicopters, planes, and jeeps scoured the desolate foothills.

Boyce took a deep breath and leaped off the cliff. He crashed into the water and knifed to the rocky bottom. Stunned, he barely made it to the bank. He began to jog again, and the yelp of the howling dogs finally began to grow distant.

For days, Boyce lived on insects and creek water as he hiked slowly toward the town of Goleta, California, about sixty miles south of the prison. Boyce had a friend there. But when Boyce finally arrived, the friend was gone. When Boyce asked a neighbor about his friend, she called the police. Boyce ran back into the woods, scavenging garbage to survive.

Eleven weeks later, Boyce showed up at the home of Cameron Johnson—the "big strong guy" who'd protected Boyce in prison. Johnson told Boyce about Celia James—who was the mother of one of Johnson's children. Johnson bought Boyce a bus ticket to Idaho, and helped him make fake ID.

By meeting with Johnson, Boyce had made his first big mistake. If he'd had the guts to tough it out alone, there would have been no one to eventually help finger him. But mutts *always* go to their buddies.

In April of 1980—around the time I was busting Rufus the Bomber to win a spot on the Boyce Task Force—Boyce arrived in Bonners Ferry.

He hitchhiked to Celia James's remote log house but found it deserted; James was at her other home, in Newport, Oregon. The log home was funky—no running water or electricity—but it beat sleeping in the woods. Boyce crashed and helped himself to canned food.

A few days later, he hiked into Canada, but remained only briefly. In Canada, he was a nobody—and to an exhibitionist like Boyce, that was intolerable.

He returned to Idaho, and met Celia James. He also met one of Celia's teenage daughters, with whom he began an affair.

Around the time I began my lengthy computer search for Boyce—looking for hits among his associates—he was having a high time with Celia and her daughter. They were growing pot, and hosting frequent parties for local losers.

Boyce bought a mule, and started hitching it in front of backwoods taverns and general stores, to show the locals what a colorful character he was. He called himself "Jim the Mule Man." But nobody gave a shit. He was just another goofball. Celia was the only person who knew who he really was.

In July of 1980, about six months after his escape, Boyce met the Perry brothers—Mike, twenty-four, and John, nineteen. The Perrys had been abandoned years before by their father, who'd split from home after failing to strike it rich in the gold fields. The Perry boys were poor and uneducated, but hip enough for Celia. Boyce and the Perrys began spending long hours in the local bars. During one of their drinking sessions, less than a month after they'd met, Boyce told Mike Perry, "What would you say if I told you my name wasn't Jim?"

Mike showed no interest.

"My name is Christopher John Boyce," he said. "Does it mean anything to you?"

"No."

Boyce was hurt. "There was a *book* written about me," Boyce squealed.

But Mike didn't care.

Then Boyce began to rob nearby banks and sponsor *legendary* parties at Celia's place. The parties would last for days, and featured the finest food and drink. Mike and John began to be more impressed with Christopher John Boyce.

Boyce enlisted the Perrys in his robberies. Mike drove the getaway car, and Celia supplied theatrical makeup and wigs. They made about $3,000 to $5,000 per robbery.

Around the time I made the Thomas-Black raid outside San Diego, Boyce was living the good life in Bonners Ferry. But he couldn't control his exhibitionism; he began to tell a growing number of people who he really was.

Boyce began pressuring the Perrys to join the army. He wanted them to get security clearance, so they could pass him information that he could sell to the Soviets. He assured them they could each make $25,000 a month. They refused.

Around the time I began to expose "soldier of fortune" Tommy Lynch, the Perrys quit helping Boyce rob banks. It was too dangerous, even for them. But Boyce refused to quit. He loved the thrill.

While I was chasing Frank Riley, Boyce relocated to the Olympic Peninsula of Washington. He was still robbing banks, and still pissing away the proceeds on parties. But he had a new plan. He bought a fishing boat, and he planned to pilot it to the Bering Strait. There was an island there, Big Diomede, that was controlled by the Soviets. Boyce was going to defect there, travel to Russia, have his features changed by plastic surgery, and then return to America as a spy.

Around the time I broke Frank Riley's story, Boyce abandoned the plan to reach Russia by boat. His boat, the *Rose M,* couldn't handle the high seas. His new plan was to hopscotch across Canada and Alaska in a small plane, then fly over the Bering Strait.

On the Olympic Peninsula, in Port Angeles, he took flying lessons. He made his first solo on August 16. He was ready to go.

We arrested him August 21.

* * *

As Boyce listened to all this, he maintained the bitter, superior little smirk that made him look like he was sucking a saltshaker. But when I finished, a look of genuine pleasure lit his face.

"That's *all?*" he asked.

"That's *enough,*" I said. "Your only *possible* hope is to plead guilty and cut a deal. Which I strongly advise."

"But you don't *have* it."

"Have what?"

"A *witness,* deputy, a *witness.*"

"I have the Perrys."

"My point exactly," he said sarcastically. He stood up, and his prison coveralls drooped down on him like a wet sack. "Thanks, buddy," he said. "You just *made my day.*" He held out his hand.

I rubbed my palm across my face. Smiled. Shook his hand.

He jerked away. "You spit in your hand, fucker!"

I laughed. But I didn't feel like it. I was afraid he was right.

After an hour and a half with John Durant, I stood up slowly, listening to the bones in my spine pop. I was still stiff from my month-long ride with the Perrys, and now I was tense as hell. Durant didn't think I had enough, either.

"The problem is the disguises," Durant said. "Out of sixteen bank jobs, we don't have a single bank employee who can positively ID Boyce. If we go before the jury with just the Perrys, it'll be a crap shoot. They're crooks, and the other side will hammer their credibility. If we could get Celia to roll over on Boyce, we'd be okay. But that's not gonna happen. She's as tough as any old con. We need another insider—but somebody who *didn't* take part in the robberies."

"Got any ideas?" I asked.

Durant shook his head.

"Did you ever hear of a kid called Rick the Spic?" I asked. "A *little* kid."

"Ricki Blanca?"

"He's a little Mexican boy who hung out at Celia's."

"Yeah. That's Ricki Blanca. But he's gone. Long gone."

"How do you know?"

"He was a ward of our court. He left his foster mother just after my car got blown up."

"Who was his foster mother?"

"Celia James."

I went to the local sheriff to see if he had anything on Ricki Blanca.

He had a file twenty pages thick, full of possible contacts and phone numbers. He told me his copy machine was down, but that he'd task somebody with compiling a complete dossier for me by the end of the day.

"I know where *I'd* go first," the sheriff drawled. He was old, and moved in slow motion. "I'd go the last place we know Blanca was. His mom's."

"Why do *you* think Blanca split?"

"Well, he was a suspect in the car bombing. Him and a *lotta* people. Maybe he just got scared."

"Where's his mom?"

"Spokane. She works the streets over there. If she don't help, try his stepdad. *He's* a piece-a work. He sniffs glue and fucks vacuum cleaners. I shit you not."

I got both their addresses and drove like hell to Spokane. We had already charged Boyce with the bank robberies— and Cameron Johnson for harboring—and we had to meet the requirements for a speedy trial. Time was evaporating.

Blanca's mom was scared as hell. Her voice had the hollow sound that people get when their guts are all clenched up. She said that the last she'd seen Ricki was the first week in August, shortly after the car bombing. She said Ricki had been on his way back to Bonners Ferry when he'd left. That was all she would say.

Blanca, I found out, was not a young child, as the Perrys had assumed. He was fourteen, but was stunted—about four feet eleven and eighty-five pounds. He was a tough little guy who'd had a miserable life. He was a congenital truant, and knew his mom was a whore. His mom had shot and badly wounded his stepfather, and had been arrested for it. Blanca had also witnessed one of his aunts kill an uncle, and bury the body in the backyard. And it was true—his stepfather really did sniff glue and have sex with vacuum cleaners.

His stepfather was much more helpful than his mom. I treated him with dignity and respect—that's the best way to play a degenerate. He fell all over himself to be helpful. He gave me some pictures of Ricki and some names of Ricki's friends.

"But you'll never find him," Blanca's stepfather said. "The earth done *swallowed him up,* like it does ever-body who don't wanna be found."

"Well, I'm pretty good at finding people," I said.

"Besta luck." He offered his hand and I shook it. There was something sticky on it. I hoped it was glue.

It was way past dark when I got back to the sheriff's office, but he was still at his desk.

"I feel like hell," he mumbled. His face was twisted with wrinkles, like a half-rotten potato. "We *lost* that Blanca file. *Damn* if I know how. There's been people in and outta the copy room all day, and one of 'em musta just *took* it."

I didn't bust his balls. There was no percentage in it.

The next morning, I went back to the sheriff's office to see if the file had turned up. It hadn't. I lost my temper, and twisted the sheriff's nuts for a while. It was counterproductive; he just got sullen. But it made me feel better. I played with his computers, looking for hits on Blanca, but his system was primitive.

Just after lunch, I headed back to the crystalline pool where I'd met Tonto the Aspiring Indian. I began hiking upstream, following a trail that hugged the bank. Again, I was almost overwhelmed by the raw, pure beauty of the place. The schemes and doubts that were racing through my mind began to recede. The whisper of the creek cooled my nerves.

Within a few minutes, I heard the sounds of The Eagles. "Hotel California." Plus some grunts and moans.

When I came upon the tepee—a big tan canvas cone—I yelled, "Knock-knock!"

Tonto stuck his head out the flap. "Muh *man!*" he enthused.

He ducked back in, and emerged shortly with a very pretty young girl who was flushed and embarrassed. She sized me up and her eyes said: *old* person. At thirty-four, I wasn't used to that look. "I've gotta boogie," she told Tonto, and scampered down the trail.

"Bring more batteries!" he called after her. He gave me a wide-eyed smile. "What it is, bro?" he said.

"Just in the neighborhood."

"Cool. Had lunch?"

"I had somethin' at the pancake house."

"Then how about some food for *thought?*" He whipped out a joint and stuck it against an ember in his campfire. "You here on *vacation?*" he asked, handing me the joint.

"Yeah, basically. But I'm also tryin' to find a friend of my little brother's. A kid named Ricki Blanca. I guess he used to hang out at Celia James'. Heard-a her?"

"*Everybody* knows Celia. But Ricki Blanca doesn't ring a bell."

"Little Mexican kid? Rick the Spic?"

"Nope." He shook his head.

My bullshit detector was going apeshit.

"You ever go to her parties?"

"*Everybody* went to her parties."

"Ever see that guy Boyce? The one in the papers?"

"Nah, never saw him." Tonto looked away.

Tonto was a lying fuck.

There was a thump in the forest, and the kid held his finger to his lips. He motioned for me to follow. We walked silently upstream for no more than a hundred yards, then slowed to crouch behind a boulder. We peeked over. A black bear—*big* sucker, all fat in the belly—sat on its haunches in the creek while a cub splashed around in the shallows. For twenty minutes we watched. The little cub was trying to cold-cock a trout. It was like something out of *National Geographic.* Huge yellow butterflies floated over the diamond-clear stream.

Even after we got back to his camp, we didn't talk. We sat by his fire, and tossed twigs into it.

After a while, I said, "You know, you've got a really nice scene goin' here."

My chin dropped toward my chest and I started breathing deeply. Soon my breaths were almost sobs. "This is *fucked,* man," I blurted. "I've *got* to tell you somethin'. My name is John Pascucci, and I'm a deputy U.S. marshal. The reason I came up here was to *squeeze* you. I got you on furnishing and manufacturing a controlled substance, and I was gonna *trade* you that for information about Ricki Blanca. I need him as a witness." I stood up. "I'm gonna go, man. This is *fucked.* I got a fucked-up job." My eyes were glassy with water.

He came over and put his hand on my forearm. "Don't sweat it, man. *Everybody's* got a shitty gig." Bewilderment flooded his face. "Jesus," he sighed, "I can't believe *you* work for Ronnie Ray-gun."

I stared at the ground. "Look," I said, "what I did was *wrong.* I'll leave ya alone now."

I started to walk away.

"Hey," he called after me, "I'll give ya a hand. It's just not somethin' that I wanted to get in the middle of. *You* know why. But you were straight with me, so I'll be straight with you."

He went into his tent, came back with a notebook, and sketched a map.

"You'll find a dude here," he said, indicating an *X.* "In a little gray travel trailer. But don't go in the trailer, cuz he cooks methedrine in there. It's *very* toxic. He's a meth monster and a neo-Nazi, and he knows all about Celia's gang. I don't really *know* the dude, 'cept for selling him a little pot. Shit! Should I have said that?"

"It don't matter. I won't come back on you. Swear to God." I started to leave. "Hey! What's your name?"

"Levy."

"Well, you're *Chief* Levy to me."

That cheered him up a little, but he still looked pretty queasy. I didn't blame him.

As I hiked back to my car, I felt elated.

I'd just done the best acting job of my life. I'd manipulated a snitch that most cops would have gotten nowhere with. And I'd flipped him with no threats, no rough stuff. And no paperwork.

I couldn't wait to tell Brick how I'd played Chief Levy.

"How-the-fuck-ya-*find*-me?" the meth monster snarled in rapid fire as he bolted out of his ratty trailer. "There's-only-three-people-know-where-I-live-and-two-of-'em-are-*me!*"

He was ghoulish: emaciated and death gray. His eyes

bounced around like marbles in a tumbler and his teeth were rotted to sharp points.

I pulled my gun from behind my back and stuck it in his face. "I'm John Pascucci, U.S. marshal, and you're in a world of *shit!* Turn around and put your hands behind your neck!" I cuffed him. "On the ground, facedown!"

I held my breath, and stuck my head inside the trailer. No one else was in it. It was crammed with chemicals and cooking apparatus. Even holding my breath, I felt a pungent stench hit my nostrils.

I jerked the meth monster up by his elbow. "This is the luckiest day of your *life,*" I snarled, "because I'm gonna forget all about you when you tell me where I can find Ricki Blanca."

"He's-not-*one*-of-us."

"I don't *care* if . . . One of who?"

"Oh-you-*wish*-you-knew." Then he blathered something like, "You-*wish*-you-could-say-rider-behold-a-pale-horse-and-*feel*-the-apocalypse-descend! Right? Right?"

I sighed. I was in over my head.

"Look," I said quietly, "let's make this easy. Where's Blanca? Did Celia James kill him?"

"*Physical*-death? *Spiritual*-death? You-think-it's-so-*easy*-to-tell-the-difference? Is-it-like, black-white, good-evil? We-*behead*-informers, is-what-it-boils-down-to."

"You're going to prison."

"I-*love*-prison. Best-drugs-in-the-world. *Brothers*-in-prison. Brothers-of-the-*skin.*"

I took a deep breath. Everybody was afraid of *somebody,* and this brain-cooked asshole was no different.

"I've got it!" I said. "I'll just turn you over to your own head Nazi. I'll tell him you've been cookin' methedrine, right under his nose."

"He-*knows.* His-*nose!* He-*knows!* You-think-it's-*cheap*-to-spread-the-word-of-Jaweh? *Cheap* to keep the niggers in Africa?"

"*That* was real bright. You just implicated your leader in racketeering. He's gonna *love* you. *Now* when you go to the joint, the Aryans will be *waiting.* You know, I heard of a case in Attica where the Aryans took *all night* killing a guy. They did it with a *fork.*"

He tensed, then seemed to sober up a little. "C'mon-c'mon-c'mon-whattaya-*want,* Jew Edgar Hoover?"

"I told ya. Ricki Blanca."

"Well-you-gotta-big-*mouth,* Wop. You-got-the-balls-to-go-*with*-it?"

"Some people think so." But I didn't feel brave. I felt scared to death.

"Then-let's-go-see-the-Man-and-if-the-Man-says, '*Sacrifice*-upon-the-altar-of-the-Zionist-Occupational-Government,' I'll-*give*-you-Spic-Blanca."

"Sounds good. Let's go see the Man."

I frisked him, uncuffed him, and then we walked about a mile to his rusty Volkswagen van. "You'll-have-to-wear-a-blindfold-and-give-me-your-gun," he said as I got in.

"Eat shit and die."

"Okay-fair-enough-you-gave-me-a-reason-and-I-*respect*-that. We're-men-of-*reason,* you-see."

We headed south on Highway 95 to Sandpoint, where the meth monster stopped to make a call at a bar called the Cowgirl Corral. Then we drove into the hills for about ten minutes. My guts were churning. I'd let the situation get out of my control, and I *hated* losing control.

As the moon climbed clear and huge over the Bitterroot Mountains, we hit the top of a rise and came to a halt. Seconds later, another Volkswagen van pulled out of the darkness and came to a stop on our driver's side. The meth monster rolled down his window, and the driver of the other Volks leaned over and rolled down his passenger-side window. Then he scooted back behind the wheel. It was too dark to see his face. "Speak," he said. Very arrogant tone.

"I'm with the U.S. Marshals. I'm here to help prosecute the Boyce case. I've got *no* interest in you. All I need, as your boy here probably told you, is a location for Ricki Blanca, who's a witness against Boyce. My deal is this: Give me Blanca, and I'll stay outta your business while I'm up here."

"We don't make deals with the Zionist Occupational Government. Our mission is to *destroy* ZOG."

173

"That's all well and good. But frankly, my dear, I don't *give* a shit. What my common sense tells me is that you came to this meeting to do one of two things: to finger Blanca, or to kill me. So whichever it is, let's get on with it, okay?" I put my hand around my gun, and tensed.

For just a moment, the driver of the other van leaned forward, so he could see me. When he did, I caught a moonlit glimpse of his face. He had a shaggy beard, and little, vacant eyes, like a fish. His lips were drawn back, as if he'd just seen something repulsive. He looked different from any other mutt I'd ever seen. Most of them were so self-involved that they always seemed to be looking inward. But the main look on this guy's face was not selfishness, but pure hatred. He didn't look egocentric at all; he looked like somebody who'd offered up his life years ago, in the quest to bring everybody else down to his own level of misery.

I remember thinking, at that time, that I was looking into the face of evil.

He pulled back into the shadows.

"Why do you want to *destroy* us?" he asked. "Our kinsmen are trying to *save* this country. From racial *suicide.*"

"I'm not here to debate. What's your answer?"

For several long minutes, there was silence. Then the guy in the other van said to the meth monster, "Give him the spic." He started his motor, and disappeared.

"Little-greaser's-in-Newport-Oregon-at-Celia's-other-place," said the meth monster. Then *he* tried to start a political debate with me. It made me nostalgic for mutts like Thomas and Black, who were ODC's—ordinary, decent criminals.

"Look," I said, "my nerves are shot, my stomach's growling, and I got what I need. So let's go. *Now.*" I smiled sweetly, and held up my gun. "Or I'll kill you."

I made him drop me in Sandpoint. A local cop there drove me back to my car. As he drove, he kept checking his rearview mirror. "I think we're being followed," he said.

"I know."

It meant I was getting closer to my target. It was almost reassuring.

* * *

174

At six the next morning, I packed my suitcase for a trip to Newport, Oregon, then met John Durant for breakfast at the pancake house.

"Who did *you* piss off yesterday?" Durant asked as he slid into the booth.

"Some red-haired Nazi asshole," I said.

"Sounds like Gerry Whitaker. He's on the muscle end of their operation. Anybody else?"

"No." I didn't mention the meth monster. When I promised to cover somebody, I did. "Why?"

He pushed a note across the table. It said "The Fed is Dead."

"This was taped to the courthouse door this morning," he said.

"Fuck 'em," I said. But it made my skin crawl.

I told Durant about my lead on Blanca as I shoveled down pancakes and gulped three or four Cokes.

About halfway through the meal, though, I felt a hot wave of sickness shoot from my belly to my mouth. "Somethin's real wrong," I said.

I started to puke—right there in the restaurant—and Durant hustled me out and drove me a couple of blocks to a doctor's office. The doctor didn't know *what* to do, except dodge my puke. I threw up until the only thing left in my stomach was a brown, sticky bile.

I told the doctor it was probably just food poisoning—and maybe it was.

I had no time to wait around, though. The trial was only weeks away. Late in the afternoon, I drove to the airport in Spokane.

As nearly as I could tell, no one followed me. There was no point in it. They knew where I was going.

A uniformed Newport cop helped me find Celia James's daughter Janice—Boyce's girlfriend. She was on the front porch of Celia's Newport house. Janice started to lip off to the cop, so he grabbed her by the arm and hauled her to the backseat of his unit. The Newport police hated Celia James and her crew just as much as the Bonners Ferry cops did.

I got into the front seat of the car and tossed a picture of Blanca onto Janice's lap. "Where *is* he?" I demanded.

"Hell if I know."

I picked up the radio and pretended to push the "call" button. "Unit one-eleven. Be advised that the harboring suspect is now in custody. Please arrange for transport to the juvenile detention center in Portland. Ten-four."

We took off for the local station to question her. I hit the siren and light switches; it was nonsensical, but it always softened people up.

In the interview room, we started throwing out questions about her sex life with Boyce, to confuse and humiliate her. Within ten minutes, she was acting like a scared kid, instead of a wise-ass gangsta.

She started to sniffle and choke. I turned off the tape recorder, as if that meant she was no longer on the record.

"Did your mother threaten you?" I asked.

Janice broke down and wept. "You don't *know* my mom," she said. "She said she'd *kill* anybody who gave up Ricki—*including* me." She convulsed into sobs. I felt sorry for her and allowed it to show on my face. That made her cry harder.

"Where is Blanca?" I asked gently. I put my hand on her shoulder.

"Go out to the Goat Farm," she said. "I'll give you directions. See Rosie and Tom. They've got him. But *please* don't say I told you."

"I'll cover for you," I said.

We drove out. Place smelled like sheep shit. It took Rosie about two seconds to roll over on Tom. Real close couple. Tom, she said, knew exactly where Blanca was. And Tom was already in custody in the Newport jail. He'd been popped for shoplifting earlier that morning. We drove back to the jail.

I sized up Tom as he walked into the interview room, and the gut feeling I got was: *soft.* Soft little hands, weak little chin. I walked up to him, hauled off, and slapped the shit out of him. "Where's Blanca?" I screamed.

"Denver! Denver! I put him on a bus last night to *Denver.*"

I cocked my fist. "Denver *what?*"

"Denver, *Colorado!*" he wailed.

I smiled softly. "I know Denver's in Colorado," I said softly. "I was just *testing* you."

I started to laugh, but Tom didn't see the humor.

I drove to Eugene and tried to catch a flight to Denver. Fogged in. I called the Marshals' office in Denver, and told them to sit on the bus station.

But the Denver office was still filled with old hacks, and they fucked up the stakeout. By the time I reached Denver, Blanca was back in the wind.

I called Kupferer with the bad news and he phoned the Denver office to scream at them. He told them to do whatever I said. It solidified my reputation as the "headquarter's hit man."

I quickly assembled a search team. I told them to do the basics, and find me whatever triggers they could. Then I called Blanca's stepfather. He gave me a strong lead: Blanca's biological father was in Denver. For a guy who fucked vacuum cleaners, Blanca's stepdad was a pretty good citizen.

Blanca's father wasn't in the phone book, so I started working the computers. I found him in the county divorce records. The records contained the vehicle identification number of the car he kept during the divorce. Using his vehicle ID number, I ran a Colorado DMV "alpha search," which gave me a complete look at all his driving-related records. I came up with his address.

When I found him, in a rundown apartment near the airport, he wouldn't even open the door. He was a paranoid old bastard. "How'd you find me?" he demanded.

"Through Ricki's stepdad. We think that you'll be eligible for a portion of Ricki's witness compensation money, through the Sole Biological Guardian Act." That was bullshit, of course, but it got the door open.

"Ricki was here yesterday," he said. "But he didn't come home last night."

I went back to my car, and spent the night parked in front of the apartment, waiting for Blanca to show. It was cold, I was tired, and I missed my wife. At times, the only way I could stay awake was to picture how Boyce had sneered when he'd told me I didn't have enough evidence to convict him.

In the morning, I called my Blanca team together.

"Okay," I began, "who checked to see if Ricki's already in

custody?" Nobody said anything. "Oh, for Christ's sake!" I snapped. "That's the *first* thing you do when you work fugitives. Fugitives *have* to commit crimes, and they usually get busted. Make *sense,* guys? *You!*" I pointed at the nearest body. "Call around and see if he's been booked anywhere."

Ten minutes later, the guy I'd pointed at came back. "I found him," he said sheepishly. "He's at Juvie Hall. Got caught boosting a car stereo night before last."

"Meeting's over," I said.

But when I went to haul Blanca out of juvenile detention, I hit a wall of government. Typical bureaucratic bullshit. Even though I had a federal material witness warrant, the pipsqueak judge in family court wouldn't hand over Blanca. As usual, the bureaucrat with the least power was the one swaggering the most.

I hit the phones, working the local judicial system from the top down. I called the area's chief federal judge, chief state judge, and the chief judge of the Arapahoe County Court. These were powerful guys, not Barney Fifes, like my jerk in family court. We cut a deal.

At midnight, I trudged through the snow to the federal courthouse, where the chief federal judge awarded me *personal custody* of Ricki Blanca. He even allowed me to take him three judicial districts away. It was an extraordinary weasel-deal, not done before or since by any federal officer.

At Juvie Hall, they told Blanca he was being released to his guardian. When he saw that *I* was his guardian, he scowled. "Where's my dad?" he barked.

I opened my arms. "Come to poppa!"

I hustled Blanca to the airport and bought two tickets to San Diego. I was taking him to my home to prepare his testimony.

When our flight attendant saw him, it was love at first sight. Easy to see why: He was as little and cuddly as a koala bear, with big brown eyes and soft, childish features. He didn't own a coat, so she brought him three fleece blankets.

But as she bent over to tuck him in, he pulled out a pack of cigarettes and lit one.

"You can't do that!" she blurted.

"Like fuck," he snarled, "I'm *in* the smoking section."

"It's not *legal*," she wailed, glaring at me.

I pulled out my badge and tinned her. "I'm a federal officer, ma'am, and this young man has a waiver on the tobacco restriction ordinances." She knew I was lying, but she left.

Later on, she came back with our snack—an eggroll, fortune cookie, and some milk. "Do you like Chinese food?" she asked Ricki, trying to be civil.

"Yeah, do you?" he said.

"Sure."

"Okay." He leered, pointing to his balls. "Then nip-on-ese."

She recoiled, and I started to cuff the back of his head. But I stopped. I needed his approval more than hers. She hurried away.

When I got him home, Betsy fell for him in about a second. I had to take her aside and tell her what a tough little bastard he was.

It was great to see Betsy. I'd been gone so much that sometimes I didn't even feel married. A lot of marshals indulged in the unwritten "five-hundred-mile rule"—if you were more than five hundred miles away from home, it was okay to cheat on your wife. But I never did. I wasn't a saint, but I loved my wife, and I was too obsessed with hunting fugitives to even think about other women.

The next morning, I started interviewing Ricki. He played dumb. Said he couldn't remember anything.

I bagged the interview and took him out for lunch. "It's on the Marshals," I said, "so let's go someplace *nice*."

"Abso-fuckin'-lutely," he said. "*I* know a place."

He wanted McDonald's.

"What's your dream in life?" I asked him as we sat down to our Big Macs.

"I dunno. Own a Walkman?"

He had no dream.

"You ever see James Bond movies?" I asked.

"Yeah."

"Guy catches spies, right? Gets laid a lot? Drives hot cars? Well, you know who's soon gonna be the biggest spy-catcher in American history?"

"No."

"Ricki W. Blanca. *You.* You're gonna put Christopher Boyce away for good, and then there's gonna be books and movies about *you,* like there are about Boyce."

"What'll I get to *drive?*" He smirked. I had to laugh; a few days with me, and the kid already had a good bullshit detector.

That night, just past midnight, I heard a shriek. I ran into Ricki's room, with Betsy just behind me. He was having a nightmare with his eyes wide open. I shook his shoulders, and he flinched awake. He started to cry. Betsy pushed past me, grabbed him, and rocked him in her arms. He cried for five minutes while she comforted him. It made me sad to watch. Life's so brutal to the vulnerable.

The same thing happened the next two nights. Then Ricki asked if our big German shepherd, Andy, could sleep in his room, and the nightmares ended.

I stopped trying to interview him. There was no way to hard-nose this kid into cooperating. I had to play him differently. I let him spend his days with Betsy, hanging out at the beach and playing video games in shopping malls. After a while, he told her the whole ugly story of his life. It seemed to make him feel a lot better. Betsy took him to an endocrinologist, who put him on a regimen of growth hormones. Apparently, Ricki had a deficit, which the doctor thought was a result of trauma.

Betsy gave him chores around the house, and we bought him some clothes and a few essentials. He took a lot of pride in his new stuff, and took good care of it. One day, we all went out together and bought a Sony Walkman. We had to shop all over for a good price, because I was still making only about $10,000 a year, which didn't go very far with inflation at 20 percent. But he treated that Walkman like it was a Rolls-Royce.

I kept talking to him about how his testimony could do a lot of good in the world—more good than most people achieve in a lifetime. And I challenged his courage; we both knew his testimony would expose him to risk. I told him he'd probably end up in the Witness Security Program.

But as the days dragged on, I was getting scared he

Chris Boyce—the "Falcon and Snowman" spy—did more damage than any other traitor in American history. Tracking him was my introduction to major-league manhunting. It taught me a lesson: To track a criminal, you have to think like one. *(U.S. Marshals)*

A portrait of the author as a young punk: Rebel without a clue, circa 1961. Shortly after this was taken, I split from home to live in the slums of New York, and be one of Bob Dylan's sycophants.

In college—as a standard-issue flower child—I majored in philosophy and minored in sex, drugs & rock 'n' roll. I fell in love with the philosophy of utilitarianism: The ends justify the means.

Herbert H. Lehman College
of The City University of New York
Bedford Park Boulevard West
Bronx, New York 10468

John Pascucci
109 Whitman Rd
Yonkers NY 10710

094-36-1277

TITLE 3gs UN Class

ATION DATE AUG 3 1 197_

SIGNATURE

As a sheriff's deputy in suburban New York City, I mowed down murderers and battled the Mob. I thought I'd seen pure evil. But I hadn't seen nothin' yet.

I'm seated to the far right in this training academy class of freshmeat Marshals. At this time, I thought I could serve justice without breaking the law myself. People change. *(U.S. Marshals)*

I loved target practice. Because targets don't shoot back. I was the best marksman in the Marshals, but I wondered: Could I look another human being in the eyes, and then blow him away? *(U.S. Marshals)*

There are two things I love most about law enforcement: (1) ensuring justice, and (2) kickin' ass and drivin' fast. *(U.S. Marshals)*

Alleged Nazi war criminal Bohdan Koziy—the Child Killer—eluded justice for forty years. He was one of the "uncatchables." But I knew more tricks about manhunting than he knew about hiding. Such as how to get into my target's psyche. OSI, the government's Nazi investigation agency, said this was what Koziy looked like, but the face looked like that of any of a million wrinkled old men. However, after I learned to think like Koziy, his evil face came alive to me, and I could have spotted him anywhere.
(Stephen Crowley, courtesy of Department of Justice)

I waded through a snake pit to get this surreptitious surveillance photo, which I.D.'d Nazi mass murderer Bohdan Koziy. What would you do in this situation? Process his case through the proper channels? Or save paperwork and blow him straight to hell?
(U.S. Marshals)

Konrad Kalejs was accused of murdering 13,000 Jews, then lived the good life in America. Ten thousand Nazi war criminals escaped to America; so, on average, every American town or neighborhood of 25,000 became home to a Nazi murderer. The horrifying thing about evil is not so much its depth in an individual, but its breadth in the everyday world. It's so common. If you look for it, you find it. If you've got the guts to look hard enough, you even find some in yourself—and that's the most horrifying thing of all. *(U.S. Marshals)*

I'm accepting an award from Howard Safir—the Boss—who was the man that made the Marshals the greatest manhunting agency on earth. Safir was a consummate administrator and a man of high intelligence, integrity, and sophistication. But he was also a former gunfighting street cop, and there were all these legends about the guy, like, that he'd gone into the desert with a gun and a burro and had come out with forty smugglers. *(U.S. Marshals)*

When you hit a house, every instinct in your body is screaming YOU DO NOT BELONG HERE! *(U.S. Marshals)*

I was one of the most decorated men in the modern era of the Marshals, but it didn't do me any good. It just made me a more visible target. *(U.S. Marshals)*

Sometimes, after months of tracking a fugitive all over the world, I'd look at this picture of my wife, Betsy (with our dog, Andy), and wonder if it was worth it. But then the trail would get hot, and I'd forget everything except the puke I was chasing.

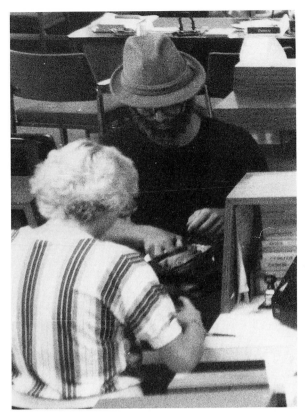

Because Soviet superspy Chris Boyce was heavily disguised in all the bank jobs he pulled while he was on the run from me, the FBI—the "Feebs"—declined to prosecute him for the robberies. Guess who inherited the job. *(Federal Bureau of Investigation)*

After I left the Marshals, I did some work for Hollywood. Here I am on a movie set. But in my heart, I'll always be a manhunter.

When I started tracking Dr. Josef Mengele—Auschwitz's "Angel of Death"—I had little more to work with than this old photo. I was determined to make the search for Mengele my greatest manhunt ever. But when I heard that his compatriots were tracking *me,* I was afraid it might be my *last* hunt. *(Department of Justice)*

Every fugitive has one fatal weakness. In a manhunt, you get inside your target's head and ferret out that weakness. You make yourself feel what he loves, because love is vulnerability. But the evil Dr. Mengele—shown here as a clean-cut young man—hated everything and everyone, except his son. His son was his one weakness. So that's what I used. *(National Museum of Auschwitz-Birkenau, courtesy of the U.S. Holocaust Memorial Museum)*

wouldn't flip in time. The trial was only two weeks away. Still, I played soft-sell.

Then, one day at the beach, a stranger mistook him for my son and said we looked a lot alike. Ricki just *glowed*. I put my arm around his shoulders. Suddenly, he began to spill his guts. He told me the whole story of life at Celia's. Ricki had seen enough to put Boyce away for thirty more years. Ricki could also lock up Celia James: He'd seen her trying to wash money that had been stained by a bank's dye bomb.

I went over that and other important scenes with him again and again, trying to get the little details that would convince the jury.

"When you went with Celia and Boyce to the laundromat," I said, "did they have the right change to wash the money with?"

"Probably not. They never did *anything* right."

"There's a convenience store across the street. Did you maybe go in *there* to get change?"

Ricki was smart; he knew how to take a cue. "Yeah, I went in there to get change. Eight quarters."

"That might not have been enough."

"Twelve quarters is what I got."

"Did you maybe buy anything else? Can of pop?"

"Yeah, a can of *orange* pop. And beef jerky."

"Good."

We went on like that for days. Of course, that kind of coaching is strictly illegal. But it's done by virtually every lawyer and prosecutor in America—not that they would *admit* it.

After ten days of rehearsal, we were ready to return to Idaho. I hated to leave. Being at home with Betsy and Ricki and the dog was the closest I'd gotten to a normal family life in three years.

Besides, the way things were in Idaho, I wasn't sure that once I went in, I'd ever come back out. I told that to Betsy, but she told me I was just paranoid.

About five minutes after Ricki and I touched down in Boise, I knew I wasn't.

* * *

I could see there was trouble when we were met at the ramp by a phalanx of local officers. They encircled us in a "security formation" and double-timed us to a waiting car.

John Durant was in the car, with an armed patrolman in the driver's seat. We squealed off.

"Things have been hot ever since you located Ricki," Durant said. Worry lines had started to cut into his eyes and mouth. "According to the sheriff, there's a hit man after one of our witnesses."

"Which witness?"

"Tony Wallinson—a kid who was occasionally out at Celia's. The sheriff found out about the hit, and told Tony. Tony came to see me, totally spooked. So I called the sheriff. And the sheriff goes, 'I didn't tell him that.' " Durant made an ugly face; he didn't trust the sheriff. He thought the sheriff was mixed up with Celia's crowd.

"So a couple of days later," said Durant, "there was a murder across the Montana border, in Libby. The victim was peripherally involved in our case. You'd recognize the name." He told me the name, and I did recognize it. "They apprehended a suspect. And get this: He had a list with five names on it. The first name was the victim's, and it was crossed off. The other four names were all witnesses in our case."

I glanced at Ricki, and he seemed to shrink within himself.

"Some people have also been calling the FBI, making death threats."

"Against who?"

"Me and you."

"Think the whole thing is Celia's work?"

"Probably. But not necessarily. FBI says there's a hit against *her,* too. But maybe that's just a cover—something she cooked up herself, to misdirect our attention."

"Could be. But I bet some of the people she dealt with want to see her gone. Back east now, any mob guy over the level of captain who gets busted is automatically whacked. They won't even *chance* a rat-out." I tapped the driver on the shoulder. "Officer, take some evasive action, will ya?" I was concerned about a red hatchback that had been behind us since we'd left the airport.

"They made a move against me last night," said Durant as

the driver took a hard left turn. "They came into my motel room and tore it up. Luckily, I was gone."

"They find anything important?"

"No, I carry all the key stuff with me." He patted his briefcase.

"Officer Pascucci?" said the driver, "I think we do have a tail."

"Red hatchback?" I asked. The driver nodded. "Good—it'll give me a chance to test this thing." I pulled out a guarded-channel radio that Kupferer had just bought from the CIA. Since our take-down of Boyce, we'd started getting better equipment and more money.

I called the local police station and requested backup.

In a couple of minutes, a sector car pulled in behind the hatchback. I got the unit on my radio. "Officers," I said, "do a felony hot-stop on this hatchback. Be advised they may be armed."

The police flashed their cherry top, and the hatchback pulled over. The police found a Mini-14 with a four-power scope. Beside it was a loaded magazine. ATF computers showed that both guys in the car were members of the Order, one of the Aryan Nations groups. But they were Idaho residents with hunting tags, so there was really nothing to charge them with. They were released.

I didn't care. I had enough to worry about. The trial was two days away.

Boyce strutted into the courtroom in a brown velvet three-piece suit, grinning at the cameras and waving to the crowd. The attention lit an inner glow in him.

While we were waiting for the judge, a line of people holding copies of the *The Falcon and the Snowman* formed in front of Boyce's table. Everybody wanted an autograph. Boyce didn't even try to hide his pleasure.

Finally, it was time for Boyce's attorney to make his opening statement. He looked confident. He told the jury that no bank teller would be able to identify Boyce, and that fingerprints taken by the FBI had not implicated Boyce. The only eyewitnesses against Boyce, he said, were the Perrys—*admitted* bank robbers who were being *paid a reward* to betray

Boyce. "A lot of what the government says is *conjecture*," he argued, "and it will *still* be conjecture after the government presents its case."

For the first couple of days, the Perrys took the stand. Their presentation was good. I'd told them about the importance of details, and their testimony was crammed with exact descriptions of the banks they'd robbed, and how they'd robbed them. By now, there were even *three* brothers ratting out Boyce. During my investigation, I'd discovered that Mike and John's other brother, Tommy, had also been involved.

All of the Perry boys looked great now, with new haircuts and nice suits. But—let's face it—they were *still* the Perrys. The jury didn't look very impressed with them.

On the second day of the trial, Mike Perry testified against Celia James, tying her to the robberies. Suddenly Boyce lunged forward in his seat and yelled, "That's all perjury, Mike! That's all perjury!" He had to be restrained.

In the gallery, I whispered to John Durant, "What was *that* all about?"

"Boyce is gonna bust his ass to keep Celia clean. The rumor around the jail is that if Boyce doesn't clear Celia, the Aryans are gonna kill him."

"Why?"

"They're scared that if she gets convicted, she'll cut a deal. If she starts talking, there's no telling *who* will go down."

After the Perrys finished, we brought out our ancillary witnesses—mostly bank tellers. But they were weak. None of them could make Boyce.

The jury did *not* look convinced. It was up to Ricki.

When Ricki took the stand, he could barely see over the microphone. The bailiff had to get a law book for him to sit on. He was wearing a suit, but it was a little boy's suit, with gold buttons on the cuffs. It was the only thing we could find that fit him. He looked cute, but I didn't want him to look cute. I wanted him to look like a tough little bastard who'd seen the inside of a crime ring.

Ricki did a good job. He didn't miss a detail. But when he stood up to leave, I didn't like how the jury looked. They were confused. They'd heard Blanca say all the right things, but their attitude seemed to be: What could this little *child* know?"

I didn't like how John Durant looked, either. Worried.

After adjournment, one of the marshals working Boyce's transport detail took me aside. "Kupferer wants a top gun on the convoy back to jail," he said. "Can you give us a hand?"

"What's up?"

"The Feebs out of Seattle said Jimmy Frattini and Tony Mulhill are in town." They were two prominent Northwest bank robbers. "Supposedly, they're gonna break Boyce out."

"Any report on what they might be carryin'?"

The marshal began to read from an FBI memo. "One .44 Magnum; one .357 Magnum; one .38-caliber pistol; one submachine gun; ten pounds of C-4 explosives; two hand grenades."

I got a sinking feeling in my belly.

I went to the back hallway, where Boyce was waiting, and grabbed one of his elbows. "Looked *bad* for you today," I chirped. I sounded much more confident than I felt.

But Boyce looked genuinely unconcerned. "It *really* doesn't matter," he snapped.

The transport went smoothly, but I couldn't fall asleep that night. *"Doesn't matter?"* What in the hell did that mean?

Was there really a breakout in the works? The ride from the courthouse to the jail would have been the easiest time for someone to make a move—but maybe the plan didn't involve violence. Maybe all the information about weapons was just a smokescreen, meant to divert attention from the real plan.

I told myself just to go to sleep. Didn't work. I was full of doubt, and wanted to do something. *Anything.*

At about midnight, I got dressed and headed for the county jail.

I made my way back to Boyce's cell in the men's security section.

It was empty.

I ran down the cellblock and grabbed a guard. "Where's Boyce?"

"They moved him to the women's security section, cuz it's empty."

I hurried over to that section. I applied for clearance to see his cell. No dice—the turnkey wouldn't admit unauthorized visitors.

"Do me a favor," I said. "Have somebody check his cell. Humor me."

He sent back a guard.

Minutes later, the guard came running back. "He's gone! His cell door was unlocked!" The turnkey started pushing buttons, and in the distance I could hear the muffled blare of alarms.

"Lemme in!" I demanded. One of the guards tossed me a gun, and I rushed into the bowels of the prison.

I ran through the cellblock, scanning the dark corners. Guards were everywhere, looking spooked.

Minutes later, an all-clear sounded, and just after that two deputy marshals quick-stepped past with Boyce.

They threw him in a cell, slammed the door, tested it, then tested it again.

Boyce stood with his face pressed against the grill-covered window of his door. He was dark with rage.

I walked around a corner and started talking softly to a guard. In the near-empty cellblock, though, our voices carried.

"How the *hell* did that happen?" I asked.

"Somebody from the sheriff's office came to visit Boyce. After the visit, the door was left unlocked."

"How far did Boyce get?"

"Too far. He almost made it."

"Well," I said, "that was his last chance. He's a dead man now."

"*Dead* man?"

"Shhh!" I put my finger to my lips, but didn't lower my voice. "The guys at Leavenworth already have a contract for him."

"From who?"

"From the Aryans. They're *tremendously* pissed. They say if he'd really wanted to save Celia's ass, he would have confessed. They say he's goin' back to jail anyhow, so he oughtta just take the whole rap and let her off."

"He's too pussy for that."

"I know. And now he's gonna pay for it."

We both laughed softly, and I left to go cover up the escape attempt. If it hit the newspapers, Safir would have my ass.

The following morning, Christopher Boyce pleaded guilty to all thirteen counts of bank robbery. He took sole responsibility and pleaded with the court to dismiss the charges against Celia James.

I'd like to think I "helped" him decide to do the right thing. But maybe he'd been planning to confess all along. I didn't know, and I didn't care. The job had gotten done. That was all that mattered.

Boyce was sentenced to twenty-five additional years.

A day after Boyce confessed, the trial continued, now focusing on Celia James.

Ricki Blanca again took the stand. He was superb. He vividly described her washing the money.

As he came off the stand, he walked past Celia. Suddenly, his face contorted into absolute grief, and he knelt and threw his arms around her. "I'm *sorry*, Celia," he sobbed—loud enough for the jury to hear—"but I *had* to tell the truth."

He stumbled out of the courtroom in dejection. I followed him. As soon as we were in the hallway, he leaped up and threw his fist into the air. "I *burned* the bitch, didn't I?" he whooped.

Celia James was found guilty of bank robbery, conspiracy, and harboring a fugitive, and was sentenced to five years in prison.

As we waited for James to be sentenced, I enrolled Ricki Blanca in the Witness Security Program. He was the first child ever admitted into the program as a protected witness.

Ricki was delighted. He felt like a hero—and he was. He had big plans for his life now. Because of the growth hormones, he was even starting to get taller.

But a day later, I had to go to him with bad news.

"It's your stepdad, Ricki. I'm really sorry, but he's dead."

Ricki got still as stone.

"Who killed him?" he asked.

"It *might* have been an accident. He was hit in the head by a limb, out in the woods. We don't have a suspect."

Ricki sat for five minutes without moving.

"I may have to roll over on you," he said.

I didn't know he knew what "roll over" meant. I had to smile.

"Celia's friends might kill me," he said, "and you won't." He shrugged his little shoulders. "It's a pretty simple choice."

"Do what you gotta do, Ricki. I don't give a shit. My work's done."

The next day, before he left for Witness Security, Ricki Blanca made a statement to the court. He said Celia James had nothing to do with the robberies, and that he'd testified against her because he'd been "manipulated and bribed with new clothes and video games."

Celia James used Ricki's statement to apply for a new trial.

The judge denied the application.

Shortly after that, the slow, old sheriff spent an entire day meeting with associates of Celia James.

That was the last the sheriff was seen. Without notice, he left town.

Money from his office treasury was missing, and it was believed that he left with it.

John Durant came to my motel room as I was packing to leave.

"John, I want you to stay," he said. "I've been authorized to offer you the position of sheriff."

"I can't stay."

"Please," he said. *"Think* about this place. Have you ever seen a more beautiful little town?" He swallowed. "You and I could make this a *good* town," he said.

But I wanted to make more than just this *town* good. I wanted to make the whole *country* good. I was the Gipper's cop—and I could do *anything*.

"John, I can't."

But I was extremely touched—not because of the offer, but

because of who it came from. John Durant was as brave as men get. I faced danger all the time—but I always left it behind. Durant stayed.

I took his hand. "Thanks, man." Over the last couple of days, I'd gotten letters of commendation from a number of prominent people, including U.S. Attorney General William French Smith and Idaho Senator Frank Church. Durant's offer meant more than all of them combined. "We'll work together again," I said.

The war between the Aryan Nations and the U.S. Marshals was just beginning. Before it was over, good men would die. Assholes, too.

John left looking lonely.

Suddenly, I yearned to be home. In my mind, I saw Betsy's face—her small Irish mouth, her green, happy eyes.

I sat on the bed for a long time. I was lonely, too.

We were in a lonely business.

Before I left, I stopped to see the Perry brothers. They were half stoned and half drunk, and were raving about some scheme to find buried silver in the Bitterroot Mountains.

"I hope you guys are gonna be a little more careful about who you hang out with," I said.

"Believe me, we are," Mike said.

But they weren't. Two years later, Mike and Tommy fell in with another bank robber, and in a panic one afternoon, Mike shot and killed a policeman. Mike was sentenced to die, and Tommy got life in prison.

When that happened, I didn't try to help them. By then, they were no longer *my* sons of bitches. They were just sons of bitches.

On my way out of town, as I headed for the airport in Boise, I went to see Levy the Indian boy. I was going to urge Chief Levy to get the hell out of here. Too many people connected to the investigation were dying.

The second I saw his campsite, I knew something was wrong.

Some of his gear was knocked over, and there was rotted

food outside his tent. Except for the buzzing of flies, the campsite was quiet as death.

Judging by the food, he'd been gone at least a couple of days.

I didn't touch anything. I drove back into town and called the acting sheriff. He said he'd send out an investigator. I told him to have someone question the meth monster, and I gave him directions.

But no one ever called me for a statement.

I felt sick. If Levy was hurt, or dead, I was to blame. Jesus Christ—how many people did I have to destroy to achieve something good?

But I couldn't sit around and worry about that. If I did, I'd get paralyzed with guilt. And I couldn't afford paralysis. To achieve *anything,* I needed action, action, action.

Levy was gone.

So be it.

Christopher Boyce and I sat side by side in a small government jet as we began to lift over the clouds. I was taking him to Leavenworth.

Boyce pulled out a stack of mail, and lifted a pink envelope off the pile.

According to the return address, it was from his mom.

The letter was less than a page, but he stared at it for ten minutes.

Finally, he whispered under his breath, "Jesus, what did I do to you?" He didn't mean for me to hear.

But I did. "You fucked her over real *good,*" I said. *"That's* what you did." I pointed to a town below us. "Just like you fucked over all those people down there, and everybody *else* in the country."

He peered out the window for a long moment. His face was dark and full of thought.

Then he pulled his face away from the window. *"Fuck* those people." His mouth twisted with contempt.

I closed my eyes, to burn the memory of his expression into my brain. In the years to come, I would need that memory, to remind me that catching him had been worth the fear and pain. There'd been so much of it lately. There had been the pain of going up against Rufus the Mob Bomber, so I could get assigned to the Boyce Task Force. There'd been the fear of running unprotected across the vast parking-lot kill zone in the Black-Thomas raid. The pain of wasting months of my life on assholes like Tommy Lynch and Frank Riley. The pain of telling Ricki Blanca his stepfather was dead. The pain of walking through Levy's deathly still campsite.

When I opened my eyes, the sneer was still frozen on Boyce's face.

After we'd been in the air about half an hour, a high-ranking marshal who'd flown in from headquarters asked me to join him in the front of the cabin. He was jovial as hell. Throughout the Service, everyone was feeling giddy. After the Boyce capture and conviction, the threat of the Marshals being disbanded had evaporated into thin air. Reagan loved us now, and let everyone know it. We were *his* kind of cops. Our arrest rates were higher than ever before, and *much* higher than the federal arrest records would later be, in the 1990s.

"Got some good news for you," said the headquarters man. "You've been promoted to G.S. nine. You're a full U.S. marshal now." He held out his hand, and I shook it. "Got somethin' else too," he said. He handed me a gold-embossed Special Achievement Award, signed by Attorney General William French Smith. "Congratulations," he said. "These things are very rare."

"Who put me in for it?"

"Chuck Kupferer. He's very happy with you," he said. "Chuck says you always get the job done, no matter what."

I didn't respond. I was getting leery of compliments. They always seemed to be attached to an ugly new assignment.

"So he wants you to stay in Idaho for a while, to work on something really big. There may be a connection between the Mafia and the neo-Nazis. Chuck tasked you with finding out what's going on."

He opened his briefcase. "I've got a dossier for you." He pulled out a legal-size enveloped marked EYES ONLY.

"Here's some of the people who may be involved," he said. He handed me a stack of photos, and I began to flip through them. Some looked like wise guys, and some looked very clean-cut. Suddenly I stopped. I saw a face I'd seen before— in a Volkswagen van on a moonlit night. It was the face of evil.

The courier gave me a long look. "Do you *know* this guy?" he asked.

"We've met."

"Well, it looks like you're gonna meet him again."

Chapter Seven

Power

• The Nazi/Neo-Nazi/Mafia
Conspiracy • Flash Money • Computerized
Manhunting • Kickin' Ass and Drivin'
Fast • Satanism • Mexican
Interrogations • Murder as a Procedural
Matter • My Dark Side • More
Necessary Evil •

"I have become what I have beheld."
—Eliot Ness

Shi-i-i-t!" I grabbed at my guts and braced for a crash.

Our plane veered headlong at a rock wall. The wall rushed at us, growing larger and more detailed by the second.

The pilot of the little Cessna gasped for breath. His hands were white on the stick.

He jammed the stick down and to the left. The wall swooshed around to our right. The wing almost smashed into it. The pilot jerked the stick back and I almost puked from the sudden increase in gravity.

Then we began to level off. The pilot slumped back in his seat. He tried to catch his breath. "That cliff's a *tall* son of a bitch," he panted.

I didn't answer.

"I'll try to take a better *run* at it," he muttered.

"Good idea." I tried to stay cool as we backtracked away from the wall, but I couldn't keep my legs from trembling.

We gained altitude. He swung the plane back toward the wall. We kept climbing. The wall got closer. Closer. I could see the cracks in the boulders.

We skated over the top.

Suddenly, an immense forest came into view—a limitless green expanse broken only by the icy white tips of the Bitterroot Mountains and a few blue dots of water.

The Northern Idaho scenery was diametrically different from where I'd been the day before—the flat plains of Kansas, where I'd dumped Boyce at Leavenworth—but it didn't look beautiful to me anymore. Now I saw the Idaho wilderness as just a vast hiding place for scum.

We were in the plane searching for a property that Kupferer had told me to find. He'd heard that the mob was building a retreat up here. He'd gotten the information from a hook in the secret Los Angeles Police Department Intelligence Unit. The unit was not supposed to exist, but it did.

The Intelligence Unit, which targeted organized crime, believed the Southern California Mafia and the Idaho neo-Nazis had started working together. The unit suspected them of running guns and drugs from border to border, moving fugitives, laundering money, and collaborating on bank robberies. The Idaho neo-Nazis were in the early stages of a three-year, twenty-million-dollar bank robbery spree, and the mob generally demanded a piece of any organized criminal entrepreneurship.

On the face of it, of course, the two groups had dramatically opposing philosophies. But as I've said before, philosophy has nothing to do with crime.

"Check that out," I said, pointing to a clearing near a lake.

The pilot zoomed low over the clearing. It was nothing but

a barn with some vehicles around it. "Let's try again," I said, "but even lower."

This time, I noticed something suspicious. There were half a dozen pickups, Blazers, and cars around the barn, and not one of them was worth less than $30,000. This was *not* Old McDonald's Farm. For whatever reason, it was a nexus for money. I plotted the place on my map, and we flew back to town.

I went to the courthouse to find out who owned it. The deed was held by a real estate holding company in San Jose, California. I spent the rest of the day on the phone, trying to scam information out of the holding company. But I hit a dead end. The paper on the place belonged to a bank in the Cayman Islands. Unraveling an offshore scheme is almost impossible. But I had an idea.

I drove out to the postal substation closest to the farm, and got with the postmaster. I asked him to look at his records on postal boxes. No dice: rules and regs. It was the usual Barney Fife bullshit, a typical government-punk power trip. But I let him know real quickly that I was the guy who'd put away Chris Boyce and Celia James, and all of a sudden the rules and regs flew right out the window. We scanned his list of box holders, and he recognized all the names, because he'd lived there since about the Jurassic era. Then he came to the name "Miguel Sanchez": someone he didn't know. Miguel Sanchez had rented the box just six months ago—on the same day that the San Jose holding company had taken title to the property.

Every box holder has to list a street address on his application, so I asked for Sanchez's address.

"He's in San Why-*sid*-roe, California."

"San Ysidro?"

"Yep."

"Great!" I was going home. San Ysidro was a suburb of San Diego. It was the seedy little border town where I'd gotten the Mexican cop out of jail for Brick, just before I'd joined the Boyce Task Force.

I was so anxious to get out of Idaho that I didn't even call Kupferer. I just grabbed a plane. I had a whole packet of airline vouchers now; they were one of the perks I'd gotten after closing the Boyce/James case. I'd also gotten a $50,000 flash-money account. Since Boyce, the Marshals Service was the federal government's Flavor of the Month, and everybody was throwing money at us. Congress suddenly loved us, and so did a few private sector "angels." The Marriott hotel chain, for example, had started offering us deep discounts. They loved the idea of being a "sponsor" of America's hottest law enforcement team.

Best of all, the Justice Department was suddenly crazy about the USMS. Reagan was pushing Justice to go easy on white-collar crime, antitrust infractions, and civil rights, and focus instead on the Marshals' primary interest: street crime. The rising star in the criminal division, a young lawyer named Rudolph Giuliani, wanted the federal government to *double* its criminal prosecutions, and was counting on the Marshals' Fugitive Program to help reach that goal.

Besides the Fugitive Program, the Service was still responsible for all its traditional duties: guarding courthouses, transporting prisoners, running the Witness Security Program, and responding to civil disturbances that violated federal law. Our real glory work, though, was Fugitives, and Justice was doing everything it could to empower us. The A.G., William French Smith, was a 24-karat puke buster and cop lover. He even favored drastic things like "preventive detention"—putting mutts away *before* they caused trouble. Smith was rumored to be leaving, but his heir apparent, Ed Meese, was even tougher. Meese hated the Bill of Rights— he said it shouldn't be enforced by the states—and he called the Miranda decision "infamous."

Under any president other than Reagan, the American public would have been freaked out by such a fascist approach. But Reagan, who *oozed* paternalism, packaged it as "tough-love," and most Americans bought it.

For an old street-fighter like me, it was a wonderful time to be the president's cop. The Marshals were flying high, and I was in the vanguard of the Marshals' ascendancy. My reputation was soaring. I was the guy who "got the job done." I had more power than ever, and with my promotion to G.S. 9—as a full U.S. marshal—I was suddenly able to make about $25,000 a year. For the first time in my life, I was able to indulge a little. I started buying myself expensive suits. I was still just thirty-four and was poised to take the next big step—into management.

Even so, I was nagged by the feeling that I still had to prove myself to the patriarchs of the Service, like Kupferer and Safir. In a way, I still felt like a kid trying to impress his dad by bringing home rolls for breakfast.

But busting a neo-Nazi/Mafia conspiracy, I figured, would impress *anybody*. It would be the type of sexy bust Safir and Kupferer loved. We'd be in the newspapers for weeks and emerge with more power and money than ever.

In San Diego, I stopped off to see Betsy—for all of forty-five minutes. Then I headed for the street address in San Ysidro. Unfortunately, it was just a mail drop—one of those commercial places people use when they need to have a street address. I tinned the guy behind the counter, but got nowhere. He was an old raisin who'd seen it all and had learned to keep his mouth shut. Probably half his clients were dope runners or illegal aliens.

But I had flash money now, and that changed everything. My new motto was, When in doubt, *buy* something. I put the guy on the books for $500, and it did amazing things for his citizenship. "Every Tuesday Mr. Sanchez comes and gets his mail," he said. "Just after we open."

When Tuesday rolled around, I was there early. At 9:05 A.M., Sanchez came in. He left in a blue Cadillac with B.C. plates—Baja, California.

I followed him across the border to Playas de Tijuana, the upscale seaside village near Tijuana. He pulled into a gated plaza, handed his keys to a uniformed valet, and disappeared into a plush private club. From behind a ten-foot stucco wall, I could hear the sounds of people splashing in a pool.

I drove to downtown T.J. and went to city hall. Even with my training academy Spanish, I was well received, because I had a complete set of Mexican Federal Judicial Police credentials. I'd gotten them from Brick's Mexican Army Intelligence hook—the guy I'd sprung from jail. The Federales credentials gave me the power to execute search warrants, make arrests, detain suspects, seize property, rape and pillage—you name it. Of course, my having the credentials was *completely* illegal—in both countries. But fuck that. I *loved* them. In America, I was a cop, but in Mexico, I was a *dictator.*

The private club, according to city hall records, belonged to a corporation controlled by Señor Luis Morada. Name didn't mean shit to me.

I hurried back across the border; as a Federale, I could zip through customs in a special lane. At the San Diego USMS office, I flipped on my computer terminal and ran Luis Morada through a number of programs, looking for triggers. I came up dry. Then I keyed him into a DEA program.

His name was plastered with red flags. Señor Morada was a suspected dope czar. I immediately lost interest in Sanchez; he was just Morada's gofer.

When I looked up from the terminal, it was dark. The office was empty. Hard to say how long I'd been there. And I didn't care. I wanted to stay all night. I grabbed five bottles of Coke, lined them up on my desk, and went back to work.

I wanted to learn everything I could about Louis Morada. So far, Morada didn't have any U.S. warrants. But I could change that. I could change *anything.* I was Rambo's cop.

I tailed a silver, chauffeur-driven Mercedes as it pulled out of the gated club in Playas de Tijuana. According to Tijuana's Motor Vehicles Division, the car belonged to Luis Morada.

I had a photo of Morada from Motor Vehicles, and it matched the guy sitting in the backseat of the Mercedes. Morada was on the move.

Morada's chauffeur didn't seem concerned about surveillance—probably for a simple reason. He was a Mexican cop.

Morada's car drove to the airport outside Tijuana, and Morada—with no luggage—disappeared into a Mexicana Airlines VIP lounge. I covered one of the exits, but he never reappeared.

Back to San Diego. I got on the phone with the hook I'd developed at Qantas Airlines during the Boyce investigation, when I'd been tracking crazy Frank Sweeney. I told my Qantas contact that his help back then had broken open the Boyce case, and that I'd just been authorized by Attorney General William French Smith to send him a token reward payment of $200, plus a Letter of Citizen Commendation from the USMS. All bullshit, needless to say, but by the time I was done, he felt like Dick Tracy.

Then I hit on him. Where had Luis Morada flown yesterday? Had he flown Mexicana? Was he going someplace he visited regularly?

My contact promised to pull some strings, and find what he could.

While I waited for him to call back, I wrote him a $200 check out of my flash-money account. Even if he couldn't help on this caper, it was still a good investment. Sooner or later, I'd need him.

Three hours later, my hook got back to me. Luis Morada had indeed flown on Mexicana Airlines, first class, to Asunción, Paraguay. He had stayed overnight, then flown back. He made the same one-day trip about once every month.

I told my hook how much the Gipper and I appreciated his work. When I hung up, he was in a postcoital glow.

Paraguay! Paraguay was not prime *dope* country. It was prime *Nazi* country. And not neo-Nazis: *old* Nazis, from World War II.

My conspiracy was getting sexier by the second. Nazis. Neo-Nazis. The Mafia.

I was electrified. I'd never felt more alive.

While my head was still rushing with adrenaline, I got a Telex. From the Central Intelligence Agency. It was a "request" for me to call a CIA agent at the Langley, Virginia, headquarters.

Though I would later be the Marshals' chief liaison officer with the CIA, I hadn't dealt with them before, and I was a little unsettled. But the guy I called—who was with the Narco-Terrorist Unit—was all charm.

"Deputy Pascucci, I got info-copied with a need-to-know memo from DEA this morning," he said. "Apparently, you ran a search through their system on Luis Morada. Am I right?"

"Yeah, you are."

"Well, DEA has no contraindications against your investigation, but I'm going to have to give you an off-the-record briefing on *our* dealings with Morada."

"Fire away."

"Any federal search on Morada triggers *our* computers," he said, "because we have an open file on him. To get straight to the point, Inspector, I'm going to have to ask you to desist your activities on him because he's part of an ongoing operation of ours."

"May I ask what *type* of operation?"

"It's a dark op, Deputy; national security is involved. I know you understand. But let me say this, and this is *strictly* off the record. Right now, the director"—he meant CIA Chief William Casey—"thinks there is a fifty-fifty chance the Mexican government will fall. In the near term. He calls Mexico 'the next Iran.' The Soviets are operating unchecked out of their Mexico City embassy, and the Cuban activity in Mexico is increasing exponentially. The Communist presence there is becoming untenable."

He stopped. He'd told me nothing but had implied everything; Morada might be a Nazi-helping, dope-running son of a bitch, but he was the CIA's *anti-Communist* Nazi-helping, dope-running son of a bitch. Therefore, he was one of the Good Guys.

A few minutes later, Kupferer phoned. He'd just gotten a call from a senior Justice official, who had been briefed earlier that morning by CIA. Kupferer told me to suspend my investigation. "Everybody's hinky all of a sudden," Kupferer said. "It's just not worth it."

I didn't argue. No point in it.

I felt empty. I sat at my desk for an hour, staring at my terminal.

I *hated* the idea of walking away.

I especially hated walking away blind, without even knowing what I'd stumbled onto. But maybe I could do something about that.

It was time to drive across the border and see somebody who owed me one.

I walked unannounced into Manuel Fuerte's office at the Mexican Army Intelligence Unit in Ensenada. "Manuel! How goes it?"

"My friend!"

I told him my story about Luis Morada and the CIA, and he nodded quietly, as if none of it were news to him.

"I'm willing to lay off this guy," I said. "But I wanna know what's goin' *on.*"

"Let's go for a walk," he said.

When we got outside, I said, "What are you worried about? Do your people bug you?"

"Noooo," he said sarcastically. *"Yours* do." He stopped and bought a sugar-drenched pastry from a street vendor. "You helped me," he said, "so I will try to help you. I believe that what you suspect is true. I believe that German refugees from the Second War, who are now in Paraguay, Brazil, and Argentina, are trying to help the neo-Nazis in North America. I *believe* this, but I do not *know* this. It appears as if Señor Morada, who is active in anti-socialist politics, is somehow involved with the two groups. We believe he provides armaments to them.

"But on this situation, my hands are tied together, for the same reasons that yours are. Your State Department, at this time, is exerting extreme pressure on my government to resist Communist influence. And that influence is very *strong* now. Mexico is a poor country, with many unhappy people. For many, many years, the Nazi elements in South America have helped to oppose the Communists, and so also have the organized-crime families. Therefore, your State Department is not very antagonistic to these people. Please understand— this is a reasonable thing."

But I already knew this stuff. I was wasting my time.

Manuel saw the dark look on my face and smiled grimly. "I know that for a simple policeman, like you or me, this is very frustrating. These forces—the Nazis, the new Nazis, the crime families—they are very"—he struggled for the right word—"they are very *interesting.* And most of what simple policemen do is very *uninteresting.* But still, our uninteresting work is *important.*" He seemed to brighten. "Come, I want to show you something."

We returned to his office, and he opened a locked file cabinet. "As you know," he said, pulling some documents out of the cabinet, "I do a certain amount of . . . consulting . . . for the U.S. government. I work primarily with your men in

201

the border towns—El Paso, Tucson, Brownsville, Yuma. *Good* men. Nice men. I also work with their counterparts on the Mexican side of the border. But it is very difficult work that we do, because this border area has the highest incidence of crime in all of the Americas. My men on the Mexican side, though, are *very* valuable in this work, because they do such thorough interrogations." He looked away from me. He meant that the Mexicans used torture.

He unfolded a United States map and spread it on the table. All along the border, on the American side, were red dots. Emanating from the dots were red lines, connecting to the larger Southwest towns. From those towns, a series of blue lines ran to major cities all over the United States. From the major cities, green lines ran to practically every town in the country. Splattered all over the map were purple dots. The map was a spider web of lines and dots.

"What am I lookin' at?" I asked.

"A picture of crime in America. The red dots on the border are landing strips used by drug smugglers. The red lines leading from those dots are the primary distribution routes. The blue lines and green lines are secondary routes. The purple dots are drug-related murders."

"How'd you get all this?"

"Very aggressive police work."

He looked away again.

Then he pulled a stack of computer printouts from the cabinet. It was four inches thick, and when he tossed it onto his desk it made a hollow thud. It was nothing but names, most accompanied by addresses. Thousands and thousands of names.

"This list goes with the map," he said. "These are the people involved."

I flipped through the list, page after page.

Never before had I seen such an extensive list of criminals who were still at large. It was unsettling.

I had already seen the ugly side of America, and I had known that surely more ugliness existed, just beneath the surface. Now I felt as if I were peeking beneath that surface for the first time. It was like walking down the hallway of a slum tenement and suddenly having all the doors flung open, and seeing the squalor behind them.

I was repulsed. And fascinated. "Who's seen this?" I asked.

"Not many people. My superiors are not very interested in American crime. They say we have enough crime of our own. And your superiors do not want to . . . reimburse me . . . so they have not seen it. I thought that perhaps you could speak to them?"

"I'll mention it." I tried not to sound encouraging. I couldn't see the U.S. government buying a list that had obviously been derived from torture. That was something the government just didn't *do*. At least, that's what I thought then.

"Well, do not worry about it," he said. "I showed you this just to make a point, because you seem so unhappy." He ran his fingers through the list. "All these people? Almost *none* of them are interesting criminals, like your Nazis. They are just common criminals who are in and out of prison all their lives. They have no intelligence, no glamour. But they commit *many* crimes."

I was always looking for ways to motivate myself, and now I'd found one. All those pukes! Running free!

Manuel must have seen a change in my face because he grinned and slapped me on the back.

All of a sudden, I felt like going out and grabbing mutts. Just common criminals. But not by the dozens, or the hundreds. I wanted to bust them by the *thousands.* And I knew of a fledgling USMS program that might be able to do that. I wanted to go see Kupferer and Safir, and volunteer for it.

I had a feeling—for no good reason whatsoever—that I would eventually catch up with the neo-Nazis—including Gerry Whitaker, the "face of evil."

And I was right. I'd meet Whitaker again soon—and I'd enjoy the meeting more than he would.

For now, though, the Nazis and neo-Nazis would have to wait.

While I stood in front of them, Kupferer and Safir talked about me as if I weren't there.

"John's *executive* material, Howard," said Kupferer. "He was indispensable on Boyce, he nailed Celia James, and he took down Rufus Donner damn near single-handedly. If he wants to work FIST, I think we oughta let him get his feet wet, and then give him a FIST of his own."

Safir's controlled, rectangular features didn't move. He hated to make a decision until he'd considered every angle. He was particularly careful about important, new programs, like FIST, which was his baby. The Fugitive Investigative Strike Team was a mass manhunt for criminals, and was Safir's latest strategy in the Fugitive Program. It was based on the same idea that Manuel had argued: America was crawling with common, recidivist criminals—ignorant punks who got almost no public attention because their crimes were so mundane. But it was these *career* criminals, Safir thought, who were at the heart of crime in America. In the mid-1980s—believe it or not—this was a hot, new concept.

"Did you know," Safir said to me, "that the hard core of career criminals, just six percent of all criminals—"

"Commit seventy percent of all crime?" I interrupted. "Yes, I did know that." I'd done my homework. I'd read the most recent Justice Department monographs on crime. What I'd learned was fascinating.

Astonishingly, by the mid-1980s, no coordinated, multi-agency program in American law enforcement had ever targeted career criminals who had become fugitives—even though a high percentage of recidivist criminals were on the run. Half of all major city police departments didn't even have a fugitive squad. Because of this reluctance to tackle a tough job, there were well over a quarter of a million fugitive felons roaming the streets of America. Almost all of them, because they were wanted, were blocked from normal sources of funds: jobs, welfare, food stamps, and government-subsidized housing. Therefore, it was almost axiomatic that they would commit more crimes to survive. In fact, each year in New York City alone, about ten thousand fugitives were arrested for a new crime.

But, it wasn't *just* their inability to make a legal living that made these people continue to commit crimes. Of all suspects out on bail—who *were* eligible for normal sources of income—thirteen percent still committed crimes to support themselves. They *liked* crime.

"I have an idea on how to *improve* FIST," I told Safir. "As we search for fugitives, we should make a computer entry on everything we do, and everything the fugitives do. Then we could write a program on fugitive hunting.''

"That's quite interesting," said Safir, in a monotone. His black bar of eyebrows lifted slightly. I couldn't tell if he meant it. Safir was impossible to read. He was the consummate bureaucrat, analytical and conservative. But there were all these *legends* about the guy—like, he'd gone into the desert with just a burro and a shotgun and had come back with forty drug smugglers. Stuff like that.

"Would you be willing to start at the bottom?" Safir asked. "In a four-man car in Detroit? We're going to run a FIST over the whole state of Michigan, and I need to task some experienced manpower with Detroit."

"I'll go wherever you send me, Boss." I could never bring myself to call him "Howard."

"Well, good luck with it," Safir said, rising to dismiss me. "Memo me on your computer idea as you develop it."

Kupferer walked me to the door. "You're gonna love FIST," he said. "It's the closest you'll ever get to bein' a TV cop. It's nuthin' but kickin' ass and drivin' fast."

"Sounds *won*-derful," I said. It really did.

And it *was* wonderful. The operation lasted about ten weeks, and it was nonstop thrills. Every day, I, another U.S. marshal, and two Detroit beat cops worked the slums of Detroit, following up leads on fugitives. Most of these skells were easy to find; they'd been ignored by the police for months or years and weren't keeping low profiles. We hit ten to fifteen houses a day, and averaged three arrests a day. We made almost every hit with our guns drawn, and we kicked the door about half the time. Because most of our targets were predicate felons—bad-ass criminals with multiple convictions—43 percent of our arrests were of armed men. In just over two months, the Michigan FIST arrested 928 felons, who had 3,631 prior arrests.

I could tell you a lot of war stories about FIST, but they'd all start to sound alike. And that was *exactly* the point of FIST: We were operating a repetitive, military-style program.

There was a big payoff in the repetition. Patterns emerged.

I began to write a computer program. Within a few years, my program would be used by the DEA, the FBI, and the USMS.

When the Detroit FIST ended, Kupferer and Safir moved me into my first executive position. We began a FIST operation over the entire state of California, and I was put in charge of the San Francisco office. I was in charge of fifteen men, and delegated virtually all of the street work. For about fourteen hours a day, six days a week, I'd sit in an office with a phone in each ear and a computer terminal in my face. I hated it. No adrenaline. But as Dick Nixon said, The measure of a man is not how well he does what he likes, but how well he does what he hates.

Safir loved my paperwork because it was so statistically detailed. William French Smith wanted a statistical analysis of crime in America, and Safir used me to provide it. If the A.G. called Safir one morning and needed to know what percentage of bank robbers were blue eyed, I'd have the answer by afternoon.

Reagan's people were thrilled with our blitzkrieg against crime and started lavishing even more perks and privileges on us. Safir was grabbing more money, equipment, and power for the Marshals than we'd seen in a century. Reagan loved to whine about cutting the federal budget, but for the war on crime, nothing was too expensive. The Justice Department's budget had ballooned to a record $2.5 billion, and personnel had shot up to 54,000 employees. An unprecedented 92 percent of all of Justice's employees were working in the criminal division. While street crime busts were soaring, white-collar arrests were down 18 percent. That was natural, of course, since Reagan and William French Smith—a former Rodeo Drive society lawyer—loved America's business elite. And it was a godsend to the Marshals, because street crime was our specialty. We were achieving the best crime/arrest ratios in history—better than any before or since.

The Marshals were entering their golden era, and I was tasting some of the rewards myself. In San Francisco, we busted a meth magnate—a crankster gangster—who owned a 1960 red Corvette convertible—the same car Todd and Buzz drove in *Route 66*. I seized the car for my own use. The meth maker had used it as a souped-up decoy car; it had traveled with a drug-loaded car, and if police gave chase, it would speed away, to draw off the cops. Therefore, it had a hot transmission and an engine the size of a rhino. After a long day, I'd take my 'Vette out on the Pacific Coast Highway and turn it loose.

In the ten-week California FIST, we made 2,116 arrests, busting mutts with a total of 10,215 prior arrests. Of the felons we arrested, 505 were armed and dangerous. At that time, it was the most successful fugitive roundup in American history. But it was nothing compared to our next two FISTs.

In late 1984, Safir organized a FIST for a seven-state area in the Northeast and put me in charge of a squad of thirty men. In that FIST, we took down about three thousand felons—seventeen hundred of them armed and dangerous—with twelve thousand priors. In the following FIST, which covered Florida and the Caribbean, we made four thousand pops on guys with eleven thousand priors.

The press loved the FIST operations, and I was given a free hand to talk to reporters. My name started to pop up in the *New York Times* and other major papers. It was a big ego trip.

By mid-1985, I felt like I'd earned the right to run a FIST of my own. I brought up the subject with Kupferer, but he shrugged me off.

I went to Brick, who was still my unofficial rabbi. He told me there was some lingering doubt about me. I always got the job done, he said, but "some people" felt that I was more interested in my own glory than the Marshals'. He gave me the old speech about always putting the Service ahead of yourself.

I *was* ambitious. I couldn't argue that.

Even so, I got pissed off. How many skells did I have to face down? How many laws did I have to break? What did it *take?*

I was about to learn. But after I did, I'd wish that I'd never found out.

While I was driving to work in Springfield, Illinois—my home base at this time—the car phone in my 'Vette rang.

"Head for the airport." It was Brick. He sounded grim. "We just lost a man. Steve Thompson, out of Florida."

"Shit. Who got him?"

"That's for you to find out. Safir wants you on this full-time."

"Any leads?"

"Yeah, a brother. But I don't think it was him. Whoever did it tortured Thompson first—cut the shit out of him. Thompson's head wasn't even on his body. Not your typical family dispute. Looks like a cult to me."

"Satanists?"

"It could be." There was far more activity by Satanic cults in the 1980s than the public ever realized. I'd seen several cases of it, mostly involving ritualistic child abuse. But most enforcement agencies tried to cover it up. Publicity just encouraged it.

"John," said Brick, "if it is a cult, keep your head down, okay? You don't want 'em knowin' where you live."

Five hours later my plane touched down in Indianapolis, where Steve Thompson's car had been found. I stopped at the airport gift shop, bought a couple of clean shirts, and headed straight to the local FBI office.

The Feebs were involved because the victim's car had crossed state lines. Officially, the FBI had jurisdiction in the case, but protocol allowed participation of the slain officer's agency.

I didn't want to work with the College Boys. The Bureau was too prissy, and they fucked up too often.

But the guys in the Indianapolis FBI office were great. They were all ex-cops—no lawyers or college kids. They knew the streets.

By the time I got to their office, it was after dark, and the only agents left were sitting around drinking beer. They stashed it in their desk drawers, in case anybody important walked in.

First thing they did was brief me on the brother, who was the prime suspect. His name was Nick, and he was the family's black sheep. Both brothers had grown up in Indianapolis, and Nick supposedly still lived around here—which certainly increased our suspicion of him, since this was where

Steve's car had ended up. Steve had been a model young-ster—a bodybuilder and good student who'd later joined the local sheriff's department. Nick, though, had become a junkie and had consorted with every puke in town.

According to the Bureau guys, witnesses had seen a recent fistfight between the two brothers.

"I'll tell you what bothers me," I told them. "The murder apparently took place under an overpass near Tampa, Flor-ida, right? Well, why would a guy whack his own brother out in public? He woulda had access to the victim in private, where it would have been easier to conceal the crime. And what about this torture business? I've never even *heard* of that in a family dispute. Let's consider somethin' else, too— Thompson was shot with his own gun. If Nick was pissed off enough to torture Steve, wouldn't he have brought his own gun to the scene?"

Some of the Bureau guys were nodding. But not all of them. "Two brothers drivin' down the highway," one of them said. "Hate each other's guts. Steve stops to take a piss. Nick can't stand it anymore. He pulls out a knife and sticks his brother. Brother's all *indignant* about it, gives Nick a raft of shit. Nick starts slicing and dicing until Steve's finally a little *respectful.* Then Nick realizes he's gone too far. He takes Steve's service revolver outta the car and—ba-bing!— Steve's dead. I could see that. I think Nick's good for it."

"Question is," said another, "if we catch this cop killer, are we gonna bring him in? Or just smoke 'im?"

Everybody got real quiet, and I could feel them stealing glances at me. The agent shouldn't have spoken so bluntly in front of a stranger. One of them said, "Heyyyy," as if he wouldn't even consider such a thing. But that was just for my benefit. The fact is, cop killers *usually* have a hard time making it safely into custody. In the large East Coast cities, particularly New York and Philly, it's common practice for police to murder cop killers. The public doesn't know that, but all the mutts do; we make *sure* they do. It's our life insurance.

To break the tension, I said, "Well, if I had my druthers, he'd come in cold." That got the discussion going again.

The next morning, an FBI agent and I worked the computers, to see if Nick was already in custody. He wasn't. So we drove out to his last known address, and started talking to the usual sources—neighbors, the landlord, the postmaster, the phone company, the relatives, and the vendors in the area: the bars, restaurants, and motels. We put out a nation-wide BOLO—"be on the lookout for"—and entered Nick into the National Crime Information Center computer. Then we prioritized our information according to credibility, and ran down our leads. But by the end of the day, we didn't have shit.

Safir wanted a daily update, and I was dreading the call. I hated to let him down. I also hated the ass chewing I knew I'd get.

The situation called for aggressiveness—and imagination.

I found a city cop, tinned him, and found out where the local drug scene was centered. It took me about two minutes to spot a street corner dealer. "This is the easiest money you'll ever make," I told him. "Tell me who's lodged in local jails for dope, and I'll give you fifty bucks." He gave me about ten names, and I paid him. I could have gotten the same information from the local authorities, but it would have taken four hours—plus bureaucrat-length coffee breaks.

I hit the city jail, but none of my dopers knew Nick. Couple of cons *said* they did, but I gave them a quick quiz on Nick and they flunked.

The reason I wanted an informant who was already in custody was because I'd have leverage on him. A junkie on the streets would never turn in Nick, but my junkies in jail were dying to help me, so that I'd help them. Of course, that also made their information suspect.

At the Marion County jail, I found my man. He was an old running mate of Nick's and had watched Nick get smacked around plenty of times by local cops who were trying to help Deputy Steve Thompson straighten out his fucked-up brother.

According to my snitch, Nick was in a halfway house for addicts in Louisville.

I called the halfway house. Nobody answered. But it was almost midnight.

Early the next morning, I went to the FBI office to call the halfway house again, but the Bureau's Agent in Charge intercepted me. He had an elderly deputy from Steve Thompson's hometown in his office, and the old guy wanted to search Steve's car for evidence. That was fine with the Agent in Charge, but the Bureau's regional crime scene specialists—who'd already searched the car—were being all pissy about it. They said the old deputy could read their reports but couldn't lay a finger on Thompson's Chevy Blazer. No good reason—just typical Bureau arrogance.

But it embarrassed the Agent in Charge. He asked if I'd get one of my superiors to call one of his superiors, to grease the skids for the deputy. According to him, that would be easier than his trying to climb the Bureau's rigid chain of command. So I called Kupferer, and he called his counterpart at the Bureau. Permission granted.

Before I could call the halfway house, the old deputy stuck his head into my cubicle to say thanks. Colorful old guy—he looked like Gabby Hayes. "Remember," I said, "those Bureau guys ain't cops, they're *specialists,* so they probably skipped the obvious places, cuz they weren't a *challenge.*"

He liked that. "I'm gonna look *ever*-where," he said. "Nobody can teach me nuthin' 'bout searchin' cars."

I finally made my call. Bad news. My snitch was right on the money. Nick was in-pocket at the time of the murder. He'd made all his roll calls on the day Steve disappeared.

Now we had no suspect. And no leads.

I had to call Safir with the news. But I procrastinated. I wrote a letter to the local DA, telling him what a good citizen my snitch in County was.

Then the old deputy sauntered in. He waltzed into my cubicle and took a seat. Big grin. He opened a billfold and started to toss its contents onto my desk. A gasoline credit card. A few receipts.

"Who's this belong to?" I asked.

"The shooter. It was in the car."

"I'll be damned. *Where?*"

"Behind the seat."

I held up my hand for a high five. But he must have thought I was just waving, because he waved back.

*   *   *

I telexed out a BOLO on our new suspect, entered him into the NCIC computer, and called Safir with the update.

To most people, the wallet might have looked almost empty—just a few receipts and one credit card—but to me, it was crammed with triggers. Each scrap of information led to something new that, in turn, triggered something newer still.

The suspect's name was Jerry Smeed, and he'd recently lived in Indianapolis. That probably explained why he'd driven Steve Thompson's car here. It also created the possibility that he had known Steve when Steve had lived here in Indy.

The crime had happened on July 13, and on July 16, Jerry Smeed had spent the night at the Salvation Army Mission in Louisville. That was another interesting coincidence: Louisville was where Steve's brother was. Conceivably, the brother had hired Jerry Smeed to kill Steve, and had then paid him off in Louisville. But if Smeed had just gotten paid, why would he have crashed at the Mission?

I was *glad,* though, to see that Smeed had stayed at the Mission. It indicated he probably wasn't a solid citizen whose wallet just *happened* to be in a murder victim's car.

While I waited for the full crime-computer profile of Smeed, I developed other information. Smeed had sold a Gold Cross pen and pencil set to an employee of the Mission. If I could tie that pen and pencil to Steve Thompson, Smeed would be in very deep shit.

Was Smeed still on the move? I hoped so. If he was, he'd leave tracks. I called the airlines, Amtrak, and Greyhound. No sign of Smeed. Then I called the police in the Indianapolis suburb where Steve Thompson's car had been found. I wanted to know if any vehicles had been stolen on the same day that Smeed abandoned Thompson's Blazer.

Bingo! On the day the Blazer was found, a 1969 Ford had been stolen—three blocks from the Blazer. Excellent news. It reinforced the probability that Smeed was a mutt. If, as I suspected, Smeed had stolen the '69 Ford, it wrapped Smeed in three thousand pounds of steel, labeled with license plates. I entered the stolen Ford into a nationwide missing vehicles computer, and amended my BOLO telex.

My crime-computer profile of Smeed came in. As I'd suspected, he had a nice long sheet—a number of arrests, and a couple of extended incarcerations.

While I was reviewing Smeed's record, one of the Indiana Bureau guys ran down a lead on some people who had arrived at the Louisville Mission with Smeed. They were low-lifes, but as nearly as I could tell, they were just hitchhikers that Smeed had picked up. Still, I had two men sit on their apartment.

I called a jail where Smeed had served a burglary sentence, and sweet-talked a woman in the warden's office into giving me Smeed's list of visitors. One of them was his mother.

I called Smeed's mom up, and did sort of a hillbilly accent. "Mizz Smeed?" I said, "My name's Bob Zimmerman, and I think I found a wallet belong to your son. At least, there's a piece-a paper in it with your number, and it says 'Mom.' So I was hopin' you could tell me how I could get 'hold of him to return it, 'cuz there's about three hundred bucks in it."

She sounded suspicious. She told me to send the wallet to her.

"Well, ma'am, I really think I oughta be givin' this straight to the person who lost it. No offense, a-course." She wouldn't budge. "Okay, I unnerstand," I said. "What I'll do is give it to the police, and let them give it to ya." She hated that idea.

It seemed as if she knew he was in trouble. And she probably knew where he was.

After I got off the phone, one of the Bureau guys gave me a note. It had the phone number of a pawnshop on it, and said: "SMEED TRIED TO PAWN RING HERE—*USMS* RING."

We had our shooter. I was gut-certain.

I called Safir's office with the news. His assistant told me that the Boss wanted me in Steve Thompson's hometown, Tampa, Florida. "Mr. Safir's not happy with the way our Tampa people are handling this. He wants you to go there and take over."

"Oh, they'll love that."

"Don't worry about them. Worry about Mr. Safir."

It was time to break things loose.

I called back Smeed's mother in my normal voice. "Mrs. Smeed, my name is John Pascucci, and I'm with the U.S.

Marshals Service. A law enforcement officer just gave me your son's billfold, which he received from a private citizen. Based on where this wallet was found, we have reason to believe your son may have knowledge of a crime. We'd like to speak to him. Do you know how we can reach Jerry?"

"No, I don't. I've had some problems with my son, and we're not in close contact." She didn't mention the call from the "hillbilly."

My bullshit detector was going batshit. She knew. And, somehow, I was going to flip her. Against her own son.

The marshal in charge of the Tampa investigation freaked when I showed up. "You *sandbagged* us, you smart son of a bitch!" he yelled. "You knifed us in the back!" I kept my cool and let the old bastard run out of steam.

Before long, he got tired of busting my balls and headed off for a Geritol break. His assistant ushered me to my office. It was the janitor's closet. They'd put a phone in it, and a folding chair.

I drove out to Steve Thompson's house, to try to get a feel for the guy. Why had this happened to *him?* Often, crime victims are just people who were in the wrong place at the wrong time. But just as often, there was something in their personality or lifestyle that had triggered their victimization and that sheds light on the crime. Maybe they were risk takers, maybe they were confrontational, maybe they were stupid—or maybe they were doing something illegal themselves.

Thompson's roommate answered the door. He seemed pretty fucked up by the whole thing, and that made me uncomfortable. I'm not good at letting people cry on my shoulder. I feel like they expect me to fix everything.

"Do you mind if I look around a little?" I asked. "Maybe it will help me understand why this happened."

"I don't mind," he said. "But I don't think there's *ever* a reason for a person to be tortured to death."

He had a point.

We wandered around. Standard "guy house"—macho, messy, and nothing matched.

"Is this Steve's office?" I asked as we walked into a room with file cabinets and a desk.

"It *was.*" He got a little teary.

I opened the door of an adjoining room. "Jesus!" I said. It looked like an office supply store. Boxes of supplies were piled ten feet high: folders, tape, pencils, typewriter cartridges—you name it. One box was crammed with thousands of loose paper clips.

Problem was, most of the boxes were labeled "USMS." Steve Thompson was a petty thief.

And maybe he was more than that. I'd come to believe that most petty thieves became major thieves—*if* they got the opportunity. And Steve had had plenty of opportunity. The whole state of Florida was floating in drug money. According to the FBI, every dollar bill in the state of Florida had at least a trace of cocaine residue on it. I wanted to find out if Steve had gotten greedy. If he had, maybe that's what had gotten him killed.

I drove to the county courthouse and punched up Steve Thompson's death records. Steve had died intestate, without leaving a will. That was good news. It meant that the local probate court would have a list of his assets, along with the names of the people that the court was considering as his probable heirs.

When I saw the list of Steve's assets, I was shocked. He owned property all over Tampa County and Manatee County. His assets far out outstripped his salary as a marshal. Maybe Steve had been independently wealthy. Not likely. Steve's parents, who were both dead, had been working-class people.

It looked to me as if Steve Thompson had been dirty.

Among the probate court's list of probable heirs was the name of Steve's junkie brother, Nick. But the court hadn't been able to find Nick. Next to Nick's name was a notation, saying that the court would hold Nick's money until they could find him, and rule on his possible claim to the inheritance. Under the notation was the name and number of a professional heir finder—a private investigator who located heirs and took a cut of their inheritance.

I called the heir finder and told him where Nick was.

"Appreciate it," he said, "but I just found Nicholas myself. My problem now is he may not get any money at *all*. Steve Thompson's roommate is now claiming that *he* oughta get

all the money, on account of an oral contract he says he had
with Steve. He says him and Steve were real close."

"Real close?"

"Yeah, *real* close. As in, they were blow-brothers."

I immediately called Brick. Things were getting messy.
Headquarters had a lot to think about. A dead agent. A dead
agent without a head. A dead, headless, and possibly *dirty*
agent. And now a dead, headless, dirty, *gay* agent.

Brick got pissed, like all this was *my* fault. "Find out what
you can," he said. "Try to find out if Jerry Smeed was homosexual. If he was, maybe this was a lover's spat. Or maybe it
was a love triangle between Smeed, Steve Thompson, and
the roommate. But be *discreet,* for God's sake. And try to
stay ahead of the Bureau. They'd love to tag us with something like this."

I took a stack of mug shots of Jerry Smeed and headed for
a little strip of gay bars just outside Tampa. I showed the
pictures around, asking guys if they'd seen Smeed.

Of course, I wasn't just fishing for information on Jerry
Smeed. I was also hoping to find out about Steve Thompson.
But you can't just go into a gay bar and start asking about
the sexual orientation of a prominent murder victim—who
just happened to have been a federal agent. That kind of
investigation always landed in the local news.

Off in one corner, nursing draft beers and gazing into each
other's eyes, were two jug-eared hillbilly characters in dirty
jeans and flowered shirts: Homer and Jethro Go Hawaiian.

I showed them the picture of Smeed. "Ever seen this guy?"
They shook their heads. "He's a suspect in the death of Steve
Thompson, the U.S. marshal."

That got a rise out of them. "No shee-yut?" said Homer.
He traded a smirk with Jethro.

"Do you know anything about Steve Thompson?" I asked.

"Nope," said Homer.

"I'm a federal officer," I said, "and I believe you're with-
holding information and obstructing justice. You're under
arrest."

"Well, then, yes," said Homer. "We knowed him. A little
bit."

Within five minutes, Homer spewed out one of the strangest stories I'd ever heard. It boiled down to this: Steve Thompson was a serious S&M freak who had paid men—including both Homer and Jethro—to sodomize him until blood had run down his legs. Then Thompson would pretend to turn the tables and "rape" his "assailant."

I took Homie and Jethie straight to a private polygraph analyst and paid cash for a test, using my flash money. I still didn't trust polys, but I knew headquarters would want some objective verification of their story. I also knew Brick would want the poly done back-channel, in case headquarters wanted to bury the story.

My hillbillies passed the test.

The Steve Thompson case was starting to look *incredibly* messy. Jerry Smeed was probably the only person who knew what had really happened. But I had a couple of theories of my own.

One theory was that Jerry Smeed had known Steve Thompson through S&M circles. That might explain Thompson's torture—which had been horrific, according to an updated report from the coroner. Thompson's penis had been cut off, his fingers had been mutilated, and his eyes had been gouged out. Maybe Smeed was just a stone sadist who'd gotten carried away.

I also had a "money theory." Maybe Smeed and Thompson had been in business together, and Thompson had double-crossed Smeed. That, too, might account for torture. Maybe Smeed had tortured Thompson to extract information.

I called Smeed's mother again. I leveled with her, and told her Jerry was a suspect. I told her we knew his license plate, and that we were closing in. Then I went for the kill.

"Mrs. Smeed, I'm going to tell you something that I'll later deny. It's this. In a few days, after we catch Jerry, he'll be dead. I overheard a conversation with the officers running the case. They said the only way to stop cop killers is to kill them. That's what's going to happen to Jerry.

"Now, Mrs. Smeed, do you know any police officers personally?" She said she did. "Good. Call that officer. Ask him, just hypothetically: Do cop killers ever get murdered by the police? You ask him that, and then you'll know that I'm on *your* side, tryin' to keep your son alive."

I was gambling, of course. The cop she knew might just bullshit her, and say cop killers never got iced. Or—if he was a small-town cop—he might never have *heard* of such things. But she lived in Jersey, just outside New York, so it was a safe gamble.

She called back early the next morning. Scared to death. I played her very sympathetically, like I was a father figure who just wanted the best for Jerry. After all, he'd been such a *good* little boy; surely it wasn't *his* fault he'd tortured someone to death.

I got her to agree to a consensual trap-and-trace. Jerry was calling home almost every day. He wouldn't tell Mom where he was, but we could figure that out.

Since the breakup of Bell Telephone, though, it had become much more difficult to trace a long-distance call. The first time Jerry called—later that afternoon—all we could tell was that he was west of the Mississippi.

The next evening, though, he called again, and we isolated him to the Northwest quadrant of the United States.

The third time he called, we determined he was in Colorado. The next phone call would give us a specific location.

I made a bet with one of the Tampa agents that Smeed would turn up in Denver, which was a nexus for fugitives. Thousands of them passed through there on their way to the Northwest, Southern California, Canada, or Mexico. Right then, though, was a bad time to be a fugitive in Denver because the city was crawling with federal agents. A Denver talk-show host, Alan Berg, had just been murdered, apparently by neo-Nazis. All the enforcement agencies were competing to break the case.

While I was waiting for Smeed's final call, Brick telephoned. He sounded frantic. He hated the way this case was unfolding. "Get up here," he said. "We've gotta figure out what we're gonna tell the Old Man." He meant Safir. "And we've gotta talk about damage control. Jesus!" he hissed, "a scandal like *this,* just when we were startin' to get some respect on the Hill!"

Just minutes after I arrived in Washington, Smeed called his mother. Smeed was in a bar in Denver. I called the Denver Marshals' office and arranged for two deputies to hit the bar. "Call the FBI first, though," I told them, "and coordinate the bust with them. Otherwise, they'll get pissed off."

By the time I got to Brick's office, Jerry Smeed was in custody. But Brick was steaming. "Those Bureau pricks!" he snarled. "You know what they did? When our deputies called them, like you asked, the Bureau guys said they'd meet 'em across the street from Smeed's bar. Our guys waited. But the Bureau guys never showed up. The Feebs went straight to the bar, popped Smeed, and recorded it as their own arrest!"

Brick couldn't sit still. His huge body was flopping around behind his desk like a beached shark. He obviously had more on his mind than just the FBI.

"At least we got Smeed," I said. I felt like saying, At least *I* got Smeed—but there was no point in grandstanding. Brick knew I was dying for a FIST of my own, and that after finding Smeed, I deserved one.

Brick kept fidgeting. "What's eatin' ya?" I asked.

"I just keep thinkin' about somethin'," he said, looking past me. "There was a story in the papers not long ago about some New York City cops who were movin' a cop killer. They were takin' him from Canada back to the city. But the mutt made a break, and they hadda shoot 'im. It made the papers cuz the puke was in *restraints* at the time, and liberals were goin', Gee-that's-*harsh*. Course, the whole thing blew over, like it always does. Internal Affairs called it 'officer discretion,' and let it go. But it just got me thinkin': Damn, I wish *Smeed* would try to rabbit, cuz this whole Steve Thompson business is gonna look like shit when Smeed goes to trial. You *know* Smeed's lawyer is gonna try to impeach Steve's character. And it's just not fair. I don't give a good goddamn if Steve was gay, or stealin' paper clips, or spankin' hillbillies, or whatever. We can probably cover all that up. The point is, he was a good agent, and by God, that's all that matters. I tell ya, John, somebody oughta *do* somethin.'" Brick's voice trailed off, and he kept staring out the window. "Know what I mean? Do somethin' *fast*, before the shit hits the fan."

I studied his face. Had he just broached the subject of murdering our suspect? I didn't say anything.

"Anyhow," Brick said, "I think I may send you out to Denver to bring Smeed in. This is a goddamn touchy situation, and I don't want it gettin' any more out of control than it is."

This time, Brick looked me straight in the eye. I didn't look away. Why should I? I was Rambo's cop. I could do anything.

I spent the night in D.C., waiting for another meeting with Brick.

It was a hard night. One of the hardest of my life. I felt scared—much more scared than I ever felt when my own life was in danger. I was scared of what I might have already become, without even knowing it.

Maybe I was just another asshole with a gun.

If I was willing to kill a prisoner *just to make Brick happy*—and to advance my own career—then I was no better than my pukes.

But there was more to it than that. Smeed deserved to die. He'd murdered someone. *Tortured* him. But Smeed would probably work the system, and eventually win release. Then he'd kill someone else.

Besides, if I allowed Smeed to discredit the Service, what would it mean to the Big Picture? We were the only agency in the country going after career-criminal fugitives; if our FIST programs got cut back because of a scandal, how many innocent people would die?

It was weird to weigh a man's life against the life of a law enforcement program, but that's what it boiled down to. Sometimes, in the federal bureaucracy, murder was just a procedural matter. It was a necessary evil.

Finally, I turned off my brain and let my feelings take over. As I've said, my own sense of morality comes from my heart, not my head. And my heart said: Go ahead.

When I dragged into Brick's office, I was half sick with nervous exhaustion. But I'd made up my mind. I was going to do the right thing.

"You look like hell," Brick said.

"I feel like hell."

"How come? You been thinkin' about what we discussed yesterday?"

"What else?"

"I understand. Look, hypothetically, if you were assigned to this prisoner transport, how would you do it?"

"I'd put just one man on the detail, because it's just a short drive from the jail to the airport. No follow car—because we have no reason to believe this skell has any friends who'd try to help him. I'd avoid the center of town, to stay out of traffic. I'd move Smeed on surface streets to Lowry Air Force Base, where we'd meet a government plane."

"Sounds like you've thought about it."

I just shrugged.

"Would you volunteer, John? To be the man to take that drive?"

"Yeah. I'll do it."

"Good man."

"But only if there's *no alternative.*" I said. "Only if we explore all the other options first."

"Well, you can count on that."

I sat there, feeling dizzy and stoned, like I was watching myself in a movie.

"You're a valuable agent, John. You're gonna go a long way in this agency."

"That's the *last* thing I want to hear."

Brick looked at me coldly. "No, it's not," he said in a monotone.

I started to argue. But he was right. Some dark part of me didn't care about anything but myself.

I stumbled out of his office.

I was still in D.C. the next afternoon, waiting for the transport assignment. My nerves were raw. I jumped every time someone spoke. I didn't like myself. I'd already made so many sacrifices to get where I was, but the more I gave, the more the Service wanted. Now they wanted my soul. It was terrifying—but not as terrifying as the fact that I was willing to give it.

To settle myself down, I went out to the Marshals' firing range. I still loved to shoot, and I was the best shot in the Service. I'd won so many awards I no longer bothered to keep them. For me, the joy was in the act—feeling the big

221

balls of lead alloy fly out of the barrel at four thousand feet per second ... hearing the roar ... seeing the blue flame burst forth. It was almost sexual. Made me fell omnipotent.

But while I was waiting to shoot, some marshals from headquarters—guys I didn't know—started to talk, and I eavesdropped. I only got about one-tenth of it, but it was enough to make my heart start pounding. The gist of it was: One of their secretaries was buddies with Brick's secretary, and Brick's secretary thought "Steve Thompson got what he deserved."

What the hell did *that* mean?

I went to Brick's office when I knew he'd be out for lunch. I acted annoyed when his secretary said he wasn't there, and told her I'd wait. I was wearing an expensive blue wool "power suit." I was going to play Brick's secretary, and I wanted to look like one of the bosses to her.

I sat there for half an hour before I said anything. Then, very casually: "So what's your take on Steve Thompson? Half the people—I'm talkin' about people who know the *real* story—say he got what he deserved, and the other half say he didn't. I don't know *what* to think."

"Oh, Brick doesn't want me talking about this stuff."

"I know, I know. And that's good. But you won't be tellin' me anything I don't already know."

She paused for a while. She wanted to talk. People *loved* to talk—and that was my most powerful weapon. She took a gulp of coffee and said, "Personally, I think he *deserved* it."

"You're probably right. You really are. But, I keep thinkin' about his family."

"Well, Steve *Thompson* should have thought about his family before he tried to rape that boy."

"You're right. I know. You're right. But you know how people are. Especially *guys.*"

"I'm sorry, there's no *excuse* for it. What goes around, comes around."

"It *does.* You're right."

Jesus H. Christ! Steve had tried to *rape* Smeed? Was *that* what Brick had wanted to cover up—by killing Smeed?

I felt like puking. My guess was that Brick had known

about the rape when he'd sounded me out about icing Smeed. Fucking *Brick!* He was *playing* me.

Now it was time to throw a fake on Brick, and get to the bottom of this.

When Brick returned, I followed him into his office. I closed the door.

"You *fuck,*" I barked. "How fuckin' dumb do you think I am?"

He sized me up. He could see I knew something. "I-know-I-know-I-know," he blurted. "I just found out about it myself. I spent half the morning talking to Smeed's lawyer. I called your hotel, to brief you."

"The hotel said I didn't have any messages."

"Deputy, in my line of work, you don't always *leave* messages."

"So brief me."

"How'd *you* hear about this?"

"I can't say. Just brief me."

"Okay. According to Smeed—who already passed a poly on this—he was hitchhiking when Steve Thompson picked him up. Then Thompson stopped his car in a deserted area, pulled a gun on Smeed, and ordered Smeed to give him a blow job. When Steve's pants were around his knees, Smeed knocked him over, grabbed Steve's gun, and emptied it into him. Then Smeed panicked and ran. When he discovered he'd killed a federal agent, he kept running."

"What about the mutilation?"

"The coroner called on that yesterday. He has a new finding. Now he's sayin' that wild animals did it."

"Animals severed the *head? Ate Steve's dick?*"

"Apparently. Florida's got all kindsa critters. *Hungry* bastards."

"When did the coroner call?"

"I just told you. Yesterday."

"I mean, before or after you saw me?"

"After," Brick snapped.

I thought he was lying. But I wasn't certain.

"Well, I'm sure as hell not gonna go ... move ... Smeed now."

"Fine. Don't. We'll work something else out. If he'll keep

223

his mouth shut, we won't file homicide charges. That won't be a sure thing, like . . . the other option. Smeed still might blab. But if we gotta do it, we'll do it, and take our chances."

I got up to leave. "But I'll tell you this, Deputy," Brick said. "Your commitment to the Service has been noted, and ya got some goodies comin'. Don't quote me on this, but you're in line for a G.S. eleven, with the rank of inspector—it's the military equivalent to a captain. Also, we already got the paperwork started on another Special Achievement Award. We just need the A.G.'s signature. Plus—and this is the part you're gonna love—it looks to me like you're ready to command your own FIST.

"Like I say, nuthin's official. But . . ."

But the fix was in.

I finally had what I wanted.

I should have felt good.

I was made executive in charge of the Southwest FIST, the largest felony-fugitive manhunt in world history.

The Southwest FIST covered California, New Mexico, Arizona, and Texas. I directed hundreds of men from the USMS, the U.S. Border Patrol, the U.S. Immigration and Naturalization Service, the Mexican Federal Judicial Police, and 31 different state, county, and city police and sheriff's departments.

The Southwest FIST—known as the Border Sweep—was the first American law enforcement program ever to officially cross our national border. We were operational in four Mexican cities.

The first thing I did when the operation started was to call my old friend, Manuel Fuerte, to inquire about "reimbursing" him for his list of American criminals. But Manuel said he'd already sold exclusive use of his list to the DEA.

I called the DEA, but they said they "never even heard of" his list.

Fuck that. I didn't need it. My own computer work was producing data that rivaled Manuel's list—and I was doing it without torture.

In the ten-week southwest FIST, we busted 3,506 felons—the most criminals ever arrested in a single operation. We

averaged one arrest for a violent crime every forty-seven minutes. We grabbed 45 murderers, 159 robbers, 82 rapists, 734
drug pushers, 553 burglars, 25 kidnappers, 23 arsonists, and
369 embezzlers and counterfeiters.

We also made the largest drug seizure in Texas history, when
one of our investigations resulted in the capture of 862 pounds
of cocaine, worth $137 million. That seizure was worth more
than the seizures from all other FISTs combined. We also seized
large amounts of heroin, vehicles, cash, and guns.

I made it a point not to bust small-time dope users, but to
go after traffickers. Normally, only 15 percent of all narcotics
arrests were for trafficking, and the rest were for possession.
But in my FIST, 54 percent of all narcotic arrests were for
trafficking.

I hope I'm not boring you with statistics, but I don't know
how else to show you that we kicked *significant* ass. As I
mentioned earlier, at this point in the Reagan administration,
our arrest statistics for serious crime were *twice* as high as
national stats are now, in the mid-1990s. Under Reagan, we
actually made America safer.

All my life, I'd wanted to do the greatest good for the greatest number, and finally I was getting my chance. It made me
feel better about having almost murdered Smeed.

As executive in charge, though, I wasn't in on much of the
street work. I missed it. But I was learning how to manipulate
on a grand scale. For example, I learned how to work the
press. One thing the press loved was our "sting roundups"—
operations in which we'd trick a number of perps out of
hiding. So I scheduled a bunch of stings, even though they
were a piss-poor tactic, compared to computerized police
work. In a Houston sting, where we offered bogus trips to
Las Vegas, we only collared six mutts. But the press ate it
up. They gave us ink, and ink meant money—and money
meant power.

Also—and this was important to me—I was operating the
way government *should* operate—without throwing away
taxpayers' money. On all the other FISTs, the average cost
per arrest ran from $900 to $1,400. *My* cost per arrest was
$495. How? Simple answer. I *gave a shit* about money. Most

government employees don't. The way they see it, it's not their money, so who cares?

I'll give you an example. When an agency starts an operation, it rents cars. If it's a big operation, with a lot of cars, the bureaucrat can get a discount, or take an upgrade. Nine times out of ten, he'll take the upgrade. In the other FIST operations, we got Cadillacs. But when I needed cars, I didn't even *rent* them. I went to the Border Patrol and borrowed a fleet of seized cars. Some of them were real pigs, but so what?

When the standard bureaucrat rents his cars, he generally finds the closest government garage, and signs a contract for maintenance. Fuck that. I shopped around until I found a private-sector garage that would give me a great price. Then I sat down with the manager and said, "Look, if you fuck me around, I'll *kill* ya." He didn't even take offense. He was private sector.

I didn't comparison-shop on just the big-ticket items, either. If the usual government vendor couldn't sell me a stapler cheaper than Kmart, I crossed him off my list. And if I could borrow a stapler, I did that.

To save even more money, I fired the Marshals' in-house SWAT team that had gone out on all the other FISTs. All they ever did was wait around and watch TV. I also sent home our government planes and government pilots, because I could fly commercial cheaper. The SWAT guys and pilots hated me for that, and Safir worried about the Service's morale. But I said, Fuck it, let's get the *job* done, and get our morale from that.

Sometimes, I even had to break the *law* to save money. Part of my job was to prepare PR press kits, and the standard procedure was to fly in two women from our headquarters press office. But their travel was going to cost a fortune—and, anyway, they were hacks. So I found a PR firm that agreed to go on the payroll as "paid informants." I falsified their payment vouchers—*highly* illegal—and they cranked out some beautiful work. Safir had me ship him the originals of their artwork to use throughout the Service.

Reagan's new attorney general, Edwin Meese III, was particularly supportive of my tight budget. At the end of my FIST, he threw a party in Washington for me and my top managers. At one point, he took me aside and said, "You were incredible down there, John. You seized six million dollars in salable assets, and you only spent three million. You're the only guy in the government who's operating at a *profit.*" He looked half-drunk, but I still appreciated the compliment. Meese was the epitome of a tough cop, and didn't seem to mind people who cut corners to get the job done. For me, he was the perfect A.G. He loved policemen and hated the ACLU, so how could I resist his charms?

Before the party ended, though, Brick put his arm around me and said he had an interesting assignment. "We're gonna put you in charge of a National Emergency Response Team. It's only the fourth one in U.S. history."

"What now?"

"You're gonna move one of those neo-Nazi assholes. He was in on the murder of the Denver talk-show host."

"Which Nazi?"

"Gerry Whitaker. We just busted him."

"Whitaker! I met that son of a bitch one night! I call him the Face of Evil. How come you want *me* on the gig?"

"We need a serious shooter. The Feebs say Whitaker's buddies are gonna ambush the movement."

I tossed down the rest of my drink. "Brick, tell me the truth. The bosses—do they think of me as an executive? Or as a hit man?"

His face twisted in puzzlement. "What's the diff?" he asked. I kept waiting for him to laugh. He never did. Brick was *made* for the Reagan era of law enforcement.

"Back in Da Nang," said Rob Armstrong—my assistant on the Whitaker movement—"whenever we were tasked with moving a high-level VC prisoner, we'd take a *green viper* and put it in a paper sack, and set it right on Charlie's *lap.* Best *possible* way to get a prisoner to sit still and shut up."

Rob was an incredible bullshitter. But also a skilled rifleman.

"Rob, I don't *have* a green viper. Want me to requisition one?"

"No *need,* my man. A rattlesnake will be fine, and I know *exactly* how to catch 'em."

He probable did. As a Green Beret, he'd lived in the bush for weeks at a time.

"I think we'd better review other options," I said. We were driving down the interstate, trying to think of the best way to avoid ambush as we moved Whitaker from northern Idaho down to Boise, three hundred miles away. The only thoroughfares were two-lane mountain roads, and we were virtually certain—based on FBI intelligence—that the neo-Nazis would hit us as soon as we were out in the boondocks.

"What we really need," Armstrong said, "is a helicopter, and a squad of Army Rangers. Toughest men in the *world*, Rangers."

"Fine. But how we gonna get a 'copter and Rangers?"

"No problem." Armstrong swiveled the wheel of the car and suddenly we were airborne, flying across the median strip of Interstate 84, just outside Boise. We landed with a huge *whump!* and Armstrong cranked the wheel again, shooting us into the eastbound lane. "There's a miltary base just down the road, in Mountain Home," he said. "I know the base commander. *He'll* take care of us."

But when we got there, the commander made us cool our heels in his outer office. "I thought you *knew* this guy," I said.

"Well, I know *of* him," said Armstrong. "Don't worry, this is gonna be a *snap.*"

A few years ago, before my management experience, I wouldn't have had the patience for this. I'd have just bought some extra ammunition, grabbed the prisoner, and hauled ass. But I operated differently now. These days, I leveraged my power. And Armstrong *did* have some clout. In Vietnam, he'd served with Colin Powell, and he had other cronies back in the Pentagon. I decided to let him play this out.

"The colonel will see you now," said the base commander's aide.

Before we'd even shaken the C.O.'s hand, Rob started ranting. "We're executing the most important prisoner movement in Idaho *history,* sir," he bellowed, "and *you're* going to be part of it. Tell you what we need. We need two 'copters, five air policemen, two helicopter technicians, *good* radio equipment, an infrared scope, six Rangers, and machine guns to secure the refueling site. Plus, maybe a case of champagne. You know, for when we finish. Beer call."

The colonel just stared at us. Finally he said, "I can't do that. We don't mix military and law enforcement."

Armstrong waved his hand like he was shooing a fly. "No prob, Colonel! We do this *all the time.*" He scribbled a phone number, and passed it to the colonel. "Check us out," he said.

The colonel handed the number to his aide, and then started to bust our balls for wasting his time.

But half a minute later, the aide reappeared. "It's the office of the secretary of defense, sir. They'd like to talk to you."

He grabbed his phone, and his face went white. All we heard was: "Yes, sir. Yes, sir. Of course, sir. Absolutely, sir." He returned the receiver delicately to its cradle.

"I'd *like* to give you what you need, gentlemen, but I'm very sorry. I can only supply you with *one* helicopter." He buzzed his aide. "Lieutenant, get our Ranger captain in here immediately."

Minutes later, the captain arrived. Very imposing figure— a bodybuilder with striking good looks. He told us he'd hand-pick our team. "Thanks, Captain," said Armstrong. "Also, we'd like you, personally, to work directly with John and me." The captain nodded.

When we got outside, I asked Armstrong what we needed the captain for.

"Waitress bait," he said.

We set up a command post from the top floor of Boise's tallest hotel and sent the helicopter north. We put our radio transmitter on the roof, then ran wires to it from our room.

The mission proceeded smoothly. The helicopter picked up Whitaker late in the afternoon and headed back toward Boise.

By nightfall, the helicopter was within twenty miles of Boise Municipal Airport, and we were getting ready to go meet them. Then the radio guys on the roof relayed a distress call from the helicopter. "They're goin' down!" the radio operator yelled into his walkie-talkie. "Small plane's forcing 'em down!"

"Gimme the coordinates!" I shouted. I was trying not to

panic. But I knew the neo-Nazis had a number of small planes. Over the past three years, they'd robbed banks and armored cars for $20 million, and had counterfeited at least another million. They had better air capability than the Marshals, and at least as much concentrated firepower. Damn! I should have anticipated their using a plane.

According to the radio operator, the downed helicopter was on a country road just north of town.

"Let's go!" I yelled.

"I've gotta call my colonel," the Ranger captain bleated. "We've got *procedures!*"

"You *can't* call anybody," I said, tossing him a shotgun.

"Why not?"

"Cuz your hands are full! Let's *go!*"

"You guys are fuckin' nuts!" he screamed. He laid down the gun and stood there as Armstrong and I leaped into a car.

I drove toward our location at about a hundred mph. The car seemed to float just above the road.

We kept in radio contact with the command post as we zeroed in on the helicopter. Within minutes, I could see the 'copter's emergency flasher. But above the helicopter I saw the red light of a small plane. It was banking into a turn. I mashed down even harder on the accelerator, and we hit 110.

I heard a sharp "click" and saw Armstrong opening an aluminum case. He pulled out a mini-Uzi machine gun. Armstrong rolled down his window and trained the Uzi on the plane, which was quickly descending toward the helicopter. A tight smile twisted his face. It wasn't a smile of malice, or even anger—just pure mischief.

"That plane *better* be full of neo-Nazis," I warned him. "If it *is,* I'll do the paperwork."

"Fuck you, Pascucci," he wailed. "If it's *not, that's* when I'll need you to do the paperwork."

"No fuckin' way."

He pulled the Uzi back in and sighed. "Damn, Pascucci, you're gettin' so *conservative.*"

We screamed up to the 'copter. The small plane roared past. It couldn't have been more than forty feet overhead. As we screeched to a halt, the plane disappeared.

I badged the Rangers in the helicopter, who were relieved as hell that we weren't neo-Nazis. I grabbed Whitaker, threw him in the back of our car, and jumped into the backseat with him.

Armstrong drove to the airport at about seventy mph. Seventy felt like slow motion.

I kept my eyes on Whitaker, who was chained hand and foot.

"Remember me?" I said. "We met one night on a country road."

I didn't see any trace of recognition in his face.

"Maybe you remember a friend of mine? A hippy kid named Levy? Lived in a tepee? Grew dope?"

This time, I saw a flash of recollection. "Never heard of him." Whitaker smirked.

"Well, Levy says hi," I said. I lifted my elbow, and drove it into Whitaker's balls. He shuddered for about half a minute, then whimpered.

He didn't look so evil anymore.

At the airport, we parked beside a government jet. The command post patched me into Brick.

Brick was delighted that we'd made it.

"Don't say I told you," Brick said, "but it looks like you got a bee-you-tiful assignment comin'. Safir wants you to go find a Nazi."

"Up here? One of the Bonners Ferry boys?"

"Noooo. Not those silly-ass pipsqueaks. They're just little troublemakers." I looked over at Whitaker, who was listening. Whitaker looked like Brick had just put a dagger into him.

"I mean a *real* Nazi," Brick said, "from the *war*. You won't *believe* this son of a bitch."

As the fear and adrenaline drained out of me, I began to feel as happy as I could ever remember feeling.

Over the last couple of years, I'd helped put away thousands of evil men. Now I was going after a Nazi war criminal: evil incarnate.

I no longer regretted the sacrifices I'd made. I didn't even regret having seen the dark side of myself.

It was all worth it.

I'd done some bad things. But they had been necessary evils. Now I had power. Now I could do some *real* good.

My life made sense.

That was the last time I ever talked to Brick. Shortly after this, he transferred to the DEA. Later, he went to the CIA.

I never knew if his departure was linked to the Jerry Smeed situation. Maybe he was being punished. Or maybe he was being rewarded. I didn't know, and I didn't want to know.

I missed him. But I no longer needed him.

Because—God help me—I'd *become* him.

Chapter Eight

Mass Murder

★

• The War Criminal • America's Anti-Nazi
Boutique • Judge Wapner and Doug
Lewellen • Follow the Money • Snitches and
Hooks • The Geriatric Death Squad •
The Master Sergeant •

*"He who fights with monsters might take care, lest he
thereby become a monster."*
— *Friedrich Nietzche*

The Marshals chief of International Operations handed me
a mug shot. It was the cruelest face I'd ever seen: a tight,
angry ball of flesh with close-set eyes and a mouth that was
just a slash.

"The FBI says this Nazi is abso-*lutely* un-*catch*-able," said
Don Ferrarone, who ran our international operations.

"They *can't* catch him, or they don't *wanna* catch him?"
I asked.

Ferrarone smiled. It was easy to be cynical about the College Boys. They just weren't interested in catching Nazis.

To understand why, you have to understand that the FBI

is basically two organizations—the criminal division and the intelligence division. The agents in the criminal division are pretty straightforward: They bust mutts. But the people in the intelligence division—who investigate spies, Communists, and other threats to national security—live in a world of shadows and politics. Ever since the end of World War II, the intelligence division had been in bed with America's Nazi immigrants. Why? For the same reason the CIA had been—because the Nazis were valuable allies against the Communists.

To me, that was twisted. But, then, I'm a simple guy.

"Let's see the Nazi's folder," I said to Ferrarone. He pushed it across his desk, then started to play with some of his new CIA gadgets. Ferrarone was frequently in foreign outposts, sharing embassy space with spooks, and they were always giving him toys.

As I scanned the folder, he fiddled with some night-vision goggles that were no bigger than a pair of Ray-Bans. Also on his desk was a camera lens that fit in the stalk of a car's radio antenna, and a parabolic microphone that could pick up a whisper at a hundred yards.

I loved Ferrarone's toys. I envied his job. And in a few years, I'd *have* his job.

"Oh, my God," I moaned.

"What?" said Ferrarone, looking at me through the goggles.

"This *asshole.* He murdered thirteen thousand people!"

"I know," said Ferrarone. "It's impossible to imagine."

"I wish." I had an excellent imagination. It was part of the reason I was becoming the Marshals' top manhunter. But it caused me a lot of pain.

"Oh, Jesus," I said, "once he killed an entire *village.*" I flashed on dozens of families—parents and kids—clumped together, holding one another, shivering with terror. A hot wave rolled through my stomach. I saw a mass of faces, white with fear. I heard children whimpering.

"John!" Ferrarone's voice cut into my reverie. "Can you *get* this guy?"

"Yes." I was certain of it. Just on instinct.

"Then go tell the Boss."

*　　*　　*

When I entered Safir's inner office, both Safir and Kupferer rose to shake my hand. Made me feel good. It was a sign of respect.

"John," said Safir as he crumpled his uptight, rigid body into a chair, "you were the first person I thought of when this case came up, because we can *not* afford to blow this one. It's right at the level of the attorney general and the president, and it's going to open a whole new panorama for the Service. This is the first time an identified Nazi has ever gone on the run in the United States, and it's the first time the Marshals have ever gotten involved with a Nazi. As you know, the Bureau has declined to act on this case." He paused. His dark, straight eyebrows lifted. "In confidence, I'll tell you that Ed Meese didn't *want* the Bureau on this. He wanted *you*. You're his type of guy."

I believed it. Ed Meese was a total pragmatist who was already famous for some of the weasel-deals he'd allegedly pulled. His confirmation as A.G. had taken a record thirteen months while all the allegations of malfeasance against him had been probed. During that time, though, Reagan had stood behind him. Everybody called the Gipper and Meese "soul mates," because they both embraced the same God and mom ethic—while they interpreted the law to fit their philosophies.

Meese had risen to prominence by busting up the 1964 Berkeley Free Speech Movement, when he'd been a local DA. After that, he'd been anointed Governor Reagan's point man on law and order. Meese was a jovial, down-to-earth back-slapper, and I couldn't help but like him.

"So, tell me," Safir asked, "can we get close to this Nazi?"

"We can get *more* than close."

I was very confident. I'd discovered why this monster seemed so elusive to the FBI, and to the Office of Special Investigations, the country's official Nazi-hunting agency. Both agencies were treating it as a civil case; instead of a criminal case. Technically, it *was* a civil case; the only American statute the Nazi had violated was lying on his immigration papers. But if you tracked him using just the proper civil-case procedures, you'd fail. If I hunted him with the tougher criminal-case methods, I could catch him. The same principle would later apply to my investigation of Bohdan Koziy, the Nazi I told you about at the beginning of the book.

But I didn't tell Safir I was going to use criminal-case procedures. I always spared him the gory details.

"How do you want to handle this?" Safir asked. "Task force?"

"No. Solo. Or with just one other agent. But make it a woman. A man and a woman can stay undercover easier than two men. And I want carte blanche—open travel vouchers, and as much money as I need. Also, I want you to clear a path in the field for me. I don't want any obstruction from local marshals when I go into their districts. I don't even wanna tell 'em I'm there. But if I need 'em to do something, I don't wanna ask twice."

Safir's eyes narrowed. "We've never operated like that before," he said. He looked at Kupferer. "What do you think?"

"I think John's never let us down." Kupferer fiddled with his droopy cowboy mustache. What I'd said made perfect sense to him; he hated bureaucracy as much as I did.

"Okay," Safir said uneasily, "go to the clerk and draw a new book of travel vouchers. You'll have open authority to fly anywhere. You'll be reporting directly to Ferrarone, so work it out with him how you'll check in."

"I don't *want* to check in," I said. "I just want to send in a progress report every couple of weeks."

Safir shot a look at Kupferer. Kupferer shrugged.

"Have it your way," Safir said. "Just keep me briefed."

"Don't I always?" I smiled.

Safir's rectangular face stayed immobile. "Get with your best computer guy," said Safir, "and draw me up a portfolio to show OSI. You and I are meeting with them at two-thirty. And look—don't say too much. Be your usual charming self, and don't piss 'em off, just for fun."

"I don't do that anymore, Boss. I'm an *executive*."

"Get outta here." Safir almost smiled. It was a rare moment.

"As you know," droned the OSI executive, "President Reagan alienated many members of his Jewish constituency recently by visiting the S.S. cemetery in Bitburg. He also estranged certain key members of the Israeli administration. In consideration of these . . . considerations . . . as well as the moral elements involved, we feel it's critical to take some positive steps toward resolution of this matter."

Leave it to a lawyer to make catching a Nazi sound boring.

All the OSI guys were lawyers. Because of OSI's high pro-file in the media, the agency was one of the most prestigious boutiques in the federal bureaucracy. It was a magnet for careeraholics. Because OSI had such a good thing going, though, most of its agents had fallen into the worst pitfall of government: They were terrified of risk. That's why they had done such a lousy job. They'd spent *millions,* and had caught about forty Nazi war criminals, out of the ten thousand hid-ing in America. If my FIST guys had performed like that, I'd have smacked them around and sent them home.

I was no longer intimidated by lawyers, or any other upper-class, academic drones. The longer I stayed in the Ser-vice, the less insecure I was about not having a college de-gree. It seemed like the more education someone had, the less heart they had—and in my line of work, heart was everything.

"We certainly do want to apprehend this man," said the OSI agent, "but we are, of course, constricted by the parame-ters of the case, insofar as it's a civil matter and not a crimi-nal prosecution."

"We understand your situation," Safir said affably, "and we're going to help you in every way we can. Inspector Pas-cucci is going to be handling this case, and he'll give your investigators whatever help they want—no more, and no less."

The OSI guy was relaxed and smiling, content to let his expense-account lunch digest as he waltzed through an-other day.

But I was fuming. All this hypocrisy about *civil* procedure! How the fuck could this be *civil* when the Nazi had mur-dered 13,000 people? He was 12,995 corpses ahead of Charles Manson—and in my book, that made him *criminal.* To me, civil meant Judge Wapner and Doug Lewellen.

But Safir was giving me a look that said: If you go off, you're *dead.* So I bit my tongue.

After the meeting ended, Safir asked me to stick around. When we were alone, he said, "Look, you're tasked with working for Ferrarone on TDY"—temporary duty—"so don't worry about hurting Kupferer's feelings by going outside the normal chain of command. But remember, above all else, you're working for *me*."

"I'm *always* working for you, Boss."

"You always know just what to say, Pascucci. But let me tell you something else. I'm Jewish myself, and this *means* something to me."

For once, I didn't have a wisecrack. "Me, too, Boss."

I went directly from Safir to the office of the senior OSI investigator, who carried their badge number one. His name was Bert Falbaum, and he impressed me as having a hell of a lot more on the ball than most of the OSI wimps. He was assigned to me for the duration of the investigation. Of course, in his mind, *I* was assigned to *him*.

"Let's look at the Nazi's file, Bert," I said as I took a seat in his office.

Falbaum looked uneasy. "Well, the director wants us to work this up properly," he said. "He wants us to go down to the archives, where the historians will give us a lecture. Then the chief attorney wants to brief us on—"

"When *can* I see the file?"

"Well, the director wants—"

"C'mon, Bert, I'm *dyin'* to see the file. I wanna get this into the NCIC crime computer."

"Oh, no-no-no-no. We can't run him through NCIC. This is *civil*."

"Okay, no problem." I'd just do it myself. "Tell you what," I said, "lemme go get a couple of Cokes, then we can crack that file."

"The *historians*," Falbaum said firmly.

"The *historians* aren't gonna help me nail this mutt."

Falbaum just sat and looked at me—until I finally stopped being a prick and went with him.

I was glad I did. What I learned made me even more willing than usual to risk my life. And that was good—because before this case was over, I'd put my life on the line more than once.

The historians' briefing turned out to be a real eye-opener. Even with my active imagination, I hadn't been able to comprehend the sadism of Nazi war criminal Konrads Kalejs (Konrad—with a silent *s*—Kuh-*laze*). I'd envisioned him directing a single, violent massacre of thirteen thousand people, with bodies falling quickly in a hail of machine-gun fire. But, according to the historians, it hadn't been like that.

It had been much slower. Much more personal. Much more cruel.

Konrads Kalejs was a strong, healthy, square-jawed eighteen-year-old when he'd allegedly joined Latvia's Arajs Kommandos in 1941. The Kommandos, directed by the bloodthirsty Viktor Arajs, were a group of Latvian punks and thugs who terrorized their own country. Before the war, Latvia—a tiny country on the Baltic Sea—had been under the domination of the Soviet Union, and the Kommandos, who hated the Soviets, had actually been *glad* to see Nazi Germany take over.

The Kommandos worked for the German Security Police, the "S.D." The S.D. was the brutal secret police branch of Heinrich Himmler's notorious "S.S." In short, they were the worst of the worst.

Kalejs—more intelligent and more vicious than most Kommandos—quickly rose to the rank of senior lieutenant, and was reportedly given his own company to command. Kalejs's company was accused of being a roving death squad, which roamed the countryside, robbing, torturing, and murdering. Their primary targets were Jews. But they also killed thousands of Gypsies, Communists, homosexuals, retarded people, handicapped people, intellectuals—and anyone else who seemed rebellious, or "anti-German." The tactics of Kalejs and his men were unspeakably cruel. They did not simply shoot people, but murdered them in ways that terrified the populace. They forced mothers to drown their own babies in buckets of water. They tied children to trees and lashed them to death. They castrated men, amputated their hands, then set them loose in the forests. They forced naked prisoners to exercise in snow, then shot them. They set elderly people on fire, then doused the flames, leaving their victims to die a slow death from their burns.

Kalejs later became a senior lieutenant at the Salispils concentration camp, where his penchant for torture and murder continued. At one point, he and his men were accused of invading the village of Sanniki and murdering the entire population. Then they reportedly went to surrounding smaller villages and did the same thing.

After the war, Kalejs gathered his loot and moved to Copenhagen. In 1950, he immigrated to Australia, and in 1959, he moved to the United States.

In America, he lived in the wealthy Chicago suburb of Winnetka, surrounded by priceless objects of stolen art. He spent his winters on both coasts of Florida, where he owned several properties. By all accounts, he was a happy man.

In the winter of 1984—about ten months before I started hunting him—he had been contacted by the OSI. The next day, he'd taken about $325,000 out of his various bank accounts and had disappeared.

When I finished the historical review, my hands were trembling.

I excused myself, and went to the men's room. I couldn't shake the image of a mother having to drown her own baby. I splashed my face with cold water. Then I vomited into the sink.

I was a little worried that I was starting to take my work too seriously.

I was waiting for Falbaum when he arrived at his office the next morning.

He gave me the complete Kalejs dossier. It was full of financial information, none of which OSI had investigated—because that wasn't "legal."

As I read it, my dark mood began to lift. My Nazi had left a money trail, and those are the easiest trails in the world to follow—they're full of triggers. Konrad Kalejs might have been pretty good at mass murder, but he wasn't very good at being a skell.

When I finished with the file, Falbaum asked me if I'd like

to be cross-designated as an agent for the Immigration and Naturalization Service.

"Only if you think it's necessary," I said.

But inside, I was jumping for joy. The INS agents, unlike marshals, could issue administrative subpoenas, or "pocket subpoenas"—writs that *compelled* people to hand over documents. If I could get my hands on those, I wouldn't have to spend half my life weasel-dealing.

"I think it would be a good idea," said Falbaum. Many OSI agents, he said, were cross-designated as INS agents so that they could legally work on cases involving aliens. Because Kalejs was a "permanent resident alien," Falbaum said, I needed INS designation to work the case properly.

"Well, let's do it properly, by all means," I said.

He hit the phones, and a couple of hours later I was being sworn in as a dual USMS/INS agent. I was the first U.S. marshal ever to be cross-designated.

After the ceremony, I asked the INS officer, "Shouldn't I get some administrative subpoenas while I'm here?"

He seemed suspicious. "You don't really need your own," he said. "Bert has 'em. We try to keep a tight rein on 'em."

I played it cool. No fuss.

We went back to Falbaum's office, and I asked him for some subpoenas. But he told me he couldn't give me one until I *needed* it. "No problem," I said. I gathered a number of documents. "Where's your copy machine?" I asked.

"I'll do it for you," said Falbaum.

"Don't be crazy, Bert; you got calls to make. Where is it? Supply room?"

He nodded. "Down the hall, take a left."

I made copies until there was nobody else in the room. Then I scoped the place out and found the only locked file cabinet. I went to work on its cylinder lock with a paper clip, and popped the lock in about ninety seconds. It only took a few moments to find the pocket subpoenas. I grabbed a couple dozen. Because they were numbered serially, I took them from the back of the booklet, so their loss wouldn't be discovered until I was long gone. But even if I got caught, so what? I figured that Ed Meese would understand. Meese lived in the real world.

I stuck my head inside Falbaum's office. "Well, I'm off," I said.

"Off where?"

"Winnetka. To hit Kalejs's neighbors."

He gave me a funny look, as if I were rushing off half-cocked. "But, John, Kalejs has been gone ten *months.* What's the hurry?"

"Tomorrow it'll be ten months and a day."

He shook his head. I liked Falbaum. He was a good man. But I was beginning to have a hard time communicating with people who weren't crazy.

I made a one-day stop in Springfield, Illinois, where I was now stationed. Springfield didn't feel much like home, but no place else did, either, since I bounced around so much. But I wanted to pick up my Corvette. Also, I wanted to enter Kalejs into every crime computer in the world. Completely illegal, of course. But fuck that. I was Ronbo's cop, and I could do what I wanted.

I punched Kalejs into NCIC, EPIC, TECS, the Illinois Department of Law Enforcement Data Processing System, the DEA's NADDIS system, the Treasury Department's system, and MIRAC. Plus, I put out multiple BOLOs on him. You know the drill by now.

That evening, I made dinner for Betsy and curled up with her in front of the fireplace. I didn't know exactly when I'd be able to see her again, or even if I'd be quite the same person when I did. Every one of these cases was changing me. I was learning how to make myself think like my pukes, and once I got them into my head, they never really left.

While I was lying there, with my arm around Betsy and my feet on the dog, Betsy tried to tell me how proud she was of my work. But I kept making jokes.

"Why can't you ever accept a compliment?" she asked. She put her hand on my neck.

"Cuz I haven't caught my Nazi yet."

"Doesn't matter."

"Doesn't *matter?*"

"No. I read a quote by Mother Teresa in the paper today.

She says, 'God doesn't require you to succeed. He only requires that you try.' "

"Well, God has lower standards than Safir."

Betsy sighed and squeezed my neck with both hands.

"You wanna strangle me, right?" I said.

"No, John." She kissed my cheek.

This could have been a peaceful moment. In fact, it could have been one of the last peaceful moments in our marriage.

But in part of my mind, all I could see was a woman drowning her baby in a bucket of water. How could a man *do* that? And what was there in that sick mind that would lead me to him?

More and more, I couldn't keep my thoughts on anything but my pukes. It was what made me a good manhunter.

It was a curse.

Nothing is more quiet than the empty house of a rich person. The thick walls, the high ceilings, and the deep carpets hush the noise of life. Kalejs's house was eerie in its silence, and forbidding.

Throughout the house were paintings, porcelain figures, and antiques. To me, they all looked ugly, because I knew where they'd come from.

Kalejs's closet was empty. Bad sign. He wasn't coming back.

Kalejs, who was seventy-one, had lived here since 1960. All those years, he'd shared the house with Dr. Fedor Vitkin, Vitkin's wife, Ausla, and the Vitkin's grown daughter, Dzentra, who had Down's syndrome. Kalejs had known the Vitkins in Latvia.

Several years earlier, Dr. Vitkin had been killed in an auto accident. But even after Dr. Vitkin's death, Kalejs had continued to live with Ausla Vitkin, and to accompany her to Florida each year. Ausla Vitkin and Kalejs jointly owned a number of assets, including several jumbo CDs.

I was extremely interested in the relationship between Ausla Vitkin and Kalejs. If I could flip Ausla, who was inpocket down in Florida, my job would be done. She had enough of Kalejs's money to reel him in. But I wasn't optimistic. It certainly looked like they were buddies.

I called our Tampa office, and asked them to sit on Ausla's house down there. They said they didn't have the manpower. They volunteered to put up a "wanted" poster. I got pissed off. Hung up.

I locked up Kalejs's house and started to canvass the neighborhood. It was an expensive neighborhood, so I dressed to fit in: starched white shirt, gold cuff links, and a beautiful new cashmere jacket.

The next-door neighbor was the former chairman of John Deere. His housekeeper had me sit in his parlor for about half an hour before he ambled downstairs. He didn't know anything about Kalejs. But he directed me to an old woman who lived in a huge white mansion across the street. Her maid opened the door and ushered me in. I waited twenty minutes before the old lady finally appeared. The rich are different from you and me. They're bigger assholes.

The old woman got all agitated when I mentioned Kalejs and the Vitkins. "There was something *not right* about them," she intoned.

"How so?"

"Well, what I'm saying, young man, is that there was something *wrong*." What? Were they mass murderers? Did they have *new money*?

But I didn't have time to pull it out of her. I'd have to come back.

I jumped in my 'Vette, put in Springsteen's only good cassette—*Born to Run*—and howled out to Elgin with the top down. The March sun was glinting, the city was scrubbed clean by rain, and I was feeling the high that came from being on the hunt.

I had appointments at Kalejs's credit card company, and at his bank. When I got to the credit card company, I was sort of shocked to see that it was mostly just a big boiler-room operation, with dozens of people sitting at long tables, answering phones. I'd always imagined a credit card company as being plush and dignified, like a nineteenth-century bank. I made a mental note to never again let them intimidate me.

I asked to see the assistant manager, but they put me with the head of security. I don't like security chiefs. Often as not, they're former Bureau guys, and their first instinct is to wimp out. But companies love to hire ex-FBI agents, because they think they're *studs.*

I didn't tell the security director what I wanted—a full rundown of all Kalejs's charges after he'd gone into the wind. Instead, I beat around the bush, trying to bore him into passing me off to a subordinate, who might be easier to play. But as I talked, I noticed that the guy's wall was full of military emblems and certificates—even a West Point diploma. He wasn't a Bureau double-dipper; he was an *army* double-dipper. So I decided to play him with some *army* bullshit.

"You know," I said, "I think I can trust you with something that's highly classified. But if you ever mention it, it'll cost me my job." He liked that; it made him feel in control. "I see by your background, though"—I waved at the military emblems—"that you'll understand. So here it is. Our military intelligence people have a top-secret folder in my target's file that implicates him in the murder of over two hundred American prisoners of war."

"Is that right!"

"Yeah, it is. It was one of the worst American POW atrocities in the European theater. He pulled them out of transport trucks, machine-gunned them, and burned the bodies. It's in books. You've probably read about it."

"I think I *have.*"

Pretty soon, he was telling *me* how to hunt my germ. "One thing we can do," he said, "is run his account number through a system that'll access all the states east of the Mississippi. I can run that system in about seven minutes."

We started running the stuff, and started finding triggers. One stood out: a charge for $1,397.63 to Qantas Airlines on January 26. After that date, the account was dormant.

Today was March 5. I'd just cut a ten-month time line down to thirty-nine days.

Maybe Kalejs was going to Australia. Maybe he was already *in* Australia.

The security guy promised to red-flag the account, and to notify me immediately of any new charges. It violated his company's right-to-privacy rules, but *now* his attitude was, fuck that. He wanted his *mutt.*

On my way to Kalejs's bank, I phoned my hook at Qantas Airlines—the guy who'd helped me with Frank Riley, and with the Mexican drug magnate. I told him that the Gipper and I needed him again.

He ran a quick search, and found that Kalejs had not yet used his ticket. Excellent news! But he also determined that Kalejs must have bought a fly-anytime "open ticket," because there was no record of it in the computers. Open tickets are negotiable documents, and the airlines don't keep track of them.

He did establish, though, that the ticket was for an overseas flight. It was too expensive to be a domestic fare.

My Qantas contact flagged the ticket, so that he'd be notified immediately if Kalejs used it. He also promised to try to figure out where Kalejs was going, based on the price of the fare.

At the bank, the woman I hooked up with was just great. Her name was Maureen something—an Irish name—and she was dying to know all about my Nazi. I *love* to see curiosity in my hooks, because it pulls them into the game. I hate it on TV when a cop comes to the door looking for somebody and the citizen asks what the mutt did and the cop says, "Oh, we can't talk about that." You *always* tell them something, because that's what catches their interest and turns them into Junior G-men.

Over the past few months, Maureen discovered, Kalejs had written only a few checks. But five of them were interesting.

One was a $165 check to a service station in Wilmette, the suburb near Kalejs's Winnetka home. I was hoping it would be for something like a major tune-up or new tires. That would mean Kalejs was probably on the run in his car—a three-thousand-pound billboard.

Another check was to the Chicago Motor Club for $30. That also bolstered the car-trip scenario.

The third was for $150 to a Chicago law firm, written shortly after OSI had visited Kalejs. A hundred fifty bucks sounded like about an hour's worth of advice—just enough for Kalejs to find out that he had very few legal options. If he was trying to stay in the country through legal maneuvers, the bill would have been much larger.

Kalejs had also spent $144.45 at the classy Bally Shoe store in the Northbrook Mall. If he'd spent that kind of money on a new pair of shoes, he'd probably sat around for a while and had talked to the clerk. Maybe he'd mentioned where he was headed.

The fifth check was the most intriguing. It was for $50, was written December 15 to a guy with a European-sounding name, and was annotated "For Lena." To me, it looked a hell of a lot like a Christmas present. Lena was probably a little kid, and the guy with the European name was probably her dad. I wanted to find that guy. If Kalejs cared enough about this guy to send his daughter a Christmas present, Kalejs would probably stay in touch with him. Also, the check gave me a frame of reference for my interview with the guy. I'd ask him, "When was the last time you heard from Konrads, even if it was just a Christmas card or a note?" If he said, "I haven't heard from Konrads in years," I'd jump on him for lying, and try to break his resolve.

I got Maureen to red-flag any future activity in Kalejs's bank account, then I bombed over to the phone company. I laid a pocket subpoena on Ma Bell for Ausla Vitkin's phone records.

Then I screamed up the Edens Expressway in the diamond lane to the Northbrook Mall, where Kalejs had bought his expensive shoes. Beautiful mall—it was where Michael Jordon shopped. Kalejs had good taste in where he spent his blood money.

At the shoe store, I showed Kalejs's picture around. No hits.

It was late, so I headed back downtown, smoked a joint, drank a six-pack of Coke by the Buckingham Fountain, and had dinner in the Pump Room. I was trying to spend more on food. Already, OSI—which was underwriting my investigation—was bitching that my per-diems were too low. In government, bureaucrats think that if you're not spending, you're not working.

The next morning my phone rang long before dawn and I grabbed my gun as I came awake.

"I got our Nazi," a voice croaked. It was my Qantas hook. "I been up all night running fares through my p.c.," he said. "And get this. Toronto to Vancouver to Sydney to Melbourne. The cost would be $1,397. And sixty-three cents. Including Canadian tax. That's *exactly* what Kalejs spent, and it's the *only* Qantas ticket combination that would come to that precise figure."

"I'll be goddamed. You're *good.*"

"Let's not celebrate until we collar our mutt, okay?" He was definitely getting into the spirit of things.

"Look," I said, "I'm gonna put you up for a Justice Department Citizen/Agent certificate. They're very rare, but if I nominate you, Ed Meese will sign off on it. Ed's still wet behind the ears, and he does whatever I tell him."

"Just doin' my job," said my hook. But I could tell he was thrilled.

I called room service and they sent me four cream cheese Danish, four Cokes, and a quart of strawberries, with cream. Didn't even get heartburn from it—can I *eat,* or what?

Then I got on the phone with the ad agency I'd used on my Southwest FIST. I told them to design a Citizen/Agent certificate, and to make it look official. When they had it finished, they were to sign my name on it and send it to my Qantas contact. Cost me $400, but it would mean more to my hook than flash money. Besides, I could keep the original artwork and use it again.

Just after nine, I got a message from the concierge (yeah, the concierge—I was moving up in the world). He had a fax for me. The bellboy brought it up.

It was Ausla Vitkin's phone records. Nothing too scintillating. I isolated the numbers she called most, went to the phone company, and subpoenaed the records on those numbers.

Then I sat down in a nice restaurant, had a couple more Cokes, and thought things over. These days, I spent almost half my time just thinking.

If Kalejs *was* planning a run to Australia—and it looked like he was—he'd need a passport. It would probably have to be an Aussie passport, since that was his last legal residence. I called Interpol to check it out.

Kalejs, Interpol told me, *had* applied for an Australian passport—shortly after OSI had visited him. No doubt about it: Konrads Kalejs was planning to stay in the wind forever. Maybe under his own name, or maybe someone else's.

I drove out to Kalejs's service station and found out his check to them was for repair work on a white Oldsmobile. I called DMV, got the pertinent numbers on the Olds, then sent out a national BOLO on it.

While I was on my way back to see the rich lady who lived across the street from Kalejs, the car phone rang. It was Betsy. Her voice was shaky. She thought somebody was watching our house.

I turned the 'Vette around, put the cruise control on eighty-five, and streaked home.

I was at our house in two hours. The whole place was dark. Betsy was sitting in an inner room with Andy, our German shepherd. She acted brave, but she was freaked.

I sat out on the porch for a while with the lights off and my gun in my hand. My instincts told me that if anybody was out to hurt us, they were probably connected to Kalejs. But I'd pissed off *so* many people over the last few years; any one of them could have been out there.

Betsy made some calls, to find a friend to stay with.

Before bedtime, I went to the kitchen to get a snack. While I was standing in front of the refrigerator, I heard a car drive slowly down our street. Reflexively, I stood away from the window. I reached into a cupboard for a glass.

Then: BOOM! Shards of glass exploded into the room. I heard a screech of tires.

I hit the floor, crawled to a dark window, and looked out. The car fishtailed around the corner with no headlights.

I yelled, "Betsy! Stay put!" I grabbed my gun. If I'd been a movie cop, I would've run outside—and gotten my ass shot off. But I was a real cop, so I just huddled into a scared little ball, listening. I should have called the police, but if I did, Safir would probably find out and reassign me.

After a minute, I crawled to the bedroom and found Betsy. She was trembling.

I put my arms around her. "All I gotta do," I said, "is report this, and Safir'll take me off the case. You shouldn't have to put *up* with this kind of shit."

Even though her whole body was still shivering, she shook her head. "Don't give up," she hissed.

I squeezed her hard. "Jesus," I said, "you're a good wife."

That was about as romantic as I could get back in those crazy days.

The next morning, I dropped Betsy at her friend's house. She was safe, but I still felt guilty about going back to Chicago. I called her on the car phone. "It's not too late for me to get reassigned," I told her.

She was quiet for almost a minute. I thought she was mulling over my offer. But she wasn't. Finally she said, "You know the only thing that hurts me, John? It's that you don't see how much alike we are. Why do you think I worked so hard to become an operating room nurse? Cuz it's *fun?* I did it for the same reason you took your job—to do something *important* for people. That *matters* to me—every bit as much as it does to you. Now let me ask you something else. Could you be out there doing what you do, if I wasn't here to give you my support?"

I knew the answer to that immediately. "Nope," I said, "I couldn't." It was true. Knowing she was at home, waiting for me, was my psychological harbor. It gave me the strength to lead the insane, isolated existence that I did.

"I know you need me," she said softly. "I know it even better than you do. We're in this together, John. I make what you do possible, and I'm *proud* of that. But, God, John, sometimes it seems like, to you, I'm just the long-suffering wife."

"But you *do* suffer. And I *don't* suffer because of *your* work."

"That's okay," she said. "I'm tougher than you."

I laughed. She didn't. Probably because it was true.

"Don't get reassigned," she said. "I mean, Jeeze, it's not like you'd be *safe* on some other assignment."

She had a point. Marshals were dying all over the country. Safir was allowing us to be the most active enforcement agency in the government, and we were making more busts than all the other federal agencies combined. But it was taking a toll. The neo-Nazis had killed several marshals, the drug cartels had killed a couple, and our FIST operations were also taking casualties. Many of the career criminals we were bringing in had nothing to lose from one more murder.

Know what you *can* do for me?" Betsy said. "Tell me you love me."

"Awww, Bets," I whined, "you're so *demanding.*" I wasn't entirely kidding. It was hard for me to tell her that.

Another call came in. It was Kupferer, so I had to take it. Saved by the bell.

I didn't mention last night's shooting to Kupferer.

Just before I got to Chicago, I called Betsy back. She was gone.

So I told the answering machine, "I, you know, love you."

Back in Kalejs's hometown of Winnetka, I got with the old, rich lady who'd told me there was "something wrong" with Kalejs and Vitkin.

I always followed up on my leads. Most cops, after an initial interview, just leave their business cards and say, "Call me if you remember anything else." I *never* did that. I'd stay in somebody's face until I had what I needed.

The old lady, though, was as pompous and tight-lipped as ever. "Doctor Vitkin," she announced aristocratically, "was not a particularly happy man, because of . . . a situation. A domestic situation."

"Situation?"

"Yes." She nodded emphatically, as if she'd just spilled her guts.

"What kind of situation?"

"The one I just *referred* to, officer. The *domestic* situation." She wouldn't make eye contact.

"Oh-my-God!" I blurted. "Konrad and Ausla were *fu—*" I stopped. "Funneling their romantic energy into their *own* relationship!"

"Please!" She went crimson.

So! They were fucking! Disgusting! But interesting. It meant my chances of flipping Ausla were just about nil.

"How did you know? If you don't mind my prying."

"The doctor would upon occasion come over here, when his wife and Mr. Kalejs . . . wanted to be alone. And he

would be weeping, poor man. I'm afraid I just don't understand foreigners."

"They're sure not like *us,* are they? But tell me. Do you
recall anything about the doctor's death?"

"I do."

"What?"

"I remember Mrs. Vitkin's concern for her automobile. The
doctor passed away in an auto accident, and when Mrs. Vitkin told me about it, she seemed quite upset about the loss
of the automobile."

"Musta been a heck of a nice *car.*"

"The point I'm trying to *make* is that she was more concerned about her auto than her husband."

"Oh, *I* see." Old bitch. "How had they been getting along,
prior to the accident?"

"The doctor was in a state of pique. Shortly before he
passed away, he alluded to something that had happened 'on
the other side.' I believe he meant the Old Country. It seemed
to be something that Mr. Kalejs had done. Dr. Vitkin seemed
very uneasy about it, and wanted to 'clear the air.' I believe
that's how he put it."

"Did the doc ever say he was *afraid* of Kalejs or Ausla?"

Her face got rigid. "I *know* they were . . . ethnics," she
said. "But one mustn't draw conclusions. Mr. Kalejs and Mrs.
Vitkin were still among the better class of people. They
weren't the type to *harm* someone."

"I dunno," I said. "Kalejs was a Nazi murderer. He killed
thirteen thousand people. Lot of 'em were old women. He
loved to kill old women."

"No!" she said. She looked like her ears were going to
burst into flame.

"Oh, yeah. You were *lucky* to survive, with him next door.
A woman like you, he'd cut your throat and drink the
blood." Her whole body went rigid. I tried not to smile.

When I interviewed people, they could bust my balls all
they wanted. But never for free.

I picked up the deputy Safir had assigned to me, a young
woman named Hinda Gottlieb, and we stopped off at an old
man's house near Northwestern University. The old guy's

phone number had turned up several times in Vitkin's telephone records.

Turns out, the old man was in the same Latvian social club as Kalejs. The Latvians were very big on social clubs.

The old man gave me the chills. He looked like he was about to jump across the table and kick my ass. His nose tapered to a sharp point, like a hawk's beak, and his cold eyes held me in a haughty stare.

When I mentioned the war, he went batshit. "You were not *there!*" he yelled. "You cannot *judge!*"

When I pulled out research that OSI had given me, he swept it off the table. "All *bullshit!*" he shouted. "Bullshit from *Jews.*"

He strutted over to a shelf and pulled down a book called *The Holocaust Myth.* "*This* is research!" he snapped. "I was *there! I know!*" He tossed the book in my lap. I started to stand, but he put his hands on my shoulders and pushed me down. "Sit! Read! *Then* you will leave us alone."

I started to get up again, but he grabbed the lapel of my suit. Made me very nervous. It was my nicest suit—a $650 gray wool Armani. I reached up to take his hand off. He grabbed my throat, and—whop!—the next thing I knew, I was lying on my back and he was on top of me, flailing away with his hard little fists.

I tried to get free of him without ripping my suit. Wasn't easy. He was a mass of fury. He kept yelling, "We are not *finished,* Jew lover, we are not *finished!*"

Even as I grappled with him, though, part of me was detached. I was asking myself a standard question: What can I learn from this that will help me catch my mutt? And what I was learning was how *arrogant* Kalejs must feel. If he was *anything* like this asshole, he was *certain* God was on his side. In a mutt, that was unusual. Most of them were riddled with insecurity and self-destruction. Kalejs's self-righteousness would make him harder to hunt. It would give him strength and increase his ability to hold the loyalty of his support group.

But if I played him right, I could *use* his arrogance. Arrogance had a downside. It made people foolhardy.

I decided to be a lot more arrogant myself. It would help me get into Kalejs's head, and even help me get my job done.

With one heave, I pushed the old man onto his ass. "You Nazi *fuck!*" I bellowed. "I can have you sent to *prison* for that!"

That quieted him down.

Hinda looked at me like I was crazy.

From now on, I *would* be crazy. At least until I had Kalejs. After that, I'd try to be my usual lovable self.

I got a call from Maureen, my hook at the bank. She had an address for the guy Kalejs had sent $50 to at Christmas.

It was wonderful to have a bank *volunteer* help. Usually, they were incredibly tight-assed. Even when we subpoenaed them—with *real* subpoenas—their attitude was: We'll get to it when we can. But now that I was a Nazi hunter, everybody was dying to help. It was great for my new sense of arrogance. I was *on a mission from God.*

I took the address, ran it against Vitkin's phone records, and got a hit. The resident, Vilni Rosinik, was one of the people Kalejs and Vitkin had called frequently. I ran Vilni through my other programs, and found his name in an Immigrations system. Vilni was the son of Kalejs's sister. He lived nearby, in Milwaukee.

I flogged the 'Vette up to Milwaukee and showed up unannounced on Vilni's doorstep. When I tinned him, he slammed the door. "Open the door at once!" I barked, "or I'll have my SWAT team use their ram!" He opened it meekly. I was starting to *like* my new attitude.

I'd already worked up Vilni on our computers, so I knew a hell of a lot more about him than he did about me—which was how I liked it.

Vilni was a standard-issue Yuppie, and that was good. Yuppies were easy to play, because they had a lot to protect. Vilni was a computer consultant with a trimmed beard, a Volvo in the driveway, and a cushy government contract. He was doing some research on SDI, Reagan's Star Wars program.

For me, Vilni's Star Wars contract was manna from heaven. If Vilni got snippy, I could threaten to kill his deal. I couldn't, of course, but Vilni wouldn't know that. People think of the federal government as a unified entity, but I had no more control over the Defense Department than I did over Ethiopia.

Vilni tried stonewalling: His poor immigrant uncle was, like, one of the Boat People.

"I don't have time for your bullshit!" I snarled. "Your uncle's a war criminal. If he's not guilty, why's he running?"

I took a step closer, and got right in his face. "Look," I said, "I could stand here all day arguing. But let's keep it simple. You believe whatever you want, but if I find out you knew where he was and didn't tell me, I'll ruin your fuckin' *life*. I won't even *bother* with the harboring statute. I'll just queer your DOD work, then go talk to your neighbors, and to the teachers at Lena's school, and to all your wife's friends. I'll tell them that you're a family of murdering Nazi *pricks*. Am I gettin' through to you?"

Vilni flipped in less than ten minutes.

He actually came to believe that his uncle was guilty. All the logic in the world would have slid right off him—but a few ugly threats changed his whole worldview.

I quieted down, and got almost friendly. "Now, I know this is a family matter, so I'll keep everything you tell me confidential. But you *are* going to help." I said it with complete conviction. "Where *is* he?"

"He's with Ausla. In Florida."

On the plane to Florida, I caught up with my mail.

One letter stood out. It said "Back off, or you'll get more."

I assumed it was from associates of Kalejs—maybe neo-Nazis, or maybe an organization of old Nazis, like ODESSA. I also assumed they were referring to the shooting at my house.

Konrads seemed to be taking this personally. That was good. I wanted him angry. It would make him easier to catch.

When my plane touched down at Tampa International, I drove straight to the local USMS office and grabbed two bodies to sit on Vitkin's house.

I could almost *smell* Kalejs. It would be stupid of him to be at Vitkin's place, of course, but when I looked at it from

255

Konrads's arrogant perspective, it made sense. He'd evaded justice for forty years, so why should he get spooked now?

I sat in the car with the stakeout guys for quite a while, giving them all the gory details on my mutt Konrads, to motivate them to stay awake for at least a *couple* of hours after I left.

At 4:00 A.M., I got my hotel's wake-up call, and had room service send up a bucket of ice and five sixteen-ounce Cokes. I needed to write a search warrant, because I wanted to hit Ausla's house. Problem was, I didn't know how to show probable cause that Kalejs was there because I'd promised Vilni I'd keep his information confidential, and I didn't want to lose him as an informant. So it was time for a weasel-deal.

I went to Vitkin's next-door neighbor and showed him a picture of Kalejs. I asked him, Ever seen this guy? He said, Yeah I saw him once. Where? Well, I think it was next door, or maybe down the block. Seen him recently? No, I've been gone a lot.

So I lied in the warrant. I wrote in the warrant that the neighbor had seen Konrads in Vitkin's house yesterday. I also wrote that Konrads was a federal fugitive. It was all total bullshit. But fuck that. Faking warrants was a necessary evil.

When I handed the warrant to the judge, I held my breath.

The judge signed off on it without blinking. And why not? I was on a mission from God.

Then I had to figure out a way to get Kalejs outside the house, if at all possible. If I could, I wanted to take him in his front yard, by surprise, before he had a chance to get his hands on a weapon. I was paranoid about the old bastard. Most of my skells had only killed *one* or *two* people. Not thirteen thousand.

I called OSI, to see if they knew someone with a Baltic accent. If they did, I'd have the guy stiff in a call to Kalejs, pretending to be a friend. He'd ask Kalejs to meet him somewhere. Then, when Kalejs came out of the house, I'd take him down.

OSI freaked. Unethical! Unthinkable! They wouldn't even consider it. The *proper* procedure was for me just to knock on the door, and get my ass shot off.

They were even pissed that I'd gotten a search warrant. They didn't think that was "appropriate."

They knew nothing about Reagan-era law enforcement.

I held my tempter until I hung up. Then I screamed at a poor innocent deputy. That's the way we arrogant bastards operate.

The next morning, Hinda Gottlieb, OSI's Bert Falbaum and I hit the house, more or less naked. We had some uniformed city cops working backup, but if Konrads came out blazing, we'd all be dead.

We stood at the door. I had my gun behind my back. Falbaum was hyperventilating. But he didn't back off. Not one inch. Neither did Hinda.

Ausla Vitkin opened the door. I scanned wildly for Kalejs—or any sign of a weapon.

I waited for the thunder of gunfire. Silence. My nerves were burning. I wanted to push past Ausla and scream through the house, like usual. But I couldn't. My warrant was too weasly for scrutiny. We had to play nice.

I gave Ausla the warrant and *ever* so politely slipped past her, keeping my gun out of sight. I hurried quietly through the house. Each time I opened a door, I tensed, waiting for a bang and a burn.

There was every evidence of Kalejs—clothes, a razor, aftershave. But no Kalejs.

"Is Konrads out of town," I asked Ausla, "or just out of the house?"

"Out of town," she said.

I went outside and told our police backup men they could leave. But I had one plainclothes car stay, to sit on the house in case Ausla was lying about Kalejs being out of town.

Back in the house, I sprawled out in one of Ausla's easy chairs. I was spent. The adrenal high began to drop me hard.

Ausla sat down, too. Ugly old witch. She was fat, short, and Slavic, with ham hock arms and rat gray hair. In my mind, I saw her and Kalejs in bed. My imagination can be cruel.

Falbaum sat down, and I turned on my microcassette recorder, as if that were the natural thing to do. We started telling Ausla that she had no problems—as long as she helped us find Konrads.

Immediately, she went on a tongue cruise of self-justification, spraying spittle in anger. "War is war!" she railed. "You *forget* how conditions at these times are!" She said that Konrads "should get an award."

She rattled on, but I interrupted. "Did you drive down here, Ausla? I'm just curious, because the roads in Illinois are pretty flooded."

"We drove. It was not flooded."

"You'd better watch it going back. You'll get stuck. Or are you gonna fly?"

"I cannot decide."

"Might be dry by then. When are you leavin'?"

"I don't know exactly. Maybe you will put me in jail."

"We don't even want to put *Konrads* in jail," I said affably. "We just want him to come to court and answer the allegations." *Then* we'd throw his ass in jail, and deport him to Israel, where he'd fry.

She told us that Konrads was out looking for witnesses who would clear his name. Like there was a *one-armed man* out there who'd *really* killed the thirteen thousand people.

"Where would the witnesses *be,* ma'am?" I asked. "After so many years? I'm just curious."

She wouldn't say. She knew I was picking her brain.

We tried a few more times to trick her into giving up information about Kalejs, but she wouldn't. She just kept bleating about how this was "the time for forgiveness," and about how Latvia had a "much, much better legal system than America."

I didn't even consider trying to hammer her, like I had Vilni. She wasn't like my Yuppie. She had balls.

As soon as we left, I checked in with Safir, and with OSI. This time, I talked to a different OSI agent.

OSI, the agent told me, *had* called the house. The night *before* the raid.

They'd spooked Kalejs.

I didn't know if their tip-off had been intentional, or just stupid.

It didn't matter.

Kalejs was back in the wind.

I grabbed a body from our Tampa–St. Pete office, and he

and I flew to Toronto, which was one segment of Kalejs's ticket to Australia. If Kalejs was ready to make his move, I wanted to be there to block it.

On the flight to Toronto, I got lost in a book about the Holocaust. It was called *Love Despite Hate.* During the investigation, I'd met a number of Holocaust survivors, and one of them had given me this book, which was about children who'd survived the death camps.

As we flew, I read about a reunification center for children and parents who'd gotten separated at the camps. Often, at this center, the children had blamed their parents for abandoning them. Many had spit on their parents, and had violently attacked them. Some children had refused to go home.

It broke my heart to read things like that because it was something I could actually comprehend—unlike exotic tortures and mass murders.

I tasked my Tampa deputy with staying at the Toronto Airport, where he would maintain surveillance for Kalejs. Then I called the Royal Canadian Mounted Police, to let them know I was in town. They were very gracious, and sent out a detective to help. The Mounties, who had their own serious problems with neo-Nazis, sent me a specialist from their anti-terrorist intelligence unit.

The Mountie and I drove straight to a rooming house owned by a man whose phone number had shown up several times on Vitkin's phone records. We showed him a picture of Kalejs, and he identified Kalejs as somebody who'd stayed with him for several weeks in December.

But there was a problem. The rooming house owner—who was a Latvian refugee himself—didn't identify our photo as "Konrads Kalejs." When he'd been here, Kalejs had gone by the name of Jazeps Laimina. It was shitty news. It meant Kalejs was building a separate identity. I called headquarters and had them run the new name. It came up as a dead relative of Vitkin. I called my deputies in Springfield, Illinois, and had them enter the new name in all the crime computers.

For the next couple of days, I interviewed people in the boardinghouse and in the neighborhood—including a travel agent who'd sold Kalejs the airline ticket to Australia. Found out something interesting from the travel agent. Kalejs had been in Toronto until January 1. That was revealing. For years, his routine had been to hang out in Chicago until January 1, then split for Florida. It looked like Kalejs was trying to stick to his old patterns. The arrogant old prick wasn't going to let something like an international fugitive investigation disrupt his routine.

That was good. It made him more predictable.

On my second evening in Toronto, my Mountie contact took me to the world's tallest building, the CN Tower. It was a place where he sometimes entertained foreign visitors—particularly *adventurous* visitors—because the Mounties had access to a freight elevator that didn't have a governor. You could take it down so fast that you were momentarily weightless. Didn't sound like much fun to me, because I hate loss of control. But I didn't want to look pussy. So up we went.

As we got close to the top, the detective told me there was another reason he'd brought me here. He wanted to tell me something in absolute privacy. The neo-Nazis in Toronto, he said, were suddenly throwing around a lot of money. A source inside the organization had told him it had come from "a rich American." Furthermore, the money was rumored to be a down payment for a hit—against an American cop.

"Am *I* the American cop?"

"It *appears* that you are," he said carefully as we paused at the top of the building. "But please understand: All of this information I'm giving you is completely confidential. And it must remain so, or my informant might be compromised."

"I understand." Good! I wouldn't have to tell Safir, and get pulled off.

He studied my face. "You don't seem particularly frightened," he said. I didn't respond. He put his hand on the "down" lever. "Are you ready?"

"How far are we gonna fall?" I asked.

"The better part of half a mile."

I knit my anal sphincter. This was *definitely* a pucker job. "Let's do it." I sighed.

He cranked the lever, and the world fell away. My guts

were in my mouth. My feet hovered just off the floor. I felt totally out of control.

I couldn't help it—I screamed. The Mountie laughed. After a while, my feet began to settle onto the floor. Suddenly, I weighed a thousand pounds. We hit bottom.

The Mountie looked happy as hell. "Would you like to try it again?" he asked.

"You're *crazy!*" I shrieked.

He gave me a funny look, as if he couldn't figure me out.

Early the next morning, Maureen from the bank called. She had four new checks from Kalejs. The most recent, made out to a Chicago company, had been cashed on March 29, just four days earlier. Interestingly, though, it had been written on March 24. That meant it had probably spent about five days in the mail.

One of the places it could have been sent from—judging by its time in the mail—was Florida. Like Boyce, Kalejs was psychopathically arrogant—arrogant enough to stay close to home. He may have found a place down the block from Ausla's house so that he could watch us as we made fools of ourselves.

I sent a Citizen/Agent certificate to Maureen, then phoned Vilni. It was time to play Bluff the Yuppie. "I paid a call on your uncle down in Florida," I said, "but he'd already split. I just found out today that he's still in Florida, but I don't know *where* in Florida. Do you?"

"No," he said. "All I know is what you know—that he's still somewhere in Florida. Ausla won't tell me anything more than that."

So: Kalejs *was* in Florida!

I called Tampa and told them to increase their surveillance of Ausla. I wanted somebody sitting on her twenty-four hours a day. I booked a flight to Florida for early the next morning.

Then I went shopping. For the first time in my life, I had more money than I could spend. With all the overtime that OSI insisted I claim, I was making well over a grand a week, but I never had time to buy anything. Toronto, though, had a number of shops that sold fine European suits for a fraction of what they'd cost in the States.

261

I shopped until late in the evening, then started walking back to my hotel with three new Italian suits. One was dark blue silk, one was linen, and one was a charcoal gray pinstripe. Beautiful materials.

I started to cross the street in front of my hotel. From out of nowhere, a car suddenly materialized, and screeched toward me. I yelled, *"Hey!"* and jumped backward. But the goddamn thing swerved right at me. It kept coming. Its engine got louder and louder. The next thing I knew, I wasn't holding the suits. My hand was on the car's fender, and I was vaulting myself upward. I skimmed over the hood, and caught the windshield with my ass. There was a hard *whop!* and my butt felt electric.

I found myself sitting in the street, with the suits scattered around me.

The hotel's doorman came running and pulled me out of the street. I felt half-drunk, and all the bones in my spine were popping. One of my hands was bright red.

"Do you want to go to a hospital?" the doorman asked.

"I wanna go home." My voice was shaky.

"Where's home?"

"America."

Right after my plane landed in Florida, I made a courtesy call to OSI, to tell them I'd shifted the primary investigation back to Tampa–St. Pete. But the OSI agent got quiet and polite, and put me on hold while he switched me to his supervisor. Then the supervisor handed me off to *his* boss. Bad sign. *Somebody* was going to bust my balls. When the Big Boss finally got on, he was all huffy. For the last week, he said, he'd been bombarded by calls from members of a Florida-based Latvian social club called the "Eagles of Riga." The Latvian-American community, which was very large in St. Petersburg, was infuriated that I'd been "hounding" Ausla Vitkin.

"I know all about the Eagles of Riga," I told him, "and I can assure you that Ausla is tied in with them. I'll bet *she's* behind all those calls. And it's *damn good* that she's doing this. It means we're closing in on our target."

He didn't seem to hear me at all. He just went on whining

that a high-powered New York lawyer, Karlis Kavlan, was representing Kalejs, and that Kavlan was unhappy with my investigative methods. I knew all about Kavlan, too. I had a deputy in New York who'd been trying to reach Kavlan for a week, and Kavlan had been ducking all his calls.

But the OSI guy didn't want to hear about my problems. "Just lay off Ausla," he snapped. "Stay away from her."

"But she's the key to the whole investigation!"

He didn't care. He ordered me to pull my people off. OSI was *so* pussy. In the bad-ass Reagan Justice Department, OSI just didn't fit in.

I took a walk around the block. I needed to think.

I did *not* want to fuck up my career by defying OSI. I finally had money, power, freedom, and the most exciting job in the world. On the other hand ... I kept flashing on the image of a mother pushing her baby's head into a bucket of water.

I stopped at a pay phone and called the car that was sitting on Ausla's house. "Look," I said, "OSI just ordered us off Ausla. So, *officially*, you're no longer there."

My guys had no problem with that. They were good men. Besides, they were on a mission from Me.

I drove over to see the Eagles of Riga. It was midday, and many of them would be at their clubhouse for lunch. Before I walked in, I steeled myself. My men had interviewed a number of these people, and some of them sounded like monsters. One of them had said, "If I find out that anybody snitched on Konrads, I'll *shoot* them." Another was a former member of the Nazi secret police and had barely evaded war crimes prosecution himself. Many of them had stated that they "understood" why Kalejs had committed atrocities. One had defended Kalejs's reluctance to explain his side of the story by claiming that "true heroes never talk about their war experience." Another had boasted to my men that the Eagles of Riga had close ties to a neo-Nazi organization—in Canada.

I pushed through their door and strode into the main hall to confront the monsters. And saw nothing but a group of bent and withered old raisins. They looked at me with friendly eyes, and held themselves in the careless, vulnerable posture of old people who no longer have to struggle for a living.

Then I told them who I was, and they underwent an immediate transformation. Their body language clenched up, and their eyes grew wary and hooded. They slowly encircled me. I pulled myself into my best Nazi pose. "You are hereby notified," I snapped, "that if there is any further hindrance of the Kalejs investigation, those responsible *will* go to prison. *Do* you understand!"

From the back of the crowd, someone snarled, "Jew lover!"

"That's the second time in a month somebody's called me that. Let me tell you: You're *right!* I *am* a Jew lover. They are the *Super Race.* They have the brains, the education, and the moral power that you *peasants* only *dream* of." I was busting their balls. But I believed it.

My new *Nazi* motto was, when in doubt, shout. So I bellowed, "Listen also to *this.* I want you to know that, on your worst day, you were *not* as bad as I am. I will *not* be stopped. My country has ordered me to find Kalejs, and I will *follow* that order. So I advise you, stay *out* of this." I pivoted and marched out.

Then I went back to the office, called my deputy in New York who'd been trying to talk to Kalejs's lawyer, and gave him an order.

That night, my New York deputy went to the exclusive Long Island neighborhood of Kalejs's lawyer, and stood on the lawyer's front lawn. "Hey, *Nazi!*" he screamed, "come out and talk! *Jewww*-killer! Come on *out!*" He went on like that until every porch light in the neighborhood was lit.

The next day, the FBI called, acting on a complaint from Kalejs's lawyer. They threatened to bring me up on harassment charges. I got pissed off and told them they'd better talk it over with Ed Meese. Never heard another word about it.

It was easy to see, though, that the FBI was starting to hate me. Ostensibly, they didn't like my outrageous conduct and weasel-deals. More than that, though, I think they hated me for my successes. I got my jobs done—and they didn't.

That night, I went to a bar. That was unusual for me, because I rarely drank during an investigation. But I needed a break. I felt like half my brain belonged to Konrads Kalejs.

It was an ugly, spirit-numbing feeling, almost like having a split personality. Part of my mind was constantly plotting how to capture Kalejs, while the other part—my "Kalejs head"—was concocting schemes of evasion and subterfuge. There was a war in my brain, and it was sucking the life out of me.

As I was sitting at the bar, a beautiful young woman— honey-colored hair and a full, sexy body—came up and asked me to dance. Reflexively, I turned her down. A lot of marshals took advantage of the "five-hundred-mile rule," but not me. She stuck around, though, and really started flirting with me. I got to thinking: This is too good to be *true.* This is a setup. I'll end up *dead.*

On the other hand . . .

Even if it *was* a setup, I could do a standard James Bond maneuver. I could take her to bed, show her a *whole new side of life,* and flip her—right on the spot. Bond practically made a *living* off that routine.

But that just wasn't my style. Next thing I knew, some good-looking college kid hit on her, and she was gone.

She was clean! I wandered out to my car.

I bombed onto the freeway, headed toward my hotel, and revved it up to seventy-five. All of a sudden, my front end started dipping and bucking. Then my right front tire shot out in front of the car, and the car collapsed in a screech of sparks. It did a one-eighty and grated to a halt. I leaped out. Ran off to the side of the road.

No cars were coming—thank God—so I jumped back in the car and forced it off the highway.

I put on the blinkers and caught my breath.

"God*damn* it!" I yelled.

I found the tire. But I couldn't find any of my lug nuts. They were probably in the pocket of some gray-haired old party from the Eagles of Riga.

I cannibalized some lug nuts from the other wheels, and put the tire back on.

I was too hyper to sleep. I drove out to see the guys who were sitting on Ausla's house. I let them go get some coffee, and I sat there alone in the steamy Florida night, listening to the crickets and water sprinklers.

I was very depressed. I was drained of adrenaline, and I felt like I was a million miles from Kalejs. In fact, I'd spent half the day arguing with Safir against canning the whole operation. I was running up big bills, with nothing to show for it.

I tried to call Betsy from the car phone. I needed to hear her tell me about some simple, little thing she'd done today that had made her happy, like picking flowers or seeing a rabbit in the backyard. Even if she'd been around tragedy all day long at the hospital, it would be the flowers that she'd want to talk about. In her own way, Betsy *was* tougher than me; she was tough enough to forget about the pain that surrounded her.

She didn't answer the phone. She was out.

Then I got an idea.

Why not just march into the house, grab Ausla, and hold her head under water until the bitch gave Kalejs up? It would be fast, it would be effective, and it wouldn't leave any marks.

It would be *cruel,* of course. But fuck that. I was Kommandant *Reagan's* cop.

I caught a glimpse of myself in the rearview mirror. My face was flushed. My eyes were cold. I began to shudder, and felt like weeping.

Early the next morning, my phone rang. "Inspector! We *got* somethin'! A *hell* of a trigger." It was one of my stakeout guys.

"What?"

"A phone number. Off a scrap of paper Ausla had. She made a call from a phone booth, but then she saw we were watching her, and she tried to tear the number up. But we pieced it together."

"Are you sure she made your surveillance?"

"Yeah, Boss, she did."

"Shit!" If Ausla had been calling Kalejs, she'd now try to warn him that we had his number. But she was probably afraid to call him from home—afraid of a phone tap. That's why she'd used a booth.

"Stay on her, and let her *know* you're on her. I don't want her making any more calls."

"You got it, Boss."

I called "Ma"—the phone company information number Brick had given me—and traced the number to a motel in Ft. Lauderdale.

Then I dialed Tony Perez, the spectacularly aggressive agent I'd worked with in San Diego. Tony was in Miami, running a FIST.

"Tony, I need you to sit on a motel in Ft. Lauderdale. And I need you to get me to Ft. Lauderdale *immediately*. You got any planes in Tampa?"

"Got a King Air sittin' at the airport. It's yours."

Ninety minutes later I was in the Ft. Lauderdale court-house, poring over property tax records.

The motel, I discovered, was owned and operated by Arvids Leontin. I called OSI to see if they had an alien file on Leontin.

They called back in ten minutes. Arvids Leontin was Latvian. He'd been in the military at the same time as Kalejs. In the same area. In the same *unit*. Arvids Leontin and Konrad Kalejs were war buddies.

Leontin, in fact, had been a master sergeant. That gave me a chill. From what I'd read, the sergeants in the German Security Police were basically just executioners.

Of course, Ausla might have just been making a routine call to Leontin's motel. But not likely. Why had she gone to a phone booth, and then tried to destroy the number?

No, it looked to me like we were closing in on action.

If we were, I wanted to know what Arvids Leontin looked like. I called DMV to see if he had a current Florida license. He did. I sent a Tallahassee deputy out to the state's main DMV office. At the same time, I sent Tony's King Air up to Tallahassee. By the time the plane got there, the deputy was waiting on the tarmac with Leontin's driver's license photo. An hour later, I was looking at it. It was an expensive way to get a photo. But fuck that.

Leontin was an *ugly* son of a bitch. Fat, bald, and brutal-looking. He was six feet four and 245. Thick, white, lumpy face, like a huge potato.

By the time I got to Leontin's motel, it was crawling with undercover cops. Word had leaked that I was about to bust my Nazi, and every agency in the area wanted in on it—for the media, of course, because media means money.

But I didn't even know if Kalejs was *here*. And if he *was* registered, but was momentarily gone, I didn't want to spook him.

There was a Denny's across the parking lot from the motel, so Tony Perez and I went in and waited for someone to leave the motel and come in for lunch. The motel was a weekly-rate place, so I was hoping a resident might recognize Kalejs.

Before long, an old couple came over, and we showed them Kalejs's photo.

They identified him. He was there!

Kalejs, they said, kept to himself. Most of the residents were Jewish retirees—many were postwar immigrants—and Kalejs was cold to them. Most of the time, the old couple said, Kalejs hung around with Leontin.

"Do we hit the place, Tony?"

"He's your mutt, John. It's your call."

My heart kicked against my shirt. *"Let's hit it.* Seal off the block."

Minutes crawled past as Tony coordinated the quarantine.

Tony was ready. "Let's go," I rasped.

We marched to the hotel's office and barged through the front door. I had my badge out.

The sergeant was behind the desk. The second he saw the badge, he leaped toward his front counter. My instincts told me he was going for a gun.

Tony hurtled toward him. He smashed his fist into the sergeant's massive chest. The sergeant absorbed the blow and kept coming. He reached behind the counter. I jumped over the counter. In midair, I kicked him in the neck. He stumbled backward. I fell forward and cracked my elbow into his guts. He went "whuh!" and collapsed.

He tried to lurch up. I stomped down on his chest.

"In the name of the United States of America," I bellowed, "I hereby order you deported for trial to the Soviet Union!"

It was bullshit—but it worked. *"He's in there!"* the sergeant squealed. He pointed to an adjacent room.

I sprinted into the room with my gun drawn.

Konrads Kalejs was sitting on a bed, surrounded by stacks of American currency. On the night table was a complete set of fake identification.

I will never forget his face. He looked at me with absolute contempt. His dead, cold eyes were filled with disgust.

"Konrads Kalejs! On behalf of the United States government, and the people of Latvia—*living and dead*—I hereby place you under arrest!"

His face did not change.

I handed Kalejs to Tony and hurried away before the press could get there. The moment was far too precious to share. I began walking down a quiet, sandy residential street. For the first time in my life, I felt whole. I felt complete.

I had years of joy ahead—years of power, love, and brotherhood—but never again would I feel so good.

I said a prayer in my head—my first in years. It was a prayer for the dead.

I summoned an image of a mother who'd been forced to drown her own child. I told her Kalejs had been caught.

In my mind, I saw her smile.

I told my father, dead for years now, what I had done. Dad, who'd fought Nazis in the war, had put his life on the line a hundred times more than I had mine.

He approved. He loved his son.

Crowding the street were jacarandas and magnolias, orange trees and lemon trees. They were in full blossom, pink and sweet, and their fragrance mixed with the ocean breeze.

Their petals fell in front of me, and laid a path in the sand.

I walked the flower-paved path like a king. Like a god. Like a newborn man.

Chapter Nine

The Angel of Death

★

• Mengele Lives! • Going Undercover for the CIA • Human Terminal Experiments • The Biggest Goatfuck in History • My James Bond Briefcase • The Forty-Year Time Line • Shaken, Not Stirred •

"And why not say, 'Let us do evil, that good may come'?"
—Romans 3:8

My eyes burned from reading. It was past midnight, and I wanted to stop. But I couldn't.

The phone rang. At first, I didn't hear it because I was so submerged in my work. I groped toward it like a man coming up for air.

It was Kupferer.

"You got your wish," he said.

"I'm on the Mengele case?"

"You're *running* the case."

"Good. I'm glad."

"I'm sure you are. God knows *why.* Did you get the dossier?"

"I'm reading it now."

"Well, have fun," he said.

But his words barely penetrated. Even as we spoke, I continued to skim the dossier.

I was back in Auschwitz.

Auschwitz was liberated, my dossier said, on January 27, 1945, by the Russian Army. Shortly after their arrival, Soviet troops marched into a filthy barracks crammed with children. There were about two hundred of them. The children seemed to be coupled into pairs. Each pair had a familial resemblance. They were twins. Initially, the little twins were terrified, and would not speak. Then, after small acts of kindness by the soldiers, the children began to tell their stories.

Their stories were about Dr. Josef Mengele.

Dr. Mengele had been their captor. During the course of his stay at Auschwitz, Dr. Mengele had gathered more than three thousand twins, most of them children. But of these three thousand twins, only those in this one small barracks had survived. The other 90 percent had died in horrifying "experiments."

Mengele was trying to understand the genetics of twins, so that he might speed production of a "master race."

However, Dr. Mengele's twins had not been given the humane treatment that most researchers give even to laboratory animals. In most cases, his experiments upon the twins had been horrendously painful. In one case, for example, three-year-old twins named Tito and Nino had been cut open, along their spines, and then sewn together, back to back, and wrist to wrist. Their wounds had been filthy, and had soon stunk of gangrene. They had screamed in pain, day and night, until finally their mother had sneaked into Mengele's laboratory and killed her two little sons.

In another criminally misguided attempt to understand genetics, Mengele had injected the eyes of his twins with dye, to change eye color. The excruciating injections had caused the eyes to swell, fester, and go blind. Still, Mengele had persisted with the experiment.

Mengele had also gouged healthy eyes from living prisoners, and had pinned them in neat rows upon the wall of his

271

lab. One prisoner recalled entering Mengele's office and seeing "a whole wall of eyes staring at me. It was as if I had died and gone to Hell."

Mengele—the favored eldest son of a rich and revered German family—had also been obsessed with dwarfism, one of several genetic conditions he considered "subhuman." At one point, he had held captive an entire family of dwarfs— Romanian circus performers. One hellish evening, Mengele had organized an exhibition of this family for two thousand Nazi officers. He had ordered the family to perform their circus act naked. As they had performed, S.S. Chief Heinrich Himmler had filmed the act as a home movie.

Attempting to control fertility, Mengele had performed many experiments on sexual organs. Some victims' genitals had been burned terribly with X rays, while the genitals of others had been injected with various substances that had caused agony and death. Thousands of women had been sterilized, a great many men had been castrated, and women's wombs had been injected with cancer cells and other foreign substances. Sometimes, Mengele had locked a naked, castrated man in a room with a naked woman, and had then furtively observed them, to note any signs of sexual arousal.

In addition to his grotesque experiments with reproduction and genetics, Mengele had also performed experiments aimed at better protecting German soldiers. He had used Auschwitz prisoners to test the limits of human endurance to cold, heat, and electrical shock. In these so-called human terminal experiments, wounds had been sliced into living prisoners, then stuffed with objects such as wood shavings, dirt, glass, and staphylococci bacteria, to produce gangrene. Then Mengele had tried various methods of quelling the infections.

In another experiment, Mengele had shot prisoners with poison-coated bullets, then charted how long it took the prisoners to begin foaming at the mouth and flailing spastically.

Mengele had also amputated arms and legs from healthy prisoners, and had then attempted to graft them onto other prisoners, who had been similarly mutilated.

Many of these experiments had been done without anesthesia. None had been successful, but still Mengele had persisted.

Prisoners had been strapped to a machine that produced electrical charges and systematically shocked. Mengele had recorded how much voltage was required before this torture became fatal.

Mengele at no time had shown the slightest remorse for his acts upon his "human guinea pigs," as his patients had called themselves. And yet, while carrying out these barbaric experiments, Mengele had exhibited a strange sentimentality. He had always been more gentle than his assistants at drawing blood and giving injections. Once, when he had administered a terribly painful injection into the eye of a little boy named Moshe, he had said, "Don't be afraid." A twin named Eva recalled, "Once I wanted to go see my twin brother. So Dr. Mengele took me by the hand and walked with me over to where my brother was staying. Mengele held my hand the whole way." Often, Mengele had brought candy to the twins he was preparing to torture and kill.

Mengele had always affected the pretension of intellectuality, and had shown little interest in the many activities that other Auschwitz officers referred to as "sport." "Sport" involved "amusing" nonscientific testing of human endurance. One "sport," for example, had been called "swim-froggy"—patients had been thrown into an open cesspool, and had been forced to croak like frogs, and swim until they drowned.

In addition to his experiments, Mengele's other primary job had been to decide who to condemn to death. He, personally, had sent approximately four hundred thousand people to the gas chambers. Four hundred thousand.

Mengele had gained a reputation as the only one of Auschwitz's twenty-two physicians who actually enjoyed the lengthy process of selecting prisoners for murder.

Usually, the selection would take place immediately upon the arrival of a freight train loaded with prisoners. If prisoners had been too young or too ill to leave the train on their own power, Mengele had ordered them thrown alive into one of the huge crematoria, or into the laundry furnace, or into a huge boiling vat of human-derived fat (which was used to make "Jew Soap").

During the selection process, endless lines of prisoners had passed before Mengele, who sentenced them either to death or slave labor. One Auschwitz survivor remembered that Mengele, immaculately dressed and groomed, "had a gentle manner and a quiet poise that almost always lay between the edge of smugness and the height of charm. He whistled a Wagnerian aria as he signaled right or left for prisoners."

The selection process was very simplistic; it was based solely upon youth and fitness, and could have been done by anyone. Mengele, however, carefully guarded his "privilege" of selection.

Selections also took place at regular "roll calls" of inmates. "It would be three A.M., four A.M., five A.M., when we would be rousted for roll call," recalled survivor Gisella Perl. "We were cold, hungry, in rags. It would last one, two, or three hours. And there was Mengele, elegantly dressed, a beautiful blue shirt, so handsome, smiling, smelling of fine soap or cologne."

But if the orderliness of a selection process was disrupted, Mengele would fly into a rage. Once, when a woman bound for the gas chambers had jumped off a truck, Mengele had beaten her savagely with a club, screaming, "You're going to burn like the others, you dirty Jew!" Afterward, he'd whistled as he'd washed his bloodstained hands with perfumed soap.

At other times, Mengele would make his selections by forcing naked female prisoners to jog for him. Anyone unable to run would be sent to death.

"Hey." A hand on my neck! I spun around. I felt groggy and sick.

It was Betsy.

"Are you coming to bed?" she asked.

"No. I don't think I can sleep right now. Kupferer called. I got the Mengele investigation."

Betsy tried to smile. But she couldn't. "Hunting these Nazis takes so much *out* of you," she said.

I couldn't argue with that. After Kalejs, I'd almost immediately gotten involved with Bohdan Koziy, the Nazi I told you about at the beginning of the book. It had only been a few weeks since the Koziy investigation had ended. By now, my nerves were tight and twisted.

I'd come out of the Kalejs investigation feeling born-again—as if I'd confronted the worst *possible* evil, and had triumphed. But as I'd studied Mengele, I'd realized that, in some people, the depths of evil are *without* limit.

That realization was overwhelming. It made me feel dizzy and weak, like you get when you look down a hole that's so deep you can't see the bottom.

I looked up at Betsy. "Tell me we're gonna get through this Mengele thing okay," I said.

"We will." But her eyes were full of pain. She was just as worried as I was.

I couldn't sleep at all. Early the next morning, Kupferer called again.

"Whattaya think, John?" Kupferer said. "Is that bastard Mengele still *alive?*"

"Looks like it. Neal Sher at OSI says he's 99 percent sure Mengele's still around. Wiesenthal's 100 percent sure. Serge Klarsfeld—the guy who caught Klaus Barbie—says Mengele's down in Paraguay, living in a villa owned by the dictator, Alfredo Stroessner. Stroessner's running a genocide program of his own against Paraguay's Indians."

"Stroessner's the reason I called. We got a lead for you. Could be a hot one. One of our guys in Southern California found Stroessner's former personal pilot. The pilot's been bragging to his friends that he used to fly Mengele around. But when we questioned him, he stonewalled."

Kupferer gave me a number for the pilot.

"Safir's going all-out on this," Kupferer said. "He wants to bring in the Israelis, the Germans, and Interpol. He says it's gonna be the biggest manhunt in world history."

"Or the biggest *goatfuck*—if we're all in each other's way."

"Oh, *you'll* stay outta the bureaucracy. Hey, how you gonna get into the head of somebody as crazy as Mengele?"

"I don't think he's crazy. Outside of Auschwitz, he never did anything abnormal. There's no sign of schizophrenia, no manic depression, not even alcoholism. Even in Auschwitz, everything he did was for a purpose."

"Is that gonna make it easier?"

"No. It's makin' *me* nuts."

After Kupferer hung up, I made a couple of calls, then dialed the pilot. He wasn't too surprised to hear from me. Our guy in the field had been riding him pretty hard.

"Look, I've *gotta* clear this lead," I told him, "but I wanna do it as quick as possible, and get on with my *real* investigation. I don't mean to insult your importance, but *somebody* in the government has gotta face facts here: Several years ago, you might have seen Mengele, right? Well, that doesn't count for much. But if you duck me, just watch—headquarters will drag you in front of a grand jury, and my whole investigation will get stalled."

"I do not want that."

"Who would? But I've got an idea. Why don't you and me meet in San Diego this Friday. I gotta *ton* of money to throw at this thing, and I can put us both up at La Costa for the weekend. It's where Reagan *himself* stays. Beautiful club. We'll talk for a couple of hours, and we'll both get a nice trip out of it."

"I could do that, probably."

"Now, one thing I've gotta say, to keep you advised of your rights, is that when we talk, you *will* be in my United States jurisdiction. So, technically, I could take you into custody. But *that's* not too likely."

Long silence.

"You know," I said, "we don't *have* to meet in the United States. Would you feel more comfortable if we drove across the border? Outta my jurisdiction?"

"Perhaps."

"Well, lemme think. I do know a beautiful resort in Ensenada. You fish?"

"Sometimes."

"Hell, we'll go to *Ensenada* and go fishin' in the Gulf. And I'll send you home with a nice little consulting fee, too. We do that all the time."

He agreed to it, and we made arrangements to meet on Friday.

Then I dialed Manuel Fuerte, my buddy with Mexican Army Intelligence.

"He went for it," I said.

"Good, my friend! So you will be visiting us?"

"This Friday."

"I will keep my most effective men on duty this weekend. Would you like to observe?"

"No way in hell. I feel bad enough about just setting it up."

"I understand. I, too, do not like to observe. But do not forget, these people, they bring this on themselves."

"I suppose."

I got off the phone with Manuel and started reading more about Mengele's atrocities. I was hoping it would make me feel better about sweating the pilot. But it had the opposite effect. It made me wonder: Was I just another brutal prick, like Mengele?

But I told myself, Fuck that. This is a necessary evil.

Late that afternoon, Kupferer called again. "Big meeting back here on Monday," he said. "Safir's got the White House *hot* for this Mengele thing. Meese is behind us all the way. But first you've gotta go meet somebody from the Agency."

"Whatta *they* want?"

"Who knows? It's probably about Mengele. They want you to take the Ozark commuter flight to Chicago tomorrow morning, and wait outside your gate. They'll approach you."

"Any reason they can't just *call?*"

"You know them. They love that secretive shit."

The next morning, I was standing outside the Ozark gate when a dapper little guy in a camel-hair jacket approached me. "Let's walk," he said. As we sauntered down a long corridor, he said softly, "We wanted to save you some trouble, and, frankly, save ourselves some trouble. We understand you've been tasked with interviewing Alfredo Stroessner's former pilot. What you'll find is that his intelligence is bona fide, but outdated—strictly feed material. Any contact you have with him, though, might jeopardize assets we have down in Paraguay."

"How so?"

"In confidence, it's because the pilot *himself* is one of our assets."

"How's he helping you?"

"I don't have a need-to-know on that."

"Well, I got no problem with leavin' him alone. I'm happy to cooperate with you guys. But I wanna say this." I stopped, and made eye contact. "I'll play ball as long as you don't fuck me around. But the first time you lie to me, that's *it*."

He didn't take offense. "I looked you up in the computer," he said, "and I can tell you this without reservation: We've never lied to you."

"What you mean is, I've never *caught* you lying."

He looked genuinely puzzled. "It amounts to the same thing, doesn't it?"

The meeting in Safir's office was strictly top level: Safir, Kupferer, international chief Don Ferrarone, and me. By this time, I was one of the most prominent men in the Service. I'd gotten another promotion after I'd bagged Kalejs. Now I was a senior inspector of the Service, with a rank of G.S. 12/ 13. I'd also gotten nominated for the Attorney General's Award, and had received considerable media attention for finding Koziy and Kalejs. At age thirty-six, I was developing a national reputation as America's top manhunter.

Safir kicked the meeting off. "What makes Josef Mengele so important?" he asked. "We know that a hundred and fifty thousand Nazi war criminals were identified after the war, and that only about thirty-five thousand were captured and prosecuted. We know that about ten thousand of them es- caped to America, and that another three thousand emigrated to Canada. So why does Mengele stand out? Because of his *style*. He's come to *personify* evil. He's a *symbol*."

"Yeah," I broke in, "but he's also an *asshole*."

"That, too," said Safir, a little annoyed. His dark eyebrows arched, and his face was tighter than I'd seen it in a year. "He's not *just* a symbol. But that *is* why we've got to catch him."

"Okay, Boss," I said, "but let's get practical. How we goin' after this mutt?"

"Two-pronged attack," said Safir. "Prong number one: a coordinated effort by the OSI, the Germans, the Israelis, the CIA, the National Security Agency, and Interpol. Prong num- ber two: Pascucci."

He was just stroking me. But he knew that I'd risk my life to nail this puke. Would anybody else?

"John," said Safir, "what's your input?"

"My input is: Go after him like any *other* mutt. Let's say he *is* a symbol. We've gotta *ignore* that, or it'll fuck us up. We've gotta let go of *all* our preconceived notions—that he's powerful, and evil, and well connected. All we know is, that's what he was *forty years ago.* We can't look for what *was;* we have to look for what *is.* We've gotta chase him like he's just a fucked-up old man trying to get what all old men want: family, friends, money, and appreciation.

"I say, let's hound the shit out of his family. And let's squeeze his *friends,* to see who's *really* his friend. Let's look for money. Let's look for bragging; in *his* head, he's a *hero.* I'm Mengele—I'm down in Paraguay with my buddy Stroessner, torturing Indians, and, to me, *Germany's* loss is just one battle in a long war. I *will* lead *again!* The Reich lives! Heil Stroessner!"

I was getting some funny looks, so I backed off.

"Basically," I said, "let's just start a time line on him and work it up.

"But! If we bring in all these other agencies, we'd better be sure everybody's working *together,* or it'll end up just like the Son of Sam investigation, where Westchester didn't know what City was doing, and the feds didn't know what *anybody* was doing. Also, don't expect too *much* from those people. The Germans have a *sickening* record on war criminals, and the Israelis gave up on Mengele twenty years ago. Israel is a lot more worried about the PLO than Mengele, and, besides, they count on Paraguay's support in the UN. And, for Christ's sake, don't trust Interpol. From what I've read, Interpol's first president was the chief of the Gestapo, and up until thirteen years ago, *all* of its presidents were former members of the S.S. One of them was hung at Nuremberg. So we've gotta be willing to shoulder most of the burden ourselves."

"Point taken," said Safir. Then he got a funny look on his big, long face. "Now, John," he said, "as you know, there's a $3.4 million reward for catching Mengele. You're not going

to close in on him, then resign and go *commercial,* are you?"
He seemed serious.

"Boss, *nobody* could pay me enough to do this shit."

"Mr. George will see you now."

I was ushered into the office of Claire George, the CIA's
deputy director of operations. Claire George was head of all
the Agency's spying and intelligence activities.

Safir had arranged for me to get CIA training. I was going
to go into South America, after Mengele, under the wing of
the Agency. I would be assigned to the American Embassy
in Argentina as an "undeclared," or secret, CIA case officer.
My cover story, or "legend," would be that I was an attaché
for the State Department.

I would also have a backup identity as an Irish national.
The CIA would supply me with forged credentials. That part
of the operation was illegal, but none of Meese's people
seemed to care.

Basically, I was being equipped to operate on my own.
And that suited me just fine.

Claire George spent about twenty minutes with me—
mostly picking my brain about how I'd located Koziy and
Kalejs—then handed me off to one of his assistants. George
looked harried and gray; he was working night and day to
negotiate the release of his Beirut station chief, William
Buckley, who was being slowly tortured to death by the Is-
lamic Jihad in Lebanon. George himself had once been the
Beirut station chief, so the situation hit him close to home.
I didn't know it at the time, but George was also busy with
the Iran arms deal.

His assistant, though, was pure elixir of collegiate charm.
Like a lot of Agency people, he came from a wealthy family.
The Agency liked its case officers to have an independent
source of money, because it made them harder to flip. He
was younger than me, very tweedy, and smoked a pipe. A
few years earlier, his collegiate demeanor would have intimidated me. Not anymore. Even though he became my rabbi at
the Agency, I can't tell you his name, because he's working
overseas now as an undeclared agent.

He began trotting me around to experts and specialists

throughout the CIA's massive headquarters. We started with countersurveillance: How not to get spied on. He took me to a room, left me alone, and had me type a couple of sentences on a regular typewriter, and on a computer. Then he stuck his head in the door and told me what I'd just typed.

"What's the trick?" I asked.

"The trick is, there's an audio bug in this room. And just by hearing you, we can tell what you typed. Every computer key emits a slightly different frequency. I taped you, then ran your tape through a computer. I monitored the typewriter the same way. Each time the typing element moves, the motor runs, and the amount of time the motor operates signals which key was struck."

"So I've got to debug the room before I type?"

"If possible. You also have to pull the shades. We now have lasers that can monitor your keyboard's vibration on window glass. We train the laser on the glass, and we can read anything you type." He gave me a happy smile, and I was hooked. I *loved* this James Bond shit.

Every day for the next couple of weeks, I went to CIA headquarters in Langley, Virginia—just across the Potomac from the Capitol—to learn CIA tradecraft. My rabbi taught me how to "sweep" a room for bugs with a spectrum analyzer, how to tap a phone, how to work a "bionic ear" for eavesdropping, and how to spray envelopes with freon, which renders them totally transparent for a few minutes. He also showed me how to detect a one-way mirror (you touch it with a sharp object, like a pencil point; if it's a regular mirror, you'll see a gap between the point and its reflection—if it's a see-through mirror, you won't see the gap).

One afternoon, we worked on evasive driving maneuvers on a deserted government runway. Using a "skid pan"—a stretch of pavement oiled to reduce friction—I learned how to pull a perfect 180-degree turn, by throwing the car into neutral and jamming on the emergency brake, to lock the rear wheels. I learned how to check a car for explosives, how to jump a curb at high speed, and how to counterram an attacking vehicle.

Can you believe I got *paid* for this?

But it wasn't all fun and games. At the same time I was

playing James Bond, I opened my investigation on Mengele. I worked closely with Safir, and the better I got to know him, the more I admired him. He had enough sophistication to interface with anybody on earth, including presidents and prime ministers, but he also had the street-smarts and balls of a good cop. Every day, he worked on pulling together the investigation's international coalition of agencies. From all over the world, computer discs and files on Mengele began to pour in.

Safir loaned me a couple of his best computer brains, and they helped me gather, correlate, and analyze all the disparate Mengele investigations. Then I distilled them into a single, unified version.

I started building my time line.

It began October 30, 1944, when Mengele and his wife fled Auschwitz after Allied bombs had begun to fall near the concentration camp. Mengele, however, soon returned to Auschwitz alone; the exit had been to extricate his wife.

That was revealing. Since he'd protected her, she would probably protect him.

Even though the war was ending, Mengele was still obsessed with his vile "experiments." When he returned to Auschwitz, he took sixteen female dwarfs out of the hospital and "experimented" upon them. Eleven died. In mid-December of 1944, as the Allies closed in on the camp, Mengele destroyed most of the records of his experiments.

On January 17, 1945, Mengele ran from Auschwitz. He was ten days ahead of the Russian Army. He took refuge at a German camp in Silesia where Soviet war prisoners had been experimented upon with bacteriological warfare. In February he left, now only eight days ahead of advancing Russian troops. On the night of May 8, when Germany surrendered, Mengele crossed into Saxony, which later became part of East Germany. In June, American troops entered the area and took custody of Mengele and thousands of other soldiers. Because the death camps had been discovered, Mengele was already an identified war criminal. But he gave the Allied soldiers a fake name. He was freed within six weeks.

He returned to his hometown of Günzburg, a beautiful little place on the Danube river. The Mengele family owned Günzburg's only large factory, and ran the town as their own little fiefdom.

Mengele got a job as a farm laborer and escaped detection for several years. During this time, his war crimes were revealed at the Nuremberg trials, and at the related "Doctors Trial," where twenty-three leading S.S. physicians were tried.

By the autumn of 1948, Mengele was alarmed at his growing notoriety, and decided to flee Europe. He traveled to Italy to seek the help of the Catholic church. The church, with the apparent blessing of its staunch anti-Communist pope—Pius XII—was operating the Rat Line, an underground network that eventually aided the escape of sixty thousand Nazi criminals—almost half of *all* Nazi war criminals. Mengele moved into a Franciscan convent near the Vatican and was issued a falsified Red Cross passport.

After Mengele got his fake passport, he set sail for South America.

All this information had been gleaned from informants, and from statements Mengele had made himself after arriving in South America. All of it was interesting, but it didn't tell me what I most needed to know: What was Mengele's primary support system? Was it the former S.S. officers' group, ODESSA? Was it *"die Spinne"* ("the Spider"), another prominent organization of ex-Nazis? Simon Wiesenthal's Nazi-hunting group seemed certain that Mengele was getting help from at least one of these well-funded organizations. Wiesenthal pictured Mengele living a life of privilege and power, jetting amongst plush villas on several continents.

But my gut told me not to believe it. When I put on my "Mengele head," I just couldn't see myself living high-profile. And I couldn't see myself trusting strangers.

I wanted to know more about Mengele's *family.*

I asked my computer guys to isolate everything on just the family.

When their report came back, I started licking my chops. Scintillating stuff! First of all: Mengele's family business was grossing about *$100 million* annually. That spoke volumes. It meant the family, with no outside help, had enough money to hide Mengele forever. And it meant something else: They really couldn't afford *not* to help him. For a family of *that* level of wealth, nothing would be more humiliating or destructive than suddenly being dragged into the world's spotlight, because of Uncle Josef's capture.

But that wasn't all I learned about the family. I found out that while Mengele had been hiding just outside his hometown, his father and his wife had been questioned. They'd both said the same thing: Josef Mengele had died on the Russian front.

When I read that, I almost jumped for joy. No doubt about it: *They* were hiding him.

I knew how I was going to catch the Angel of Death.

"I've got a couple of presents for you," my CIA rabbi said. "Sign here."

I signed an Agency requisition form, and he pulled a small box out of his desk. In it was a little disc that looked like a hearing aid. It was attached by a wire to a small battery pack. "Let's test it out," he said. "Put this in your ear, and stay here."

A minute later, he appeared on the lawn outside, holding a walkie-talkie. I saw him put the walkie-talkie to his mouth.

Suddenly my earpiece crackled with sound. "Can you hear me?" It was him.

I nodded and waved.

"Talk to me," he said.

"Can you hear *me?*"

"I hear you fine."

"How?"

"Your earpiece is also a transmitter. It picks up the vibrations in your ear canal and sends them to any two-way radio."

"Slick!"

A minute later, he was back. "Here's something else," he said. He pushed a briefcase across his desk.

"What's *this* do?" I asked.

"It does audio recording through a voice-activated mike. It does video recording through a fish-eye lens. It shoots a silenced twenty-two-caliber bullet. If it's opened without its proper code, it activates a dye-gas canister and an alarm. If it's even *picked up* in the wrong way, it can throw off a thousand volts of nonlethal electricity. It has a detector that lets you know if somebody's taping. It can stop bullets. It has a receiver that picks up signals, boosts them, and allows rebroadcast to another location. *Plus,* you can even put your *papers* and *pencils* in it."

"Briefcase, I think I *love* you," I said. "I wanna know for sure." I ran my hands over it, feeling the smooth cowhide. I caressed the magnesium tooling. I smelled the fresh leather. "Briefcase, I *love* you."

"I know how you feel," my rabbi said solemnly. "I remember my first time with an Agency briefcase."

We both sat silently for a moment. I adored my briefcase.

But fuck that. I had a Nazi to catch. I hauled ass back to USMS headquarters, to pick up a dossier. On Rolf Mengele: Josef Mengele's only son.

Rolf Mengele, the dossier said, was the black sheep of the family. A forty-one-year-old attorney, he was slightly left of center, which made him a pariah among his rich, ultraconservative relatives in Günzburg.

Rolf had grown up thinking that his father had died on the Russian front. When he was sixteen, however, he'd been told that his father was alive. In fact, he'd even met his father, on a skiing vacation in the Swiss Alps in 1956. At that time, the man had been identified to him as "Uncle Fritz."

I called Interpol, to get a workup on any international travel by Rolf Mengele. I was becoming less cynical about Interpol. They may have been dominated by Nazis in the past, but now they seemed to be helpful. In fact, so did the Germans and the Israelis. I suspected, though, that all of them had been cowed by Safir, who was extremely active in this investigation. Safir had convened a summit on Mengele and had used the full force of his personality to demand cooperation.

Interpol had some tasty information. Rolf had flown to São Paulo, Brazil, in 1977, under his own name and passport. Did that mean Mengele was in Brazil? Not necessarily. Rolf could have driven from Brazil to Paraguay in a matter of hours. And Paraguay, according to my research, was the most likely location of Mengele.

When Mengele had arrived in South America in the summer of 1949, my research indicated, he'd settled in Buenos Aires, Argentina. Buenos Aires was the most sophisticated city in South America, and had an extremely large German community. Of the city's eighteen daily newspapers, three were in German.

The Germans, along with other European immigrants, dominated the economic and political structure of Argentina. They lived aristocratically, and held the impoverished local Indians in contempt. The Germans held great sway with Argentine dictator Juan Peron, who in 1946 had set aside ten thousand blank Argentine passports and identity cards for Nazi fugitives. These Nazi emigrés, in turn, lavished stolen wealth on Peron. As early as 1942, Peron had begun to receive crates carrying millions of dollars' worth of diamonds, jewelry, gold (much of it still in teeth), artwork, and currency. The crates, many postmarked "Auschwitz" and "Treblinka," had been stored in a depository controlled by Eva Peron.

In the early 1950s, Mengele met another Buenos Aires resident, Holocaust organizer Adolph Eichmann. Eichmann, like Mengele, had been aided in his flight by the Catholic church. Both men, my research showed, lived in virtual poverty in Argentina. They probably didn't have to live poorly, but they were both extremely shrewd. They kept their lifestyles diametrically different from their former lifestyles. That's always the smartest thing a fugitive can do.

In 1959, Mengele moved to neighboring Paraguay. He believed he would be safer in that much more primitive country. Eichmann stayed in Buenos Aires—and was later captured by the Israeli intelligence agency, Mossad. Mossad had intended to grab Mengele in the same sweep.

Mengele settled in the German-dominated section of Paraguay known as New Bavaria, where a great many people still displayed swastikas and hated Jews.

In Paraguay, Mengele came under the apparent protection of President for Life Alfredo Stroessner, the grandson of a Bavarian cavalry officer. Mengele was granted citizenship under the name "José Mengele." He was rumored to be Stroessner's personal physician. He was also rumored to be

Stroessner's primary consultant on torturing and terrorizing Paraguay's Aché Indians. Some people also believed Mengele exported heroin.

But after Mengele's arrival in Paraguay, rumors were all I had. In Paraguay, his trail had grown cold. A number of Nazi hunters had gone into the jungles of Paraguay after Mengele. Some had never come out. Alfredo Stroessner's Paraguay was treacherously dangerous. Nazi-hiding organizations like ODESSA and *die Spinne* were extremely strong there. If they caught you snooping around, you were dead.

After the early 1960s, there were only two significant leads. The first was Rolf Mengele's trip to Brazil in 1977.

The second was the cancellation of Mengele's Paraguayan citizenship in 1979. But that was a weak lead; it was widely believed that Mengele had simply changed his name again, and gotten new citizenship.

I was at a dead end. Just like everyone else.

But whenever I hit a dead end, I'd just start down a different trail. When in doubt, do something.

After reviewing all the research on Mengele's family, I decided to isolate and reexamine my information on a family friend named Hans Sedlmeier. Many family members had mentioned him. They referred to him as one of the company's bookkeepers. But in a large company like the Mengeles' farm machine corporation, how come they all seemed to know this one bookkeeper?

My researchers brought me the separate file on Sedlmeier late one afternoon, after everyone but Safir had gone home. I started scanning it. And: Bingo! Buried in all the paperwork was a newspaper article that had been published by the *New York Times* syndicate in the early 1970s. Long forgotten by virtually everyone, the article, by journalist Flora Rheta Schreiber, quoted Hans Sedlmeier as saying that he had helped Mengele several years earlier.

My heart started bumping against my ribs. I skimmed for more details. Who *was* Sedlmeier? What *exactly* did he do?

Jesus! He was no *bookkeeper.* He was the company's comptroller. *Hans Sedlmeier was the family's money man.*

Not only that: He was a lifelong resident of Günzburg. And a childhood friend of Josef Mengele.

After the war, when the Americans had briefly removed all former Nazis from control of important businesses, the Mengeles had turned their company over to Hans Sedlmeier. Then, when the Americans had left, Sedlmeier had given the business back. He was practically a member of the family.

If *anyone* was sending money to Josef Mengele, I was betting that it was Sedlmeier.

I stayed in the office late, until it was morning in West Germany. Then I called the head of the police department in Günzburg. He couldn't speak English, so he passed me off to his captain. I asked the captain if anybody had ever searched Sedlmeier's home, looking for evidence about Mengele. I waited while he looked for a file.

Yes, he said. There had been two searches of Hans Sedlmeier's home. One in 1964, and one in 1971. Neither had yielded any results. Sedlmeier had also been questioned extensively, he said, with negative results. Around Günzburg, he told me, Hans Sedlmeier was *very* highly regarded.

For two minutes, the captain yapped about what a *citizen* Hans was.

I hung up the phone and got depressed. Shit! How was I ever going to close a forty-year-old case? All I was learning was how many people loved Nazis.

I felt like saying, fuck it, this guy's *permanently* in the wind, I'm going *home,* I'm gonna see my *wife.* Safir had recently insisted I move to D.C. and work at headquarters. As usual, Betsy had been given no input on the decision, and—as usual—she'd made the move without complaint.

But instead of going home, I grabbed my Sedlmeier folder and found the closest all-night diner. I started chain-drinking Coca-Cola, and ordered about nine waffles and four hot-fudge sundaes. I'd long ago burned out my adrenal glands, and now I was living from one sugar/caffeine rush to the next.

Around 4:00 A.M., when my eyes felt like hot coals, I started in on Interpol's Sedlmeier research. In 1964 and 1971, Interpol said, raids had been conducted on Sedlmeier's house. I knew that. But these raids had been "compromised," the file said, by "an apparent tip-off." Someone inside the local *police department* had told Sedlmeier they were coming.

I slept in the backseat of my car until the sun came up, then I stumbled into Safir's office. He was well into his day's work, looking fresh and bright.

"We *gotta* do a raid on Hans Sedlmeier," I said. "And we gotta make sure he's not warned. Can you set it up?"

"Yes," he said. I loved Safir. Any other bureaucrat would've said, "I'll try," or "Let's see." Not Howard Safir.

"Thanks, Boss."

"Thank *you,* John."

I was slurping black bean soup in the CIA cafeteria when a polyester-type guy approached me. He was sort of short, with a pot belly, a belt too wide, and a tie too narrow.

"Mr. Pass-gucci?" he said, in an indeterminable European accent. "May I intrude? You have been pointed out to me as the man who found Bohdan Koziy and Konrads Kalejs. I congratulate you for that. You see, I myself live in the Middle East."

"In Israel?" I stood to shake his hand.

"Around that part of the world, yes."

"Have a seat. What brings you to D.C.?"

"My employer believed it would be good for training for me to study here briefly. You know, you and I, we have similar interests. It would be good to talk, away from all this noise."

I didn't trust the guy. As far as I knew, he was an Agency officer, testing my discretion.

"Your suit is very beautiful," he said. "Perhaps you could show me where you purchased it?"

On the other hand, I'd never gotten anywhere by playing safe.

"Where are you staying?" I asked.

"In the Hilton hotel, off Chain Bridge Road."

"Tell you what, I'll meet you in the Hilton lobby at 4:00 P.M. The Tysons Corner mall is right around the corner, and they got a Bloomingdale's. Wanna do that?"

"That would be very fine."

When I picked him up, he was much more forthright. He worked for Shin Beth, the Israeli secret police. Hearing that gave me the chills, because some of the Shin Beth people were real monsters. Torture was still common in Israel, and even legal—as long as you called it "physical pressure."

We drove around awhile, and I showed off some of my new CIA knowledge, pointing out some of the intelligence agencies. Besides the CIA, there was the National Security Agency (which was even bigger than the CIA), the State Department's Bureau of Intelligence, the Defense Intelligence Agency, the intelligence branches of the four armed services, and the super-secret National Reconnaissance Agency. A lot of them were in Tysons, which had more office space than the entire city of Miami.

In the mall, we found a quiet bar. We sat at a table in the corner.

When the waitress came over, I said, "Vodka martini. Shaken, not stirred."

"Forgive my boldness," said my Shin Beth friend, "but I have been given to learn that you are running the investigation of Dr. Mengele. Yes?"

"Howard Safir's in charge of it."

"But you personally will be traveling to South America—yes?"

"Who told you *that?*"

"Our two countries are working *together* on this mission, as we should be," he said. "Allow me, please, to get to my point. And you *must* forgive my boldness. In 1977, Prime Minister Begin, with no public announcement about it, changed our policy on Dr. Mengele. The prime minister privately informed our intelligence officers that it would be in the best interests of our nation not to bring Dr. Mengele to trial. It would embarrass our South American allies, who buy from us many armaments, and are agreeable with us in the United Nations. And there was also the chance that Dr. Mengele might be pitied, as an old, sick man. You see, even our own Supreme Court sometimes finds ... easy ... solutions. We have become a nation of laws, instead of a nation of conscience.

"So the prime minister said that if we were to find Dr. Mengele, we were to terminate his situation. Immediately." He stared into his drink.

"Our *current* policy," he continued, "is somewhat more

flexible. But this gives me curiosity about your feelings. I am curious how you would react if a policy similar to Prime Minister Begin's were to become operational?"

I took a deep breath. I knew I should be coy. But fuck that. I was the Gipper's cop. I could act however I felt. "I'll be honest with you," I said, "even if you're not really who you *say* you are. A guy like Mengele? If it was up to me, I'd just fuckin' whack the guy."

"Wack?"

"*Whack*. Terminate. Blow his brains out."

His face brightened dramatically, like the sun climbing over a cloud. "Ah, yes! Whack!"

Then he became even more serious. "Now I must ask. Would you, personally . . . play a part? Perhaps the *primary* part?"

"If it was done right? Where I don't get hung out to dry? You bet."

He beamed at me. "Then we have an understanding." He reached across the table and shook my hand.

He gave me a number to call if I wanted to contact him, or his agency. He said they'd contact me if it "became appropriate."

On the way out—wouldn't you know?—we ran into one of the guys I'd met at the Agency. He recognized me, and seemed to recognize my Israeli buddy, too. The Agency, like the Marshals, had offices in the mall. I wasn't supposed to know that, but I did. "What're you guys up to?" the Agency guy asked. "Shoppin'?"

"No," said my buddy. "We're just whacking time."

The Agency guy gave us a hell of a funny look, so I hustled my buddy off.

I took my Agency rabbi and three of his colleagues out to the USMS shooting range, and weasel-dealed them in with fake Marshals credentials. They loved me for that because the CIA had no facility for weapons practice. The liberals in Congress has mandated that. To me, it was scary: All these Agency guys, all over the world, fighting off terrorists—and they didn't know how to shoot a goddamn gun!

During a break, I said to my rabbi, "I know you don't do

this kinda stuff anymore, but back in the Nixon days, when you *did* do it, how'd you guys go about whacking people?"

He got edgy. "I think that was all exaggerated. And I can flat *guarantee* you we don't do it now."

"He's right," said one of his colleagues—a heavy guy who looked like Santa Claus. "We don't do it. but if we *did*, I'll tell you exactly how." He slipped his gun into a shoulder holster and ignored the nervous looks my rabbi was giving him. Out here, he felt like a gunfighter, not a bureaucrat. "We'd farm it out," he said. "Why should *we* risk trained manpower on that kinda bullshit? We'd buy a hitter from organized crime."

"Like, a professional assassin?" I asked.

"That's *another* myth," said Santa. "There are virtually no pro assassins. Most all the mob hitters are just punks tryin' to make their bones and get away from the heavy liftin'. The bosses give the dirty work to somebody who's expendable— a kid with no special training, who's not smart enough to say no. Only reason these punks usually get away with it is—nine times outta ten—it's against another wise guy. So the authorities never pursue it. And that's the same kinda punk that they'd sell *us*. Hell of it is, it used to work out just fine. That's why we never had to set up our own Wet Department."

"Wet Department?"

"Wet work. That's what the KGB calls it. Assassination."

"Well," I said, "what if your guy couldn't just go in there *blastin'*? What if it had to be discreet?"

"You gonna whack *Mengele?*" my rabbi blurted.

"Fuck youuu. I'm just interested. How many chances do I get to talk about this shit with real Agency guys?"

"*I'll* tell you how," said Santa. He caressed his gun. He was feeling bad-ass. "*Ricin*. Distilled from castor beans. It's as deadly as poison gets. It just needs to get under the skin, or even be inhaled. It's not even hard to get hold of. And here's the beauty part. No symptoms for three days! Then, boom! Your whole body goes to hell. And it's impossible to trace."

"Is that right?" I said.

"*You're* gonna whack *Mengele*," accused my rabbi.

"No," I said, "I'm gonna go to *Chile* and whack Salvador Allende's *kids*—finish the job you guys *started*."

My rabbi choked out a little laugh. And shut up.

Safir was twisting in his chair when I walked into his office. He looked as if he were about to implode from tension. He kept plowing his hands through his short black hair.

"The German authorities say they don't have enough probable cause to raid Hans Sedlmeier," he said.

"Maybe I should go to Germany. Look for triggers. Break things loose."

"You'd break *something*," he said. "No. I think we should just try to build a preponderance of evidence that shows cause."

I trudged down the hall and got with my two computer brainiacs. I had them bring me all the ancillary stuff they had on Sedlmeier.

Nine hours later, I found something. About six months earlier, Sedlmeier had gotten drunk and had mentioned to a university professor that he'd sent money to Mengele. The professor had reported the conversation to a German prosecutor, but no one had done anything with it. After all, it was hearsay. Plus, the original source had been intoxicated.

Still, I hurried to Safir with it.

"It's better than nothing," he said, "but I think they've already heard about this. I'll call anyway. At least it'll get the dialogue going again."

"Boss, you oughta try your own special motivational technique."

"Whattaya mean?"

"Bust his hump so bad that he'll do anything to get you outta his face."

Safir nodded cheerfully. It didn't even occur to him to take offense.

I finished my CIA training, collected my fake identification, and caught a plane for South America. My spirits were shaky. I still didn't have any solid leads, and I couldn't get rid of the feeling that my life would never again be the same.

Part of my dark mood was based on the duration of the trip. Safir had told me to plan on being gone seven or eight months. Another part of it was the danger. I knew I might be captured down there, and tortured or killed. And part of it was just instinct.

As the plane began to climb, I picked out Betsy in the airport parking lot, standing next to our car. She was waving. I waved back. I knew she couldn't see me. I didn't care. I craned around in my seat and watched her disappear. My stomach felt like I'd swallowed something hot.

Before takeoff, Betsy had broken down and started to cry. She'd even asked me—for the first time ever—not to go. Made me feel like hell. She'd composed herself, and had smiled as she'd kissed me good-bye. But I could see she felt empty inside.

I pulled down my window shade and started studying my research materials. According to Wiesenthal's people, there had been several sightings of Mengele in Southern Paraguay in the last five months. I'd start by following each of those five leads.

I'd also learned that there was another Nazi support group that might be helping Mengele. It was called Kameraden-werk. Turns out, it was the largest of the underground Nazi organizations. It was also the richest, having extorted a fortune from wealthy former Nazis. The scary thing, though, was that it was the group that nobody knew anything about.

I had to infiltrate them. Preferably, without dying.

We stopped in Miami to refuel. Next thing I knew, a guy was taking me by the arm and leading me off the plane. "Mr. Safir's waiting," he said.

"What's Safir doing here?"

"Monitoring a Miami FIST."

When I walked into the reception area of the Miami Marshals' office, Safir sprang off the couch. "We got a *body!*" he sang.

"*Whose* body?"

"Mengele's! I hope."

He filled me in. After my last meeting with him, he'd leaned on the Germans again, and they'd finally agreed to hit Sedlmeier's house. Safir had made sure it was done as a top-level operation this time, with no chance for leaks.

At Sedlmeier's, the police had found the "smoking gun":

letters from Mengele. Sedlmeier's wife had *kept* them. Stupid bitch. The letters had led them to an address in Brazil— not Paraguay—and they'd hit the Brazil house. There, an old couple had given Mengele up. Mengele, they'd said, was dead. He'd had a stroke in 1978 while swimming, and had drowned. Based on the couple's testimony, local police had exhumed the body.

My task now was to go to São Paulo, Brazil, and make a positive ID on the corpse. Safir would collect a group of forensic specialists and ship them down to me.

"Two things to remember," said Safir. "One: Wiesenthal says he's almost certain this is a hoax—so be careful. Two: If this *is* Mengele, it may be more dangerous than ever. The same forces will still be lined up against you, trying to screw this up, and now they'll know exactly where to find you."

"I'll be careful."

"John, I want to say something else. As somebody who's Jewish, I want to thank you. This wouldn't have happened without you."

"Or *you*, Boss," I said. I held out my hand. He took it.

And then, for once, Howard Safir allowed himself to smile.

Moments after I stepped off my plane in Brazil, a burly federal policeman grabbed me by the arm. "You are under arrest!"

"For what?"

"Illegal entry! This document is not properly stamped."

"There's nothing *wrong* with this passport," I snarled. "I want to see your supervisor! At once!"

He sneered at my demand and motioned for me to follow him. Another Brazilian cop, carrying an Uzi, trailed behind us.

They led me to a deserted airport lounge, then left, locking the door behind them. They took my diplomatic passport. Unfortunately, it was a crude fake.

When Safir and I had suddenly discovered that I needed to go to Brazil, instead of Argentina, I'd weasel-dealed the visa in great haste.

In a matter of hours, the Brazilian cops would figure out how phony it was. That's when things would get interesting.

They'd either treat me like a high-ranking American with a glitch in his paperwork—or they'd do God-knows-what. Brazil had an ugly record on human rights.

I sat there wishing some OSI guys had been on the plane, so that they could vouch for me. But I'd already made sure no OSI guys were on it. After I'd arranged to go to Brazil, I'd started worrying that OSI would go down there and start legalizing the situation into chaos. So, as Dick Nixon used to say, I rat-fucked them. I called my airline to see if they were on the same flight, and found that they were. So I canceled their reservations. Canceled their hotel, too, just for fun.

And look where it had gotten me. As Nixon wrote in *Beyond Peace,* "If you live by the rat-fuck, you die by the rat-fuck."

I checked out the lounge and found a liquor cabinet. Poured myself a drink. For all I knew, I was going to spend the rest of the day with electrodes attached to my testicles. I needed a drink.

Then a well-dressed guy bustled in and started kissing my ass. He was the head of the Immigration Police, and he hand-wrote on my passport that I could go anywhere I wanted. Looked to me like he'd called the CIA.

I grabbed the next plane to Brasília, and reported to the Agency's top man in Brazil, the chief of station. He handed me off to a subordinate, and we went out and hopped in his car. "I know just how to grease the skids for you," he said.

He sort of reminded me of my rabbi in Langley—collegiate and cheerful. He acted like he had the world by the balls, and that the world didn't even know it. "You've got to remember," he said, "that Brazil is a totalitarian government, and if you get on their bad side, you've got a *serious* problem." He looked over the top of his bifocals, to make sure I knew what *serious* meant. "The Brazilians are concerned about you coming in here and taking over; it offends their machismo. But we'll go ingratiate you with a very prominent colonel in military intelligence.

"Open that," he said, nodding at a briefcase on the seat. I hesitated. "Go ahead; it's not armed."

I popped it open. Inside were bundles of hundred-dollar bills.

"I'll let you hand that over to him yourself. I take care of him all the time, but if *you* give it to him, he'll like you."

"He'll help me?"

"Not necessarily. But he won't hurt you."

"The colonel's a hurtin' kinda guy, huh?"

He made a face. "We don't have the same number of disappearances that they had in Chile under the generals," he said, "but this is a rough country. The colonel's primary job is to keep the press in line, and to discourage dissidents. It's one of *those* kinds of jobs."

"You mean, he whacks people."

"No. Not always. Sometimes he just tortures them." All the cheer left his face. "He's a devil," he said flatly.

"But I should *deal* with him?"

"You'd *better* deal with him."

We pulled up in front of a castle. It had an enormous concrete face, with two towers at each corner. We showed ID to a guard at the gate, and pulled in. "This is his house," said the Agency guy.

We followed a guard in a military uniform down long hallways, past thick masonry walls, toward the center of the castle. It was quiet as a tomb, the kind of place where Hell could exist without anyone knowing it.

Finally, we walked under a carved archway into a vast, plush office. The colonel, sitting behind a desk, did not rise to greet us. He was big, bloated with fat, and had a white mustache.

The Agency guy greeted the colonel in Portuguese, then turned to me. "I'll translate," he said.

"Tell him, 'Cute house.' "

The Agency guy gave me a dark look, then exchanged words with the colonel.

"The colonel says, 'Thank you, I decorated it myself.' "

"Tell him I have brought a token of my esteem, in appreciation for his work on behalf of America."

As the CIA guy spoke, I handed over the briefcase full of money. When the colonel saw it, he smiled broadly, and lumbered over to a walk-in safe. He unlocked it, and unselfconsciously stacked the money onto a massive pile of U.S.

dollars. There were also stacks of currencies from many other countries.

The colonel said something to my CIA buddy, and then they talked for a couple of minutes.

The Agency guy turned to me. "He has tasked Mr. Sung with helping you. Mr. Sung is the colonel's contact within the Brazilian Federal Police, who are in charge of the Mengele investigation."

At that moment, an Asian man in a black suit and black tie suddenly materialized from the other side of the room. I could have sworn no one else was around.

Mr. Sung languidly extended his hand. "I am at your service, Inspector Pascucci," he said in flawless English. The thin, saffron skin around his mouth tightened, in what was meant to be a smile. His eyes pierced mine.

Just looking at him scared the shit out of me.

I hustled down to São Paulo, to greet the forensic team that Safir had sent down. Also at the airport was a forensic team assembled by Nazi-hunter Simon Wiesenthal. Part of my job was to coordinate the two teams' efforts.

The other part was to keep all of them from getting killed. That wouldn't be easy, because I was not allowed to have a gun here.

To be honest, I was frightened, because this was the best moment in history for a hit against the world's top Nazi hunters. They were descending in droves on São Paulo and grouping around my two teams.

The hit against us could come from *die Spinne,* ODESSA, Kameradenwerk, any neo-Nazi group, or maybe an anti-Jewish Mideast group, like the PLO. Take your pick.

It could even come from somebody hired by Mengele himself—because *many* of the experts were still convinced this was a hoax, and that Mengele was still out there, plotting against us. Wiesenthal, Serge Klarsfeld, and even Isser Harrel—the Mossad guy who'd grabbed Eichmann—were all extremely skeptical.

Even the two forensic teams were in sharp conflict. After I got them safely to our hotel, they started ripping each other apart. Based on the preliminary information, Safir's team (a medical examiner, a former CIA handwriting expert, a medical anthropologist, and a dentist) thought we'd found Mengele. But Wiesenthal's team (a radiologist, a medical examiner, and a medical anthropologist) thought this was just a charade. The feelings of Wiesenthal's team seemed to go beyond simple scientific skepticism. I wasn't sure why. It seemed to me that they'd be as anxious as anybody to think that Mengele was already in hell.

I did know that some of these doctors already hated one another's guts, because they'd locked horns previously in criminal trials. They were all prominent "hired guns"—doctors who worked for defense lawyers and prosecutors—and for years they'd dumped on one another in various courtrooms. Supposedly, that didn't matter in a serious situation like this. But it did.

I held a get-together dinner, then sat and listened to these learned colleagues shit all over one another. Highly educated people are different from you and me. They're meaner. By the end of dinner, I was dying to get away.

I wanted to catch a cab and sightsee. But I ignored the ones parked in front of our hotel. My CIA rabbi had told me never to take a cab parked in front of an embassy, or in front of your hotel. Often, he said, they were driven by agents.

So I walked a couple of blocks away to look for a cab. São Paulo was beautiful—a rich, cosmopolitan city that twinkled like Disneyland at night.

On impulse, I stopped at a fine jewelry store. I decided to buy a Rolex. These days, I was making more money than I knew what to do with. I don't even remember how much I was making—*that's* how much I was making.

I could have paid for the Rolex out of my slush fund for the docs, because they were each on a $1,000-a-day expense account, and nobody was watching overages. As a matter of fact, one of my docs ended up spending $37,000 down there. But I wasn't into thievery. I was leaving that to some of my fellow marshals. With the advent of the drug forfeiture laws—which allowed law enforcement agencies to confiscate property used in illegal drug deals—the USMS was now custodian of about $1.4 *billion* in seized assets. A number of marshals had given in to greed, and had grifted some of these assets. In LA, for example, several marshals were selling seized goods directly out of storage lockers—while getting kickbacks from the guards they hired to *watch* the lockers. I loved the Service's increased power, but God knows there was a dark side to it.

In the jewelry shop, the young woman who waited on me was absolutely gorgeous. Just breathtaking—one of the prettiest women I'd ever seen. She had glossy black hair, creamy skin, and blue eyes that shone like two bright stars.

Amazingly, she started coming on to me. Don't tell me she came on to every American guy who paid cash for a Rolex, because I *don't* wanna hear it. She was too intelligent for that. But I had this James Bond thing going for me that was practically irresistible. Right?

I left with the watch but not the girl. I could, of course, have invoked the five-hundred-mile rule. Or even the five-*thousand*-mile rule, which covered five women, a Persian cat, and a gallon of Mazola oil.

But fuck that. I was married.

As I stepped out the door, a cab pulled up, and I hopped in.

"Speak English?" I asked.

The driver spread his thumb and forefinger, indicating "a little."

"American Embassy," I said. I wasn't sure where it was, but I was positive it would be in the nice part of town, and that's where I wanted to sightsee. I'd heard that shantytown, where the Indians lived, was pretty horrifying.

We began driving through a prosperous shopping district, past people who were almost all Caucasians. Brazil, which has half the population of the entire continent, is 75 percent European stock, and only 5 percent Indian. At first, I'd been surprised at how few Indians there were. But I guess that's like driving through Kansas City and being shocked at how few Sioux you see. We came, we saw, we conquered.

I saw a newsstand, and asked the driver to pull over. But he didn't seem to understand.

He took a turn into a residential neighborhood, and gradually the houses began to grow poor and ugly.

"American Embassy?" I said.

He turned, nodded, and smiled. But he began to speed up.

Then he ran a stop sign, and really floored it. Suddenly we were ripping down the street, and he wasn't smiling at all. "Hey!" I yelled. "Stop! *Alto!*" He didn't look at me. I punched him in the shoulder. *"Stop!"* I was just about to smack him when a car pulled right in front of us. He hit his brakes and swerved.

I jumped out.

I ran like a bastard through somebody's backyard, then barged right into the living room of the first house I got to.

A man and his wife jumped up. I badged them, and they went stiff with fear. Apparently, the cops here were scarier than the robbers. "Telephone?" I blurted. *"Telefono?"*

The man pointed at his phone. I didn't know whether to call the cops, or a taxi. I called both. The cab arrived first.

I jumped in. "Speak English?"

"Yes."

I had him take me back to the hotel.

I needed to get a gun. And I needed more than that.

I needed help. No matter what I'd told myself, I wasn't James Bond. I was just an American cop who was in over his head.

Early the next morning, I asked each of my docs not to leave the hotel, and then I went to the São Paulo CIA office.

The CIA was at the American Embassy. To get to their office, you had to walk into a supply closet, close the door behind you, then knock on another door that had a fish-eye peephole. If they recognized you, they let you in.

I got with my CIA counterpart and told him about the cab ride.

"Shit!" he said. "I'll brief you, but you have to hold this in confidence. Nobody else on your team has a need-to-know. We got a teletype this morning, one our intelligence analysts think we should take seriously. It's from Langley, based on leads generated in Brasília and Algiers. The slant headquarters put on the leads is this: The PLO apparently wants to disrupt your activities down here. Or terminate them. They don't like the Jews getting sympathetic publicity. Plus, they're unhappy that one of your doctors is originally from Lebanon."

"Ali Hameli?"

"That's right."

"Did you know he was the medical consultant on *Quincy?*"

"No kidding!" CIA guys loved information, no matter how trivial.

"Also," he said, "the PLO is suspicious about your handwriting guy being a former Agency officer. They think this investigation has a hidden agenda.

"But, bottom line, we don't know who the primary target is, or even if there *is* a primary target. As you know, terrorists often prefer random attacks, to keep *everybody* off-balance."

I took his warning very seriously. A few weeks before, Lebanese Shiites had hijacked a TWA plane, and used the hostages to win the release of 735 Lebanese prisoners.

"So," I asked, "can you give me some *help?*"

"Of course. That's *very* possible. But we'd like you to help us, too. Tell you what we need. We don't trust OSI. We believe that they want to blame the Agency for Mengele remaining at large as long as he did, to deflect criticism of their own ineptitude. Obviously, we *did* help Klaus Barbie, and a number of other Nazis who helped us fight the Communists. But Mengele was *not* one of them. How could *he* help? He was small potatoes.

"As far as trust goes," he continued, "we don't trust Wiesenthal's people, either. Wiesenthal himself seems to be a straight arrow, but we think some of his people are up to no good."

"Such as?"

"Such as debunking your investigation, regardless of its validity. And we *don't* want that. We want this thing *over,* before it causes a rift with the Brazilians. To be blunt, in the big picture of U.S. relations with South America, Josef Mengele is quite trivial."

That pissed me off, but I swallowed the anger.

"Why would Wiesenthal's people want to discredit our investigation?" I asked.

"Fund-raising, Inspector! Mengele's their poster boy. As

long as he stays in the wind, they can raise money to find him. He's their last Nazi with any real box office appeal."

"So you want me to keep my eye on OSI and Wiesenthal's people?"

"If you don't *mind,"* he said cordially.

"Why would I mind?" I tried not to sound sarcastic.

"Also," he said, "I'd like you to pick up a package for me. Won't take you a minute. It'll be in the hotel next to yours."

"What's in it? Microfilm?"

He shook me off. "Between you and me? Hog futures."

Yeah, sure. "Why do you want *me* to get it?"

"You're a fresh face," he said. "They've seen all the rest of us so many times."

I didn't ask who "they" were. I didn't ask anything. It was obvious that he wasn't going to give me any help until he owed me one. It reminded me of the old days in the Marshals, when favors were all we had to offer. Now we had money. But now we were playing for higher stakes, and needed things money couldn't buy.

I went back to the hotel and interrupted an OSI meeting. I told them I was instituting stricter security measures. Some of them whined, but not Neal Sher, their director. He was accustomed to being a target, and I've got to admit, he was a courageous man. As I finished, I left my James Bond briefcase in the room. With the recording device on.

Then I went downstairs to the front desk, and told them I needed to see the outgoing mail for OSI and the Wiesenthal team. The bell captain balked, until I badged him—then he started trembling. Jesus! What did the cops *do* to people down here?

I went back to my room and pulled out my canister of freon. Without opening the envelopes, I sprayed them with freon, like my CIA rabbi had shown me, and pretty soon they were clear as glass. There was nothing in the letters, as far as I could tell, that trashed the CIA. In a few minutes, the envelopes returned to normal, and I took them back to the bell captain.

I composed some telexes to headquarters, then picked up my James Bond briefcase.

At the prearranged time, I went to the hotel to pick up the

CIA's package. This was a "dead drop" operation. I sat where I was supposed to, and waited for someone to come and leave the package near me. When he did, I picked it up and walked out.

To tell you the truth, my heart was thumping like hell—just like it did when I kicked a door. There were too many unknowns in this.

When I handed the package to my CIA contact, it was moist with fear-sweat.

Then I gave him the tape of the OSI meeting. "Can I get a receipt for that?" I asked, smiling. It was my way of reminding him that I'd just committed a felony on his behalf, by spying on American citizens.

"No. No receipt," he said. No smile, either.

He punched his intercom and said, "Hank, the hog futures are in."

"Those really *are* hog futures?" I asked.

He nodded. Everybody always assumed, he said, that the CIA was out stealing secrets from rocket scientists. But a lot of what they did was just gather information about the finances of other countries. Uncle Sam wanted to know in advance which way the money was blowing. That way, the president could protect our national interests—and our multinational corporations—by having some senator make a speech, or by announcing some kind of trade deal.

After my CIA contact handed off the OSI tape to a transcriber, I asked, "So *now* can I have some protection?"

"You bet, Inspector. I'll put a man on your hotel. Right away."

"*A* man? As in, one man?"

"Hey, we're not the United States *Marines.* I'm *already* overstepping our charter."

I got the hell out of there and called the number I'd gotten from my Israeli Shin Beth friend.

The guy who answered the phone—a declared Mossad agent—agreed to meet me.

Before I could ask for help, he started pumping me with questions about the identity of the body.

"All we're certain of at this moment," I said, "is that Mengele definitely was living near São Paulo for some time. I talked to our handwriting expert this morning, and he says that documents recovered from São Paulo *were* written by Mengele. But we still aren't certain if the body is Mengele."

"So he may still be alive?"

"He may be."

Then he started going through the same song and dance as the Shin Beth guy in Langley, using the same basic rhetoric. Long story short: Would I ice Mengele?

Yeah, sure, I told him—but how about *first* helping me keep my *own* ass from getting shot off?

He gave me the same sob story the CIA guy had: limited resources, love to help, can't, let's have lunch.

It was time to talk to somebody *serious.* I needed Mr. Sung, my hook in the Brazilian Federal Police. But first, I wanted to pick up a present for him. I hit the nearest phone booth, called the airline I'd flown in on, and asked them if a package for me had arrived. It had.

The prior evening, just after the Cab Ride from Hell, I'd called a stateside marshal and had asked him to dip into his flash-money account and send me half a dozen Smith & Wesson revolvers. He'd sent them down by courier, giving them directly to the pilot. It had been illegal as hell, of course, but fuck that. I needed *help.*

I kept one of the illegal guns for myself, then went to see Mr. Sung.

Mr. Sung's eyes lit up when he saw the guns. "Smith and Wesson! You certainly understand the peccadillos of our enforcement officers, Inspector!" He meant that I knew South American cops had a hard-on for S & W.

Then I asked him for help.

"Why, I'd be delighted to help!" he said. "I'll put a squad of plainclothes men around your people at all times."

I did not want to like this guy. I was sure he was a monster. But when you feel like somebody's saving your life, it's hard not to get all warm and fuzzy about them.

It made me want to introduce Mr. Sung to the Gipper. Ronbo would love this guy.

Day after day, my docs did their workups on the skeleton. It was hard work, and I had them all crammed together in one safe spot. Everybody except Neal Sher bitched about my security measures. The docs were practically under house arrest, and when they did go out, I made sure they were covered by me, my lone CIA security officer, or by one of Mr. Sung's hit men.

Gradually, the physical characteristics of the corpse were determined. The easiest characteristic to ascertain was sex; this was a male, because of the shape of the pelvis. Height was determined by measuring the lengths of the major arm and leg bones, and it was clear that the skeleton's height had been close to Mengele's five foot eight. Age was harder to determine. To do that, they put a cross-section of bone under a microscope, and counted its blood-carrying canals, which increase with age. According to this test, the age of the body was between sixty-four and seventy-four; Mengele would have been 69 when he supposedly died.

Race was easy to determine. The skull was that of a Caucasian.

Our most impressive findings came from X rays. The skull showed evidence of an especially wide nerve at the top of the mouth, which indicated a probable gap between the teeth. Mengele had a gap. Also, the skeleton had suffered a hip fracture. So had Mengele.

Dental records would have been conclusive, but none existed. Therefore, we had to begin a painstaking process called photosuperimposition—mathematically matching the shape of the skull against photos taken of Mengele. From this procedure, it began to appear certain that the corpse was, indeed, Mengele.

While the docs finished their tests, I helped the Federal Police piece together the details of Mengele's life in South America. We based it primarily on interviews of people who'd known him.

When Josef Mengele moved from Buenos Aires to Paraguay in 1959—one step ahead of the Mossad—he thought he'd found a safe haven. Paraguay was a backward, fascist nation that would have hidden Mengele forever. In Paraguay's "New Bavaria," Mengele took refuge on the farm of Alban Krug, a diehard Nazi.

But Mengele stayed in Paraguay for only fifteen months.

Convinced that the Israelis were closing in on him, Mengele left for Brazil.

There he met a fanatical Nazi emigré named Wolfgang Gerhard, who was locally famous for placing a swastika atop his Christmas tree, and for giving out bars of authentic "Jew Soap" as special Yuletide gifts. Gerhard hooked up Mengele with a couple he knew, Geza and Gitta Stammer. The Stammers were sympathetic to Nazism, but Mengele still took the precaution of introducing himself under a phony name.

For about fifteen years, Mengele lived with the Stammers, and at some point apparently began to have an affair with Mrs. Stammer, who was quite attractive. But Mengele was not an easy man to live with. Authoritarian and overbearing, Mengele eventually alienated the Stammers and most of the other people he met. But he didn't make many new acquaintances because he was extremely paranoid about being exposed as a war criminal. He always wore a hat, and pulled it over his face whenever a stranger appeared.

In 1962, the Stammers discovered Mengele's true identity, when a photo of him appeared in a newspaper. But still they hid him, partly because they were afraid of him, and partly because he was giving them money that he received from Hans Sedlmeier. Sedlmeier sent Mengele tens of thousands of dollars, as well as a regular monthly stipend of $150, which was a princely sum in rural Brazil.

Mengele spent much of his time working on a self-serving, narcissistic autobiography, which included forty pages about his birth—with a page and a half devoted exclusively to a description of his placenta.

Mengele ventured away from the Stammers' humble farm only when protected by a pack of fifteen dogs. He also built a watchtower, where he scanned the horizon for Nazi hunters.

In 1969, Mengele and the Stammers moved to a comfortable four-bedroom home outside São Paulo, purchased primarily with money from Sedlmeier. But Mengele had begun to bicker constantly with the Stammers, and felt lonely and isolated. He was so stressed out that he developed a "hair ball" from chewing the ends of his mustache. The hair ball was surgically removed from his rectum.

At this time, Klaus Barbie, the notorious "Butcher of

Lyon," offered to let Mengele live with him. Mengele shrewdly refused. He was safer living in total obscurity. Barbie was later captured.

In late 1969, Mengele met another couple, Wolfram and Liselotte Bossert, who welcomed him into their home. The Bosserts, fervent Nazis, knew Mengele's true identity, and greatly admired what he'd done during the war. The Bosserts believed in forced sterilization of the "lower classes," and hated Jews.

In the bosom of the admiring Bossert family, Mengele experienced a rebirth of security and peace. He corresponded with his son, Rolf, and was visited by Sedlmeier.

Even in this supportive atmosphere, however, Mengele remained critical, self-pitying, and cold. He constantly censured Rolf and other family members in his letters. He also exhibited an unhealthy fixation upon Rolf's wife, who was a twin. Gradually, Mengele's family stopped writing to him.

In the mid-1970s, Mengele's health began to fail, and he felt increasingly sorry for himself. His ugly personality grew even more unbearable. He worried that he didn't have enough money. He developed a romantic crush on a household servant, but nothing came of it.

In 1977, Rolf visited, but the reunion broke down when Rolf gently tried to question Mengele about the war. Mengele became enraged.

By 1978, Mengele's health was nosediving. He told an acquaintance, "I am going to the beach because my life is at an end."

Then, according to the Bosserts, Mengele suffered a stroke while swimming and inhaled water as he was pulled to shore. Efforts to revive him, the Bosserts said, were futile. They told police that they buried him using a false name.

To me, the story held together. I went over it repeatedly, looking for inconsistencies. I couldn't find any. Also, it had the ring of truth. Mengele hadn't lived the grand lifestyle of a monarch in exile. And he hadn't continued his butchery, killing local Indians. Either of those acts would have been stupid. They would have invited capture. And Josef Mengele was anything but stupid.

I was going through my documents on Mengele's life when I heard a knock.

There was a tall, dark-skinned man at the door, wearing what looked like a chauffeur's uniform. "Inspector Pascucci? I was sent to drive you to the American Embassy."

"By whom?"

He gave me the name of my primary contact.

"Hang on," I said, "I'll get my papers." I put some documents in my James Bond briefcase, put on a jacket and tie, and grabbed an umbrella. "Let's roll."

In the hallway, he said, "May I take your things?" He reached for the umbrella and briefcase. I heard a little beep from my gut-meter.

"Hang on a second," I said. "I forgot to make a call."

"The Embassy did say this was rather urgent," he said. "Perhaps you could call from there?"

BEEEEP!

I left him in the hall and called my CIA contact. "You wanted to see me?" I asked.

"We're *always* glad to see you."

"I mean, did you send a car for me?"

"Not me, personally. Hang on." I heard him shout, "Anybody send a car for the marshal?" He came back on. "No. What's goin' on?" I told him about the chauffeur. "Call Sher. Tell him to stay put. Lock your door, and I'll send somebody over."

I got my Smith & Wesson and put it under a raincoat. I walked out into the hallway.

The chauffeur was gone.

"You're going to have to ratchet down the security even tighter," said my CIA contact, leaning back in his office chair while he tamped his pipe.

"Maybe you could give me even *more* help," I said. "Like, an extra Boy Scout."

He grimaced. "I understand your anxiety," he muttered. "But we are *not* policemen. Even under President *Reagan,* there are *some* restraints."

He stood up and pushed his door shut. "You know who

you *oughta* be going after? Not some piece of old news like Mengele. Go after that prick Agee."

He meant Philip Agee, an ex-Agency guy who'd written a scathing exposé of CIA shenanigans.

"From what I hear," he said, "good people *died* after Agee exposed their activities. Now, I'm not speaking on behalf of the Agency, you understand. But taking out Agee *would* be the right thing to do. And it *could* be done."

"I've got no time for Agee," I said.

"Just a thought," he said.

After that, he just sat there.

I wasn't going to get any more help.

I went straight to Mr. Sung.

"This is gettin' outta control," I told him. "We've gotta take the initiative. Be proactive. Break things loose."

"What were you considering?"

"How about this? Tonight I go for a walk. Alone. Put two of your feds on my tail—but discreetly. Make sure they've got a radio, and can speak English. I'll stay in contact with them, and if I spot somebody following me, we move against them. Maybe we can find out who the troublemakers are."

"I'll arrange it."

At nine o'clock, I left the hotel. I was wearing the in-ear receiver/transmitter my CIA rabbi had given me. As I stepped out the door, I said, "This is Pascucci. You with me?"

In my ear, I heard, "Yes, Inspector."

"Let's go."

At the first corner, I left the main commercial street and headed for a less-populated area.

As the streets became less crowded, I started using all the tricks Frank Sweeney had used against us during the Boyce investigation. I waited until just before the traffic light changed, and then jumped into the pedestrian crosswalk, just ahead of traffic. As nearly as I could tell, no one followed. I walked half a block, then abruptly changed directions. Still no takers. But then I crossed the street suddenly, and I could have sworn a guy half a block away also crossed. He was wearing a gray windbreaker.

"See a guy in a dark windbreaker?" I asked.

In my ear I heard, "We see him."

I walked around the block, then headed down a nearly deserted residential street. I looked around. I saw the guy in the windbreaker. He was walking toward me. He began to jog. "Take him!" I hissed.

I heard a squeal of tires, and a tan sedan appeared from out of nowhere. It jumped over the curb and sliced to within a foot of the guy in the windbreaker. Two men rushed out, and all I heard was one solid *thunk*. The guy in the windbreaker went limp, and they threw him in the back of the car.

The car proceeded down the street—not fast, not slow.

As it passed me, no one even looked my way.

First thing the next morning, I called Mr. Sung. He was in a jovial mood. I wasn't. I'd spent a bad night thinking about what was happening to the guy in the windbreaker.

I hated being involved in this. But it was a necessary evil.

"Inspector!" enthused Mr. Sung. "I believe we have defused your security problems. The rest of your visit should be safe."

"That guy talked?"

"What guy?"

"The guy in the windbreaker—the guy your men brought in last night."

"Oh, him. No. He was just a pickpocket. A petty thief."

"What happened, then?"

"We had been following another lead. It led to a terrorist group. I'm not at liberty to say it was the Palestinians. But you know who your enemies are."

My bullshit detector was going apeshit. "So it's just a *coincidence* you grabbed the guy who was following me, then *happened* to break the case off another lead, the same day."

"A coincidence. Yes."

"And you can't tell me what the other lead *was?*"

"No." He was starting to get annoyed.

"Can I *talk to* the guy who was following me?"

"I'm sorry, he's gone."

"Gone."

"Yes, we really had no reason to hold him. So ... he's gone."

"Can I get his *name?*"

311

"Inspector! Haven't I done *enough?* I have made you safe. And last night I indulged you in your little adventure. Why do you *insult* me?"

"Please, I meant no offense. I'm just uptight. I can't wait to close this goddamn case."

"But, Inspector. The case *is* closed. Mengele has escaped you."

"Escaped?"

"Yes. Through *death.* The game is over. You have lost."

I started pushing my docs hard to wrap this thing up so we could get the hell out of here. I called them all together, locked them in a room, and told them to get their asses in gear.

An OSI guy started shouting at me about not being able to leave, and I grabbed him and held him out over the tenth-floor balcony. "Will you *please* stop your goddamn *bitching?*" I yelled. "I'm trying to *help* you!"

"I'll stop," he croaked.

Everybody looked at me like I was insane. That suited me fine. Crazy people get their way in this world.

I told the docs they had twenty-four hours to finish their report. After that, I'd pull all security, and they'd be on their own. For some reason, they believed me, and started hustling.

All day and all night, the doctors fought over the wording of their report. Safir's team wanted to say that the skeleton was Mengele, "within a reasonable scientific certainty." But Wiesenthal's team held out for something more vague.

At 2:00 A.M., I lost my composure and started screaming. I told Wiesenthal's people the report would say "reasonable scientific certainty," whether they liked it or not. If they wanted, I told them, they could file their own "chickenshit little report."

They weren't used to being talked to like that. They caved in, and went to bed.

After all the docs crashed, I stayed up all night making sure the report was properly typed and collated.

The next morning, we scheduled a press conference. The doctors were supposed to sign the report, then answer questions. But just before it began, one of Wiesenthal's docs came to me and started sniveling that he couldn't sign the report. I reminded him that he'd already agreed to.

"I know," he said. "But fuck it."

"Fuck it?"

"Yeah. And fuck you, too."

"Fuck *me?"*

"Yeah, fuck *you."* He reached out to push past me, and I batted his hands away. He hauled back a fist, and—BAM!— Mr. Sung's federal cops just *engulfed* him. They swallowed him up.

"Hey, hey, hey!" I cried. "Don't *hurt* the little pipsqueak."

"But he *insulted* you, Captain." All the federales called me "Captain." They loved me. Or at least they loved my guns.

I started pulling *federales* off the pile, and when I got to the bottom, there was the little doc, all teary-eyed and shaky from his one short brush with the real world.

"All right, for God's sake," he whimpered. "I'll *sign* the goddamn thing. I don't *need* this."

He signed it. Joseph Mengele was officially dead.

Thus was history made.

I got all my docs safely to the airport. I put them on several different planes, to several destinations.

When they were all boarded, safe from harm, I went to the ticket counter and bought my own ticket.

I began to walk toward my gate.

Then I put my ticket in my wallet, and walked out of the airport.

I had unfinished business. In my own head and my heart, Mengele was still alive. I had to do what I could to kill him.

I hailed the first cab I saw.

I stood in Josef Mengele's former living room. The electricity had been shut off, and the shades were pulled. It was dark. An Oriental rug was stretched across the floor. Three easy chairs sat against the walls. A footrest stood in front of one of the chairs. Opposite that chair was a television set. The chair by the TV was more worn than the rest. It held a faint outline, where Mengele had often sat.

I stared at the outline until the rest of the room receded.

I felt as if I were looking at the ghost of Josef Mengele.

My mind, feverish from stress and lack of sleep, began to crowd with images of Mengele's victims. They flew into my brain, and I could not stop them. I saw the family of dwarfs performing their circus act naked while Mengele laughed. I saw children trembling with fear as Mengele brought hypodermic needles to their eyes. I saw the two twins Mengele had sewn together.

But what were the twins' names? What were their *names? What were their names?* I couldn't remember.

I saw Mengele, standing before an endless line of people, jerking his thumb to the right—for life—or to the left, for death.

I pointed at the ghost of Mengele in his chair. I jerked my thumb to the left.

It did not work. I felt nothing.

I heard the words of Mr. Sung: "Mengele escaped. The game is over. You have lost."

I stumbled out of the dark house into daylight. But the light just blinded me. Still I was in darkness.

My downfall had begun.

Chapter Ten
The Whore on Drugs

★

• The Noriega Plot • The Black-Bag Job • Brazilian Terrorists • The Pascucci War on Drugs •

"Extremism in the pursuit of justice is no vice."
—*Barry Goldwater*

Someday, you may reach a point in your life where you say, "This is as good as I'm ever going to look. This is as much money as I'm ever going to make. This is the highest position I'll ever achieve. *And it's not enough.*"

But I hope you *never* reach that point. Because that's how I felt when I got home from Brazil.

And I wouldn't wish that feeling on a goddamn dog.

"I want the toughest thing you've got," I told Safir.

He studied me across the expanse of his desk. His taut, boxy face seemed more rigid than usual. "What's the problem, John?"

"No problem. I just wanna *do* something."

He kept staring at me. I looked away.

"I can't shake this *feeling,*" I blurted. "I keep feeling like my Nazi *beat* me. I wanted to *grab* the son of a bitch. I didn't even know how *bad* I wanted it until we found out for sure that he was dead."

Safir's dark eyebrows dropped into an angry V. "That's ridiculous, Pascucci! You *closed the case.* People have been trying to close Mengele for forty years, and you *did* it. Hell, I just nominated you for the Federal Investigator of the Year Award. *And* for another Attorney General's Award." He exhaled. "I think what you need is a vacation."

I shook him off. "No! I mean it. What's the toughest thing you got?"

His eyes fastened onto my face for at least half a minute. I didn't look away.

Finally, he said, "You want the toughest thing I've got? I'll give it to you. I was going to give it to you anyway." He pulled a fat file out of his desk. "I'm putting you in charge of the biggest program we've ever run," he said. "Right now, there's only one crime issue the president really cares about. The war on drugs."

Like everyone in America, I was well aware of that. Basketball player Len Bias had recently died from an overdose, and it had triggered a tidal wave of public fear about narcotics. Reagan's pollster, Richard Wirthlin, had just discovered the considerable depth of that alarm, so suddenly the Gipper—who'd never before given us much encouragement to fight narcotics—had declared "war" on drugs.

"There's a major element of the war on drugs," Safir said, "that I want you in charge of. Narcotics fugitives."

"How many are out there?"

"Four thousand two hundred and twenty-five. Give or take."

"So it's gonna be another computer operation?"

"Right. I'm going to put you with the very best computer guy in the federal government. Kid named Ron Wutrich. He's so good it's scary."

"What kinda dollars are we lookin' at?" I meant, what was the dollar value of the drugs that the fugitives had been busted for.

"According to Wutrich, about six billion."

"Jee-*zus!*"

"Lotta money, huh? Wutrich says the average *Fortune* five hundred company does only *four* billion a year. These guys are *huge,* John. If you can make a dent on them, I think you'll forget about your Nazi."

"Where do I start?"

"At the top."

"Meaning?"

"Meaning 75 percent of America's cocaine and 60 percent of its marijuana comes from Colombia—and a *hell* of a lot of Colombian dope gets here via Panama. If somebody asked me who's the biggest single drug trafficker in the world, I'd say it was Panama's Manuel Noriega. Our sources say he alone is pocketing a million dollars a *month* from the cartels."

"So what's *my* job?"

"Get with this guy. Direct his operation." Safir wrote down the name of a Seattle deputy.

"What's he doing?"

"He's going to go south," said Safir. "And grab Noriega."

"You're kidding."

Safir shook his head. He stared at me.

"John," he said, "it's good to see you *smile* again."

Then Safir came around the desk and put his hand on my shoulder. It was an unusual gesture for him. "You know, John," he said, "I'm *happy* to let you work at the highest levels of government law enforcement, but I've got to say something to you. We can *not* tolerate *any* unethical conduct at this level. No cutting corners, okay? The FBI's already convinced you're a loose cannon, and you can't give them any reason to build a case against you. The Service needs you too much."

"Sure, Boss. No problem." I smiled sweetly.

But inside I was seething. God-*damn!* Safir wanted me to solve his toughest problems—*without* weasel-deals? Howard Safir, quite obviously, no longer lived in the real world.

"Listen up, guys!" said the chief deputy marshal of Peoria, Illinois. All the deputies hushed.

"This is Inspector Pascucci," he said, "and he's come to Peoria to show us how to run a FIST. Howard Safir says that

John Pascucci is the best fugitive investigator in the country, so please give him your full attention."

He sat down and I took over.

Noriega was not the only project that Safir tasked me with. He also put me in charge of one-third of the country's fugitive programs, as well as a national program of "mini-FIST" operations in smaller towns, like Peoria.

In addition, I was developing the entire federal narcotic fugitives program. I'd gotten together with computer ace Ron Wutrich, who was just as brilliant as Safir had said. I'd thought *I* was pretty good with computers—until I met Wutrich. The program we were putting together was a "relational data base," which not only ferreted out clues, but also established links between various leads. In many ways, it was similar to the program I'd written for FIST. But it was much more sophisticated, thanks to Wutrich.

The program *had* to be sophisticated, though, because narcotics fugitives were different from other fugitives: They had more money. The average narcotics fugitive, for example, had skipped on an $80,000 bail. And after these guys had gone into the wind, most of them had gone right back into the drug business, which had made them even richer. Because of their money, they were able to stay well concealed. The average drug fugitive had been on the run for three years, and some of them had been gone for more than ten years. The rule of thumb was, if you couldn't grab a narcotics fugitive within forty-eight hours of his skip, he was gone forever.

Somehow, I had to change that. But at the same time, I had to run FISTs all over the country—*and* black-bag Noriega.

I'd never had so much responsibility. It looked like Safir was grooming me for a top management job. My goal was to become chief of International Operations, and I'd let Safir know. I wasn't so shy with him anymore. Why should I be? I'd handed over my entire *life* to the Marshals. The Service owed me one.

I could tell, as I traveled around the country, that Safir had put out the word that I was a rising star. The other marshals treated me with respect, and even fear. Some almost seemed to be in awe of me.

But I didn't feel like I deserved it. In my mind, I still hadn't proven myself. Mengele's "escape" was eating away at me. Once again, I *had* to do something spectacular.

Like fly into Miami with Noriega in chains.

The beauty of my Noriega plan was that it was completely legal. Technically, it wouldn't even be a kidnapping.

The marshal in Seattle that Safir had put me in touch with had hooked up with a close crony of Noriega's—the dictator's personal pilot—and had flipped him. Like most men involved in criminal operations, the pilot's loyalty had been only to the highest bidder, and we'd made him an offer he couldn't refuse. For one million dollars, cash, he agreed to fake engine trouble while Noriega was in his plane. Then he would land at a prearranged site, outside Panama. If we grabbed Noriega outside Panama, the abduction would be legal, because we had an outstanding warrant for Noriega's arrest.

When Noriega's plane would touch down, a small cadre of gunmen—including me—would overpower his bodyguards. Then we'd throw him in the trunk of a car, and haul ass to a Lear jet.

It was a beautiful plan, cheap and efficient, which utilized a classic technique for busting mutts: using their own buddies to bring them in.

But there was something about the plan that bothered me. The people who'd been briefing me about the war on drugs were convinced that Noriega was as much our *ally* as our enemy.

Panama, they said, was one of the most cooperative countries on extraditions, expulsions, and deportations. Noriega had helped us more than any other Latin American leader.

The more I studied it, the more I saw that the entire war on drugs was filled with bizarre contradictions and twisted mysteries. Down in Florida, where most of the Caribbean drugs were coming in, the State of Florida drug interdiction people were ready to mutiny. About a month earlier, they'd told me, they had busted a freighter full of drug smugglers. But within a week, the same smugglers had been back in business, with beautiful new ID's. The fake ID's, said the

Florida cops, practically *had* to have come from the U.S. government.

Shortly after that incident, the same state investigators had busted a drug smuggler taking a shipment of machine guns out of the United States. But almost immediately, U.S. Customs had confiscated the machine guns. Then the guns had "disappeared."

One rumor surrounding these mysteries was that the Agency was sending guns to the Contras, and helping finance the operation with drug smuggling. Some of the drugs, people said, were coming straight from the Contras.

At this point, that was easy to believe. The Iran-Contra connection had recently been exposed, and it had made Reagan look capable of *anything.* I'd thought *I* knew how to weasel-deal, until I heard about Reagan's deal with the Ayatollah.

The Iran-Contra scandal—as well as the recent "Black Monday" stock market crash—had hurt Reagan badly. Reagan's administration had clearly peaked, and now he was just trying to hang on for the remainder of his term, amidst a storm of major and minor scandals. Ed Meese, in particular, was in trouble, mostly because of an apparent scam with a company called Wedtech.

We all felt the change in the political climate. We also felt the erosion of Reagan's moral mandate. It was getting much harder to feel like a noble warrior in the service of the Gipper.

It was also tougher to pull weasel-deals, because the entire Reagan administration was now under scrutiny. Even so, I was pulling more of them than ever—despite Safir's warning. I couldn't see how I could achieve my goals without them.

In any case, it was clear that Noriega was working both sides of the fence. Unfortunately for Noriega, though, the Reagan administration's chief of drug interdiction, Vice President Bush, needed a sexy bust. Bush was gearing up for a run at the presidency, and Noriega was his designated chump.

Truth be told, we *all* needed a sexy bust. The election of 1988 was on the horizon, and every time there was a new administration, every high-level federal job went up for grabs. Nobody was safe. Not Safir. Not Kupferer. Not even me.

Then, one afternoon, while I was refining the Noriega plan, I got a call from Safir.

"Drop everything," he said.

By late that evening, I was in Washington. I took a cab straight to headquarters. All the offices were dark and still—except for Safir's, which was blazing with light and activity.

Safir gave me a quick briefing. Two DEA agents in Brazil had just been shot. The shooter had been identified. The DEA wanted the Marshals to go into Brazil and bring the killer out.

"You want it?" asked Safir.

"Of course."

Safir sent me directly to the office of a major DEA administrator. The DEA bigshot was waiting for me.

"I can do what you want," I told the DEA guy, "but I'm going to need some *heavy* resources."

"Like what?"

"Like money, for starters. But more than that, I need you to put me with somebody who has access to the target. If this job isn't done from the inside, it's not gonna *get* done."

He tried to weasel on me: We're too *poor,* we don't *have* anybody inside, yadda-yadda-yadda.

"Well," I said, standing up, "they're *your* men—if *you* don't care, *I* don't care."

He made a motion for me to stay. But then he just sat there silently, fretting. Finally, he said, "Contact this man." He wrote down a Spanish name, and a Brazilian phone number. "This guy's . . . got contacts . . . with the Brazilian terrorist group M-19. M-19 is—let's just say—*rumored* to have close ties to the cartels. And they'll do anything you want—for the right price."

I called the number. The guy who answered was vague and noncommittal. But he agreed to meet with me or my representatives.

The next morning, I put a deputy on a plane to Rio de Janeiro. About thirty hours later, he was back. With a proposition.

For $60,000, he said, a splinter group of M-19 would kidnap the shooter and drive him across the border to Argentina. From there, we could fly him back to the United States. The only problem would be refueling. With a kidnapped man on board, we would have to stop for fuel in a country that was very "pragmatic."

The logical place to refuel would be Panama. I needed to contact Noriega. *Next* month, he'd be my mutt again, but for now, he was my citizen. It was a necessary evil.

I told my contact at DEA that I needed $60,000.

"For what?" he asked.

"For a guy in Brazil. He says he operates a 'transportation service,' and that this is a reasonable fee for transporting a dangerous man."

The DEA administrator made a call, and the money was waiting in his outer office before our meeting was over. The bundle of cash was about five inches thick, and was wrapped in brown paper. No one asked me to sign a receipt.

I called my rabbi at the Agency, and asked him how to contact Noriega. He gave me a number to call in Panama City.

When I called Panama, I got the feeling that my rabbi had already paved the way for me. Noriega's boys greeted me with open arms. Made me nervous. When the Noriega snatch went down, they'd remember my double-cross.

I sent my deputy south with the sixty thousand, then camped by the phone.

Twenty hours later, he called. "It's a done deal," he said.

"They got the target?"

"He's already in the trunk of a car, heading for the border."

"Take the next plane out," I told him.

I located a Lear jet, and put together a flight crew. I was going to fly to Panama, to ramrod the refueling. If it got messy down there, I'd have some heavy ordnance to apply to the situation.

But then I got a call from my Agency rabbi. "What the *hell's* going on in Brazil?" he asked.

"It's goin' smoothly," I said. "We located our target. He's on the way out."

"What about the *senator?*"

"What senator?"

"A Brazilian senator was kidnapped this afternoon. M-19 took credit. So Brazil closed all its borders."

"Shit! How am I gonna get my target out?"

"Beats me."

I paged my deputy at the airport, and told him to sit tight. Then I called everybody in Brazil that I knew. Including Mr. Sung. Nobody could help. M-19, they told me, was out of control.

There was nothing to do but wait.

I sat there all day. And the next day. And the next.

A week later, my deputy called. "They opened the borders," he said, "and M-19's ready to roll. But there's a glitch."

"What?"

"Well, this whole time, our target's been in the trunk of their car."

"Oh, my God," I groaned. I had an awful image of him trying to claw his way out. I imagined the stench in the car. "Well," I said, "get the goddamn money back." We couldn't afford any tie to a murder.

"On what *grounds?*" he wailed.

"Delivery of spoiled goods."

My Seattle deputy and I put the finishing touches on our plan to kidnap Noriega.

I was itching to get back into action. I was sick of sitting at a desk.

Safir communicated the plan to his counterpart at Justice. The A.G.'s man loved it. He took it to the White House.

We waited for two weeks. No word. I was getting nervous.

Then Reagan vetoed it.

Shocked me. This was obviously the "new Gipper." The Old Gipper would never have backed away from a weasel-deal. All the scandals were taking a toll. Even the *Gipper* was getting afraid to cut corners. He wasn't himself.

Or maybe something else was in the works that I didn't know about. There was a lot of grumbling that the DEA still depended heavily on Noriega.

Later on, when America sent troops to Panama, I was

dumbfounded. Even *I* couldn't imagine invading a country to make a single arrest.

But that's how the war on drugs was waged: stupidly. And strangely.

After months of fine-tuning, our computer program for catching narcotics fugitives was finished.

Out of the original 4,225 narcotics fugitives, we identified 700 prime targets, ranked by importance. We thought that if we could eliminate a healthy percentage of these key figures, the drug business would be badly damaged: Kill the head, and the body will die.

Our plan was to run a ten-week blitzkrieg in the eight cities most linked to drug trafficking: Miami, San Diego, Houston, Chicago, LA, San Francisco, New York, and Baltimore. It would take place from March 3 to May 8, 1987.

I flew to each of the eight cities to introduce the program. My last stop was San Francisco.

After the San Francisco seminar ended, a group of us went to dinner at Fisherman's Wharf. When dinner was over, I invited the guys to stop by my suite.

These days, I never stayed at the same hotel as my deputies. Their hotels were bare-bones, but I had carte blanche to stay wherever I wanted. So I usually took a suite at the finest hotel in town. A few years earlier, I would've considered that decadent. Not anymore. The Service owed me one.

Besides, I didn't want my troops to know everything I was doing, and I'm sure they didn't want me to know everything *they* were doing.

While the deputies wandered around my suite, enjoying the view of the San Francisco Bay, I called room service for a couple of bottles of good liquor. I thought the other marshals might like a drink, though I still didn't drink on the job myself. In fact, I didn't do much of *anything*—including pot. I was afraid to buy it, because I could see the headline: "Top Drug Cop Busted with Baggie." So I'd started growing a couple of pot plants in my basement. But I hadn't even had time to sample them. I was caught in a cycle of overwork. The more burned out I got, the harder I pushed, to show myself I could still hack it. And the harder I pushed, the more Safir tasked me with. I didn't really feel like myself these days; I felt like a work robot.

I stood by a ten-foot-tall window, looking at a classy little flower shop on the street below. These days, I had a new fantasy: I wanted to open a flower shop on Polk Street in San Francisco, and sit there all day, reading books. I thought about it all the time.

Here I was, finally living a life of luxury and privilege, worlds away from my working-class roots. But I was miserable.

The Gipper wasn't the Gipper anymore—and I wasn't me. I wanted out.

From San Francisco, I traveled to El Paso, to supervise a massive FIST. My first day in Texas, I got a call from Tony Perez, the balls-to-the-wall marshal who'd been with me at Konrads Kalejs's arrest.

"Got a hot one goin', John!" he crowed. "Need your help. We're drivin' across the border tomorrow night. Gonna rescue the families of the men who helped us on Verdugo."

René Verdugo was a Mexican drug criminal who had engineered the abduction, torture, and murder of DEA agent Enrique Camarena a couple of years earlier. Verdugo was a monster; he'd tortured Camarena for about thirty hours before the agent had died. A year after the murder, Tony had gone into Mexico and black-bagged Verdugo, bringing him across the border to eventually face a 240-year prison sentence. During Verdugo's kidnapping, Tony had gotten help from more than a dozen men in the Mexican national police, but recently Verdugo's men had identified these policemen. Now these men and their families were in grave danger. Tony had arranged for them to be put into the Witness Security Program. It looked as if a hit against them was imminent.

Tony needed to take all of them out of Mexico at once. If the cartel operators saw one or two leave, the slaughter would begin.

"Whattaya need?" I asked Tony.

"The first thing I need is vehicles. Enough for forty people. They gotta be fast, have big gas tanks, and go offroad. And I'm gonna need four men—the best sharpshooters you have."

I spent the next twenty-four hours hustling offroad trucks and modified vans.

When Tony arrived, the vehicles were gleaming in a row, and three marshals and I had packed our favorite weapons. I was sick with nerves, but it was a good kind of sick.

When Tony saw my three men, he asked, "Where's the fourth guy?"

"Right here," I said.

"Jesus, John, Safir doesn't want *you* to go! You're a *boss* now, buddy."

When he saw the look on my face, he said softly, "I didn't mean to mislead you."

Tony didn't feel *too* sorry for me, though, because I had what he wanted: a top-level management job. I doubted, though, that Tony was suitable for high-level management. He and I were generally considered the Marshals' two toughest guys, but I thought Tony lacked the managerial skills to oversee a large number of men.

Still, at this moment, I envied him very much. As he drove off, my sick feeling stayed. But it wasn't a good feeling anymore.

I went back to my computer and my telephone. I still had a FIST to run, and this was one of the biggest ever. I'd give you a bunch of statistics to show you how effective this FIST was, but you'd probably just get bored. You're only happy when I kick doors and blow people away, right? Well, don't feel guilty, because even *I* was bored with this stage of my career. As a top-level manager, I was finally able to do the greatest good for the greatest number. But I *hated* it. No street action.

That's one of the problems with us baby boomers. We're *extremely* idealistic—but only as long as we're having fun.

I guess we watched too much *Batman*.

While I was moping around at my desk, I got a call from a friend in trouble. To be honest, this person—a young woman—was more than a friend. A few months earlier, while I'd been in the depths of my funk over Mengele, I'd had a brief affair with her. After all those years of manhunting, the pain and sadness from my job had finally overwhelmed me and had made me desperate for escape. For a short time, the affair had soothed my pain. The young woman had been an oasis of peace; she'd made me forget about the real world. She also gave me something else: absolute approval. She was very impressionable, and to her, I was Sherlock Holmes and the Lone Ranger all rolled into one. Betsy, of course, admired me, but this girl *worshipped* me. At this low point in my life, that's what I thought I needed.

But there was no real love between us—not the kind of love two people have when they struggle together to build a life in the real world, as Betsy and I had. So the affair didn't last.

We parted as friends, though, and I learned another important lesson about life: When your pain comes from inside, you can't escape from it. You can only face it down, and try to kill it before it kills you.

For the most part, I'd succeeded in doing that. I'd rechanneled my energy into a case I was investigating, and once again used my *work* to feed my need for appreciation.

But now the woman I'd been seeing had a problem. She was being harrassed by an old boyfriend, a guy she'd dumped, and she wanted my help.

I told her I'd call up the dickhead, and get him to apologize and act like a gentleman. I was trying to be nice to her—but to be painfully honest, I also just felt like busting somebody's balls. I was completely burned out, and was feeling pretty mean.

So I called the guy, and racked his balls for a while. Because this had nothing to do with the Marshals, I didn't tell him who I really was. I told him I was a private investigator, and gave him a fake name.

But he was a real asshole and wouldn't promise to behave.

I made a note to keep calling him until I had him housebroken.

That was a mistake. God knows it wasn't the *only* mistake I'd made—but that was part of my problem. Mistakes add up.

After the El Paso FIST, I kicked off the operational phase of the narcotics fugitive program. The Warrant Apprehension Narcotics Team—WANT—was a massive operation, encompassing seventeen agencies, hundreds of men, and four countries.

I ran WANT from the ninth floor of the Federal Building in San Francisco, and practically lived in the office. For two and a half months, I worked fourteen-hour days, seven days a week, as we made bust after bust. At the end of it, we'd compiled some amazing statistics. Of the 700 primary targets, we'd busted 166, and had cleared the warrants of 158 more, by determining that they were dead, out of the country, or in jail on another charge. That gave us a total of 324 cleared warrants. In comparison, every state, local, and national agency *combined* had cleared only about *half* that many drug fugitive warrants the year before.

Plus—you know how cheap *I* am—I ran the whole program at virtually no taxpayer cost. We spent $1.1 million, but we seized over $1 million in usable assets—cash, cars, personal property, weapons, and real estate. In addition, we seized about a quarter of a million dollars' worth of dope.

After the program ended, I went back to headquarters to help put together our press materials. Safir wanted maximum media on WANT.

Wherever I went in D.C., I was glad-handed. One afternoon, I was in the Old Executive Office Building, across from the White House, and George Bush, the administration's drug boss, danced into our meeting between his final presidential campaign stops. The election was only days away, and Bush had a lock on the Oval Office.

"Terrific job, guys," Bush said to us. Since I was boss of the operation, Bush singled me out for special praise. "Ed Meese says you're a helluva cop," said Bush. Bush was just stroking me, but it made me wish my dad was alive, so that I could have told him about it.

Safir and I went out and did some regional press conferences, gloating about what a great success WANT had been. Ed Meese came to one of them and told the press that when *Pascucci* was after drug dealers, "they can run, but they can't hide." Suddenly, I was on more D.C. invitation lists than ever. Still didn't feel satisfied, though. I felt like I didn't deserve all the attention.

After WANT, I was so exhausted that I slacked off for a

while: ten-hour days, six days a week. I began studying the most recent DEA statistics, to see how much of an impact WANT had made.

Slowly, it became apparent to me: WANT hadn't done *anything*. Not *shit*.

The reason for its failure was painfully obvious: There was too much *money* in drugs. When one doper got busted, another immediately took his place.

So I sat down at my computer, loaded it with every drug statistic I could find, and devised the Pascucci War on Drugs.

Then I went to Safir to sell it.

Safir listened patiently while I explained why the war on drugs was a colossal disaster. First of all, it was inept; only 25 percent of all drugs were being intercepted. And 25 percent wasn't enough to affect consumption. Whatever we pulled out of the pipeline, the pushers just added back in. Second: cost—we were diverting $20 billion a year into a useless program. The USMS, like many other law enforcement agencies, was spending *half* its resources fighting drugs. Third, and most important: jail clogging. In the early years of the drug epidemic—the 1960s—about 15 percent of all federal prisoners had been druggies. Now *50 percent* of those prisoners were in for drugs. In the state prisons, the rates were almost as high. Since the mid-1970s, the prison population had doubled. Soon it would triple, to about one million. We had more prisoners per capita than any country on earth, including police states, like South Africa and the Soviet Union. But there hadn't been *any* corresponding decrease in violent crime.

The country couldn't afford to keep building more prison cells, because it cost $100,000 to build one, and about $70,000 a year to maintain it. Because the jails were packed with drug offenders, there was an absurd shortage of prison space for violent repeat offenders. By this time, only about eighteen percent of all felons were going to jail, and most who did go in were released early. The Bureau of Prisons was operating at 150 percent over capacity, and held far too many small-time, drug-related ODCs—ordinary, decent criminals. The *real* bad guys—the violent, predicate felons—had never had it so good. They were bouncing out of jail in record time. They *loved* the war on drugs.

"So what's your alternative?" Safir asked. He was starting to look restless—a bad sign.

I told him the Pascucci Plan: If we were going to have controlled substances, we had to *control* them. Meaning: The government should take over big warehouses in every city, and turn them into government-run bases for addicts. Addicts could receive maintenance doses of heroin, or cocaine, or whatever, for as long as they chose to be addicts. They'd have to take the drugs on the premises, and submit to counseling and therapy. Of course, many of them would die. About sixty thousand addicts died every year now, and that figure might increase at first, as it had in other countries that had decriminalized drugs.

But then it would probably decline, as it had in the decriminalized countries. Once the profit motive was eliminated, drugs would no longer be pushed onto people—particularly kids. After drugs had been decriminalized in the Netherlands, hard-drug use by young people had declined by 600 percent.

It would be tragic, of course, to lose those 60,000 lives, but no more tragic than losing 325,000 lives a year to tobacco-related diseases.

"But guess what," I said to Safir, "I don't really give a shit if sixty thousand people want to be self-destructive. The person *I* care about is the guy who gets robbed or killed by some junkie or gangbanger. *Most* street crime revolves around drug trafficking, and we could stop that in about six *weeks,* with this warehouse idea. We could put the Crips and Bloods outta business in a year. The streets would be fairly *safe* again.

"If we did it *my* way, we'd pull $50 billion a year of drug profits out of criminal enterprise. And we'd have room in jail for the *real* pukes. I'm tellin' ya, Boss, this whole war on drugs is just Reagan and Bush whoring for public approval. But, goddamnit, guys like you and me could do this job *right.*"

Safir looked as if he hadn't heard a word I'd said. "That's interesting, John, but that's not what we need to talk about."

"Whatta we need to talk about?"

"The *real* world. Here's what's happening. Justice was so happy with WANT that they asked me to do it again. So we're going to launch WANT II, and I want you to run it. Plus, DEA also wants us to go after all of *their* fugitives, along with the FBI fugitives. So I want you to work up a program for them, too."

"Sounds like a helluva lotta work." It also sounded like bullshit. I started to bitch again. Louder, this time.

Safir bolted up from his desk. "I thought you wanted to work," he snapped.

It was time to back down. "Okay," I said, "we'll do it your way. But let's do this—let's fold all the DEA fugitives into the WANT II program. Kill two birds."

"Good idea." He sat back down, calm again. "Exactly the idea I would have had."

"Oh, sorry."

"For what?"

"For havin' your idea before you did."

"Pascucci, you make a good pain in the ass, but a lousy wise-ass. *Please* get outta here."

Before I got to the door, Safir blurted, "Hey! I almost forgot to tell you! You've been nominated for Narcotics Investigator of the Year."

"What an honor."

Safir stared hard at me. "Come here," he said. "Sit down. Tell me what you need."

But I couldn't sit. Too wound up. I paced. "I need to do something *real*, Boss. Something like Koziy. Kalejs. Boyce. Mengele. Something that's gonna do some *good*."

Safir sat in his chair for a couple of minutes. Then he went to a cabinet and pulled out a file. He tossed it to me. It was labeled FRANK TERPIL.

"Terpil!" I cried. "You're gonna task me with *Terpil?*" Everybody in law enforcement knew about Frank Terpil.

"Why not?" said Safir. "I think he's the most dangerous man on earth. You and Terpil were *made* for each other. But, John, play it straight. No corner cutting."

"Of course, Boss."

I was swept by a rush of joy. Another chance to *do* something! Another great adventure! Maybe I could *still* be the Gipper's cop—even if the Gipper was no longer the Gipper.

I was certain, gut certain, that Terpil would be my greatest case ever.

I had no idea it would be my last.

Ronald Reagan and I were *both* on the way out.

Chapter Eleven

The Most Dangerous Man on Earth

• The Mutt Who Killed Manhunters • Idi
Amin's Enforcer • Selling Terror to
Kaddafi • Palestinian Warriors •
My Downfall •

*"Politics is not a bad profession. If you succeed, there are
many rewards. If you disgrace yourself, you can always
write a book."*

—Ronald Reagan

I photocopied the Terpil file and ran from Safir's office to the
nearest coffee shop, where I couldn't be interrupted. I ordered
four jumbo Cokes with crushed ice, and began devouring the file.

According to the dossier, Frank Terpil had been one of the
Boss's pet projects for six years. In fact, several years earlier,
Safir had personally directed a worldwide manhunt for Terpil and had busted Terpil's evil running mate, the infamous
spy Edwin Wilson.

What was so important about Frank Terpil? Simply this: He was a leading candidate to start World War III.

World War III, many foreign policy experts by this time believed, would probably not be a full-scale nuclear exchange between two superpowers. Instead, it would be a widespread war of terror.

It would be a war in which great nations would be deviled to near-destruction by the concentrated, extended assault of terrorism. This terrorism could be perpetrated by any small country that was willing to abandon the conventions of civilized behavior. All that country would need would be the tools of terror—explosives, weaponry, and instruments of espionage.

Fortunately for the world, though, most of the sophisticated instruments of terrorism were owned by reasonable, civilized nations. Even totalitarian countries like the Soviet Union tended not to do business with terrorists, because they feared global destabilization. After Gorbachev had taken over, the Soviets had become extremely wary of selling to terrorists.

But that's where Frank Terpil came in.

Terpil, a rich ex-CIA agent with close ties to weapons manufacturers, had access to the products that terrorists needed but were generally unable to buy. Terpil, though, would sell to *anyone.* He was a man with absolutely no conscience. On the contrary, it apparently gave him pleasure to cause suffering. For a time, he had been the chief of security for Ugandan dictator Idi Amin. In that position, Terpil had presided over the torture and murder of thousands of men and women. He had actually laughed once when describing one of his favorite tortures: placing a heavy steel pot upside down on a man's stomach, then putting a large, starving rat under the pot, so that the rat would have to eat through the victim's stomach to escape.

During Amin's reign, more than five hundred thousand Ugandans had been murdered by the government.

But Terpil's primary motivation had never been simple sadism. His main motivation was greed—and that was what made him so dangerous. To satisfy his limitless lust for money, he had to act out his evil on a grand scale. Even in Uganda, his foremost preoccupation had not been torture, but the *selling* of instruments of torture to Amin, along with $3.2 million worth of weapons, poisons, and explosives.

Amin had not been the first monster Terpil had served. In the mid-1970s—shortly after Terpil had been fired from the CIA for running a currency scam—he'd signed a $31 million contract with Libya's Muammar Kaddafi. The contract had called for Terpil to supply American-made, time-delayed detonators for explosives. Kaddafi had wanted *five hundred thousand* of them.

Terpil had been unable to supply most of the detonators, but the implications of the deal were staggering. If Kaddafi, then the world's most active terrorist, had been able to get that many detonators, he could have wreaked havoc everywhere on earth. Including America. In fact, Terpil often pitched his clients on America's vulnerability to terrorism. "The United States is not immune," he'd once said. "There are a great many Palestinians in New York, Miami, and California who consider themselves warriors." In fact, my CIA sources had told me, Kaddafi had about thirty-five American targets under surveillance, as well as ten American embassies overseas.

Terpil, who was burly, fast talking, and streetwise, was always available to the highest bidder. He'd once sold sophisticated surveillance equipment to a U.S. ally—the Shah of Iran's dreaded secret police, Savak. And he'd also sold weapons to an enemy of America, the PLO's Yasir Arafat. He'd sold U.S.-made Redeye missiles and plastique explosives to Kaddafi, and had also sold them to enemies of Kaddafi.

Terpil had also hired out as a trainer of terrorists. He and his primary partner—fellow CIA renegade Edwin Wilson— had run a terrorist training school in Libya. One of Terpil's prize students had been Carlos "The Jackal" Ramirez, who had organized the murder of Israeli athletes at the 1972 Munich Olympics.

In addition, Terpil had organized and carried out assassinations. He'd been a "wet boy." He'd recruited ex-CIA agents to assassinate Libyan dissenters living abroad, and he'd blown up the airplane of one of Idi Amin's enemies. Once, Terpil had participated in the assassination of one of Amin's cabinet members, whose severed head had been served to Amin in a covered dish at a banquet.

Terpil's evil schemes had made him extremely wealthy. He owned estates in the Caribbean, London, and the Far East, and lived lavishly.

Terpil had been on the run since 1981, when he'd been sentenced "in absentia" to fifty-three years for selling machine guns in New York.

Toward the end of the dossier, though, was a cautionary note. Someone had circled it with a red Magic Marker. It said: "Investigators who try to apprehend Terpil tend to die suddenly and unexpectedly."

When I read about the manhunters dying, I got a little shaky. I ordered a couple more Cokes, and thought it over.

Maybe, instead of locating Terpil and arresting him, I should find him and just whack him. It might be the safest thing to do, because he'd probably die before he'd submit to capture. And even if I busted him without incident, he might later have one of his associates take me out, for revenge.

I went to a pay phone to call Betsy, to tell her we were going to a reception for the Canadian ambassador that night at the Kennedy Center. We were doing that kind of a thing a lot lately. I hated the schmoozing, but now it was part of my job.

Betsy was thrilled about it. The secretary of state was going to be there, and there was a rumor that George Bush, who'd just been elected president, would drop by.

"What should I wear?" Betsy asked. "How formal is it?"

But I was plotting an assassination, and was in no mood to discuss hemlines. "Call Barbara Bush," I snapped, "and ask Babs what *she's* wearing."

As soon as I said it, I felt like shit. Why was I bitching at the one person who really cared about me? Lately, I'd been barking at Betsy practically every day. Too much stress.

"I know it's not important," Betsy said.

That made me feel even worse. "I'm sorry, I'm sorry. I'm just up to my ass in mutts."

After I got off the phone, I sank into a grim depression. I didn't like my life anymore. I was whoring around with the war on drugs. I was just another Beltway phony on the cocktail circuit. And I wasn't even a decent husband.

What good was I?

Safir burst into my office. Stuck out his hand. "Congratulations!" he boomed.

"For what?"

"For being named the United States Marshals' new chief of International Operations. It carries the rank of chief inspector, G.S. fourteen—it's almost the highest grade you can get without congressional approval. It's equivalent to the military rank of brigadier general."

Safir's face was lit with happiness. He'd brought me up from the bottom, and this was his victory, too. At this point, Safir and I were very close. Ever since he'd warned me about unethical conduct, I'd taken great pains to conceal all my weasel-deals. In reality, though, I was cutting more corners than I had at any time in my career. Since the day Mengele had "escaped" from me—through death—I'd felt compelled to accomplish greater and greater things, and I just *couldn't* reach my goals without pulling weasel-deals.

My office began to crowd with well-wishers.

As I shook hands, I tried to affect the demeanor of a Boss: careful, cool, and conservative.

Meanwhile, the wheels in my mind were spinning. I wondered: What if I hired a mob hitter to get rid of Terpil? What if I hired somebody like Mr. Sung?

Would that work? Would it?

Who knew? Who knew?

I began an exhaustive review of everything Safir had done during the initial Terpil investigation. Safir's investigation had been a standard, well-organized search. Confidential informants had been developed, surveillance had been placed on Terpil's friends and family, and marshals had been sent all over the world to follow up leads.

But, considering the target, the investigation had been all wrong. Not proactive enough. Terpil had worked for the Agency for six years, and after that, he'd been associated with many clandestine operations. He knew everything about evasion and subterfuge, and had left virtually no clues or triggers.

The only sure way to nail him would be to get *him* to come to *us*.

To do that, I'd play him the same way I'd played Boyce: I'd hang him with his own ego. Terpil, like most pukes, was proud of his sick deeds, and I'd use his criminal vanity against him.

I called up a contact I'd made during the Mengele investigation. Back then, when I'd been planning to work undercover out of Argentina, Safir had hooked me up with a former Argentine drug smuggler named Juan Hernandez. Juan had flipped for the government during the famous "French Connection" case and had been instrumental in its success. Now he was living in New York, as a member of the Witness Security Program.

"Juan!" I said. "How'd you like to go home for a while?"

"To Argentina? For what reason?"

"For the *best* reason. Money! I can give you seven thousand dollars a month, plus all expenses."

He was silent for a moment. Then he asked, softly, "Is it wet work?"

"No! That's the beauty of it. All I want you to do is pretend to be a movie producer. Your main job is to interview starlets."

His other job was to lure Frank Terpil. My plan was to have Juan contact Terpil through an intermediary, and interest Terpil in a movie about his life. It would portray Terpil as a hard-hitting soldier-of-fortune—Indiana Jones, with an edge. It would show the world the *real* Frank Terpil. Best of all—for Terpil—it would set the record straight on Terpil's relationship with his partner, Edwin Wilson. Journalists had generally portrayed Wilson—who was now in federal prison, thanks to Safir—as the dominant partner. But Juan Hernandez—the great Argentine producer—would show that it was *Terpil* who'd called the shots.

"Why me?" Juan asked. "Why Argentina?"

"I don't want Terpil to get any whiff of 'U.S. government.' Argentina's a good cover. And you're an invisible man. He won't be able to find out anything about you."

"Why not just set up a dummy corporation?"

"A guy like him would see through a paper corp in two seconds. No, I need you down there interviewing starlets, going to the best restaurants, and renting the nicest villa in town."

"Do I have to work the muscle end?"

"No. You just bring him out. We'll take him down."

"How *many* starlets?"

"At a time? Or total?"

"Total."

"I'd have to call the General Accounting Office. I'm bad at higher math."

He was on the next plane to Buenos Aires.

My next job was to find an intermediary who could get word of the "movie" to Terpil. I found a candidate in my dossier. A couple of years earlier, a London television producer had done a documentary about Terpil called "Portrait of a Dangerous Man." It had been a fawning portrayal. Because it had been such a whitewash, I assumed the TV producer still had access to Terpil.

So I had Juan write a letter to the producer, on Juan's new movie company stationery. The letter said that Juan wanted to do a sympathetic movie about Terpil. It stressed that we'd buy film rights to the TV producer's documentary, and hinted at big bucks. It also asked if the producer would sign on as a technical consultant.

The greedy little producer called Juan about ninety seconds after he got the letter. He'd *love* to help.

Fish on! Reel him in!

Of course, the producer said, *he* couldn't call Frank, because *nobody* knew where *Frank* was, but he'd put out the word, and he was *sure* Frank would contact him.

I immediately tasked two deputies with going to London, to sit on the producer. When they arrived in England, I had them go straight to Scotland Yard to try to get a tap on the producer's phone. But they couldn't swing it. I called Scotland Yard myself and begged and yelled for a while. No dice. Safir tried, too, but didn't get anywhere.

After we struck out on the phone tap, I called the producer's house to see if he had an answering machine. He did.

So I had my computer guys make me a list of all the possible three-digit access codes. *Long* list. We started with the most obvious possibilities, like 1-1-1, or 1-2-3. Finally, we hit the right number, and started monitoring his messages. But Terpil didn't leave any.

Then the FBI got wind of my investigation, and Bureau Director William Sessions had a tantrum. *His* boys hadn't been doing *dick* on Terpil, but now that somebody else was after him, Sessions wanted the attorney general to give Terpil back to the Feebs.

One of Sessions's big criticisms—which he laid out in a long memo to the A.G.—was that I'd tried to get a wiretap in London. He claimed that the tap "could have jeopardized a successful prosecution of Terpil." Well, for Christ's sake! We didn't need a *new* prosecution. Terpil was already *down* for fifty-three years, and a mutt like him would be certain to max out.

I went to work on justifying our investigation to the attorney general. Unfortunately, I didn't have a personal relationship with Bush's new A.G., Richard Thornburgh, and that made my job much harder. If Ed Meese had still held the job, I could have just called him and asked him to castrate Bill Sessions.

My other problem was that I just didn't have time for Sessions's nonsense. As chief of International Operations, I was now the Marshals' primary liaison with Interpol, and the primary liaison with the CIA. I also had an office to operate, and a staff to coordinate. Plus, I was directing mini-FISTs all over the country, and I was running WANT II in America, Mexico, and the Caribbean. On top of all that, Safir had me writing the Justice Department's position paper on crack cocaine.

Still, I dropped everything and put together a justification for why the USMS should have Terpil.

To make my case, I went to other agencies that had been involved with Terpil, such as the Customs Service, the Manhattan County district attorney's office, and ATF. I asked each of them: Do you want us to grab your puke for you? They all said, Sure, grab him. So I wrote a long memo to the A.G. explaining that we were just serving the wishes of the involved agencies.

In the process, though, I picked up a few leads that Customs and ATF had on Terpil. So it wasn't a complete waste of time.

When the A.G. got my memo, he told Sessions to shut the hell up. I got an irate phone call from the FBI, accusing me of "knifing the Bureau in the back." But I just screamed back at them. My relationship with the FBI was at an all-time low. They clearly despised me. But I didn't care. I went back to more serious matters—like my mutt, Frank.

My leads on Terpil, however, were thin. The investigation looked bleak.

Then I got a call. It was Juan.

"I just received a letter," Juan said. "From Terpil."

Juan read me the letter. Terpil was interested in our movie. But he was wary. The most revealing thing about the letter was its point of origin. It had come from Prague, Czechoslovakia. It even had a post office box number as its return address.

I called one of my contacts at the CIA. As chief of International Operations, I could now get to anybody at the Agency. I asked my Agency hook if he could find out three things. Was the post office box really Terpil's? Was it active? Was it just a mail-forwarding point?

My Agency guy hemmed and hawed. He explained to me that Czechoslovakia was a Communist Bloc nation—like I was too dumb to know—and that Agency resources in Czechoslovakia were very limited. Pissed me off. Terpil had been one of the *Agency's* guys, and if *anybody* should have wanted him nailed, it ought to have been them.

I gave my Agency guy some shit, then called the State Department. They wouldn't help, either. To State, penetrating a Commie country was like traveling to Mars.

So—fuck it—I called the Commies myself. Why not? When in doubt, do something.

I got on the phone with the Soviet consulate and asked for a meeting. Since I was the USMS chief of International Ops, protocol said he had to see me. It was good to be king.

When I got with my Commie, I didn't beat around the

bush: This is what I need, this is why. If he helped me nail
Terpil, I said, it would be good for international stabilization.

He obviously didn't give a shit.

So I told him it was widely believed that Terpil was still
running black-ops for the CIA. *That* got his attention.

But he wanted to know: Why are *you* after Terpil, if Terpil
is still working for your government?

"He's not working for *me*," I said. "In *my* agency, he's a
mutt. The rest of the government can go fuck itself. That's
democracy. You're gonna love it."

Three days later, my Commie called back. Yes, he said, the
post office box was Terpil's. And it was active. Also, it had
turnaround capabilities, which meant that Terpil could send
a package of letters to it from anywhere in the world, and
that people at the mail drop would open the package and
forward the letters.

I kissed my Commie's ass so hard I left a tattoo. Then
I asked him not to tell anyone that Terpil still worked for
the Agency.

But he would, of course. I was hoping the rumor would
get back to the CIA, and motivate them to give me some help.

I returned to headquarters and tried to figure out a way to
penetrate Terpil's mail drop. I needed to know where Terpil's
letters were really coming from. Unfortunately, I couldn't just
waltz into Czechoslovakia and lay a pile of flash money on
the proprietor.

While I was wrestling with that problem, I got a call from
one of my guys at the Agency. He sounded worried. All of
a sudden, he said, there was a big buzz that Terpil was still
an active Agency case officer. The rumor had been sourced
to the Israelis, and to Yugoslavia. He wanted to know if I'd
heard it. He was nervous that the Bureau would get wind of
the rumor, and use it to sandbag the CIA.

"I hear that rumor all the time," I said. "I tell everybody
it's bullshit, but they don't believe me. People can be so
cynical."

I made another pitch for help. He said he'd run it by his
bosses again.

Juan called. He was doing such a good job as a movie

producer that the Argentine government wanted to give him a grant to make a historical film.

"I'm going to accept it," he said. "It's the kind of film I've always *wanted* to make—and they gave me final cut."

"Juan, you crazy fuck! The most important thing in this business is to never believe your own bullshit."

"But they *love my work.* And what I really want to do is *direct.*"

I got him to turn down the grant, but he was never quite the same after that.

Over the next few days, I called all around the world, trying to find a way to bust into Terpil's mail drop. I also followed up some of the leads I'd gotten from ATF. One looked interesting. An executive for a major computer company seemed to have several links to Terpil. I wanted to put somebody on the exec, but I was stretched too thin.

One afternoon, just before six, a journalist working for a Brazilian magazine called me. He said he was doing a story on manhunting. He wanted an interview. Why not? For the last year or so, I'd been getting quite a bit of press. Safir encouraged it. Media meant money.

I met the reporter in front of the Bloomingdale's at the Tysons Corner mall. His questions were pretty standard: who, what, when, where, why. But then he veered off into the subject of Cuba. Had I ever gone after a fugitive in Cuba? Was it legal for me to go into Cuba? How would I do it?

Hell! This guy wasn't a *journalist.* He was probably an agent for Cuba's intelligence agency, DGI. He'd more than likely heard from the Soviets that I was after Terpil. But why did *he* care?

Was Terpil in Cuba?

That scenario made sense. Cuba would be a safe haven for Terpil, and with his wealth, it would probably be a very pleasant place to live. I'm sure it beat the hell out of Libya.

I called my most highly placed contact at the CIA. I told him that an agent from the FBI had just called me, wanting to know if it was true that Terpil was still working for the Agency. He freaked out when I told him that.

Then I said that a confidential informant had just told me Terpil was in Cuba. Could he confirm or deny?

He said he'd get back to me.

Ninety minutes later, he called and invited me to his office.

When I got there, he looked grim and gray. He swore me to secrecy. "You have to be *extremely* careful about poking around in Cuba after Terpil," he said.

"How come?"

"Because that's where he is."

His head drooped apologetically. "Some of us have been wanting to tell you that, but you've gotta understand, our balls are in a *vise.*" The problem, he said, was that the Agency had discovered Terpil's whereabouts from HUMINT (or, "human intelligence"). The CIA, he said, was running an agent in the Hemingway Marina, where Terpil lived, and if Terpil's cover were blown, the agent would be in jeopardy.

I got pissed. "If you'd fucking *told* me that," I said, "we could have worked together, instead of turning this into the standard agency-versus-agency goatfuck. I'm not gonna screw your guy up," I said, "if I *know he's there.* But you gotta *level* with me."

He apologized for not trusting me, and I apologized for losing my temper. All in all, I liked the Agency. Unlike the Federal Bureaucracy of Investigation, the Agency usually got their jobs done.

I asked my contact if it was feasible for me to go into Cuba and "terminate Terpil's situation."

No way, he said. Castro had just shot a couple of generals for drug trafficking, so suddenly George Bush *liked* Fidel. He wanted Castro to join the war on drugs.

Poor George. He was a likeable guy, but he sure had his head up his ass.

Before I left the CIA building, my Agency contact gave me a warning. He told me he'd heard the FBI was infuriated that I'd cut them out of the Terpil investigation, and that they were looking for ways to sandbag me.

"Don't worry about it," I told him. "I've been bustin' the Feebs' balls for years."

"That's what I heard," he said. "That's part of the problem."

As I drove back to headquarters, I got more and more pissed off at the Bureau. America's *national security* was being threatened, but all the FBI could think about was its own role in the federal bureaucracy. I felt like calling up Bill Sessions and biting his ass off.

But I couldn't do that kind of thing anymore. I was a Boss now. So I settled for just some garden-variety ball busting. I grabbed my car phone and called back the dickhead who was bugging the woman I'd had the brief affair with. By now, I'd called him several times, and he was beginning to soften up. But I was sick of dealing with him; I had more important things to do. So this time, I told him that if he didn't start acting like a gentleman, I'd call his boss at work, and find a way to fuck up his employment.

He got outraged, and flicked me some shit. But I just flicked it back—and I was better at it than him. Practice makes perfect.

After a while, he got all quiet. I stayed on the line, silent as a stone, waiting. Finally, he started whining, and gave in. He offered not only to apologize, but also to send her a gift, to show he was sincere.

Suddenly, it seemed, he'd turned into a nice guy, thus proving an old adage: Get 'em by the balls, and their hearts and minds will follow.

Good! Now I could get back to my *real* problem: my mutt Frank, the most dangerous man on earth.

Back at the office, I played with my computer until 1:00 A.M. Betsy called a couple of times, but I was too wrapped up in Terpil to go home. My computer could do amazing things these days. Some of Ron Wutrich's protégés had souped it up so much that if a flea farted in Bolivia, I could tell you what he'd had for lunch.

As I traced my info, I became fascinated by the lead on the computer executive that ATF had given me.

Interesting character. He had a good career, but he was a spy-wannabe. There were thousands of twerps like him all over the country—guys who'd read too many spy novels and were bored with their real lives. They periodically got together at Security and Surveillance conventions, where they'd do silly "spook" things, like meet somebody at midnight to pay $4,000 for night-vision goggles that they could have gotten for $750 at army surplus.

Deep in the ATF's file on the executive was a brief notation, tossed into the middle of a paragraph: "Believed to have traveled with Terpil to PLO conventions."

That note jumped off my monitor and slapped me in the face.

If it was true, I'd found my way to get Terpil out of Cuba.

I wouldn't even need the movie scam. I'd just wait for Terpil and my computer executive to head to a PLO convention, then grab them on the way.

First, though, I had to determine if the lead was valid. I called State, Interpol, and the CIA, and had them send me everything they could on major PLO events.

While I was waiting, I started running my computer executive through every possible government computer. It took longer than ever these days, because the number of federal data bases was growing geometrically. Reagan and Bush had always *talked* a lot about ending government invasion of private lives, but that was bullshit. They both *loved* having their noses into everybody's business. By now, there were almost nine *hundred* government data banks. Within the past few years, computers had revolutionized federal law enforcement. They had obliterated the concept of privacy, even for "good" citizens, like my computer exec.

My exec, whose name was Terrence McWilliams, showed up in dozens of programs, even though he had a spotless record.

One source on McWilliams, of course, was the IRS. They had a hot trigger. For years, McWilliams's income had stayed at a plateau, reflecting his stable corporate salary. But one recent year, his income had suddenly spiked. His tax return, however, showed no second source of income, like investments or inheritance. The following year, his income had returned to the plateau.

Had McWilliams done a weapons deal with Terpil that year?

To find out if McWilliams had been traveling internationally, I got a copy of his Treasury Enforcement Communications System printout, which noted reentry into the United States.

My mutt Terrence had been a busy boy! He'd traveled abroad frequently.

I cross-checked the dates of McWilliams's travels with the dates of the major PLO events. I got four hits. On four occasions, McWilliams had been out of the country during a PLO event.

Then I went to McWilliams's phone company with a photocopy of one of my old bogus pocket subpoenas, and got his phone records. Pay dirt! McWilliams had placed several calls to a telephone number in Cuba. I got a deputy who could speak Spanish to call the Cuban number. For over a minute, the phone rang. Finally, somebody picked it up. It was a pay phone in a walkway of the Hemingway Marina.

I had my link! McWilliams was dirty. I felt flushed and happy. Adrenaline hot-wired my brain.

Then I did an unusual thing. Instead of hitting the phones at ninety miles an hour, I sat back and put my feet on my desk. I wanted to savor the moment.

My nerves relaxed and my muscles went soft and warm. "I love this," I whispered to myself. I took a deep breath, and the air was sweet and cool.

Then I grabbed my phone like a mad dog.

I wanted a Title III wiretap on my mutt McWilliams—the power to listen in on *all* his calls. So I called one of my favorite U.S. magistrates, a real blue-chipper who usually gave me whatever I wanted. I told him that the Agency had located Terpil in Cuba, and that McWilliams was apparently calling Terpil there.

But my magistrate busted my balls. He said that all I had was evidence McWilliams was calling *Cuba*—not Terpil. Furthermore, he said, I had no evidence at all that Terpil, or anyone else in Cuba, was calling McWilliams.

Wiretap denied.

So I set out to build a phony preponderance of evidence that Terpil was calling McWilliams from Cuba. I got with a deputy who had relatives in Cuba. His relatives agreed to call McWilliams. They called him collect, so that it would show up on his phone records.

I got the phone company to provide me with an immediate

record of the call. I took the record to the magistrate. But he still wouldn't go for it.

What a prick! Every time I tried to be even slightly straight, I got slapped down. The government made it so *easy* to do nothing, and so *hard* to do something good.

Once again, it was time for a weasel-deal—regardless of Safir's repeated warnings.

I called in some of Wutrich's top computer nerds and tasked them with Operation Password. Their mission was to figure out how to break into McWilliams's home computer, and use his own secret "password" to raid his files. I was assuming that McWilliams entered almost everything into his p.c., because he was a genuine computer nut.

At first glance, it seemed impossible to determine his password, because it could have been anything. But I had a hunch that an amateur "secret agent" like McWilliams would use something that related to spying, or international intrigue—probably something cutesy, like "007," or "Secret Agent Man." To a punk like McWilliams, this had to be just a game. If he knew what he was *really* into—things like having a rat eat someone's stomach—he'd run like hell.

So I loaded my computer guys with booklets on Agency terminology, and with spy novels, and told them to enter every piece of spy lingo they saw.

I took off for an Interpol convention, and when I got back, they had a program of about 2,500 possible passwords. We called McWilliams's number while he was at work and started force-feeding his computer with passwords. None of them worked.

But then one of my supernerds worked up a "sniffer" program, designed specifically to crash into a system by stealing its passwords.

The sniffer program worked. The password was "I Spy."

I found a complete set of McWilliams's travel records. He'd gone to some exotic places, like Yugoslavia and Morocco. Not your normal vacation spots.

I ran his travel records against his credit card records. It looked to me, based on car rentals and hotels, as if McWilliams's pattern had been to fly to someplace like Tangier,

Morocco, then drive across the border to Algeria. Algiers, Algeria, was where many of the PLO events had been held.

I doubted that McWilliams had made these trips alone. Somewhere, he'd probably met Terpil.

I felt like I was getting close to Terpil. But I still didn't have what I needed. I needed to know the *future,* not the past. When would Terpil and McWilliams meet *next?* And where?

Once more, I was at a dead end. I had to shake things loose. When in doubt, do something. I called McWilliams.

"Mr. McWilliams? How do you do? You're not gonna believe this, but my name is Terrence McWilliams, too."

"It *is?"*

"Yeah—even spelled the same. No relation, though. Just a coincidence."

"Small world."

I'd used the same-name gimmick a dozen times. It caught people off guard, and made them more receptive.

"Here's why I called," I said. "I'm with Compsource Services, the networking firm, and our market research shows that you're an avid computer user. We think that we can fill your needs better than any of our competitors."

"Well, my current service is satisfactory."

"I'm sure it is. But I think you deserve more than just 'satisfactory.' Who are you with now, if you don't mind my asking?"

"InterCom."

"They're very good. But we offer services that they don't. For example, did you know that Compsource has an international telex network? Have you ever sent an overseas telex?"

"Yeah."

"And you used?"

"RCA."

"RCA. Let me punch in a couple of codes. Let's see. If your telex was to Western Europe, we could have saved you 18 percent over RCA. Where *did* your cable go?"

"Oh, I don't even remember." He was starting to sound uncomfortable. I didn't care. I had what I needed. I got off.

349

I filled out a couple of pocket subpoenas and hit the road. Both RCA and InterCom had regional offices nearby.

I went to RCA first. Jackpot. McWilliams had sent five telexes in the last two years to a "Mr. F. Terpid" in Cuba. Obviously, it was Terpil, with his name changed just enough to keep it from triggering computerized "alarms."

Within a matter of minutes, I had hard copy on three of the five telexes, including the most recent. The recent one was highly coded—not exactly gibberish, but close. But a three-syllable series made sense to me. It was: Cub-Tor-Prag. My guess: Cuba to Toronto to Prague. Unless I was wrong, that was Terpil's itinerary for their next trip.

I called my hook at Qantas—my favorite Junior G-man— and asked him to find out how a person could travel from Cuba to Prague.

He was overjoyed that I'd called. "I'll task my best man with it, and get right back to ya, Boss," he said. "Who's our skell?"

"International terrorist."

"Check." His voice was all trembly and slow, like he was close to orgasm.

An hour later, he called back. The only possible carrier was the Soviet airline, Aeroflot. The only routing was through Toronto.

My heart started to thump. I could smell Terpil's blood.

This was going to be the *big* one—the bust that would memorialize me forever as someone who'd *done* something in this world.

Grabbing Terpil would be even better than taking down Nazis. Terpil was just as evil as my Nazis had been—but *he was still in business.* If I grabbed him, I could stop evil before it happened.

It would probably be a violent bust, though. Terpil was *always* armed, and would have nothing to lose. I'd abandoned the idea of hiring a hit, though. Under Bush, we weren't getting the same go-for-it vibes that Reagan had put out in his glory years.

But I didn't care. I *wanted* to do it myself. This was the bust that was going to make me feel satisfied. With myself. With my life.

After Terpil, I'd be able to look at what I had achieved, and say: "It's *enough*."

And then I was going to buy that flower shop in San Francisco. Nobody knew that. Not Safir. Not even Betsy. But, in my heart, I knew it for a fact.

I'd just turned forty. But I felt like I was sixty.

I'd had enough.

Before the day ended, I hit InterCom. But they didn't want to show me their clients' records.

I laid the subpoena on their assistant chief of security. I badged him. I begged him. But he stonewalled. So I implied that if he didn't help me *immediately,* I'd go crazy and just fucking *kill* him, right then and there.

He reassessed policy.

I got a copy of McWilliams's records. He had recently used InterCom to plan a trip. The trip was coming up in three weeks.

McWilliams would travel from New York, to Toronto, to Prague. From Toronto to Prague, he would be flying on Aeroflot.

His Aeroflot plane in Toronto would have just arrived from Cuba.

I started working up a plan for the takedown.

I'd have to be fast and efficient, and be able to meet force with force. My only window of opportunity would be in Toronto.

I'd have to get Terpil off the plane. While he was still on it, he'd technically not be on Canadian soil, and I'd have no legal way to arrest him and bring him back to the United States.

I called my Mountie friend from the Koziy investigation, and explained my dilemma.

"I gotta get Terpil off that plane," I said. "What if there was a bomb threat? While the plane was being refueled? Wouldn't they have to evacuate the plane?"

"Are you saying *you'd* call in a bomb threat?"

"I'm not *sayin'* that, but you could reasonably infer that I am."

"Sounds a bit dicey."

"Okay, what about this? While they're refueling, a mechanic happens to leave a petcock open, and the ground around the plane is flooded with fuel. They'd have to evacuate, right?"

"They would indeed. I suppose something of that nature *could* be arranged. But what happens when your man comes off the airplane?"

"He'll probably be in first class, so he'll be one of the first people off. Your men will have cleared the area. We'll have just a few plainclothes cops milling around. I don't want him to see an empty terminal and run back onto the plane. As he comes off, I'll face him down. Your men will provide backup."

"Will he be armed?"

"Probably. Our intelligence indicates he's close enough to Cuba's DGI to have weapons clearance."

"So there may be shots fired?"

"Yeah. He'll have nuthin' to lose."

"Why would the chief of International Operations volunteer for a gunfight?"

"I'm the best shot in the Marshals. And I've done this before." He didn't respond. "Why *not* me?"

"Just asking."

I wrote up the plan and took it to Safir.

Safir's office—and mine, too—had recently been moved to the Marshals' magnificent new glass and granite headquarters in Arlington, Virginia. After two hundred years, the Service finally had its own building, thanks to Safir. We were finally out of the shopping center.

Safir stared at my memo for a long time. Finally, he said, "Normally, this plan would be way out of line. But considering the circumstances, I'm willing to at least *submit* this to Justice."

"Good. Tell 'em not to dick around. We've got two and a half weeks."

I stood to leave. "There's something else we need to talk about," said Safir. "I've been hearing rumors. Some people say you're still cutting corners and taking chances. John, we *talked* about that."

"So?"

"So, it's not good. It's bad for our image of professionalism."

"Our *image* of professionalism! Our *image?* God *damn* our image! Who's given more to the Service than *me?*"

"Calm down. All I'm saying is, you've gotta go by the book, even if it doesn't serve your own goals."

I stood there waiting for him to give me the speech about Always put the Service ahead of yourself.

But he didn't say anything. After standing there for a few more seconds, I wheeled around and bolted out the door.

Not very good office politics.

But fuck that.

A few days later, Safir called me into his office. He was grim. "I'll get right to the point," he said. "Justice forwarded your Terpil plan to the White House. And the White House killed it. They said it had 'too many variables.'"

"What if I eliminate some of the variables?"

Safir shook his head. "Forget about it." Safir looked even more tense than usual. "George Bush," he said, "is *not* Ronald Reagan." Safir smiled sadly. "The party's over, John," he said.

"Where do we go from here?" I asked.

"Nowhere."

"Nowhere" wasn't my style.

Too many variables? Okay, how about *this* variable? When Terpil goes to Toronto, so do I, on the slim chance that he *might* be stupid enough to step off the plane.

And, lo and behold, there *is* a bomb threat. Not from *me,* of course. It just *happens.* God knows, I'm not Terpil's only enemy.

Everybody deplanes.

And—BAM!—I make my pop. End of story.

I drag Terpil's ass back home. I get accused of being the person who made the bomb threat. I deny it. And then I get another promotion.

Simple as that.

It would work. I knew it.

I *would* get the job done. No matter what.

The party wasn't over.

Just before my trip to Toronto, I went to Tucson, to give a speech on fugitives at a major law enforcement conference.

I stood offstage in the ballroom of the El Conquistador Hotel as an administrator from Justice began my introduction.

The ballroom was full of fugitive investigators, detectives, police chiefs, sheriffs, and men from the DEA, Customs, and the ATF.

"If you know anything about fugitive apprehension," said the guy at the podium, "you know the name of our next presenter, John Pascucci. Inspector Pascucci, chief of International Operations for the U.S. Marshals, has risen to the forefront of this field in just the past nine years. His caseload reads like a *Who's Who* of the criminal world. Christopher Boyce. Konrads Kalejs. Bohdan Koziy. Josef Mengele. And dozens more. He has apprehended Nazis, neo-Nazis, murderers, bombers, drug smugglers, terrorists, and spies. Many times, he has risked his life in the line of duty. But every time that he has gone after a major fugitive—*every time—he has succeeded.* Former Attorney General Edwin Meese once said that 'When John Pascucci is after you, you can run, but you can't hide.' Ladies and gentlemen—John Pascucci."

I stepped out to the podium as people began to applaud. To my surprise, there was an enthusiasm to their applause, as if they really meant it. I had no idea so many people knew who I was. The applause continued, and got even louder.

Then a guy from the Service stood up as he applauded, and somebody I didn't recognize also stood. A few more rose, and suddenly everybody in the room was standing and applauding. Somebody yelled, "Way-to-go-*John!*" and the applause continued.

I felt a catch in my throat. Many of these people were true warriors. They had risked their lives to stand against America's predators. Their approval meant more to me than anything in the world.

Finally, I felt like I was one of them.

My eyes began to float with tears. I didn't try to brush them away.

For the first time in my life, I didn't feel the need to be tough. I was with my family.

After my speech, I hurried out to a waiting car. I had to get back east.

I had a rendezvous in Toronto with Terpil.

One of my deputies jogged down the stairs after me. "Great job, Boss!" he crowed.

I paused at the front desk to pick up a Federal Express package; it was the note of apology and gift from the guy who'd hassled my ex-girlfriend. I'd arranged for him to ship it here.

I grabbed the package and tucked it under my arm.

"Let's hit it," I said.

My other men fell in behind me.

Again, I paused to savor the moment. What could be better than this? I was surrounded by warriors. I was preparing for another great adventure. Once again, I had the chance actually to *do* something.

I felt very lucky.

I was truly happy. For the first time in my life.

At the bottom of the stairs, I suddenly felt a hand on my arm. "Hold it! Now!" The hand clamped down hard. "FBI. You're under arrest."

"What! For *what?*"

"Interference with interstate commerce."

"Interference with *what?*"

Jesus! What weasel-deal was coming back to haunt me? Was it something I'd done on Terpil? Kalejs? Koziy? Mengele?

A fat kid ambled over and badged me. "Get your mutt?" he asked.

"Huh?" I said. "What mutt?"

"Shut up! I'm not talkin' to you!" He looked at the other Bureau guy. "Your mutt has a big mouth on him."

The other guy shrugged. "I know," he said. "They're all alike."

I was out on my own recognizance in a matter of hours.

But I was finished, and I knew it. I would soon lose my job. That was certain.

My lawyer said that the FBI was in an uproar, and that I might even have to do some jail time.

I'd made a fatal mistake.

The citizen I'd been hassling—the ex-boyfriend of the woman I'd had the affair with—had decided to report my actions against him to the authorities. He hadn't been able to interest the local police, the state police, or a federal prosecutor in the case, because it was just too petty. But the FBI had agreed to at least look into it. To gain jurisdiction, the College Boys had concocted the theory that if somebody was threatening this citizen's job security, they were, technically, "interfering with interstate commerce." By proving that kind of minor violation, the Bureau could compel the trouble-maker to back off, and leave the citizen alone.

However, when the FBI had made the pop, and had discovered that the perpetrator was their old nemesis, John Pascucci, they'd had a field day. They threw the book at me. Normally, discipline on an offense of this nature would be handed over to the offending officer's own agency. There, it would typically be handled internally, with slap on the wrist—an administrative sanction, or a brief suspension. But the Feebs—for their own reasons—had insisted on drawing up the paperwork on me themselves. They wanted me prosecuted to the fullest extent of the law.

After all, interstate commerce *had* to be protected.

The whole thing was, in my humble opinion, a weasel-deal.

But it had gotten the job done. The ends, they had apparently felt, had justified the means.

I was finished.

I didn't call Safir.

What was the point?

I had pulled one weasel-deal too many. Safir had warned me, but I'd ignored him.

If I'd committed a crime to further an investigation, and serve the Marshals, maybe Safir would have stuck up for me. *Maybe.* But my harassment of the citizen had been for strictly personal reasons. I'd done it without worrying that it might backfire, and embarrass the Marshals.

I had, in short, put myself ahead of the Service.

So there was no reason to call Howard Safir.

If Safir was going to protect me, he would call me.

He didn't.

I was finished.

I called Betsy.

"Go down to the basement and get rid of my pot plants," I told her. "Some people from the FBI may come over to search the place."

"Why?"

I told her the whole truth. It was the hardest call of my life.

The next morning, I felt sick at my stomach before I even opened my eyes.

What was I going to do with my life?

What had been the *point* of my life?

Suddenly, I needed desperately to know for certain that Koziy and Kalejs were dead, or in prison.

I needed to know I'd done something good.

I called the foundation run by Simon Wiesenthal, the Nazi hunter.

But when I mentioned Koziy and Kalejs to one of Wiesenthal's associates, he sounded dispirited.

"Those two," he said. "Yes, I know about those two. Koziy is still sitting in Costa Rica. He was imprisoned for a time, but was later released. For a while, he was rumored to be dead, but he surfaced again. Kalejs, we believe, is living in Australia. Living *well,* we understand."

I groaned. "Oh, my God."

"What's wrong?"

"My name's John Pascucci. I was—"

"I know who you are! Pleasure to talk to you! Really, it's an honor! Are you after someone else now?"

"No, no. I'm not with the Marshals anymore. Actually . . . I may be going to prison." I told him why.

"That doesn't make any sense at *all*," he said.

"Well, the real world doesn't always make sense."

He didn't say anything.

So I tried to cheer him up.

Epilogue

• A Reagan Family Reunion •

"God doesn't require you to succeed. He only requires that you try."

—*Mother Teresa*

Four of us stood outside a massive oak door, guns drawn, gulping down air. I reared back to kick the door. As usual, I'd be the first man into the house. I wiped my sweat-slick hands on my windbreaker, which had DEA plastered across the chest.

"Pucker up, men," I hissed.

Then I screamed, "DEA! Open up!" And: *Boom!* I crashed my heel into the door and shattered the deadbolt.

I ran screaming into the living room, with my finger on the trigger of my gun.

Three swarthy men stood stock-still by the fireplace, frozen with shock. Then one jammed his hand into his sport coat.

I yelled, "Freeze!" as I drove the butt of my Colt .45 into his cheek. He collapsed, and I pulled his gun out of his jacket before he even hit the floor.

"Everybody on the couch!" I barked. "Hands behind your neck!" One of my men cuffed them, then he ran off with the other two to cover the rest of the house.

I glared at the men on the couch.

"Where's our guy?" I asked softly, my voice dark with menace.

"What guy?" said the best dressed of the three pukes on the couch. He had a heavy Spanish accent.

"The one you assholes kidnapped."

He shrugged. The other two watched him carefully. He was apparently the leader.

"Before my men get back," I said to the well-dressed mutt, "we're gonna get some *work* done." I pointed my gun at his thigh. "Tell me where our agent is *right now,* or I'm gonna shoot you in the leg."

"This is *America,*" he sneered. "You can't do that."

"Wrong, asshole!" I bellowed. *"I'm* America."

Then: BAM! The guy's leg exploded in red and pink. He began to thrash and wail. I sang: "God bless A-meri-ca, land that I love."

Then I turned to one of the others. "Do *you* know where he is?"

"In the basement!" he bawled.

From behind me came a voice . . . "And, *cut!*"

The three men on the couch stood up, and I turned to face the voice. It belonged to the director of the movie we were shooting.

"Terrific work, John!" he said. "Man, you've got the moves of an experienced actor."

"Thanks, Boss."

Truth be told, I'd had *years* of acting experience. As a manhunter.

But I was a manhunter no longer. After my arrest in Tucson, I lost my job.

I even did a short stint in a "country club" federal correctional camp. It was a beautiful place, deep in the heart of the Oregon forest. The regimen there reminded me of the army. It wasn't very difficult, but it got boring.

I did, however, make some good friends in Club Fed. Several were former Reagan administration officials. Almost a hundred prominent Reagan-era administrators had been accused of crimes, and some had ended up serving time. So had an even larger number of lesser officials—from Customs, ATF, Treasury, DEA, and the USMS. Hundreds of us, it appeared, had played fast and loose during the Reagan years.

Some of the former officials in camp were there because

they'd gotten greedy and had tried to use their power to get rich. Others, like me, hadn't been money hungry but had taken Reagan's "Rambo" attitude far too seriously. We'd thought we could get away with *anything*, as long as our motives had been good.

But we'd been naive. We'd been self-absorbed. We'd been self-righteous. And we'd paid the price.

Even my old drinking buddy Ed Meese had been threatened with jail for some of *his* apparent weasel-deals, including the Wedtech scandal, and what appeared to be a criminal cover-up of the Iran-Contra scam. But Ed had skated, just like Ollie North. In the real world, the top dogs get off easy.

After camp, as I began to restructure my career, I often thought about the Reagan era. For good or ill, it had been an extraordinary epoch. It had been a violent, greedy, and chaotic time, but it had also been one of those rare times—like the 1960s—when people in government had felt they could actually *do something*.

That feeling no longer seems to exist. It was suffocated by failure and inertia. Now, most people in government seem to feel helpless and cynical. And the American public no longer expects much from government—so that's about what they get.

After my release, I explored various opportunities to work as a private investigator. Because of my conviction, I could no longer work for the government. Several private investigation firms wanted me to go after bail jumpers, but after the career I'd had, chasing petty bail-bond violators just didn't seem like enough.

I eventually decided to work as an independent consultant to several prominent investigation firms, including that of Anthony Pellicano, the top-gun PI in Hollywood. Pellicano's work led me to security consulting for film production companies, and from that, I drifted into acting, mostly just for fun.

The film I was currently working on, *Psittacine Caine* (pronounced like *Citizen Kane*), was a high-action cop movie that the director thought I was perfect for. Besides having a small part, I was also the film's director of security.

I loved working in the film industry. It had the same

adrenaline-fired punch as detective work, and the people around me were smart and ambitious.

But it wasn't the same as manhunting. I missed the life-or-death action, and I missed my buddies from the Service.

I lived a quiet and safe life in the suburbs of Washington, D.C., with Betsy, and our dog, Andy. For a while, after Betsy had found out about my affair, I'd been afraid she wouldn't be able to forgive me. We went through a rocky period. After all, she'd been absolutely faithful to me in times of real hell: during long absences, the shooting of our home, and the constant possibility that I'd get killed. Under those circumstances, my betrayal of her faith had been doubly painful for her.

But Betsy came through for me—as usual—and worked past the hurt. Could I have done the same? Honest answer? Maybe. Maybe not. But Betsy was—as she always claimed—stronger than me.

Occasionally, my old buddies from law enforcement dropped by our suburban Washington, D.C., home to visit Betsy and me. Whenever they came over, they always told me what a raw deal I'd gotten. Many government officials, they said, had done far worse things than I had, without losing their jobs. They said: If only you'd done *this,* if only you'd done *that,* you could have escaped your fate.

I totally disagreed.

Because *I was my fate.* If I hadn't fallen when I did, I'd have stumbled over some other kind of weasel-deal.

But let's be realistic: Without all the weasel-deals, I'd never have gotten *anywhere*—not against *my* mutts. My mutts didn't fight fair.

But I didn't see myself as a star-crossed victim. I saw myself as a star-crossed jerk. Because, let's not forget, I didn't go down fighting an evil man; I went down fighting an *ex-girlfriend's ex-boyfriend.* And I'd fought him mostly just for *fun.*

Remember how I told you, early on, that the horrifying thing about evil is that you can find it anywhere, if you look for it, and that you can even find it in yourself, if you look hard enough? Well, I found I could enjoy hurting people—and if that's not evil, I don't know what is.

Since my downfall, I've tried to overcome that part of myself, and I think I've succeeded. But I'll always know that, at least for a while, it was there. That knowledge is my punishment, and it's as painful to me as my fall from the heights of government service. It's my burden to bear, and I'll have to live with it the rest of my life.

Sometimes, when my buddies would come visit, we'd talk about our old comrades, and what had become of them. Safir, as you might well imagine, had distinguished himself. When Safir's former boss from Justice, Rudolph Giuliani, had become mayor of New York, he'd brought in Safir as the city's powerful fire commissioner. Someday Safir, I believe, will be one of America's most prominent public officials. Chuck Kupferer—Safir's number two man—retained his power throughout the Bush administration, and retired with honor in 1994. And war hero Tony Perez—my old competition as the Marshals' toughest man—laid to rest my doubts about his being management material when he became chief of the Enforcement Division.

My old buddies—virtually all of whom had desk jobs now—were wistful about the Reagan era. It was different now, they said.

But maybe it was just that *we* were different. We were all older now. We were more responsible, less naive. And less alive.

Invariably, toward the end of these evenings, we ended up telling war stories. We talked deep into the night. We talked about kicking doors, and facing down killers, and risking our lives in a dozen idiotic and glorious ways. We talked about the sinking, sliding feeling we used to get in our bowels before we hit a house. We talked about the mutts who'd tried to kill us, and about the ones we'd killed. We talked about evil men, and about the necessary evil that we'd committed to capture them.

For hour after hour, we talked about the bad old days of power and glory.

I always seemed to have more war stories than anyone else, and every time I told them, they grew more real and immediate. I loved telling my stories. It was the only way I could momentarily recapture my past. I told my buddies about Son of Sam, and Rufus the Mob Bomber, and about Chris Boyce and Celia James and the prisoner I almost murdered. I told them about crazy bastards like Tommy Lynch and Frank Riley, and about my little buddy Ricki Blanca. I told them all about Levy the Indian, and the day we watched a bear catch a trout. I told them about Mr. Sung, and about my midnight ride with the meth monster, and about getting hit by a car in Toronto. I told them about Koziy. Kalejs. Terpil. My James Bond briefcase.

I told them about talking to the ghost of Josef Mengele.

Sometimes I'd talk about how high I used to get when I closed the time line on an evil man. When I described that feeling, I could almost feel it again. The memory was that strong. But the high never lasted—not like it had during an investigation—and when it left, I always felt hollow.

When the evenings would end, I'd usually have a hard time falling asleep. I'd lay there and ask myself: What's next? What's next?

To be honest, at this point in my life, I don't *know* what's next. I still have half my life ahead of me, and I'm determined to make the most of it. I still want to do good things.

The media, I know, likes to say that all us baby boomers have slowed down and sold out. But I don't buy that. Most of us are still out here struggling. We're trying to invent the last half of our lives, and fighting to make them something we can be proud of.

But if I do manage to do something worthwhile with my life, it won't be as the president's manhunter.

Those days are gone.

And so, too, is the best part of my life. And the best part of me.

I suppose I could say, Oh, those days will be *back*—I'll find a way to *recreate* my years of glory and grace: Just wait, be patient, the best is yet to come!

But that's not how the real world works, is it?

The glorious days of pain have disappeared—they're in the wind—and they'll never return.

These days, my life is easy. It's rich with comfort and security.

But I would trade everything to go back on the hunt. I long

for the search. For the rest of my life, I'll desperately miss the long dark trail that leads to God knows where.

I can't help but feel that somewhere, out in the darkness of that trail, the best part of me still exists, cut off forever from the rest of what I am or ever will be.

I'll never see that part of me again.

The awful days of grace are gone.

The hunt is over.

Index

(In this index, JP is used for John Pascucci)

Agee, Philip, 310
Allende, Salvador, 131, 293
Amin, Idi, 334–36
Anka, Paul, 73
Arafat, Yasir, 335
Arajs, Viktor, 239
Arajs Kommandos, 239
ARJIS (Automated Regional Justice
    Information System), 94, 123
Armstrong, Rob, 227–31
Aryan Nations, 158, 172–73, 183,
    184, 186, 189
Auschwitz, 270, 271–74, 275, 282,
    286

Barbie, Klaus, 275, 302, 307–08
Begin, Menachim, 290, 291
Berg, Alan, 218
Bias, Len, 316
Black (accomplice to Boyce),
    124–28, 129, 135, 140, 147,
    151, 166, 174, 191
Blanca, Ricki (Rick the Spic), 162,
    167–74, 175–85, 187–88,
    191, 364
Bossert, Liselotte, 308
Bossert, Wolfram, 308
Boyce, Christopher, 61, 85, 86,
    119–53, 198, 261, 310, 331,
    338, 354, 364
    bank robberies, 155, 156, 157,
    158–59, 160, 161, 162,

163–67, 168, 170, 173, 175,
    176, 177, 180, 181
    capture and conviction, 190–91,
    194, 195, 196, 203
    trial, 183–87
Boyce Task Force, 84–85, 86, 88,
    93, 94, 106, 109, 111, 118,
    120, 121–22, 129, 165, 191, 195
Brick (agent), 99–104, 106, 108–11,
    118, 158–59, 171, 195, 197,
    207, 208, 216, 218–20, 222–24,
    227, 231–32, 267
Brown, Edmund G. (Jerry), 106,
    108, 109–10, 118
Buckley, William, 280
Bureau of Alcohol, Tobacco and
    Firearms (ATF), 97, 98–99,
    116, 183, 340, 341, 343,
    345–46, 354, 360
Bureau of Prisons, 14, 329
Bush, George, 320, 328, 336, 340,
    344, 346, 350, 353
Bush administration, 363
Butler, Richard, 157–58

California FIST, 206, 207
Camarena, Enrique, 325
Caputo, Danny, 16
Carta, Señor, 41, 44, 45–46, 47–49,
    60
Carter, Jimmy, 26, 77, 78, 85, 91,
    103, 106–07
Casey, William, 200

Castro, Fidel, 132, 344
Catholic church, 283, 286
CIA (the Agency), 33, 34, 35, 44, 45,
    46, 47, 99, 121, 138, 183,
    199–200, 201, 232, 234, 290
  and Contras, 320
  JP liaison with, 340
  Mengele case, 277–78, 291–92,
    296, 297–98, 301–05, 306,
    309–10
  Narco-Terrorist Unit, 199
  Terpil case, 335, 337–38, 341,
    342, 343, 344, 346, 347
  training, for JP, 280–81, 384–85,
    293, 299
Chicago Marshals office, 97, 98,
    104–05
Christian Identity movement, 158
Church, Frank, 189
Churchill, Winston, 14
Civiletti, Benjamin, 85
Cludy, Joe, 144
Cold War, 14, 121, 148
CompuServe, 94
Conseula, Joanne, 30–32, 34, 39,
    40–43, 52, 59
Contras, 38, 320

Dachau trials, 13
Defense Intelligence Agency, 290
Denver Marshals' Office, 177, 218
DGI, 343, 352
Dighera, Bob, 84–90, 94, 117–18,
    119, 123–28, 131, 132, 135,
    140, 148–50, 151, 152
DMV system(s), 22
"Doctors Trial," 283
Donner, Rufus, 93–94, 97–99, 105,
    107–16, 118, 139, 165, 191,
    203, 364
Donteri, Bill, 23, 26, 51, 52
Drug Enforcement Agency (DEA),
    14, 22, 33, 43, 59, 136, 199,
    206, 224, 232, 254, 359
  agents killed in Brazil, 321–23
  fugitives, 331
  NADDIS system, 242
Durant, John, 153, 155, 156–57,
    159–60, 167–68, 175, 182–83,
    184–85, 188–89
Dylan, Bob, 16, 17, 59, 68

Eagles of Riga, 262, 263–64, 265
Earp, Virgil, 2, 104, 117
Edwards, LaDonna, 105, 107, 108,
    111, 114, 115

Eichmann, Adolph, 286, 298
EPIC (computer bank), 22, 242

Falbaum, Bert, 238, 240–42, 257
Falcon and the Snowman, The,
    122, 163–64, 183
"Falcon and Snowman" spy, 61, 85
  see also Boyce, Christopher
FBI, 8, 14, 86–87, 91, 101, 206,
    228, 317
  arrest of JP, 355–56
  and Boyce case, 121, 159, 160,
    161, 162–63, 182, 183, 184
  computer systems, 135
  fugitives, 331
  and Nazis, 233–34, 235, 264
  relationship with U.S. Marshals,
    122, 216
  and Terpil case, 340, 341, 343,
    344–45
  and Thompson case, 208–11, 219
Ferrarone, Don, 233, 234, 236,
    238, 278
Final Solution, 13
Florida Department of Law
    Enforcement Data Processing
    System, 22
Florida DMV, 267
Frattini, Jimmy, 185
"French Connection" case, 338
Fuerte, Manuel, 111, 200–03, 204,
    224, 276–77
Fugitive Investigative Strike Team
    (FIST), 8, 204–07, 219, 220,
    224–27, 237, 250–51, 267, 318,
    325, 340
Fugitive Program, 16, 129, 145,
    196, 204
  assigned to U.S. Marshals
    Service, 85, 86–87, 91, 100
Fusaro, Flora, 65

Garcia, Captain, 40–41, 43–45,
    46–52, 53, 59–60
Garrett, Pat, 2, 104
George, Claire, 280
Gerhard, Wolfgang, 307
German Security Police (S.D.),
    239, 267
Germans
  and Mengele case, 275, 278, 279,
    285, 293
Gipper (the), 26, 33, 56, 305, 325
  see also Reagan, Ronald
Gipper's cop(s), 18, 55, 188, 291,
    332
Giuliani, Rudolph, 196, 363

Godchaux, Simone, 146, 147, 148
Gorbachev, Mikhail, 56, 334
Gottlieb, Hinda, 252–54, 257

Hameli, Ali, 302
Harrel, Isser, 298
Hernandez, Juan, 338–39, 341–43
Hickock, Wild Bill, 2, 104, 117
Himmler, Heinrich, 239, 272
Holocaust, 259
Homenick, Larry, 135, 143–44
Hudson, Colonel Paul, 143–44, 146
HUMINT (human intelligence), 344
Humperdinck, Engelbert, 72–73

InterCom, 349, 350, 351
Interpol, 248, 275, 278, 279, 285,
    288, 340, 346, 348
Iran-Contra scandal, 280, 320, 361
IRS, 346
Israelis
    and Mengele case, 275, 277, 279,
    285, 290–91

James, Celia, 157, 158, 162, 164,
    165–66, 167–68, 170, 171,
    172, 174, 175, 176, 179, 182,
    184, 186, 187, 188, 195, 196,
    203, 364
James, Janice, 175–76
Jews, 18–20, 26, 158, 162, 239, 253,
    264, 268, 308
Johnson, Cameron, 149, 164–65,
    168
Judenfrei (Free of Jews), 18
Justice Department, 12, 14, 15, 26,
    51, 101, 137, 159, 263, 323,
    340
    budget, 206
    historical library, 18
    monograph on crime, 204
    and Terpil case, 352, 353
    and U.S. Marshals Service, 196

Kaddafi, Muammar, 335
Kalejs, Konrads, 61, 239–69, 274,
    275, 280, 289, 331, 354, 355,
    357–58, 364
    arrest of, 269, 278, 325
Kameradenwerk, 294, 298
Kavlan, Karlis, 262, 263
Kennedy, Teddy, 106
KGB, 34, 35–36, 37–40, 49, 55–59,
    60, 86, 132, 138, 292
Klarsfeld, Serge, 275, 298
Koziy, Anatoly, 25–26
Koziy, Bohdan, 13–14, 15, 17–20,

21–30, 35–60, 236, 274, 278,
    280, 289, 331, 354, 355, 357,
    364
Koziy, Yaraslava, 41, 44, 50, 51, 52
Krug, Alban, 306
Kupferer, Chuck, 177, 183, 185,
    191, 194, 200, 211, 235, 236,
    238, 251, 321
    and Boyce case, 128–30, 132,
    133, 134, 135, 136, 137, 138,
    139, 140, 141, 143, 144,
    145–46, 147, 148, 150, 151,
    152–53
    career, 363
    and FIST, 203–05, 206
    JP relationship with, 197
    and Mengele case, 270–71, 274,
    275–76, 277, 278

Lennon, John, 140, 145
Leontin, Arvids, 267–68
LeRon (prisoner), 149
Lincoln, Colonel Raymond, 143
Los Angeles Police Department
    Intelligence Unit, 194
Lynch, Tommy, 128–34, 135–36,
    138–39, 147, 151, 166, 191,
    364

M-19 (terrorist group), 321, 322,
    323
McCue, Harry, 123
McWilliams, Terrence, 346–50, 351
Mafia, 191, 194, 197, 199
Meese, Ed, 15, 26, 40, 54, 196,
    226–27, 235, 241, 248, 264,
    277, 320, 328, 340, 361
    on JP, 354
Mengele, Josef, 22, 61, 270–314,
    316, 319, 326, 331, 337, 338,
    354, 355, 364
Mengele, Rolf, 285, 287, 308
Michigan FIST, 205, 206
MIRAC (computer network), 22,
    242
Morada, Luis, 198, 199–200, 201
Morelli, Gina, 29–30, 32
Mossad, 286, 298, 306
Moynihan, Daniel Patrick, 85
Mulhill, Tony, 185

NADDIS (computer system), 22,
    242
National Crime Information Center
    (NCIC), 135, 210, 212, 238,
    242

National Emergency Response
    Team, 227
National Reconnaissance Agency,
    290
National Security Agency, 278, 290
Nazi support groups, 283, 294
Nazis, 12–14, 22, 31, 40, 41, 56,
    199, 231, 274–75, 278, 283,
    350, 354
  anti-Communism, 19
  FBI and, 233–34
  Kalejs case, 235–69
  Mengele case, 270–314
  in South America, 286
Neff, Dave, 148–49, 150
Neo-Nazis, 31, 74–75, 152, 156,
    157–58, 171, 172, 175,
    191–92, 218, 227–31, 250, 255,
    298, 354
  in Canada, 259, 260, 263
  German refugees and, 201
  and Mafia, 191–92, 194, 197, 199
New York Police Department, 69,
    70
Nixon, Richard, 69, 93, 106, 110,
    117, 118, 123, 131, 206, 292,
    296
Non-Immigrant Immigration
    System, 22
Noriega, Manuel, 23, 124, 317,
    318–21, 322, 323
North, Don, 130–31
North, Ollie, 33, 361
Nuremberg trials, 13, 279, 283

ODESSA, 31, 35, 255, 283, 287, 298
Office of Special Investigations
    (OSI), 12–13, 14, 17–18, 19,
    20, 26, 45, 51, 54, 60
  and Kalejs case, 235, 236–37,
    238, 240, 241, 246, 247, 248,
    253, 256–57, 258, 261,
    262–63, 267
  and Mengele case, 275, 278, 296,
    302, 303, 304, 312
O'Neill, Tip, 94, 109, 117
Operation Password, 348
Order (the), 183

Pascucci, Betsy, 20, 59, 78, 91, 133,
    153, 177, 188, 197, 242–43,
    249–51, 266, 274–75, 288, 294,
    327, 336, 345, 351
  and end of JP career, 357, 362
  and Ricki Blanca, 179, 180, 181
  support for JP, 160
  threats to, 34

Pascucci, John
  awards, honors, 191, 224, 278,
    316, 331
  career, 69–83
  career with Marshals, 83, 84–118,
    152, 159, 191, 196–97, 206,
    220, 263, 278, 326
  career with Marshals, end of,
    326–27, 337, 345, 354–56,
    362–63
  desire to do good, 70, 188, 331–32
  early life, 16–17, 63–70
  marksmanship, 73, 75, 118,
    221–22
  post Marshals career, 360–65
Pellicano, Anthony, 361
Peoria FIST, 317–18
Perez, Tony, 23, 51, 124, 131, 135,
    268, 269, 273, 325–26, 363
Perl, Gisella, 274
Peron, Eva, 286
Peron, Juan, 286
Perry, John, 161–63, 165, 166, 167,
    184, 189
Perry, Mike, 160–63, 165–66, 167,
    184, 189
Perry, Tommy, 184, 189
Pius XII, pope, 283
PLO, 162, 279, 298, 301–02, 346,
    347, 349
Powell, Colin, 228
Psittacine Caine (film), 361

Rabinowitz, Henry, 140, 142, 144,
    145–47
Ramirez, Carlos "the Jackal," 130,
    335
Rat Line, 283
Reagan, Ronald, 3, 14, 22, 34, 41,
    54, 55, 59, 103, 129, 134,
    137–38, 140–41, 145, 159, 162,
    206, 235, 266, 276, 309, 332,
    346, 350, 353
  and Iran-Contra scandal, 320
  Justice Department under, 263
  and Noriega case, 323
  Star Wars program, 254
  and U.S. Marshals Service, 191
  visit to Bitburg, 236–37
  and war on drugs, 316
  see also Gipper (the)
Reagan administration, 225, 360–61
Reagan era of law enforcement, 3,
    5, 15, 25, 138, 196, 227, 257,
    361, 363
Riley, Frank Burton, 139–48, 151,
    166, 191, 246, 364

Ronstadt, Linda, 110
Roscoe (cop), 71–72, 74, 75–76
Rosinik, Vilni, 254–55, 256, 258, 261
Royal Canadian Mounted Police, 259, 260–61, 351–52

Sadat, Anwar, 161–62
Safir, Howard, 11–16, 17–18, 25, 104, 187, 218, 249
  career, 15–16, 363
  and FIST, 203–05, 206, 207
  and JP, 197, 315–18, 320, 325, 326, 337, 348, 356–57
  and Kalejs case, 235–36, 237–38
  and killing of DEA agents in Brazil, 321
  and Koziy case, 29, 30, 32, 44, 45, 47, 48, 53, 54–55
  and Mengele case, 275, 277, 278–80, 282, 285, 288, 289, 290, 293–95, 298, 312
  and Nazi war crimes, 252, 258, 260
  and Noriega case, 319, 323
  and Terpil case, 333, 337, 338, 352–53
  and Thompson murder, 208, 210, 211, 213
  and U.S. Marshals Service, 111, 118, 129, 130, 135, 152, 159, 226, 231, 250, 343
  and war on drugs, 328, 329–31
San Diego Marshals office, 84–85, 91, 93, 198
Sanchez, Miguel, 195, 197, 198
Savak, 335
Schreiber, Flora Rheta, 287
SDI, 254–55
Sedlmeier, Hans, 287–89, 293, 294–95, 307, 308
Sessions, William, 340, 341, 345
Sher, Neal, 275, 303, 305–06, 309
Shin Beth, 289–91, 304–05
Sinatra, Frank, 73
Smeed, Jerry, 212–14, 216, 217–20, 222–24, 225
Smith, Jerry, 124, 135
Smith, William French, 159, 189, 191, 196, 198–99, 206
Son of Sam, 70, 72, 279, 364
Southern California Mafia, 194
Southwest FIST (Border Sweep), 224–27, 248
Soviet Union, 13, 14, 34, 54, 55, 60, 121, 166, 200, 239, 271, 334
Spinne, die, 283, 287, 298

S.S., 239, 279, 283
Stammer, Geza, 307
Stammer, Gitta, 307
State Department, 34, 54, 94, 125, 201, 341, 346
  Bureau of Intelligence, 290
Stroessner, Alfredo, 275, 277, 279, 288–89
Sung, Mr., 298, 305, 306, 310, 311–12, 313, 314, 323, 337, 364
Sutton, Willie, 15
SWAT team, 6–7, 226
Sweeney, Frank, 198, 310

Thomas (accomplice to Boyce), 124–28, 129, 135, 140, 147, 151, 166, 174, 191
Thompson, Nick, 208–10, 211, 212, 215
Thompson, Steve, 208–17, 219, 222–24
Thornburgh, Richard, 340
Treasury Department, 242, 360
Treasury Enforcement Communications System, 22, 346

United Nations, 290
U.S. Border Patrol, 224, 226
U.S. Customs Service, 320, 340, 341, 354, 360
U.S. Immigration and Naturalization Service (INS), 14, 224, 241
U.S. Marshals, 2, 3, 14, 101, 250–51
  female agents, 30
  status of, 85
U.S. Marshals Service, 11, 12, 79, 81, 151, 203, 206, 224, 318, 360
  arrest rates, 191, 206, 225
  and drug forfeiture laws, 299–300, 328
  duties of, 196
  and federal government, 122, 196
  Glynco, Georgia, training academy, 90, 91
  history of, 104
  JP career with, 83, 84–118, 152, 159, 191, 196–97, 206, 263, 278, 326, 354–55, 362–63
  JP chief of International Operations, 1–2, 3, 337, 340, 341, 352
  JP "headquarter's hit man" for, 141, 177
  patronage system, 90–91

U.S. Marshals Service (*cont.*)
  professionalization of, 15–16
  putting ahead of self, 104, 111, 207, 353

Verdugo, René, 325
Vitkin, Ausla, 243–44, 247, 248, 251–52, 255–58, 261, 262–63, 265, 266–67
Vitkin, Dzentra, 243
Vitkin, Fedor, 243, 244, 251–53, 254, 259

Wallinson, Tony, 182
Wambaugh, Joseph, 77
Warrant Apprehension Narcotics Team (WANT), 327–29, 331
  WANT II, 331, 340
Washington, George, 2

Westchester County Sheriff's Department, 70–78, 80–82
Wet Department, 292
Whitaker, Gerry, 175, 227–31
Whitaker, Tommy (the Skeleton), 86–89, 91–92, 94–97, 98, 99, 103, 104, 111–16, 117
Wiesenthal, Simon, 22, 275, 283, 294, 295, 298, 299, 302–03, 312–13, 357–58
Wilson, Edwin, 333, 335, 338
Wirthlin, Richard, 316
Witness Security Program, 15, 180, 187, 188, 196, 325, 338
World War III, 334
Wutrich, Ron, 316–17, 318, 345, 348

Zinger, Monica, 46